4

What can you say about this book except that it contains a wealth of information encapsulating the aura and mystique of the greatest football club in the world?

Edwin van der Sar

Just open this book at any page and you will be amazed with at least one entry contained within. I found myself just wanting to read it over and over again; it is simply that good.

Cristiano Ronaldo

The Official Manchester United Almanac is one of those books about the club that comes along every now and again that you simply must have for your collection. It will amaze and please you in equal measure.

Paul Scholes

Other Manchester United Books
available from Orion:

The Official Manchester United Annual
The Champions' Story
The Official Illustrated History of Manchester United
Manchester United: The Complete Record
Behind the Scenes at Manchester United
Sir Alex
Legends of United

THE OFFICIAL
MANCHESTER
UNITED
ALMANAC

John D. T. White

Copyright © Manchester United Football Club Limited 2008

The right of Manchester United Football Club Limited to be identified as
the author of this work has been asserted by them in accordance with the
Copyright, Designs and Patents Act 1988.

This edition produced for The Book People Ltd.
Hall Wood Avenue,
Haydock, St Helens WA11 9UL

First published in hardback in Great Britain in 2008 by
Orion Books
an imprint of the Orion Publishing Group Ltd
Orion House, 5 Upper St Martin's Lane,
London WC2H 9EA

An Hachette Livre UK Company

1 3 5 7 9 10 8 6 4 2

A CIP catalogue record for this book is available
from the British Library.

ISBN: 978 1 4072 1352 1

Typeset by Input Data Services Ltd, Frome

Printed in Great Britain by Clays Ltd, St Ives, plc

The Orion Publishing Group's policy is to use papers that are natural,
renewable and recyclable and made from wood grown in sustainable forests.
The logging and manufacturing processes are expected to conform
to the environmental regulations of the country oforigin.

Every effort has been made to fulfil requirements with regard to
reproducing copyright material. The author and publisher will
be glad to rectify any omissions at the earliest opportunity.

www.orionbooks.co.uk

CONTENTS

Acknowledgements   vii
Foreword by Sir Alex Ferguson CBE ix
Author's note   x

JANUARY   1

FEBRUARY   33

MARCH   63

APRIL   91

MAY   132

JUNE   164

JULY   182

AUGUST   202

SEPTEMBER   229

OCTOBER   259

NOVEMBER   290

DECEMBER   317

Bibliography   343
Index   345

ACKNOWLEDGEMENTS

How do you conceivably dedicate a book to individuals whose very lives have been affected by the exploits of Manchester United Football Club as much as your own life has? Well, if you are a Red, then you will know what I mean and if you are a named Red then 'Come On United!' (Wilson, your Red Flag will always guide us, mate.)

Firstly, I am very honoured that Sir Alex agreed to write the Foreword to this book for me. I am so very deeply honoured that The Boss has been so kind, but then again, if you know him, this is a true reflection of the man. This is the fourth time Sir Alex has very kindly contributed a Foreword to one of my books and I have nothing but the utmost respect for the man I consider to be the greatest football manager of all time. Boss, you know you will always have the unwavering loyalty of the members of the George Best Carryduff Manchester United Supporters Club.

I would like to dedicate this book to a number of very deserving Reds including: Adrian and Andrew Abbott, Stuart Anderson, Davy Campbell, Bill Clarkson, Big Geordie Crossett and family, Anne Cullen and family, Addy Dearnaley, Big Dee (Nicole and Patricia), John, Maria and Martin Dempsey, Frankie Dodds, Marty Ferguson, Mark Gibson, Granville and Levi, Big Mike Hartley, Gordon and Rebecca Kerr, Big Jim Kyle, John McGettrick, the McGrandles clan, Malachy McMahon, Wee Stevie McMenemy, Mickey and Pat Morrison, Brendy Neeson, Robbie Robinson and family, Mervyn and Darren Shaw, Heather Torrens, Danny Young and family, my mother-in-law and father-in-law Bobby and Ruth McWilliams, my mum Rosaleen Doherty White, my brother David, sisters Danielle, Donna and Michelle, and all my nephews and nieces. Not forgetting two special people who are no longer with us, my father John McDermot White and my good mate and a huge Red, Wilson Steele.

But, above all else, I would like to dedicate my fifth book on the club I adore to my wife Janice and our sons, Marc and Paul. Just as Manchester United enjoys the loyal support and dedication of us the fans, I too have this very same encouragement to succeed in all that I do from my wife and boys. Without them I am nothing.

And never ever forget the legend that is Manchester United, the most famous and greatest football club in the world.

Come On United!

John White
March 2008

FOREWORD

I must admit that the first day I looked up in John's book was my own birthday, 31 December. Of course I already knew I would see one of my old warhorses on the page, Steve Bruce, who was born a couple of years after me (only kidding Brucey!), but what I didn't know was that United set a post-war attendance record on 31 December 1955 when a crowd of 60,956 spilled into Old Trafford to witness United beat City in the Manchester derby. Naturally the record has been surpassed several times since with the expansion of Old Trafford, but it was still a huge crowd when you consider that the game was played more than 50 years ago.

Another day I just had to look up was 29 February, hoping I would catch out John, but then I noticed he had two entries for this date and I can still recall one of them very vividly, being named the Carling Manager of the Month on 29 February 1996.

Just opening the book at any page really takes you on a tour of the history and mystique that universally attracts and surrounds Manchester United. Like any good book, John has not missed a thing because he has taken the time to painstakingly research all there is to know about events in the history of the club. John records many of the proudest days in the club's history (first League Championship success, first FA Cup final win, first European game, Sir Matt Busby's arrival at the club and not forgetting our truly wonderful Treble achievement in 1999), but he also recalls many of the club's bleakest and saddest days (including the club's bankruptcy, the bombing of Old Trafford, the Munich Air Disaster and Eric's sending off at Selhurst Park).

This book is a history of the club examined from a day-to-day point of view. From the inception of the club in 1878 as the Newton Heath Lancashire & Yorkshire Railway Football Club right up to the global stars of today who have helped make Manchester United the world's most famous football club, John's book encapsulates all that you ever wanted to know about the Red Devils and so much more you would never even dream had happened.

In closing, I would like to take this opportunity to remember the past 21 years I have been the manager of Manchester United, the highs and the lows, none of which I would change for anything, and the wonderful support you the fans have always given to both my players and myself throughout my time in charge. To the best fans in the world – I thank you one and all.

Best wishes

Sir Alex Ferguson CBE
Manchester United Manager
March 2008

AUTHOR'S NOTE

Where I have supplied career statistics for players, in some cases the totals for appearances and goals will not be the sum of the previous entries. This is because there are a small number of 'other' official fixtures, including the Charity Shield, the Inter-Continental Cup and the Club World Championship. The European Super Cup forms part of the European figures.

Abbreviations used in the career records: *EUR*=European competitions (European Cup/Champions League, European Cup-Winners' Cup, Inter-Cities' Fairs Cup/UEFA Cup, European Super Cup); *FAC*=FA Cup; *FL*=Football League (Divison One and Division Two); *FLC*=League Cup; *PL*=Premier League.

JANUARY

1

1886

Harold James Halse (Forward 1907–12) was born in Stratford, East London. Halse scored six goals in succession for United when they hammered Swindon Town 8–4 in the 1911 FA Charity Shield.

Appearances: FL: 109, goals 41 FAC: 15, goals 9 TOTAL: 124 apps, 50 goals.

1903 THE BANK BUSTERS

United signed Ayr Parkhouse's centre-forward Alexander Bell for £700, smashing their previous record transfer fee paid for a player (Gilbert Godsmark for £40 from Ashford FC in 1900 – United were still Newton Heath at this time). Bell, who went on to make over 300 appearances, was converted to a centre-half by United and was a member of United's famous half-back line of Bell, Duckworth and Roberts. Bell helped United to their inaugural First Division League Championship success in 1908 and a second in 1911 as well as their inaugural FA Cup triumph in 1909. In July 1913, Bell left Old Trafford for Ewood Park and helped Blackburn Rovers win the First Division League Championship in his first season at the club, 1913–14.

BELL, Alexander *(Defender 1903–13)*
Appearances: FL: 278, goals 10 FAC: 28, goals 0 TOTAL: 306 apps, 10 goals.

1907 QUAD MAKE THEIR DEBUT

Manchester United 1   Aston Villa 0
Legendary Welsh international, Billy Meredith, who had also played for Manchester City, made his Manchester United debut in this 1–0 First Division win over Aston Villa. Meredith, along with Jimmy Bannister, Herbert Burgess and Sandy Turnbull, joined United from City in May 1906 amid a bribes and illegal payments scandal that resulted in all four of them receiving lengthy suspensions. All four made their United debut against Villa with Sandy Turnbull scoring the only goal of the game.

MEREDITH, William Henry 'Billy' *(Forward 1906–21) – debut in the above game.*
Appearances: FL: 303, goals 35 FAC: 29, goals 0 TOTAL: 335 apps, 36 goals.

BANNISTER, James (Forward 1906–10) – debut in the above game.
  Appearances: FL: 57, goals 7 FAC: 4, goals 1 TOTAL: 63 apps, 8 goals.
BURGESS, Herbert (Full-back 1906–10) – debut in the above game.
  Appearances: FL: 49, goals 0 FAC: 3, goals 0 TOTAL: 54 apps, 0 goals.
  (The medals Burgess won with United are on display in the Old Trafford Museum.)
TURNBULL, Alexander 'Sandy' (Forward 1906–10) – debut in the above game.
  Appearances: FL: 220, goals 90 FAC: 25, goals 10 TOTAL: 247 apps, 101 goals.

1953 BABY FACED CHARLTON ARRIVES AT UNITED

A 15-year-old Bobby Charlton, nephew of the legendary Newcastle United forward, Jackie Milburn ('Wor Jackie'), arrived at Old Trafford as an amateur. Wilf McGuinness, also aged 15, signed for United as an amateur.

1962 VIOLLET SOLD TO POTTERS

Dennis Viollet was sold to Stoke City for £25,000, a move that surprised many United fans at the time. Dennis won two full England caps, scoring once and found the back of the net 178 times for the Reds in 291 appearances.

1974 GEORGE BEST SAYS FAREWELL AND STEWART HOUSTON
MAKES HIS DEBUT

Queens Park Rangers 3   Manchester United 0
This game at Loftus Road brought the curtain down on George Best's career with Manchester United, an association that had lasted over 10 years and brought so much joy to United fans the world over. In this, his last ever game for his beloved United, the Red Devils' manager Tommy Docherty gave Stewart Houston his debut in the United defence. Houston went on to become a loyal servant of United until he left Old Trafford for Bramall Lane in July 1980 to sign for Sheffield United.

HOUSTON, Stewart Mackie (Full-back 1973–80) – debut in the above game.
  Appearances: FL: 204 (1), goals 13 FAC: 22, goals 1 FLC: 16, goals 2
  EUR: 6 (1), goals 0 TOTAL: 248 (2) apps, 16 goals.

1989 UNITED KINGS OF THE NORTH WEST

Manchester United 3   Liverpool 1
Manchester United sent their fans home delighted following a 3–1 win over their bitter rivals at Old Trafford. The United goals came from Brian McClair, Mark Hughes and Russell Beardsmore.

1995 DAVID MEEK SAYS FAREWELL TO OLD TRAFFORD

David Meek was the *Manchester Evening News'* Manchester United correspondent from 5 March 1958 until his retirement in January 1995. He took up his post less than one month after the tragic Munich Air Disaster. David reported on the highs and lows of the club, home and abroad, for 37 years. After his retirement he continued as a shrewd and well-informed observer of all things United, and was much sought after for his insights by many media outlets.

2006 THE BULLDOG SPIRIT

Almost nine years after his painting *The Art of the Game* caused uproar among Church groups because it depicted Eric Cantona as Jesus Christ, the Manchester-born artist Michael Browne found himself at the centre of controversy once again with his latest painting. His painting was accused of attempting to promote anti-German feelings in the lead-up to the 2006 World Cup finals in Germany. It depicts Wayne Rooney and Rio Ferdinand alongside Sir Winston Churchill but football officials elected to disassociate themselves from the work, claiming the iconic British wartime leader had nothing to do with the England football team. Meanwhile, Rio and Wayne liked it that much they had to toss a coin to decide who could buy it; Rio won.

2007 NEW YEAR'S DAY HALF CENTURY

Newcastle United 2   Manchester United 2
United drew 2–2 (scorer: Paul Scholes 2) with Newcastle United at St James' Park in this Premier League encounter. It was United's 50th New Year's Day game.

2

1959 GILES BECOMES THE REPUBLIC OF IRELAND'S YOUNGEST INTERNATIONAL

United's Johnny Giles became the youngest player to be capped by the Republic of Ireland when he played for his country against Sweden. Johnny was aged just 18 years 361 days and went on to win an FA Cup winners' medal with the Reds in 1963 before joining Leeds United shortly after his Wembley triumph. Giles enjoyed even greater success at Elland Road, winning countless trophies with United's Yorkshire rivals over the following 12 years.

1960 SEVENTOON

Newcastle United 7   Manchester United 3
Goalkeeper David Caskell had a day to forget at St James' Park when a New Year hangover saw United concede a record-equalling seven goals to the Magpies. He was not selected again for the rest of the season, but would go on to make 119 appearances until 1966–67. Newcastle are the only club to have achieved this feat

three times (also on 10 September 1927 and 13 September 1930). The United scorers were Albert Quixall (2) and Alex Dawson.

3

1905 14 ON THE TROT

Bolton Wanderers 2   Manchester United 4
United's 4–2 First Division win over the Trotters at Burnden Park was their 14th successive victory in Division Two (scorers: John Allan 2, John Peddie, Henry Williams). The winning run was an all-time League record although the feat was subsequently equalled by both Bristol City and Preston North End. However, United's form fluctuated during the 1904–05 season and the Reds missed out on clinching promotion to the top flight after ending the campaign third in the table. In the first seven games of the 14-match unbeaten run, United scored 14 goals without reply, while their run of seven successive clean sheets was equalled again in season 1924–25.

4

1951

Patrick Joseph Christopher Roche (Goalkeeper 1974–82) was born in Dublin.

1972 BESTIE GOES AWOL

George Best failed to turn up at The Cliff training ground and missed training for a full week. He spent the time in the arms of Miss Great Britain, Carolyn Moore, and was dropped for United's home game against Wolverhampton Wanderers on 8 January. He was handed a fine by the club, two weeks' wages, amounting to £400.

1987

Danny Simpson (Defender 2003–present) was born in Salford, Greater Manchester.

1994 ANFIELD THRILLER TIME

Liverpool 3   Manchester United 3

United, chasing their second successive FA Premier League crown, travelled to Anfield for an important game against their arch-rivals Liverpool. United turned on the style and much to the amazement of the watching Kop, United went 3–0 up inside the first 24 minutes with goals from Steve Bruce, Ryan Giggs and Denis Irwin. However, Liverpool managed to claw their way back into the game and salvage a 3–3 draw. The game also marked Eric Cantona's 50th appearance for United and remarkably *Le Roi* had only tasted defeat twice in the 50 games.

1998 BLUE HEAVEN FOR REDS

Chelsea 3   Manchester United 5

David Beckham and Andy Cole scored twice and Teddy Sheringham once as United stunned the home crowd by taking a 5–0 lead at Stamford Bridge. However, the Blues fought back but could only manage three late goals to save their blushes in this FA Cup third round encounter at Stamford Bridge.

5

1932 JAMES W. GIBSON BECOMES A DIRECTOR

At a board meeting at Old Trafford James W. Gibson was elected as a director of the club. Just as John H. Davies had done before him, James Gibson proved to be the club's saviour when in December 1931 he placed £2,000 at the club's disposal to pay the mortgage on Old Trafford and the monies owing to the Inland Revenue as well as honouring the outstanding wages owing to the players.

William Anthony 'Bill' Foulkes (Defender 1952–70) was born in St Helens, Lancashire.

1974 THE UNSEEN MATCH PROGRAMME

Plymouth Argyle visited Old Trafford for an FA Cup third round tie. Plymouth took the decision to print a programme for a replay before a ball was kicked in the tie, but a replay was not required thanks to a goal from Lou Macari. Plymouth decided to have the programme printed in advance as a precaution against power cuts during the three day week.

1993 A RISING IRISH STAR

Manchester United 2   Bury 0
Keith Gillespie marked his senior Manchester United debut with a goal against
Bury in a 2–0 FA Cup third round win at Old Trafford (Mike Phelan also scored).

> GILLESPIE, Keith *(Forward 1992–4)* – *debut in the above game.*
> *Appearances: PL: 3 (6), goals 1 FAC: 1 (1), goals 1 FLC: 3, goals 0 TOTAL: 7 (7) apps, 2
> goals.*

1997 CUP HOLDERS EXTEND GOOD RUN

Manchester United 2   Tottenham Hotspur 0
In season 1996–97, Manchester United began the defence of the FA Cup with a
comfortable 2–0 home win over Tottenham Hotspur. A Paul Scholes strike and
a sensational free-kick from David Beckham extended United's recent record in
the competition to just one defeat (the 1–0 loss to Everton in the 1995 final) in
their last 22 FA Cup ties.

2006 ROCKY IV

Manchester United signed Spartak Moscow's Serbian international defender
Nemanja Vidic for £7m. Vidic started his football life at Red Star Belgrade
although the Serbian side farmed him out on loan to Spartak Moscow to gain
experience. As he gradually progressed in Russian football he returned to Red
Star before they agreed to sell him permanently to Spartak for 6m euros in July
2004. The Russian club's fans adored Vidic's no-nonsense aggressive style of play
and nicknamed him 'Drago' after the Russian boxer with the same name, played
by Dolph Lundgren in the *Rocky IV* movie.

6

1958 MATT – THIS IS YOUR LIFE

Matt Busby made the first of his two appearances on the famous television show
This Is Your Life.

1973 STROLLER STROLLS OUT FOR UNITED

Arsenal 3   Manchester United 1
George Graham (nicknamed 'Stroller') made his Manchester United debut in
this 3–1 First Division defeat by Arsenal at Highbury (scorer: Brian Kidd). In a
strange treble for the player, United signed Graham from Arsenal, he made his

United debut against Arsenal and when he hung up his boots he guided Arsenal to two First Division League Championships (1989 and 1991).

> GRAHAM, George *(Midfielder 1972–5) – debut in the above game.*
> *Appearances: FL: 41 (2), goals 2 FAC: 2, goals 0 FLC: 1, goals 0*
> *TOTAL: 44 (2) apps, 2 goals.*

1996 RUSH PASSES LAW

Liverpool's Ian Rush overtook Denis Law as the record goalscorer in the history of the FA Cup when the Welsh international scored his 42nd goal in the competition.

2000 BECKS OFF

Necaxa 1   Manchester United 1

The Reds failed to beat this relatively unheard-of Mexican side in the inaugural FIFA World Club Championship played in Brazil (scorer: Dwight Yorke). And to make matters worse, David Beckham was sent off.

2005 NO STRAWBERRY DELIGHT FOR RIO

Rio Ferdinand blew his top with his team-mates after he emerged from United's Carrington training complex following a hard morning's workout. When he got outside he could not believe his eyes when he saw his brand new £200,000 6.8 litre Bentley Arnage convertible completely covered with strawberry yoghurt. His team-mates could not contain their laughter when they saw the expression on Rio's face although wisely they did look on from a relatively safe distance. A furious Rio stormed off in the car and had to have it professionally cleaned.

7

1893 GOALIE MISSES HIS TRAIN

Stoke City 7   Newton Heath 1

Newton Heath's first-ever season in the Football League (1892–93) had already begun badly and things just got worse when on 7 January 1893 their goalkeeper, Jimmy Warner, didn't turn up for an away game at Stoke City. With no substitutes permitted at the time, the Heathens' 10 men – without a recognised goalkeeper – were no match for Stoke, who thrashed them 7–1. An embarrassed Warner later explained to club directors that he had missed his train to Stoke, but the directors were highly unimpressed and suspended him. It marked the end of his career at Newton Heath and he appeared only twice more after the missed match before signing for Walsall Town Swifts in September 1893. Warner won an FA Cup winners' medal when Aston Villa won the trophy for the first time in 1887. He made just 22 appearances for the Heathens after joining them in July 1892.

1905 ROBINS TAME DEVILS

Bristol City became the first team in 15 attempts to prevent United winning a League game when they held United to a 1–1 draw at Ashton Gate (scorer: Thomas Arkesden).

1911 OLD TRAFFORD'S FIRST AWAY O.G.

Manchester United 4   Nottingham Forest 2
David Needham of Nottingham Forest became the first visiting player to score an own goal at Old Trafford in his side's 4–2 First Division defeat (other scorers: Thomas Homer, John Picken, George Wall).

1975 WHEN DAVID BEAT GOLIATH

Walsall 3   Manchester United 2
United were dumped out of the 1974–75 FA Cup in humiliating fashion by Walsall from the Third Division. The Reds lost this third round replay at Fellows Park 3–2 (scorers: Gerry Daly, Sammy McIlroy) after drawing 0–0 at Old Trafford three days earlier.

1984 CUP HOLDERS' EARLY EXIT

AFC Bournemouth 2   Manchester United 0
United, the reigning FA Cup holders, were on the receiving end of a Cup upset when they were beaten 2–0 at AFC Bournemouth in the third round. The match also marked the debut of Graeme Hogg.

> HOGG, Graeme James *(Defender 1984–8) – debut in the above game.*
> *Appearances: FL: 82 (1), goals 1 FAC: 8, goals 0 FLC: 7 (1), goals 0 EUR: 10, goals 0*
> *TOTAL: 108 (2) apps, 1 goal.*

1990 SACK FERGIE!

Nottingham Forest 0   Manchester United 1
Following a sequence of poor League performances Alex Ferguson, less than four years into his job, was, according to the headline-hungry media, facing the sack. The United manager hoped that his fortunes would take a turn for the better when the draw for the third round of the FA Cup was made. Fergie's heart must have skipped a beat when United's name was drawn from the bag to face Nottingham Forest at their City Ground. However, United won the game 1–0 with a well-taken goal from their diminutive striker Mark Robins. The rest, as they say, is history because not only did United go on to win the 1990 FA Cup

but it also marked the beginning of the most successful decade ever by an English League club as United swept all before them during the 1990s, even surpassing the exploits of the famous Liverpool side of the 1980s.

2000 FROM THE CLIFF TO CARRINGTON

Manchester United enjoyed their first training session at their new purpose-built state-of-the-art training complex at Carrington, Manchester. The new training complex replaced the old Cliff training ground. Manchester City and Sale Sharks (Rugby League) also have training centres in the Carrington area. However, the official opening ceremony did not take place until 26 July 2000.

2007 SUPER SWEDE SCORES ON HIS DEBUT

Manchester United 2   Aston Villa 1
Henrik Larsson made his debut for Manchester United and scored in the Reds' 2–1 FA Cup third round win over Aston Villa at Old Trafford (Ole Gunnar Solskjaer also scored). Henrik was born in Helsingborg, Sweden on 20 September 1971 and played for his home-town team before moving to Feyenoord, winning his first Swedish cap in 1993 and starring in the World Cup of 1994. However, he was more or less a complete unknown in Scotland when the Glasgow Celtic manager, Wim Jansen, brought him to Parkhead in the summer of 1997. Henrik went on to firmly establish himself as a Celtic legend after scoring an incredible 242 goals in 314 games for the Scottish giants.

8

1898 BROTHERS UNITED

Woolwich Arsenal 5   Manchester United 1
Fred and Harry Erentz became the second pair of brothers to play for United (at the time the club was still known as Newton Heath) when Fred Erentz made a scoring debut for the club in a 5–1 away defeat to Woolwich Arsenal. Jack and Roger Doughty were the first set of brothers to represent the club.

1947

Edward John 'Ted' MacDougall (Forward 1972–3) was born in Inverness, Scotland.

1949 CUP FOOTBALL RETURNS TO OLD TRAFFORD

Manchester United 6   Bournemouth & Boscombe Athletic 0
This third round FA Cup tie was the first FA Cup match played at Old Trafford in almost 10 years. The 55,012 who paid to see United were not disappointed as they swept aside Bournemouth & Boscombe Athletic 6–0 (scorers: Ronald Burke 2, Jack Rowley 2, Stan Pearson, Charlie Mitten). United's previous FA Cup fixture at Old Trafford took place on 11 January 1939 when West Bromwich Albion beat the Reds 5–1 in a third round replay (scorer: Hubert Redwood).

1971 BEST SCORES OFF THE FIELD

Chelsea 1   Manchester United 2
George Best missed the train taking the team to London for their game in the capital against Chelsea. While United scored twice at Stamford Bridge to beat Chelsea 2–1 (scorers: Alan Gowling, Willie Morgan), George also scored off the field by spending the weekend with the actress Sinead Cusack.

1992 LEAGUE CUP WAR OF THE ROSES

Leeds United 1   Manchester United 3
United were drawn away to Yorkshire rivals Leeds United, their main challengers for the 1991–92 First Division Championship, in the fifth round of the League Cup. United won the game 3–1 with goals from Clayton Blackmore, Andrei Kanchelskis and Ryan Giggs. It was the only game Leeds lost all season at Elland Road, and while United went all the way to Wembley and won the Cup, it was Leeds who were crowned League champions.

2000 NO SOUTH AMERICAN SAMBA

Vasco da Gama 3   Manchester United 1
United were soundly beaten 3–1 (scorer: Nicky Butt) by the Brazilian side Vasco da Gama in the inaugural FIFA World Club Championship in Rio de Janeiro, Brazil. The game was played in the magnificent Maracana Stadium with Romario scoring twice for the home side. The result ended United's hopes of winning the tournament, the 2–0 defeat (scorer: Quinton Fortune 2) by South Melbourne of Australia in their third match being academic.

2005 MINNOWS EMBARRASS UNITED

Manchester United 0   Exeter City 0
United were held scoreless at Old Trafford by non-league minnows Exeter City in their FA Cup third round encounter. Even the introduction of Paul Scholes, Cristiano Ronaldo and Alan Smith in the second half made no difference as the

defiant Conference side held out for a highly respectable draw to force a replay at their St James Park ground.

9

1902 FROM CUP DONATION TO BANKRUPTCY PROCEEDINGS

In 1898 William Healey, the President of Newton Heath, donated a Cup that was to be contested by Newton Heath and Manchester City. City won the Cup in 1898 (4–2 at Bank Street) and again in 1899 (2–1 at Bank Street). However, on 9 January 1902, Healey took the Heathens to court for an outstanding amount owed to him of £242.17s. Healey, one of the club's principal creditors, sought a compulsory winding-up order and with total debts of £2,600 the club was forced into bankruptcy. Prior to the Heathens' next home game against Blackpool the Official Receiver sent the bailiffs in to take control of the club's offices and assets. The bailiffs removed a clock from the club and locked the gates to the Bank Street ground. Harry Stafford, the Newton Heath captain and full-back, managed to secure an interim ground for the Heathens to play their home games situated at Harpurhey, Manchester. By 1900 Newton Heath were in such desperate financial straits that very often the supporters had to hold a 'whip-round' to raise money just to pay for the players' rail fares to away games. And unlike the lavish lunches on offer to players today, the Newton Heath players' pre-match lunch usually consisted of a bottle of beer and some cheese.

1946 AN UNHAPPY SCORING DEBUT

Manchester United 5   Accrington Stanley 1
William Bainbridge made his Manchester United debut in this FA Cup third round, second leg tie against Accrington Stanley at Old Trafford. Bainbridge made it a debut to remember by scoring, with further goals from Jack Rowley (2), William Wrigglesworth and an own goal. Bainbridge never pulled on a United shirt again and four months later he joined Bury. The Reds won the tie 7–3 on aggregate.

1954 FOULKES BEGINS HIS LONG FA CUP MARCH

Burnley 5   Manchester United 3
Bill Foulkes played the first of 61 consecutive FA Cup ties for United. United lost their third round trip to Lancashire rivals Burnley, 5–3 (scorers: Jackie Blanchflower, Tommy Taylor, Dennis Viollet).

1965 ONE GAME, ONE GOAL

Manchester United 2   Chester 1
Albert Kinsey made his Manchester United debut in this FA Cup third round tie against Chester at Old Trafford. Despite scoring in the game, along with George Best, he never played for United again. Kinsey signed for United as an amateur in June 1961 from Liverpool schoolboys and turned professional at Old Trafford in October 1962. In March 1966 he signed for Wrexham.

1991 STYLISH VIV TEAMS UP WITH BIG RON

Viv Anderson, who along with Brian McClair was Alex Ferguson's first signing for Manchester United during the 1987 close season, was allowed to leave the Reds on a free transfer. Anderson, a cultured and stylish full-back for Nottingham Forest, Arsenal, United and England, teamed up with former United manager Ron Atkinson at Sheffield Wednesday.

1995 ERIC MAGNIFIQUE

Sheffield United 0   Manchester United 2
Eric Cantona scored one of his best-ever goals for United, a chip from 20 yards on a cold, wet and blustery evening at Bramall Lane. Mark Hughes also scored for the Reds in the FA Cup third round tie. The Red Devils wore an unusual new away strip of blue and white stripes in their 2–0 victory over Sheffield United. The shirt had the names of the Manchester United first-team players and many former Old Trafford legends printed on it.

2005 RONALDO HELPS TSUNAMI VICTIMS

Cristiano Ronaldo flew to Indonesia to visit the areas affected by the tsunami and to help raise funds for the victims of the disaster, which occurred on 26 December 2004. During his visit he helped raise £66,000 by selling some of his personal sports items in a charity auction held in Jakarta.

10

1948 THRILLER TIME

Aston Villa 4   Manchester United 6
Manchester United opened their 1947–48 FA Cup campaign with a tough third round away tie against Aston Villa at Villa Park. Things did not go well for the Reds when they fell behind after just 13 seconds of play. However, this jolt to the system merely inspired United and by half-time they led the home side 5–1 with

goals from Johnny Morris (2), Jimmy Delaney, Stan Pearson and Jack Rowley. After the interval Villa fought back well in terrible playing conditions to trail 4–5 but Pearson's second goal of the game gave United a 6–4 victory in the mud and rain. The win proved the catalyst for a successful Cup campaign as the Reds went all the way to Wembley and beat Blackpool 4–2 in the final to claim the FA Cup for the second time in the club's history.

1954

John Gidman (Full-back 1981–6) was born in Liverpool.

1987 UNITED–CITY CUP DUEL

Manchester United 1   Manchester City 0
United met neighbours Manchester City in the third round of the FA Cup at Old Trafford. Norman Whiteside scored the only goal of the game to send the Red half of Manchester home very happy.

1995 COLE PURCHASE BREAKS TRANSFER RECORD

United purchased Andy Cole from Newcastle United in a deal worth £7m – £6m cash plus Keith Gillespie (valued at £1m) going in the opposite direction. Cole scored 12 goals in his first 18 Premiership games for United, including five in one game in the 9–0 rout of Ipswich Town, but endured two near misses at West Ham United on the final day of the season that would have meant United winning the first three FA Premier League titles. In the end the title made its way from Manchester to Ewood Park and Kenny Dalglish's Blackburn Rovers side. Cole's transfer smashed the United record transfer deal for a player, which was the £3.75m needed to buy Roy Keane from Nottingham Forest in July 1993.

1999 UNITED LOSE POWER

Manchester United 4   West Ham United 1
Manchester United's Premier League game against West Ham United at Old Trafford was delayed due to a power failure in the Trafford area of Manchester. The evening kick-off time was put back 45 minutes but the delay failed to affect United's play as they hammered the London side 4–1 with goals from Andy Cole (2), Ole Gunnar Solskjaer and Dwight Yorke.

2006 FROM OLD TRAFFORD TO CHURCH

United signed the French full-back Patrice Evra from AS Monaco for a reported £5.5m. Although he was born in Dakar, Senegal, Evra represents France at international level. On his first day at Old Trafford Evra is said to have asked

Gary Neville for the location of the closest church, 'So I can thank God for letting me join the biggest club in the world.'

11

1904 CLUB'S LONGEST FA CUP TIE

Newton Heath 3   Small Heath 1

When Newton Heath finally beat Small Heath (subsequently Birmingham City) 3–1 at Hyde Road in the FA Cup (scorers: Thomas Arkesden 2, William Grassam) it ended the most protracted FA Cup tie in the club's history. The game was the third replay between the two clubs – they had previously drawn 1–1, 1–1 aet and 1–1 aet. It took a mammoth seven hours to decide a winner. The Heathens' reward for winning the marathon tie was a place in the first round proper, an away tie at Notts County.

1922 ROBSON DIES OF PNEUMONIA

John Robson, Manchester United manager 1914–21, died of pneumonia. During Robson's time in charge of United, Old Trafford witnessed both its highest and lowest attendance figures recorded. The highest was on 27 December 1920 versus Aston Villa when a massive 70,504 packed into the ground. The lowest attendance recorded was just 13 people, who came to Old Trafford to see a Second Division match between Stockport County and Leicester City. The *Manchester Chronicle* summed up Robson by saying: 'John Robson was a kindly man of great football experience, whose chief characteristic was probably loyalty to his employer. In his long experience of well over thirty years in the official life of the Football League, he won a reputation as one of the really shrewd judges, he believed in making his players comfortable and on the one hand he expected respect from them.'

1957

Bryan Robson (Midfielder 1981–94) was born in Chester-le-Street, Durham.

1975 MCCALLIOG BRACE DOWNS OWLS

Manchester United 2   Sheffield Wednesday 0

Jim McCalliog scored both goals (including a penalty) for United in their 2–0 Second Division win over Sheffield Wednesday at Old Trafford. Amazingly, McCalliog failed to find the net again for the rest of the season.

2002 UNITED'S FIRST HAWTHORNS PREMIERSHIP VISIT

West Bromwich Albion 1   Manchester United 3

United visited The Hawthorns for the first time in a Premiership encounter and came home with all three points thanks to goals from Paul Scholes, Ole Gunnar Solskjaer and Ruud van Nistelrooy.

12

1921 SOLO CUP TIE

Liverpool 2   Manchester United 1

After drawing 1–1 with Liverpool at Old Trafford four days earlier (scorer: Thomas Miller) in the first round of the FA Cup, United lost the replay 2–1 (scorer: Edward Partridge) at Anfield. George Albinson made his one and only appearance for the Reds in the Cup exit.

1955 LOWEST POST-WAR ATTENDANCE FOR AN FA CUP TIE AT OLD TRAFFORD

Manchester United 4   Reading 1

Only 24,578 fans turned up to see Colin Webster (2), Dennis Viollet and Jack Rowley score the goals that put United into the hat for the fourth round of the FA Cup. The gate is United's lowest post-war home attendance for an FA Cup tie at Old Trafford.

1980 TWO FANS DIE WATCHING UNITED

Middlesbrough 1   Manchester United 1

Manchester United travelled to Ayresome Park for a First Division game against Middlesbrough. The game ended 1–1 (scorer: Mickey Thomas) but was sadly marred by the death of two spectators when a gate at the ground collapsed.

1997 CASPER'S NORTH LONDON BOW

Tottenham Hotspur 1   Manchester United 2

Chris Casper (Defender 1993–8) made his Premier League debut for United versus Tottenham Hotspur at White Hart Lane. Chris replaced Ronny Johnsen as a second-half substitute in the Premiership encounter. United won the game 2–1 with goals from Ole Gunnar Solskjaer and David Beckham.

13

1972

Mark Bosnich (Goalkeeper 1989–91 and 1999–2001) was born in Fairfield, Sydney, Australia.

1973 CHARLTON CLOCKS UP 75 IN A ROW

Wolverhampton Wanderers 1   Manchester United 0

Manchester United visited Wolverhampton Wanderers' Molineux ground for this FA Cup third round tie. The encounter marked Bobby Charlton's 75th consecutive and last FA Cup game for the Reds (79 in total). Wolves ensured it was their name, and not United's, in the hat for the fourth round draw with a 1–0 win. However, after he left Old Trafford in May 1973 to become the player-manager of Preston North End, Charlton made a further 4 FA Cup appearances for the Lilywhites to bring his career tally to 83 FA Cup appearances, scoring 19 goals.

1995 CAR THEFT

Nicky Butt's Renault Clio car was stolen from outside his local pub, The Cotton Tree, in Gorton, and the thieves set fire to the vehicle. His team-mate Paul Ince was told that he would have to serve a three-match ban following his sending off against IFK Gothenburg in the UEFA Champions League.

1996 BROTHERS APPEAR IN THE BOOK

Manchester United 0   Aston Villa 0

Gary and Phil Neville were both booked in Manchester United's 0–0 draw with Aston Villa at Old Trafford. They became the first pair of brothers to be booked in the same game while playing for United.

2000 REACH FOR THE SKY

Further building redevelopment work at Old Trafford added a second tier to the East Stand giving the stadium a capacity of 61,000.

14

1961 ONLY BLANK IN DOUBLE-WINNING SEASON

Manchester United 2   Tottenham Hotspur 0
Manchester United beat the high-flying Tottenham Hotspur 2–0 at Old Trafford in this First Division match, with goals from Mark Pearson and Nobby Stiles. It was the only occasion during the 1960–61 season that the London club, who went on to clinch the first domestic Double of the 20th century, failed to score in a game.

1969 A GOLDEN ERA DRAWS TO A CLOSE

Almost 24 years to the day after taking charge of Manchester United, Sir Matt Busby announced his retirement from football.

1994 FERGIE LEAVES UNITED

Darren Ferguson, the son of United boss Alex, was sold to Wolverhampton Wanderers.

15

1977 206 NOT OUT

Manchester United 2   Coventry City 0
Steve Coppell made the first of his 206 consecutive Football League appearances for Manchester United in a 2–0 First Division home win over Coventry City (scorer: Lou Macari 2). His 206th game was United's 5–1 away win over Sunderland on 7 November 1981 (scorers: Frank Stapleton 2, Garry Birtles, Kevin Moran, Bryan Robson).

1979 NO LEAGUE GAMES FOR UNITED

Manchester United 3   Chelsea 0
During the month of January 1979 Manchester United did not play any League games. However, they did entertain Chelsea in the third round of the FA Cup at Old Trafford. Steve Coppell, Jimmy Greenhoff and Ashley Grimes all scored in a comprehensive 3–0 win.

2005 ROONEY PELTED WITH COINS AND A MOBILE PHONE

Liverpool 0   Manchester United 1

Maybe the Liverpool fans thought Wayne Rooney needed to phone home, despite the fact that nearly all of his family were at Anfield to watch him play. They rained coins down on him, and one fan even chucked a mobile phone at the local lad. Despite going down to 10 men following Wes Brown's red card, United won this FA Premier League encounter 1–0 with a goal from none other than Wayne Rooney. It was United's third consecutive League win at Anfield.

16

1909 RECORD CUP LOW FOR 'UNATTRACTIVE' UNITED

Manchester United 1   Brighton & Hove Albion 0

A paltry crowd of 8,074 watched United beat Brighton & Hove Albion 1–0 in the first round of the 1908–09 FA Cup (scorer: Harold Halse). The attendance remains a club record low for the Reds in an FA Cup tie (excludes games as Newton Heath from 1878–1902). However, the 'unattractive Reds' made it all the way to the FA Cup final in 1909 and they beat Bristol City 1–0 at the Crystal Palace (scorer: Sandy Turnbull).

1954 DERBY GAME BROADCAST LIVE TO LOCAL HOSPITALS

Manchester United 1   Manchester City 1

A live commentary of the Manchester derby game between United and City at Old Trafford was broadcast to hospitals in the Manchester area for the first time. All of the patients were given a copy of the match programme, the *United Review*. The game ended 1–1 (scorer: Johnny Berry).

1999 JAAP'S FIRST UNITED GOAL

Leicester City 2   Manchester United 6

United was in irresistible form at Filbert Street in what proved to be their Treble-winning season, hammering Leicester City 6–2 thanks to a Dwight Yorke hat-trick, two goals from Andy Cole and Jaap Stam's first ever goal for the Reds.

17

1921

Charles Mitten (Forward 1946–50) was born in Rangoon, Burma.

1931 UNITED 10 UNITED 0

Newcastle United 4   Manchester United 3
United lost 4–3 to Newcastle United in the First Division at St James' Park (scorers: Arthur Warburton 2, Thomas Reid). It was the 10th season in a row that United lost to the Geordies in the League.

1948 FOOTBALL LEAGUE ATTENDANCE RECORD AT MAINE ROAD

Manchester United 1   Arsenal 1
In season 1947–48 United were still renting neighbouring Manchester City's ground to play their home League and FA Cup matches. Old Trafford was under reconstruction at the time after being damaged in 1941 when German bombs fell on it. A mammoth crowd of 82,950 packed into Maine Road to watch Arsenal hold the Reds to a 1–1 draw (scorer: Jack Rowley). The attendance remains a record for an English Football League game.

18

1890 HIT FOR SIX

Preston North End 6   Newton Heath 1
Newton Heath's first FA Cup campaign came during the 1886–87 season but after drawing 2–2 away to Fleetwood Rangers in the first round the Heathens refused to play extra-time. The referee had no other option but to award the tie to the home side. The Heathens did not enter the Cup again until season 1889–90 when they lost 6–1 away to the reigning League Champions and FA Cup holders, Preston North End, at Deepdale in the first round on 18 January 1890 (scorer: T. Craig on his debut). Preston went on to retain the First Division Championship.

1961

Peter Andrew Beardsley (Forward 1982–3) was born in Longbottom, Newcastle-upon-Tyne.

1964 LAW, BEST AND CHARLTON UNITED

West Bromwich Albion 1   Manchester United 4

This was the first game in which Matt Busby played the magnificently gifted trio of Denis Law, George Best and Bobby Charlton together in the same match. United, with the predatory instinct of Law, the class of Charlton and the genius of the young Irishman, were simply too good for the home side, running out 4–1 winners at The Hawthorns. Naturally the four goals were scored by the players who would become known as 'The Holy Trinity' at Old Trafford, Law (2), Best and Charlton. The trio went on to immortality in the famous 1960s iconic red shirts of United, winning two Championships (1964–65 and 1966–67) and the Holy Grail, the European Cup in 1968.

1973 BREAKING THE BANK IN SCOTLAND

When Lou Macari joined Manchester United from Glasgow Celtic for £200,000 the transfer fee set a new Scottish transfer record.

1994 HERO OF '90 JOINS CELTIC

Lee Martin, scorer of the winning goal in the 1990 FA Cup final replay against Crystal Palace, was sold to Glasgow Celtic.

2005 GRECIANS FALL TO DEVILS

Exeter City 0   Manchester United 2

Exeter City pushed United, the FA Cup holders, all the way in their third round replay at their St James Park ground before the Conference side finally succumbed 2–0. After holding United to a 0–0 draw 10 days earlier at Old Trafford, the Grecians were dreaming of causing the biggest Cup upset of all time. However, goals from Ronaldo and Rooney gave United a deserved win.

19

1977 ROBINS PUT TO FLIGHT

Manchester United 2   Bristol City 1

Brian Greenhoff and Stuart Pearson were both on the score sheet for United as they beat Bristol City 2–1 at Old Trafford in a Division One game. It was United's first home victory over the Robins in more than 50 years.

1996 BIGGEST DERBY TRANSFER

Tony Coton moved across Manchester to join the Reds from the Blues. The £500,000 transfer fee remains the most expensive transfer between United and City.

2002 SAME AGAIN PLEASE

Manchester United 2   Blackburn Rovers 1
When United beat Blackburn Rovers 2–1 in the Premiership it was the first time in 50 games that Sir Alex had chosen the same starting XI. Ruud van Nistelrooy and Roy Keane scored the goals.

20

1932 J. W. GIBSON IS ELECTED CHAIRMAN AND PRESIDENT OF THE COMPANY

James W. Gibson was elected chairman and president of Manchester United Ltd and Messrs Westcott, Shaw, Newton and Thomson were elected as the company's new directors.

1968 UNITED SET UNBEATEN HOME RECORD

Manchester United 4   Sheffield Wednesday 2
When United beat Sheffield Wednesday 4–2 at Old Trafford (scorers: George Best 2, Bobby Charlton, Brian Kidd) they set a new club record for the longest run of undefeated home League games, at 37. The run began on 27 April 1966 with a 2–1 victory over Blackpool (scorers: Charlton, Law).

1973 HOLTON AND MACARI MAKE THEIR DEBUTS

Manchester United 2   West Ham United 2
Following their transfers from Glasgow Celtic and Shrewsbury Town respectively, Lou Macari and Jim Holton made their Manchester United debuts in a First Division game at Old Trafford. Macari celebrated his debut with United's second goal of the game while Bobby Charlton also found the net for the Reds. Macari later went on to manage the Hammers during his career.

> HOLTON, James 'Jim' Allan *(Defender 1972–5) – debut in the above game.*
> *Appearances: FL: 63, goals 5 FAC: 2, goals 0 FLC: 4, goals 0 TOTAL: 69 apps, 5 goals.*
> MACARI, Luigi 'Lou' Forward *(1972–84) – debut in the above game.*
> *Appearances: FL: 311 (18), goals 78 FAC: 31 (3), goals 8 FLC: 22 (5), goals 10*
> *EUR: 9 (1), goals 1 TOTAL: 374 (27) apps, 97 goals.*

1981

Owen Lee Hargreaves (Midfielder 2007–present) born in Calgary, Canada.

1994 FOOTBALL SAYS FAREWELL TO A GREAT

The football world was united in mourning the death of Sir Matt Busby, the man regarded as the Father of Manchester United, aged 84. Such was the public outpouring of grief that the City of Manchester had not witnessed such scenes of sadness since the Munich Air Disaster on 6 February 1958.

21

1893 RAILWAY TAG DROPPED

Blackburn Rovers 4   Newton Heath 0
Midway through the 1892–93 season Newton Heath Lancashire & Yorkshire Railway decided that the club would become simply known as Newton Heath Football Club. The Heathens' first-ever FA Cup game under their new name was a 4–0 away defeat to Blackburn Rovers at Ewood Park on 21 January 1893 in the first round.

1951 FANS LOCKED OUT

Manchester United 4   Leeds United 0
United's fourth round FA Cup tie with Leeds United at Old Trafford attracted a bumper crowd of 55,000 fans. The United faithful went home happy after demolishing their Yorkshire rivals 4–0 thanks to a Stan Pearson hat-trick and a goal from Jack Rowley. Such was the demand to see the game that thousands found themselves locked out shortly after arriving at the stadium.

1956 LAST DEFEAT UNTIL OCTOBER

Preston North End 3   Manchester United 1
United lost 3–1 (scorer: Liam Whelan) to Preston North End at Deepdale in a First Division game and then remained unbeaten in their next 14 League games until the end of the season to clinch the League Championship by 11 points over their nearest rivals, Blackpool. The excellent League form continued into season 1956–57 when United were unbeaten in their opening 12 fixtures.

1964

David Lloyd 'Danny' Wallace (Forward 1989–93) was born in Greenwich, London.

21 JANUARY

1971 THE LAST BUSBY BABE

Sammy McIlroy, the last player Sir Matt Busby signed for Manchester United, played for the first team aged just 16 years 172 days in a friendly against Bohemians in Dublin. However, it would be another 10 months before the young Irishman made his League debut for the Reds.

1975

Nicky Butt (Midfielder 1992–2004) was born in Manchester.

1977

Phil Neville (Defender 1994–2005) was born in Bury, Greater Manchester.

1984 SPARKY SPARKLES

Manchester United 3   Southampton 2

'Sparky' or 'Hughesie', as he was known by the Manchester United faithful, is one of the greatest players ever to have pulled on a Red shirt. He joined United as an apprentice in May 1980 and was a member of the United youth team that lost the 1982 FA Youth Cup final. He made his first-team debut in a League Cup tie against Port Vale in October 1983 and after establishing himself in the first team his name was always one of the first on the team-sheet. Strong and powerfully built, Hughes was a handful for any defender. He left Old Trafford in August 1986 for Barcelona but never really settled abroad, which included a brief loan spell with Bayern Munich. Alex Ferguson wasted no time in bringing Sparky back to United in the summer of 1988 and Hughes repaid the faith placed in him by scoring many spectacular and important goals for United, including both goals in the 1991 European Cup-Winners' Cup final victory over Barcelona and the equalising goal against Oldham Athletic in the 1994 FA Cup semi-final. A Welsh international, he won 3 FA Cup winners' medals with United (1985, 1990 and 1994), a European Cup-Winners' Cup and European Super Cup winners' medal in 1991, a League Cup winners' medal in 1992 and two Premier League winners' medals in 1993 and 1994.

During his Old Trafford career he also won the PFA Young Player of the Year Award in 1985 and was twice named as the PFA Player of the Year, in 1989 and 1991. In the summer of 1995 he joined Chelsea where he won a record fourth FA Cup winners' medal in 1997.

HUGHES, Mark (Forward 1983–5 and 1988–94) – League debut in the above game.
Appearances: FL: 336 (9), goals 120 FAC: 45 (1), goals 17 FLC: 37 (1), goals 16
EUR: 30 (3), goals 9 TOTAL: 453 (14) apps, 163 goals.

22

1910 LAST GAME AT BANK STREET, CLAYTON

Manchester United 5   Tottenham Hotspur 0

This game marked the last ever occasion Manchester United played a home game at their Bank Street ground before the grand opening of their new purpose-built stadium at Old Trafford. The game against the Londoners should have actually been United's first at their new home, but the building work had not been completed on time (scorers: Charlie Roberts 2, Edward Connor, Arthur Hooper, Billy Meredith).

1938 LONG THROW BLUNDER

Barnsley 2   Manchester United 2

Manchester United visited Oakwell for an FA Cup fourth round tie against Barnsley. An error by United's Irish goalkeeper, Tommy Breen, cost the visitors victory as the game ended 2–2 (scorers: Henry Baird, Johnny Carey). In a bizarre incident Breen conceded a goal directly from a long throw-in and is credited with conceding the first goal ever scored directly from a throw-in in English football. As the ball was thrown into the Manchester United box Breen went to collect it but misjudged its flight and could only watch in horror as it hit his hand and rolled over the line into the net.

1994 IN MEMORY OF A GREAT MAN

Manchester United 1   Everton 0

A full house of 44,750 crammed into Old Trafford for United's FA Premier League game against Everton just two days after United fans mourned the loss of the man who practically single-handedly built United after World War II, Sir Matt Busby. Up and down the country football fans remembered the Great Man by holding a minute's silence prior to games. Sadly, a number of Leeds United fans chanted 'Revie' (the surname of the Yorkshire club's most successful manager) prior to their own Premiership game away to Blackburn Rovers. However, thankfully the Everton fans had more respect for one of the greatest managers British football has ever seen and behaved impeccably. United gave Sir Matt a winning send off by beating the Toffees 1–0 thanks to a rare headed goal from Ryan Giggs. Meanwhile, the bumper crowd of 44,750 set a new FA Premier League attendance record at the time.

1995 ANDY'S UNITED DEBUT

Manchester United 1   Blackburn Rovers 0

Following his much publicised £7m transfer from Newcastle United, Andy Cole made his Premiership debut for the Reds in a crucial 1–0 win over their nearest title challengers, Blackburn Rovers, at Old Trafford before an appreciative audience of 43,742 fans. United talisman Eric Cantona scored the all-important winning goal with an angled far-post header from a Ryan Giggs cross.

23

1919

John Joseph Carey (Full-back 1937–53) was born in Dublin.

1926 DERBY DAY MASSACRE

Manchester City 6   Manchester United 1

This biggest ever Manchester derby win came in a First Division game played at Maine Road with the Blues annihilating the Reds 6–1 (scorer: Clatworthy Rennox).

1969

Andrei Kanchelskis (Forward 1990–95) was born in Kirovograd, Ukraine.

1989 THREE BITES AT THE CHERRY

Manchester United 3   Queens Park Rangers 0

Manchester United met Queens Park Rangers for the third time in the third round of the 1988–89 FA Cup. The first game ended in a scoreless draw at Old Trafford and four days later the replay produced a 2–2 draw after extra-time (scorers: Anthony Gill, Deiniol Graham). United won the second replay 3–0 with two goals from Brian McClair and one from the skipper, Bryan Robson.

1993 FERGIE'S SEPTET OF FLEDGLINGS

Seven trainees at Manchester United – David Beckham, Nicky Butt, Chris Casper, Gary Neville, John O'Kane, Paul Scholes and Ben Thornley – all made the step into the big time by signing professional terms with United. The famous septet was nicknamed 'Fergie's Fledglings' by the press and helped United win the FA Youth Cup in 1992, United's seventh triumph in the competition.

24

1948 IN OUR LIVERPOOL HOME

Manchester United 3   Liverpool 0
During the 1947–48 season Old Trafford was still under reconstruction after suffering bomb damage during World War II, and when the FA Cup fourth round draw was made United came out of the hat at home to Liverpool. However, the game had to be played at Everton's Goodison Park because Manchester City (United rented City's Maine Road ground for home games during the reconstruction period) had also been drawn at home in their fourth round game. United won 3–0 with goals from Charlie Mitten, Johnny Morris and Jack Rowley.

1976 NOEL CANTWELL RETURNS TO OLD TRAFFORD

Manchester United 3   Peterborough United 1
Noel Cantwell, United's 1963 FA Cup-winning captain, brought his Peterborough United team to Old Trafford for a third-round FA Cup tie. United won 3–1 thanks to goals from Alex Forsyth, Sammy McIlroy and Gordon Hill.

1987 GIBSON GRABS HIS ONLY GOAL

Manchester United 2   Arsenal 0
Terry Gibson scored the first and only goal of his United career for the Red Devils in their 2–0 home First Division win over Arsenal. Gordon Strachan also scored.

1999 PUTTING ON A LATE, LATE SHOW

Manchester United 2   Liverpool 1
Just when the Liverpool fans, who made the short trip to Old Trafford for their FA Cup fourth round game against United, thought that they were about to put the Red Devils out of the Cup, up stepped Dwight Yorke and Ole Gunnar Solskjaer with two goals in the dying moments of the game to put United in the hat for the fifth round to keep their Treble hopes alive.

2000 ONWARDS AND UPWARDS

Manchester United 1   Arsenal 1
United opened their new East Stand upper deck for the first time when Arsenal came to Old Trafford for a Premiership game. The match finished 1–1 (scorer: Teddy Sheringham) while the attendance of 58,293 set a new FA Premier League record.

2006 SCHOLESY'S SEASON ENDED

Paul Scholes's season was brought to an end when Manchester United announced that the dynamic midfielder had an eye problem. Scholesy had been suffering from double vision in his right eye since sustaining a blow to the head in United's 2–2 draw with Birmingham City at St Andrew's on 28 December 2005. 'Paul Scholes has a medical condition affecting the vision in his right eye. It is not a football related injury. A number of specialists have all agreed that he needs three months' rest,' said a club statement.

25

1958 BUSBY BABES' LAST GAME AT OLD TRAFFORD

Manchester United 2   Ipswich Town 0
This was the last occasion the Manchester United faithful saw the famous Busby Babes play at Old Trafford. Matt Busby's all-conquering Babes beat Ipswich Town 2–0 in an FA Cup fourth round tie thanks to two goals from Bobby Charlton.

1964 A KING'S HAT-TRICK

Manchester United 4   Bristol Rovers 1
Denis Law scored a hat-trick in United's 4–1 FA Cup fourth round win over Bristol Rovers at Old Trafford. David Herd also scored.

1986 ROBBO SENT OFF FOR THE FIRST TIME

Sunderland 0   Manchester United 0
United, the FA Cup holders, visited Sunderland's Roker Park ground for an FA Cup fourth-round tie. The game marked the return of club and England captain Bryan Robson after an injury and finished 0–0. However, Robbo received his marching orders following a collision with Barry Venison. Both players went for the ball resulting in the pair lying on the pitch and as Robbo got to his feet he caught the Black Cats' defender on the head with his boot as he attempted to step over him. However, the linesman waved his flag in the air and when the referee spoke to him he was informed that Robbo had intentionally kicked out at Venison resulting in the red card. It was the first time he was sent off in his professional career.

1995 ERIC'S KUNG-FU FIGHTING

Crystal Palace 1   Manchester United 1
Manchester United travelled to London to face Crystal Palace in an FA Premier

League game at Selhurst Park. The game was a spiteful affair and ended in a 1–1 draw (scorer: David May). However, the game will always be remembered for Eric Cantona's kung-fu attack on a Palace fan in the crowd who hurled abuse at Eric as he walked down the sideline to the dressing rooms after being sent off. A resulting FA Premier League hearing suspended Le King for nine months.

2007 DONG TO STAY

Manchester United's Chinese international striker Dong Fangzhou signed a new contract with United. The 21-year-old, who was signed from Dalian Shide in January 2004, was granted a work permit in December 2006 after being sent out on loan to Royal Antwerp in Belgium. His new contract will keep him at Old Trafford until 2010.

26

1946 UNITED WIN BUT EXIT FA CUP

Manchester United 1   Preston North End 0
Despite beating Lancashire rivals Preston North End 1–0 at Old Trafford (scorer: John Hanlon) in the fourth round of the FA Cup, United were not in the hat for the fifth round draw of the competition. During the 1945–46 season, shortly after the end of World War II, no League games were played while all early FA Cup ties were played over two legs. United lost the second leg at Deepdale just four days later 3–1, with John Hanlon finding the net again.

1991 SPARKY TROTS UNITED INTO FIFTH ROUND

Manchester United 1   Bolton Wanderers 0
Manchester United, the reigning FA Cup holders, entertained Lancashire rivals Bolton Wanderers at Old Trafford in the fourth round of the 1990–91 competition. Mark Hughes scored against the Trotters to earn the Red Devils a fifth round tie at Norwich City.

2003 HAMMERS HAMMERED

Manchester United 6   West Ham United 0
Manchester United hammered the Hammers 6–0 at Old Trafford in an FA Cup fourth round tie with goals from Ryan Giggs (2), Ruud van Nistelrooy (2), Phil Neville and Ole Gunnar Solskjaer.

27

1973 SEASON'S FIRST FOR BIG JIM

Coventry City 1   Manchester United 1

Jim Holton scored his first League goal of the season when United drew 1–1 at Highfield Road with Coventry City.

2007 ERIC'S CRYSTAL BALL

In an interview with BBC's *North West Tonight* programme, former Manchester United idol Eric Cantona had no doubts that United would win the 2006–07 Premier League: 'For sure they will be champions. It's a new era, a new generation. They have a great team but they have a lot to prove.' Eric's gaze into his crystal ball proved to be right as United were crowned champions at the end of the season, their ninth Premier league crown.

28

1967 FOULKES FA CUP FAREWELL

Manchester United 2   Stoke City 0

Bill Foulkes played his last ever FA Cup game for his beloved Manchester United in their 2–0 win over Stoke City in the third round at Old Trafford (scorers: David Herd, Denis Law). It was the big defender's 61st FA Cup game for United, all made consecutively, having played his first game in the competition on 9 January 1954.

1995 WELSH DRAGON SLAIN

Manchester United 5   Wrexham 2

Wrexham visited Old Trafford for an FA Cup fourth round tie and looked to be heading for an upset when they took the lead inside the opening 10 minutes. However, the Welsh side were soon brought back down to earth when Denis Irwin scored in the 17th minute. Following Irwin's goal, United eased into top gear and rattled home four more (Irwin, Giggs, McClair, o.g.) before Wrexham added a consolation second goal in the last minute of the game. Wrexham's opening goal of the game was the first they had ever scored against United while their second goal was the 150th conceded by the Red Devils at Old Trafford in the FA Cup. The game marked the fifth time the two sides had played each other with Manchester United retaining a 100% win record with 17 goals scored and just two conceded.

2001 STRANGE BUT TRUE

Manchester United 0   West Ham United 1

West Ham United beat United 1–0 at Old Trafford in this fourth-round FA Cup tie played at Old Trafford. Paolo di Canio slipped the ball past Fabien Barthez, who tried to fool the Italian master into believing that he was offside. Amazingly, it was United's first FA Cup defeat since their exit to Barnsley in the 1997–98 competition. United won the Cup in their Treble-winning year of 1999 but did not defend the Cup in season 1999–2000 after opting instead to play in the inaugural FIFA World Club Championship tournament in Brazil.

29

1932

Tommy Taylor (Forward 1953–8) was born in Barnsley, Yorkshire.

1955 CHILTON BECOMES FIRST DERBY EXIT

Manchester City 2   Manchester United 0

Allenby Chilton of Manchester United became the first player to be sent off in a Manchester derby game when the Red Devils lost 2–0 to City in the fourth round of the FA Cup at Maine Road. A crowd of 75,000 attended the game.

1997 UNITED GO TOP OF THE LEAGUE

Manchester United 2   Wimbledon 1

Manchester United recorded their biggest home FA Premier League gate of the season when Wimbledon came to play the defending champions. A mammoth crowd of 55,314 saw United come from a goal down to beat the Dons 2–1 (scorers: Ryan Giggs, Andy Cole). The victory sent United to the top of the FA Premier League where they remained, winning their fourth Premiership title in five years at the end of the season.

2000 THE MAIN ATTRACTION

Manchester United 1   Middlesbrough 0

Just five days after Old Trafford set a new FA Premier League record attendance of 58,293 in a 1–1 draw with London rivals, Arsenal (scorer: Teddy Sheringham), a massive crowd of 61,267 packed into Old Trafford to see United beat Middlesbrough 1–0 (scorer: David Beckham).

30

1932 LAL HILDITCH SAYS FAREWELL

Manchester United 3   Nottingham Forest 2

Clarence 'Lal' Hilditch played 13 seasons at Old Trafford and to this day is the only player-manager in the history of Manchester United. Lal was appointed player-manager in 1924 after United's previous manager, John Chapman, was suspended indefinitely by the Football Association. Lal coupled his new managerial responsibility with his playing career, although he was most reluctant to pick himself for the team, for a year until Herbert Bamlett took over. A loyal servant from 1919–32, this was his 322nd and final game for his beloved United (301 League appearances scoring 7 goals, and 21 FA Cup appearances) who beat Nottingham Forest 3–2 at Old Trafford with a hat-trick from Thomas Reid.

1960 ANFIELD CUP JOY

Liverpool 1   Manchester United 3

United beat Liverpool 3–1 at Anfield in the fourth round of the FA Cup (scorers: Bobby Charlton 2, Warren Bradley).

31

1953 CUP UPSET NARROWLY AVOIDED

Manchester United 1   Walthamstow Avenue 1

In what was supposed to be one of the most one-sided FA Cup games of all time, Walthamstow Avenue, a non-league side, visited Old Trafford in the fourth round of the competition. The visitors had the Essex and England cricketer Trevor Bailey in their starting line-up and fought hard for a 1–1 draw to earn a well-deserved replay (scorer: Edward Lewis). However, United won 5–2 five days later at Arsenal's Highbury Stadium with goals from Jack Rowley (2), Roger Byrne, Edward Lewis and Stan Pearson.

1976 ALEX OFF THE MARK

Manchester United 3   Birmingham City 1

Manchester United's full-back Alex Forsyth scored his first League goal of the season in the 3–1 home victory over Birmingham City. Lou Macari and Sammy McIlroy scored United's other two goals in the game.

1978 JAWS SEEN AT OLD TRAFFORD

Manchester United signed the Leeds United and Scotland striker, Joe Jordan (nicknamed 'Jaws'), for £350,000, smashing their record transfer fee (United paid Nottingham Forest £200,000 for Ian Storey-Moore in March 1972).

2004 SAHA SCORES ON DEBUT

Manchester United 3   Southampton 2

Louis Saha scored 17 minutes into his Manchester United debut in United's 3–2 win over Southampton in the FA Premier League. Paul Scholes and Ruud van Nistelrooy also scored.

FEBRUARY

1

1946 BUSBY MAKES HIS FIRST SIGNING

Matt Busby entered the transfer market for the first time since taking charge of United in October 1945 and moved swiftly to sign the prolific Glasgow Celtic striker, Jimmy Delaney. Delaney cost Manchester United £4,000 but had to wait until season 1946–47 to make his Football League debut for United as wartime League football was still being played. However, Delaney helped United to fourth place in the Football League North in season 1945–46. Delaney scored 79 goals in 178 League and Cup games for the Scottish giants and won two Championship winners' medals (1936 and 1938) and a Scottish FA Cup winners' medal (1937). He also won nine caps for Scotland as a Celtic player and added a further four during his five-year Old Trafford career.

1954 STAN BIDS FARWELL

After spending 19 years at Old Trafford (1935–54), Stan Pearson left United and joined Bury for £4,500, after which he became player-manager at Chester where he continued to play until he hung up his boots aged 40. Pearson won the FA Cup with United in 1948 and the First Division Championship in 1951–52 (runner-up four times) and played 345 times for United, scoring 139 goals.

1958 BABES' ENGLISH FAREWELL

Arsenal 4   Manchester United 5
The Busby Babes played their last game on English soil when Manchester United beat Arsenal in this First Division encounter at Highbury. United were chasing their third consecutive First Division Championship and led the home side 3–0 at half-time with goals from Duncan Edwards, Tommy Taylor and Bobby Charlton. In the second half Arsenal scored three times in under three minutes (the first Arsenal goal was scored by David Herd, who later became a United player) and suddenly the score was level at 3–3. The home side's fightback did no more than lift United's game and they scored twice more through Dennis Viollet and a second from Tommy Taylor. The Gunners pulled a late goal back but it wasn't enough. Five days after the game five of the team died in the Munich

Air Disaster. A sixth player, Duncan Edwards, died later in hospital of his injuries.

Manchester United: Gregg, Foulkes, Byrne, Colman, Jones, Edwards, Morgan, Charlton, Taylor, Viollet, Scanlon.

1961 WORST HOME POST-WAR DEFEAT

Manchester United 2   Sheffield Wednesday 7
United were completely humiliated by the Owls in this FA Cup fourth round replay, Wednesday claiming a 7–2 win at Old Trafford. Alex Dawson and Mark Pearson scored for United. Amazingly, just four days earlier United had held Sheffield Wednesday 0–0 at Hillsborough in the Cup.

1982 END OF AN ERA AS THE LAST BABE LEAVES

On 1 February 1982, the United manager, Ron Atkinson, sold Sammy McIlroy to Stoke City for £350,000. Sir Matt Busby signed the 14-year-old Irish schoolboy on 1 August 1969, his last signing for Manchester United. McIlroy, a Northern Ireland international, spent 13 years at Old Trafford clocking up 419 appearances, scoring 71 goals.

1984

Darren Barr Fletcher (Midfielder 2000–present) was born in Edinburgh.

2005 KEANO SHOWS VIEIRA WHO IS THE BOSS

Arsenal 2   Manchester United 4
United ended Arsenal's 33 game unbeaten run in the League at home (record of 63 held by Liverpool) when they beat them 4–2 in this pulsating FA Premier League encounter. United played superbly despite going down to 10 men after Mikael Silvestre was sent off for head-butting Freddie Ljungberg. However, the game will be remembered more for the pre-match tunnel bust-up between the opposing captains, Keano and Patrick Vieira, with referee Graham Poll having to separate them. After the match, Keano accused Vieira of starting the row: 'Patrick Vieira is 6ft 4in and having a go at Gary Neville. So I said, "Have a go at me." If he wants to intimidate our players and thinks that Gary Neville is an easy target, I'm not having it.'

2

1895 BANK STREET VAULT BREACHED

Newton Heath 2   Stoke City 3
Newton Heath lost 3–2 at home to Stoke City in the first round of the FA Cup
(scorers: Richard Smith, James Peters). It was the only time the Heathens were
beaten at Bank Street, Clayton, during the 1894–95 season in all competitions,
including 15 League games and one FA Cup tie.

1980 YUGOSLAVIAN BRICK WALL

Derby County 1   Manchester United 3
Shortly after arriving at Old Trafford from Red Star Belgrade, Nikola Jovanovic
made his debut for United in a First Division game against Derby County at the
Baseball Ground. United won the game 3–1 (scorers: Sammy McIlroy, Mickey
Thomas, Powell o.g.).

> JOVANOVIC, Nikola *(Defender 1979–81) – debut in the above game.*
> *Appearances: FL: 20 (1), goals 4 FAC: 1, goals 0 FLC: 2, goals 0 EUR: 2, goals 0*
> *TOTAL: 25 (1) apps, 4 goals.*

1999 WORLD'S RICHEST CLUB

With a turnover of £88m disclosed for the 1997–98 financial year, Manchester
United officially became the richest football club in the world when the figures
were announced to the press on 2 February 1999.

3

1968 NOT YOU AGAIN

Tottenham Hotspur 1   Manchester United 2
United won this First Division game 2–1 at White Hart Lane thanks to goals
from George Best and Bobby Charlton. It was the fifth time the pair had met
during the season: they drew 3–3 at Old Trafford in the FA Charity Shield,
United won 3–1 at Old Trafford in the First Division, they drew 2–2 at Old
Trafford in the third round of the FA Cup and Spurs beat United 1–0 after extra
time in the Cup replay.

1984 MAXWELL BID FAILS

Robert Maxwell entered into negotiations with Martin Edwards to purchase Manchester United for £10m. To the delight of many United fans, the deal never materialised.

4

1928 THE ICE-CREAM TRANSFER

Tottenham Hotspur 4   Manchester United 1
Hughie McLenahan made his debut for the Reds in a 4–1 defeat at White Hart Lane (scorer: William Johnston). Louis Rocca, United's assistant manager, gave Stockport County a freezer of ice-cream in return for the Lancashire club releasing McLenahan from his amateur contract. Stockport were in financial difficulties and so Rocca, a Manchester-based ice-cream manufacturer, decided to help them out with the sweet-tasting donation.

> *McLENAHAN, Hugh (Half-back 1927–37) – debut in the above game.*
> *Appearances: FL: 112, goals 11 FAC: 4, goals 1 TOTAL: 116 apps, 12 goals.*

1992 UNITED STAR TAKES HIS OWN LIFE

Alan Davies took his own life in Gower, near Swansea, aged just 30. Davies played for United in the 1983 FA Cup final and final replay against Brighton & Hove Albion.

1995 COLE THE GOAL OFF THE MARK

Manchester United 1   Aston Villa 0
Andy Cole scored his first goal for Manchester United as a packed Old Trafford watched United beat Aston Villa 1–0 in the Premiership.

5

1946

David Sadler (Defender/Midfielder 1963–74) was born in Yalding, Kent.

1947 UNATTRACTIVE REDS

Manchester United 1   Stoke City 1
A crowd of just 8,456 showed up at Manchester City's Maine Road ground on a

Wednesday afternoon to watch United draw this First Division game 1–1 (scorer: Edward Buckle) with Stoke City. The gate remains United's lowest post-war League home attendance.

1953 UNITED WALTZ PAST WALTHAMSTOW

Walthamstow Avenue 2   Manchester United 5
United defeated non-league Walthamstow Avenue 5–2 (scorers: Jack Rowley 2, Roger Byrne (pen), Stan Pearson, Edward Lewis) in their FA Cup fourth round replay. The match was played at Highbury.

1958 THE LAST LINE-UP

Red Star Belgrade 3   Manchester United 3
On 5 February 1958, Manchester United played Red Star Belgrade, champions of Yugoslavia, in the quarter-final, second leg of the European Cup. United, seeking their second successive semi-final appearance in the competition, went into the game with a slender 2–1 lead from the home leg played on 14 January 1958 (scorers: Eddie Colman, Bobby Charlton). The Busby Babes walked out on to the pitch on a cold Belgrade evening and were greeted by a partisan 55,000 crowd. The home fans fancied Red Star's chances of overturning United's one-goal advantage but fell silent when United, playing some truly magnificent football, took a 3–0 lead to go 5–1 up in the tie. Bobby Charlton scored twice and Dennis Viollet grabbed the third. The half-time score looked bleak for the Yugoslavs, Red Star 0 United 3. Inexplicably, other than fearing for his own post-match safety, the Austrian referee, Karl Kainer, then started to give what can only be described as hugely questionable decisions in favour of the home team. Two minutes into the second half Kostic scored (Red Star 1 United 3) and then Kainer gave Red Star a penalty for an infringement only he had seen. Tasic scored his second and the home fans smelt blood. Despite scoring again to level the game at 3–3 on the night, United held on for a 5–4 aggregate victory.

1968

Lee Andrew Martin (Defender 1988–94) was born in Hyde, Greater Manchester.

1984

Carlos Alberto Tevez (Forward 2007–present) was born in Ciudadela, Buenos Aires, Argentina.

1985

Cristiano Ronaldo dos Santos Aveiro (Winger 2003–present) was born on the island of Madeira.

1992 UNITED PAY THE PENALTY

Manchester United 2   Southampton 2

United became the first top-division side to lose an FA Cup tie on penalties. Southampton were the visitors to Old Trafford for an FA Cup fourth round replay and drew the game 2–2 after extra time (scorers: Andrei Kanchelskis, Brian McClair). United lost the penalty shoot-out 4–2.

2005 6,666 DAYS

Manchester United 2   Birmingham City 0

This Premiership game, for which former United hero Steve Bruce brought his Birmingham City side to Old Trafford, celebrated Sir Alex Ferguson's 6,666th day in charge of the Red Devils. Wayne Rooney and skipper Roy Keane scored for the Reds. Keano's goal was his 50th for the club in what was his 460th appearance for United.

6

1957 REDS' LAST EUROPEAN CUP GAME AT BLUES

Manchester United 3   Atletico Bilbao 0

Manchester United went into this second-leg European Cup quarter-final tie trailing 5–3 from the first but reached the semi-final at the first attempt with a 3–0 'home' win at Maine Road (scorers: Johnny Berry, Tommy Taylor, Dennis Viollet) for an aggregate victory of 6–5 over the Spaniards. It was United's last European Cup game at Manchester City's ground as the Old Trafford floodlights were ready in time for their semi-final tie with Real Madrid.

1958 THE MUNICH AIR DISASTER

The day after their 3–3 draw with Red Star Belgrade the United team, together with club officials and journalists, left Belgrade for Manchester, with a brief scheduled stop-off at Munich Airport en route. At approximately 2.00 p.m. the twin-engine Elizabethan jet, named *Lord Burghley*, was ready for take-off with Captain Kenneth Rayment, second in command, at the controls. Captain James Thain had flown the plane out to Belgrade but handed over the wheel to Captain Rayment for the flight home.

At 2.31 p.m. the aircraft control tower were informed that '609 Zulu Uniform is rolling.' As the plane taxied down the runway Captain Thain noticed the port pressure gauge fluctuating shortly after full power had been engaged and the engine sounded strange during acceleration. Captain Rayment abandoned take-off within 40 seconds of the start. The problem had been that of boost surge whereby the engines over-accelerated because of the very rich mixture of fuel. Apparently this was quite a common problem with the Elizabethan. At 2.34 p.m. 609 Zulu Uniform was given permission to attempt a second take-off by air traffic control but once again the plane came to a halt. After this second aborted attempt to take off the passengers returned to the airport lounge. It had started to snow heavily.

Many of the players were of the opinion that they would not be flying home that afternoon because of the bad weather. Duncan Edwards sent a telegram to his landlady back home in Manchester, which read: 'All flights cancelled, flying tomorrow. Duncan.' After a 15-minute delay everyone boarded the plane again. A number of the passengers, notably Duncan Edwards, Mark Jones, Tommy Taylor, Eddie Colman and Frank Swift, decided to move to the rear of the plane, where they believed it to be a safer place to sit. Following discussions between Captain Thain, Captain Rayment and William Black, (the airport engineer), 609 Zulu Uniform was on the move again. Problems ensued once more as the plane sped down the runway, the air speed indicator first reading 117 knots and then dropping to 105 knots. The jet shot off the runway and went straight through a fence, then across a road before its port wing struck a nearby house. Part of the jet's tail and its wing were instantly ripped off while the house caught fire. The cockpit hit a tree, and the starboard side of the fuselage hit a wooden hut that contained a truck loaded with fuel and tyres. The truck exploded upon impact.

Speaking after the crash, Bill Foulkes recalled hearing a bang, then after a few minutes' unconsciousness, remembered seeing a hole in the plane directly in front of him. Foulkes and goalkeeper Harry Gregg performed heroics as time after time they helped team-mates and passengers from the smouldering wreckage. The injured, including a seriously hurt Matt Busby, were taken to the nearby Rechts der Isar Hospital. However, it was not until the next day that the world became aware of the true horror of the crash. Duncan Edwards' telegram was delivered at approximately 5.00 p.m., less than two hours after the crash.

Matt Busby lay in an oxygen tent, Bobby Charlton had a bandage wrapped around his head, Jackie Blanchflower had a badly gashed arm, Ray Wood suffered a cut face and concussion, Albert Scanlon's skull was fractured, Duncan Edwards had serious injuries, Dennis Viollet had a gashed head together with injuries to his face while both Ken Morgans and Johnny Berry lay motionless in bed. Close by the United players lay journalist Frank Taylor.

The Busby Babes killed instantly were: Geoff Bent, Roger Byrne, Eddie Colman, Mark Jones, David Pegg, Tommy Taylor and Liam Whelan. Walter Crickmer, the club secretary, first-team trainer Tom Curry and coach Bert Whalley also perished in the crash. Eight of the nine journalists on the flight – Alf Clarke, Don Davies, George Follows, Tom Jackson, Archie Ledbrooke, Henry Rose, Frank Swift and Eric Thompson – died in the crash as did one of the aircrew, the travel agent who arranged the trip, a supporter and two other passengers. In all, 23 people died in the disaster – Duncan Edwards and Captain

Rayment died in hospital from their injuries – and there were 16 survivors. Two of the players who survived the crash, Jackie Blanchflower and Johnny Berry, never played competitive football again. The Munich Air Disaster is undoubtedly one of football's blackest days.

1989 MOSES CALLS IT A DAY

After numerous operations on his ankle injuries Remi Moses decided to retire from football on the advice of specialists.

1999 CITY GROUND MASSACRE

Nottingham Forest 1   Manchester United 8
Manchester United beat Nottingham Forest 8–1 at the City Ground with Ole Gunnar Solskjaer coming on as a second-half substitute to score four goals in the last 10 minutes. Andy Cole and Dwight Yorke also scored two each. The 8–1 trouncing remains the biggest ever away win in Premiership history.

7

1925 FROM BLUE TO RED IN AN HOUR

Manchester United 4   Clapton Orient 1
Clapton Orient (later named Leyton Orient) arrived at Old Trafford with Albert Pape named in their starting line-up for a Second Division League game. Pape was a no-nonsense forward and a good friend of United's Frank Barson. Less than an hour to the kick-off the United directors met with the Clapton directors with the latter agreeing to transfer Pape to United with immediate effect. So instead of running out at Old Trafford in Clapton's blue away strip, Pape made his United debut, and just to show that he did not hold any grudges against his former employers, he scored in the game. Fred Kennedy (2) and Francis McPherson also scored in United's 4–1 win. Pape scored four more League goals for United from 15 games during season 1924–25, helping them to runners-up spot in the League and promotion back to the big time. Surprisingly, after just two more League games at the beginning of the 1925–26 season, Pape left United and joined Fulham. During his career he also played for a host of other clubs including Hurst FC, Notts County, Rhyl Athletic and Rotherham County scoring 103 League goals in 266 games.

> PAPE, Albert Arthur (Forward 1924–6) – debut in the above game.
> Appearances: FL: 18, goals 5 TOTAL: 18 apps, 5 goals.

1970 BEST'S MAGIC SHOW

Northampton Town 2   Manchester United 8

Manchester United were drawn away to Northampton Town in the fifth round of the FA Cup but all eyes were not focusing on a major Cup upset as the game marked the return of the Genius himself, George Best, after serving a suspension. Best was in spellbinding form weaving his way through the Cobblers defence like a hot knife glides through butter, scoring two hat-tricks in this one-sided affair. At one point Bestie almost looked apologetic for scoring with such ease as he clasped the upright and gently kicked the mud from his boots after finding the net again. United won comfortably 8–2 with Brian Kidd adding two more for the rampant Red Devils.

2004 RUUD THE CENTURION

Everton 3   Manchester United 4

Ruud van Nistelrooy scored his first goal for Manchester United on his debut against Arsenal in the Charity Shield on 12 August 2001. Less than three years later Ruud netted his 100th goal for United in their pulsating 4–3 away win at Everton on 7 February 2004. Amazingly, it took Ruud only 131 games to reach his century of goals for United.

8

1929

Roger William Byrne (Full-back 1951–8) was born in Gorton, Manchester.

1958 A FITTING MARK OF RESPECT

United were due to play Wolverhampton Wanderers in a First Division game on the Saturday following their midweek European Cup tie in Belgrade but the match was postponed as a mark of respect for those who had lost their lives in the Munich Air Disaster. A *United Review* from this postponed First Division game was sold in 1997 for £1,925. The price slightly bettered the £1,887 a collector paid for a match programme from United's game with Red Star Belgrade in Belgrade on 5 February 1958, the last game the Busby Babes played together.

1978 TOOTHLESS JOE PULLS ON A RED SHIRT

Manchester United 1   Bristol City 1

Following his £350,000 transfer from Leeds United, Big Joe Jordan made his debut for the Reds in a 1–1 draw with Bristol City at Old Trafford. Ironically, after returning from a spell in Italian football, Joe played for and also managed Bristol City.

> JORDAN, Joseph 'Joe' (Forward 1978–81) – debut in the above game.
>   Appearances: FL: 109, goals 37, FAC: 11 (1), goals 2 FLC: 4, goals 2
>   EUR: 1, goals 0 TOTAL: 125 (1) apps, 41 goals.

9

1929 MAGPIES DEVOUR DEVILS

Newcastle United 5   Manchester United 0
United were beaten 5–0 away by Newcastle United in this First Division game. Earlier in the season United had beaten the Magpies 5–0 in the League clash at Old Trafford (scorers: William Rawlings 2, James Hanson, William Johnston, Joe Spence).

1957

Gordon David Strachan (Midfielder 1984–9) was born in Edinburgh.

1972

Darren Ferguson (Midfielder 1990–4) was born in Glasgow.

1974

Jordi Cruyff (Midfielder 1996–2000) was born in Amsterdam.

1986 MISSILES AND TEAR GAS THROWN

Liverpool 1   Manchester United 1
United's team bus was pelted with missiles, and tear gas was thrown in the direction of the players when they arrived at Anfield for this First Division game with Liverpool. The game ended 1–1 (scorer: Colin Gibson).

10

1912 ERIN GO BRAGH'S FIRST

Michael Hamill became the first Manchester United player to be capped by Ireland (prior to 1924 Northern Ireland and the Republic of Ireland, as they are known today, were one country). Born in Belfast on 19 January 1885, Hamill made his international debut in Ireland's 6–1 defeat in Dublin by England. Hamill made it a debut to remember by scoring the Irish goal.

1948

John James 'Jimmy' Rimmer (Goalkeeper 1967–73) was born in Southport, Lancashire.

1991 REDS BEAT THE WHITES IN RUMBELOWS CUP

Manchester United 2 Leeds United 1
Leeds United visited Old Trafford for the first leg of this Rumbelows League Cup semi-final and were packed off back across the Pennines on the end of a 2–1 defeat (scorers : Lee Sharpe, Brian McClair).

2006 FASHIONABLE RONALDO

Cristiano Ronaldo opened his very own fashion store, 'CR7', in his home town of Funchal, Madeira and placed his older sisters in charge of it. However, he was not the first Red to enter this line of business as George Best was United's original trendsetter back in the early 1960s.

2008 SILENT TRIBUTE TO THE BUSBY BABES

Manchester United 1 Manchester City 2
Prior to United's Premier League game against Manchester City at Old Trafford, a minute's silence was held as a mark of respect to the 23 people who tragically lost their lives in the Munich Air Disaster on 6 February 1958. The Manchester City fans played their part in commemorating the 50th anniversary of the disaster by behaving impeccably throughout the silent tribute when you could have heard a pin drop inside Old Trafford. United lost the game 2–1, with Michael Carrick scoring United's goal.

11

1978 HILL NETS AT THE BRIDGE

Chelsea 2 Manchester United 2
United's exciting winger Gordon Hill scored for the third consecutive game, his fourth in three games, in United's 2–2 First Division draw with Chelsea at Stamford Bridge. Sammy McIlroy also scored for the Reds.

1995 PHIL SINGS THE BLUES

Manchester City 0   Manchester United 3

Phil Neville (Defender 1994–2005) made his Manchester United debut in this 3–0 Premier League win over local rivals Manchester City (scorers: Andy Cole, Paul Ince, Andrei Kanchelskis). Meanwhile, David and Ian Brightwell became the first pair of brothers to play for Manchester City in a Manchester derby game in over 100 years. The meagre crowd of 26,368 was the lowest derby crowd in over 73 years (24,000 were at Maine Road on 2 October 1921). Including this game there had been 122 Manchester League derbies: United had won 46, City had won 32 with 44 draws.

12

1949 UNITED'S RECORD 'HOME' ATTENDANCE

Manchester United 8   Yeovil Town 0

Jack Rowley smacked in five of United's eight goals against a hapless Yeovil Town in the fifth round of the FA Cup. United played the home tie at City's Maine Road ground due to bomb damage caused to Old Trafford during the war while the crowd of 81,565 is United's record 'home' attendance and the highest ever attendance to watch a non-League team in an FA Cup tie. The 8–0 win (Ronald Burke 2 and Charlie Mitten also scored) is United's record FA Cup victory.

1955 FIVE TIMES THE BLUES

Manchester United 0   Manchester City 5

Neighbours City thrashed United 5–0 at Old Trafford in the Manchester derby game.

2005 WORLD'S RICHEST FOR EIGHTH TIME ON THE BOUNCE

Manchester United were named the world's richest football club for the eighth consecutive year with an income of £171.5m for the 2003–04 season. Real Madrid were second with an income of £156.3m while AC Milan occupied third place on £147.2m.

13

1901 RECORD FA CUP DEFEAT

Burnley 7   Manchester United 1
Four days after drawing 0–0 at Old Trafford with Lancashire rivals Burnley in the first round of the 1901–02 FA Cup, United were thrashed 7–1 at Turf Moor in the replay (scorer: Alfred Schofield). It was, and remains, United's worst ever defeat in the FA Cup.

1994 RECORD-BREAKING UNBEATEN HOME RUN

Manchester United 1   Sheffield Wednesday 0
Manchester United set a new club record of 36 games unbeaten at home in all competitions when they beat Sheffield Wednesday 1–0 (scorer: Ryan Giggs) in the first leg of the Coca-Cola Cup semi-final. The run began on 21 November 1992 with a 3–0 Premiership win over Oldham Athletic.

2005 GIGGS JOINS 400 CLUB

Manchester City 0   Manchester United 2
When Ryan Giggs came on as a second-half substitute for Darren Fletcher in United's 2–0 derby win over Manchester City at the City of Manchester Stadium on 13 February 2005 (scorers: Wayne Rooney, o.g.), it marked the Welsh winger's 400th Premier League game for United. Giggs wore protective tights in the game to shield his hamstring and almost marked the occasion with a goal but the ball struck the foot of the post.

14

1900 HEATHENS IN DOCK OVER TRANSFER

In January 1900 Newton Heath signed Gilbert Godsmark from the Kent League side Ashford FC. The agreed fee between the two clubs was £40 with half of the fee being paid upon the player signing and the remainder to be paid after a satisfactory trial period had been served. After only nine appearances for the Heathens, in which he scored four times, Godsmark was called up in April 1900 as a reservist to fight in the Boer War. The Heathens retained his playing registration for season 1900–01 but sadly Godsmark was killed in action in

February 1901. Following his death Ashford FC served a writ on Newton Heath for the outstanding £20.

2004 FIERY CUP DERBY

Manchester United 4   Manchester City 2

In the FA Cup fifth round United beat Manchester City 4–2 at Old Trafford despite being reduced to 10 men after Gary Neville was sent off for head-butting Steve McManaman. The United scorers were Ruud van Nistelrooy (2), Cristiano Ronaldo and Paul Scholes. United have not lost to City in the FA Cup since 1955.

15

1945 MATT BUSBY ACCEPTS UNITED JOB

Matt Busby was appointed the manager of Manchester United and the legend began although he did not officially take up his new post until he was demobbed from the army on 1 October 1945. Matt Busby was born in Bellshill, Lanarkshire in 1909. His father was a miner, who died on the Somme in World War I, and the young Busby followed his father's footsteps down the pit. The young Busby always had a dream that one day he would earn his living as a footballer and in 1928 that dream became a reality when he joined Manchester City. An outstanding right-half for City, he won an FA Cup winners' medal with them in 1934 and then moved on to Liverpool in 1936. He captained Scotland and the British Services' team during the Second World War.

Upon taking up his appointment at United he inherited an old team while Old Trafford was a pile of rubble following its bombing by the Germans during the war. However, ably assisted by his right-hand man, Jimmy Murphy, Matt Busby began the rebuilding process. He built his first team around Johnny Carey and is enshrined forever in the history of Manchester United for building three great teams at Old Trafford. His first great team were First Division runners-up in 1947, 1948 and 1949 and winners of the FA Cup in 1948. Busby's style of management was a breath of fresh air and unlike his predecessors he joined his players on the training field, a concept unheard of at the time. Matt Busby built a dynasty at Old Trafford and put all his faith and trust in youth. Who will ever forget his Busby Babes side of the 1950s, which dominated the domestic game? During the 1950s United won the First Division Championship three times (1952, 1956 and 1957), were runners-up twice (1951 and 1959), FA Cup finalists in 1957 and 1958, FA Charity Shield winners three times (1952, 1956 and 1957) and United's youth team won the first five FA Youth Cups (1953–7). The football world was at the feet of the Babes – Duncan Edwards, Geoff Bent, Roger Byrne, Eddie Colman, Liam Whelan, David Pegg, Mark Jones, Bill Foulkes, Johnny

Berry, Bobby Charlton and many others, all products of Matt Busby's youth policy. However, on the 6 February 1958 the heart was ripped out of Manchester United by the Munich Air Disaster.

Most ordinary men would have given up football after going through what Matt Busby suffered, but this was no ordinary man. He was like a father to the young players who lost their lives that fateful day in Munich and in their memory he commenced the almost impossible task of rebuilding the team. Matt Busby built his third great side during the 1960s, a team containing United legends such as Law, Best and Charlton. The team of the 1960s thrilled fans up and down the country with their swashbuckling style, instilled in them by Matt Busby. Matt's philosophy for his players was simply for them to go on to the field and enjoy themselves. United won the FA Cup in 1963, were First Division champions in 1965 and 1967, First Division runners-up in 1964 and 1968, joint holders of the FA Charity Shield in 1965 and 1967 and winners of the FA Youth Cup for the sixth time under his leadership in 1964. But the greatest night in Matt Busby's football life came at Wembley in May 1968. That night his dream came true. United, the pioneers of English football in European club competitions when Matt Busby defied FA orders and entered United in the 1956–57 European Cup, became the first English side to win the tournament. On that hot May evening his third great side beat Benfica of Portugal 4–1 after extra-time at Wembley Stadium.

In 1968 Matt Busby was named Manager of the Year, awarded the freedom of Manchester and given a knighthood by the Queen. Matt Busby was a man of the people, honest and hard working, respected by everyone and loved by the fans of his beloved Manchester United. He was, and always will be remembered as, 'The Father of Manchester United'.

2003 BEWARE OF LOW-FLYING BOOTS

Manchester United 0   Arsenal 2
David Beckham was injured when a furious Sir Alex Ferguson kicked a football boot across the dressing room at Old Trafford as he berated his players for losing an FA Cup tie to Arsenal. The boot hit Beckham in the face leaving the England captain with a gash that required two stitches. Sir Alex said: 'It was one of these freak acts of nature that happens and it's over. It was a freak act, it will never happen again.'

16

2006 UNITED DETHRONED AS WORLD'S RICHEST CLUB

According to a report issued by the accountants Deloitte Touche, Real Madrid overtook Manchester United to become the world's richest football club in terms of income. United had been named the richest club side in the world for the past eight years but based on revenues from the 2004–05 season the Spanish giants took their rich-list crown. United, acquired by the US business tycoon Malcolm Glazer during the season, saw their income fall from £171.5m to £166.4m. However, United still generated more income from matchday revenues (ticket sales, corporate hospitality etc.) than any other club. Deloitte did expect United to reclaim the world's richest-club tag as soon as the further expansion of Old Trafford was completed, which in turn would generate more matchday income.

2008 SIR ALEX'S CUP CENTURY

Manchester United 4   Arsenal 0
Manchester United's 4–0 thumping of Arsenal at Old Trafford in the fifth round of the FA Cup was Sir Alex Ferguson's 100th game in charge of the Red Devils for an FA Cup tie, equalling the total achieved by Sir Matt Busby in his reign. Goals from Wayne Rooney, Darren Fletcher (2) and Nani gave Sir Alex his 68th FA Cup victory (10 more than achieved by Sir Matt). The tie was the 12th time the two sides had been drawn together in the FA Cup, United edging the Gunners with six wins to their five plus one draw (the 1999 FA Cup semi-final).

17

1910 GALES DESTROY UNITED'S BANK STREET GROUND

Two days before the official opening of United's new home at Old Trafford fierce gales struck the Manchester area. The old wooden stand at Bank Street was ripped apart by the gales as wreckage from it blew across the roadway, damaging a number of houses in the vicinity. Thankfully it wasn't a matchday and no one was injured.

1962 FAMILIAR OLD BIRD

Manchester United 0   Sheffield Wednesday 0
United met Sheffield Wednesday in the FA Cup for the fourth time in the last

five seasons. The two teams played out a 0–0 draw in this fifth round tie at Old Trafford but United beat the Owls 2–0 in the replay at Hillsborough four days later (scorers: Bobby Charlton, Johnny Giles).

18

1953 THE EVER VERSATILE CAREY

Sunderland 2   Manchester United 2
United visited Roker Park for a First Division game against Sunderland. However, the Reds travelled to the North East without a goalkeeper following an injury to Ray Wood and so Matt Busby asked his captain, Johnny Carey, to play in goal. Carey answered the call to arms and helped United to a memorable 2–2 draw (scorers: Edward Lewis, David Pegg). During his career with United, the highly versatile Northern Ireland and Republic of Ireland full-back played for United in every position except outside-left.

1957 UNLUCKY CHARLTON

Charlton Athletic 1   Manchester United 5
Bobby Charlton made his debut for Manchester United against Charlton Athletic at Old Trafford on 6 October 1956 and scored twice in a 4–2 win. Later that same season, on 18 February 1957, he scored his first hat-trick for United, against Charlton Athletic at The Valley in United's 5–1 First Division win, Tommy Taylor scored the other two goals for United.

1975

Gary Neville (Defender 1993–present) was born in Bury, Greater Manchester.
Keith Robert Gillespie (Forward 1992–5) was born in Larne, Northern Ireland.

2006 REDS V REDS FA CUP RECORD

Liverpool 1   Manchester United 0
This was the 12th time United were drawn against Liverpool in the FA Cup while the 1–0 win for the Merseysiders was their first FA Cup win over United in 85 years. United's substitute Alan Smith suffered a broken leg after he blocked a free-kick late in the game. Distastefully, the ambulance that took the United striker to hospital was attacked by so-called Liverpool fans.

19

1910 OLD TRAFFORD OPENS ITS DOORS

Manchester United 3   Liverpool 4

'The most handsomest [*sic*], the most spacious and the most remarkable arena I have ever seen. As a football ground it is unrivalled in the world, it is an honour to Manchester and the home of a team who can do wonders when they are so disposed' (*Sporting Chronicle*: Saturday 19 February 1910). Manchester United's move from their old Bank Street ground to the splendour of their new home was completed when the Reds played their inaugural game at the brand new purpose-built Old Trafford. The centrepiece of the new stadium was a magnificent stand that could seat 12,000 fans while the architect, Archibald Leitch, originally planned for the stadium to accommodate 100,000 fans (later reduced to 80,000). Leitch went on to design new stands in Glasgow for both Celtic and Rangers during the 1920s. When the doors to Old Trafford opened for business for the first time, a crowd of 45,000 came along to watch United play Liverpool in the First Division. Despite going into the game without several of their key players, United took a 3–1 lead (scorers: Thomas Homer, Sandy Turnbull, George Wall) and looked set to give their new home a winning baptism. However, the Merseysiders fought back to score three more goals and put the dampeners on an otherwise special occasion. Liverpool ended the season runners-up to Aston Villa while United finished in fifth position.

1939

Patrick Timothy 'Pat' Crerand (Half-back 1962–71) was born in Glasgow.

1958 A PHOENIX RISES FROM THE ASHES

Manchester United 3   Sheffield Wednesday 0

Just 13 days after the horrific Munich Air Disaster, Manchester United had to pick the club up, almost like a phoenix rising from the ashes, to play their first game of football while still mourning the death of seven of the greatest players ever to have worn the Red shirt of United. Almost 60,000 fans poured into Old Trafford and men, women and children could not hold back the tears, weeping uncontrollably as they opened the match programme to find the United line-up completely blank where once appeared the names of Geoff Bent, Roger Byrne, Eddie Colman, Mark Jones, David Pegg, Tommy Taylor and Liam Whelan. All seven had perished in the crash, lost for ever, while an eighth Busby Babe, and perhaps the greatest of them all, Duncan Edwards, would lose his own brave battle for life 48 hours later. The fans attached black ribbons to their red and white scarves in memory of everyone who lost their lives on that snowy Munich Airport runway, and United later incorporated black into their kits as a mark of respect. However, life had somehow to go on and it was Sheffield Wednesday who visited Old Trafford for this fifth round FA Cup tie. With a wave of emotion pouring out on to the pitch from the stands, a relatively inexperienced and youthful United won 3–0 with debut boy Shay Brennan scoring twice and a third coming from Alex Dawson. Amazingly, United had played their Yorkshire rivals three times previously in the FA Cup and lost all three without scoring in any of the ties (0–6, 0–1 and 0–2). The Sheffield Wednesday captain on the night, Albert Quixall, joined United in September 1958, winning an FA Cup winners' medal with the Reds in 1963. Apart from Brennan, Stan Crowther also made his debut for United in the game. However, Crowther only came along to Old Trafford to watch the game alongside his manager at Aston Villa, Eric Houghton. But one hour before kick-off he signed for United and played after the FA, sympathetic to United's plight, generously waived their rule that a player cannot appear for two different teams in the FA Cup in the same season. Crowther reached the 1958 FA Cup final with United, losing 2–0 to Bolton Wanderers, resulting in Stan becoming the only FA Cup finalist in the history of the competition to appear for two different clubs in the FA Cup in the same season.

Manchester United: Gregg, Foulkes, Greaves, Goodwin, Cope, Crowther, Webster, E. Taylor, Dawson, Pearson, Brennan.

BRENNAN, Seamus Anthony 'Shay' (Full-back 1957–70) – debut in the above game. Appearances: FL: 291(1), goals 3 FAC: 36, goals 3 FLC: 4, goals 0 EUR: 24, goals 0 TOTAL: 358(1) apps, 6 goals.

1958 THE MOST FAMOUS *UNITED REVIEW*

The *United Review* is the name of the official matchday programme sold by Manchester United at Old Trafford. The most highly sought-after edition is the programme printed for the above game, the FA Cup fifth round tie against Sheffield Wednesday. The programme for this evening kick-off game was given the title 'United Will Go On' and contained a lot of information and photographs from the horrific Munich Air Disaster, which had occurred less than two weeks earlier. Traditionally, the centre pages of the *United Review* used to be a double page spread in the shape of a football pitch with one page devoted to each team's line-up and formation. However, although the *United Review* for 19 February 1958 did indeed show all of the Wednesday players, the Manchester United half was left completely blank because Manchester United's caretaker manager at the time, Jimmy Murphy (Matt Busby was still lying in a hospital bed in Munich recovering from his injuries), simply did not know what players he could choose from until shortly before kick-off.

1995 FA CUP WAR OF THE ROSES

Manchester United 3   Leeds United 1

United beat Leeds United 3–1 at Old Trafford in the fifth round of the FA Cup. Leeds had gone into the game unbeaten in 1995 but a goal in the very first minute from Steve Bruce followed by further goals from Brian McClair and Mark Hughes made sure the Yorkshire visitors' unbeaten run came to an end. Leeds United have never beaten the Reds at Old Trafford in any Cup tie.

1997 WRIGHT-SCHMEICHEL AFFAIR BOILS OVER

Arsenal 1   Manchester United 2

Even without the suspended Cantona, Manchester United produced one of their finest performances of the season against a side that was also challenging hard for the Premiership. However, the game will be remembered more for Ian Wright's two-footed lunge on Peter Schmeichel and the subsequent allegations concerning racist remarks between the two players. Andy Cole (against his former club) and Ole Gunnar Solskjaer scored the all-important goals for United at Highbury en route to retaining the Premiership title in 1996–97.

2005 TOFFEES COME UNSTUCK

Everton 0   Manchester United 2

Everton entertained the visit of Manchester United to Goodison Park for this important FA Cup fifth round tie. In the five previous meetings in the competition between the two clubs the games all ended 1–0, including a 1–0 win for United in the 1985 final and a 1–0 win for Everton in the 1995 final. However, the tradition was broken with United winning this meeting 2–0 thanks to goals from Quinton Fortune and Cristiano Ronaldo.

20

1960 RECORD POST-WAR OLD TRAFFORD ATTENDANCE

Manchester United 0   Sheffield Wednesday 1

The crowd of 66,350 for this FA Cup fourth round replay was at the time United's record post-war attendance for a home game at Old Trafford in all competitions.

1971 WHEN THE DEVILS MAULED THE SAINTS

Manchester United 5   Southampton 1

Alan Gowling scored four goals in United's 5–1 First Division win over Southampton at Old Trafford. Willie Morgan also scored against The Saints.

1994 *TRÈS BIEN*

Wimbledon 0   Manchester United 3

Manchester United visited the home of Crystal Palace, Selhurst Park, to play their tenants, Wimbledon, in this FA Cup fifth round tie. Denis Irwin scored a superb solo goal with Paul Ince also adding his name to the score sheet. However, the game will always be remembered for the magnificent cushioned volley Eric Cantona scored from the edge of the penalty area. It was, as they say in France, *très bien*. Some years later the goal led to the creation of a poster by Nike (Eric's football boot sponsors) with the strap-line 'I'll never forget that night at Selhurst Park ... when you scored that wonderful goal against Wimbledon.' The advertisement made a play on Eric's infamous kung-fu attack at the same ground in January 1995 that led to him receiving an eight-month ban.

2007 A CONTROVERSIAL FREE KICK

LOSC Lille Metropole 0   Manchester United 1

A quickly taken free kick from Ryan Giggs in the 84th minute gave United a priceless 1–0 win in a controversial UEFA Champions League last 16 tie with LOSC Lille Metropole in Stade Felix-Bollaert. After Giggs scored the French were furious, Sylva in the Lille goal claiming he was still lining up his wall when Giggs curled the ball into the net from 25 yards. Sylva was booked for his protestations while several Lille players looked set to walk off the pitch in protest.

2008 GIGGS'S EUROPEAN CENTURY

Olympique Lyonnais 1   Manchester United 1

When Ryan Giggs captained Manchester United in their last 16 UEFA Champions League first leg tie away to Olympique Lyonnais, it was his 100th Champions League game for United. Giggs, aged 34, became the eighth player to reach the landmark following his tournament debut in 1994. Meanwhile, United complained to UEFA prior to the 1–1 draw (scorer: Carlos Tevez) in France that Cristiano Ronaldo had been dazzled by a laser beam during his pre-match warm-up.

21

1903 UNITED CHANGE THEIR KIT AT HALF-TIME

Everton 3   Manchester United 1

In an FA Cup second round encounter with Everton at Goodison Park, Manchester United wore two different kits during the game. In the first half United wore their traditional red shirts, but as a result of atrocious weather conditions,

United decided to wear a different kit for the second half. After the interval they turned out in blue and white stripes. However, neither did the Reds/Blues any good as they lost the game 3–1 (scorer: William Griffiths).

1931 TRAVEL-SICK REDS

Arsenal 4   Manchester United 1
When Arsenal beat United 4–1 in this First Division game at Highbury it was their 17th successive away League defeat (scorer: Arthur Thomson). The unwanted winless streak began back on 26 April 1930 with a 3–1 reversal at Leeds United (scorer: Joe Spence).

1940

Alexander Downie Dawson (Forward 1956–62) was born in Aberdeen.

1958 DUNCAN EDWARDS' LAST STAND

Duncan Edwards lost his brave battle for life in the Rechts der Isar Hospital, Munich, 15 days after he and his team-mates were passengers on board an Elizabethan jet that crashed on take-off at Munich Airport. He became the eighth Busby Babe to lose his life in the crash when his blood circulation gave up on him following severe damage to his kidney. Once again football fans everywhere mourned the loss of a football giant. Aged just 21, he had already played for United 177 times, scoring 21 goals, and represented England 18 times, scoring five times. Edwards was an extremely popular player and, since his death, has been paid tribute to by Matt Busby and his team-mates:

Sir Matt Busby: 'He is the greatest player of his age I have ever seen. Yet though he has soared up among the stars, his feet are still on the ground.'

Jimmy Murphy: 'When I used to hear Muhammad Ali proclaim to the world that he was the greatest, I used to smile. You see, the greatest of them all was an English footballer named Duncan Edwards.'

Wilf McGuinness: 'He could play as an attacker, creator or defender and be the best player on the pitch. Once he was playing for the English League XI against the Scottish League: 2–0 down, Duncan was moved from wing-half to centre-forward. He scored a hat-trick to win the game.'

Sir Bobby Charlton: 'The best player I've ever seen, the best footballer I've ever played with, the only player who ever made me feel inferior.'

Bill Foulkes: 'He had everything. He was powerful, technically gifted as good as anyone. He was a freak to be honest, mature beyond his years. He was one of the boys but also a gentleman, the model professional.'

Today a stained-glass window in the Church of St Francis in the Priory, Dudley, Worcestershire is a fitting permanent memorial to him.

1995 CANTONA CHARGED

The Metropolitan Police formally charged Eric Cantona following his 'kung-fu' style attack on a Crystal Palace fan the previous month. Eric was charged with common assault, the lowest form of the offence.

22

1947 PROGRAMME MISSING

Manchester United 3   Blackpool 0
Manchester United, still having to play their 'home' games at Maine Road, beat Blackpool 3–0 in this First Division encounter (scorers: Jack Rowley 2, John Hanlon). However, those fans hoping to purchase a match programme were sent home empty handed as a direct result of a strike by the printers.

1958 A PHOENIX RISES FROM THE ASHES

Manchester United 1   Nottingham Forest 1
Sixteen days after the fateful Munich Air Disaster, Manchester United had to resume their domestic League campaign with a home game against Nottingham Forest. A barely recognisable United, selected by Jimmy Murphy as Matt Busby was still in hospital in Munich, took to the pitch and drew 1–1 (scorer: Alex Dawson). At the time, the crowd of 66,123 was United's record post-war League attendance at Old Trafford.

Lancelot Holliday Richardson (Goalkeeper 1925–9) died in Cordoba, Argentina, aged 58.

1975 UNITED'S SUPERSUB

Aston Villa 2   Manchester United 0
Ron Tudor Davies made his 10th and final appearance for Manchester United in their 2–0 Second Division loss to Aston Villa at Villa Park. Remarkably, all 10 of his appearances for the Reds (8 League, 2 FA Cup) were as a substitute.

1995 UNITED TEAM IN NEAR MISS

Norwich City 0   Manchester United 2
Manchester United hired a charter plane and flew to Norwich for their Premiership game against the Canaries. However, just as the plane was landing it was hit by a crosswind and almost tipped over. Goals from Paul Ince and Andrei Kanchelskis secured a 2–0 win and all three points for the Reds at Carrow Road. Both goals were landmark strikes for the club. Ince's goal was

United's 2,500th away goal while Kanchelskis's strike was the Reds' 200th goal in the FA Premier League.

23

1963 PADDY TIME

Manchester United 1   Blackpool 1

Matt Busby paid Glasgow Celtic £56,000 for the services of his fellow countryman Paddy Crerand. Three months after arriving at Old Trafford Crerand won an FA Cup winners' medal with United in the 3–1 win over Leicester City. Always a fierce competitor, Crerand went on to serve United loyally for almost 10 years. In addition to his FA Cup medal, Paddy played a major part in United's revival during the 1960s and also won two League Championships (1965 and 1967) and a European Cup winners' medal in 1968 with the Reds. After his career ended, midway through the 1971–72 season, he was appointed assistant manager to Tommy Docherty at Old Trafford. Paddy also won 16 caps for Scotland and enjoys legendary status among United fans as a result of his unquestionable loyalty to the club regardless of events on or off the field, a firm fans' favourite.

> CRERAND, Patrick Timothy 'Paddy' (Half-back 1962–71) – debut in the above game.
> Appearances: FL: 304, goals 10 FAC: 43, goals 4 FLC: 4, goals 0 EUR: 41, goals 1
> TOTAL: 397 apps, 15 goals.

2002 IN TRIBUTE TO THE KING

Manchester United 1   Aston Villa 0

A 10-foot-high statue honouring Denis Law was unveiled by The King himself on the concourse of the Stretford End at Old Trafford prior to United's 1–0 FA Premier League win over Aston Villa (scorer: Ruud van Nistelrooy). Law's journey to United followed a long and winding road that started off at Huddersfield in 1955, before he signed for Manchester City in 1960 for a British record transfer fee. He then moved on to Torino in Italy in 1961. Law didn't take to Italian football and within a year he was back in Manchester, this time to play in the Red of United. By this time he was a regular in the Scottish national side having been given his first cap in 1958 at the age of 18 by the Scotland manager Matt Busby (he managed both United and Scotland at the time). The King's Old Trafford reign lasted for 13 glorious years, most of them spent in the same team as Bobby Charlton and George Best.

24

1940 THE KING IS BORN

Denis Law (Forward 1962–73) was born in Aberdeen.

1991 RED ROSE v WHITE ROSE WEMBLEY REUNION

Leeds United 0   Manchester United 1
United travelled to Elland Road to face Leeds United in the second leg of their Rumbelows League Cup semi-final clash. The red rose of Lancashire triumphed over Yorkshire's white rose with a 1–0 victory courtesy of a Lee Sharpe strike in the last minute. Having already won the home leg 2–1, the 3–1 aggregate result put United into the final at Wembley against Sheffield Wednesday.

1995 ERIC CANTONA BANNED BY THE FA

Following his sending off at Selhurst Park, the Football Association banned Eric Cantona from all football until 1 October 1995.

2001 IRRESISTIBLE REDS

Manchester United 6   Arsenal 1
Arsenal, the pretenders to United's throne and out to prevent the Reds from winning their third consecutive Premiership crown, were given a football lesson by United at Old Trafford. The Gunners were on the receiving end of a non-stop artillery attack from a rampant United who fired six past their so-called well-marshalled defence (scorers: Dwight Yorke 3, Roy Keane, Teddy Sheringham, Ole Gunnar Solskjaer). United went on to clinch their hat-trick of successive titles while Arsenal finished runners-up, 10 points adrift of the champions.

25

1960 MUNICH MEMORIALS UNVEILED

Dan Marsden, Chairman of the Ground Committee at Old Trafford, performed the official unveiling of the Munich Clock, which can still be seen at Old Trafford today. Later that afternoon Matt Busby unveiled the Munich plaque at the United Road corner of the K stand at Old Trafford. Both memorials are lasting tributes to all those who lost their lives as a result of the plane crash on 6 February 1958.

1978 BIG GORDON'S DEBUT

Liverpool 3   Manchester United 1

Gordon McQueen received a baptism of fire when he made his Manchester United debut away to Liverpool in Division One, United losing 3–1 (scorer: Sammy McIlroy). United manager Dave Sexton signed the big no-nonsense Scottish centre-half for £450,000 from Yorkshire rivals Leeds United and McQueen arrived at Old Trafford just four weeks after his friend and former Leeds United team-mate Joe Jordan had made a similar switch. McQueen's fee broke the English League transfer record but over the following seven seasons he was a solid, calming presence at the heart of the United defence. Big Gordon scored United's first goal in the 1979 FA Cup final defeat by Arsenal but returned to Wembley with the Reds four years later and took home an FA Cup winners' medal after United beat Brighton & Hove Albion 4–0 in a replay (the first game ended 2–2). Gordon won 30 caps for Scotland, scoring five times for his country.

> **McQUEEN, Gordon** (*Defender 1978–85*) – *debut in the above game.*
> *Appearances: FL: 184, goals 20   FAC: 21, goals 2   FLC: 16, goals 4   EUR: 7, goals 0*
> *TOTAL: 229 apps, 26 goals.*

1981

Ji-Sung Park (Midfielder 2005–present) was born in Seoul, South Korea.

1996 LAST TROT AT BURNDEN PARK

Bolton Wanderers 0   Manchester United 6

Manchester United visited Burnden Park, home of Bolton Wanderers, for the very last time. United were simply too hot for the Trotters, winning this Premier League game 6–0 (scorers: Paul Scholes 2, David Beckham, Steve Bruce, Andy Cole, Nicky Butt). United went on to win the Premier League (and a second Double) while Bolton were relegated to Nationwide Division One. This game was the last time the two teams met at Burnden Park because, by the time Bolton returned to the Premier League for the 1997–98 season, they had moved to their new purpose-built Reebok Stadium.

2003 UNITED MUG OLD LADY

Juventus 0   Manchester United 3

Manchester United beat Juventus 3–0 at Stadio delle Alpi in a memorable UEFA Champions League second stage group game with Ryan Giggs scoring a truly memorable goal preceded by a mazy 50-yard dribble. Giggsy scored twice in the game while Ruud van Nistelrooy was also on target against The Old Lady.

26

1972 OLD ACQUAINTANCES

Manchester United 0   Middlesbrough 0
United met Middlesbrough in the FA Cup for the third season running. The two sides drew 0–0 at Old Trafford in the fifth round.

1973

Ole Gunnar Solskjaer (Forward 1996–2007) was born in Kristiansund, Norway.

1980 LOUIS EDWARDS DIES

Louis Edwards, the former chairman of Manchester United, died following a heart attack. Only a few weeks earlier a *World In Action* television investigation probed into Mr Edwards' business dealings and his alleged involvement in illegal share trading and slush funds. However, nothing was ever proven. His son Martin succeeded him as the chairman of Manchester United.

1994 SIX-SHOOTER THWARTS UNITED

West Ham United 2   Manchester United 2
Lee Chapman's goal for West Ham United in their 2–2 draw with United on 25 February 1994 meant he had now scored for six different clubs against Manchester United. The Reds looked to be on the wrong end of a 2–1 scoreline until former Hammer Paul Ince scored United's equaliser with only minutes remaining. Ben Thornley made his United League debut in the game when he replaced Denis Irwin as a 79th-minute substitute. Mark Hughes also scored.

2005 A CAPTAIN'S TALE

Manchester United 2   Portsmouth 1
When Roy Keane, the Manchester United captain, was rested by Sir Alex for the Premier League home game versus Portsmouth the captain's armband was handed to Gary Neville to lead out the side. During the 2–1 win (scorer: Wayne Rooney 2) Neville sustained a foot injury and as he limped off the pitch he tossed the armband to Ruud van Nistelrooy. However, the Dutch striker was taken off towards the end of the game and United had their third captain in the game when Ryan Giggs slipped on the armband as Keano looked on. The 67,989 attendance was a record Premier League crowd at the time.

2006 MILLENNIUM MASSACRE

Manchester United 4   Wigan Athletic 0

In 2006 United reached their sixth League Cup final (known as the Carling Cup in 2006) having lost four of the previous finals to Liverpool (1983), Sheffield Wednesday (1991), Aston Villa (1994) and Liverpool (2003). Their sole success in the competition came in 1992 with a 1–0 win over Nottingham Forest (scorer: Brian McClair). United's opponents were Wigan Athletic, enjoying their first-ever season in the top flight and playing in their first major final. The final was played in the Millennium Stadium and on their way to the Cardiff showdown against their new Lancashire rivals the Reds had seen off Barnet, West Bromwich Albion, Birmingham City and Blackburn Rovers. The Latics appeared to freeze on their big day out and the final became one of the biggest mismatches in the competition's history with United romping home 4–0 victors (scorers: Wayne Rooney 2, Cristiano Ronaldo, Louis Saha), a record score for a League Cup final. Two-goal Wayne Rooney was voted Man of the Match and was presented with the Alan Hardaker Trophy. The omission of Ruud van Nistelrooy from the United starting line-up would eventually lead to the Dutch striker leaving United for Real Madrid at the end of the season. Meanwhile, Wigan Athletic's rise to the top flight was meteoric given that they had only been elected to the Football League in 1978, the same year Manchester celebrated their Centenary Year.

Manchester United: Van der Sar, Neville, Brown (Vidic), Ferdinand, Silvestre (Evra), Ronaldo (Richardson), O'Shea, Giggs, Park, Saha, Rooney. Subs not used: Howard, van Nistelrooy.

27

1902 GRAND BAZAAR HELD TO STAVE OFF BANKRUPTCY

From 27 February to 2 March 1902, a Grand Bazaar was organised by the club captain, Harry Stafford, in St James's Hall, Oxford Street, Manchester to raise funds for the club, which was facing bankruptcy at the time. Tickets cost 2s 6d for the first day and 6d all day on the final day (children were admitted half-price). Stafford's idea of holding a bazaar did not prove to be as financially lucrative as he had hoped, and he suffered even more bad luck when his much-loved St Bernard dog, 'Major', got lost. Major had been used as an overnight guard-dog at the bazaar, but managed to escape the attention of his keeper, Louis Rocca, and ran from the hall into Oxford Street still wearing a bazaar collection box. Stafford was heartbroken and placed an advertisement in the local press for the return of his beloved pet. Enter John H. Davies, a local brewery owner, at whose house, according to stories, Major had turned up. Mr Davies contacted Harry Stafford who called at the Davies' household to collect his dog. When

Harry met John H. Davies the two men chatted for a while until Harry brought up the reason why Major was wearing a collection box and sooned learned of the severe financial difficulties Newton Heath had found themselves in. Mr Davies then purchased the dog as a birthday present for his daughter and installed Stafford as the landlord of one of his public houses. On 25 April 1902 an emergency meeting of the club was held at Islington Public Hall, Ancoats. Harry Stafford addressed the audience and announced that he and Davies had a plan to save the club. Davies and three other local businessmen pledged to invest £500 each, thus guaranteeing the continued existence of the club. At the meeting the club changed its name to Manchester United and John H. Davies was appointed as their new president. And what of Major, the St Bernard dog? Well, had he not escaped from St James's Hall it is doubtful whether we would even have a Manchester United today.

1971 KNIFE-THROWER CLOSES OLD TRAFFORD

Manchester United 1   Newcastle United 0
Manchester United beat Newcastle United 1–0 in this First Division game thanks to a goal from Brian Kidd. However, a fan threw a knife on to the pitch, which fortunately did not hit anyone, resulting in the Football Association eventually punishing United by ordering them to close Old Trafford and play their opening two home games of the 1971–72 season at a neutral venue. Throughout the club's history United has played a 'home' game at six grounds other than their own. The grounds are: Anfield (Liverpool), Goodison Park (Liverpool), Home Park (Plymouth), Leeds Road (Huddersfield), Maine Road (Manchester) and The Victoria Ground (Stoke).

28

1932

Noel Cantwell (Full-back 1960–67) was born in Cork, Ireland.

1956

James Michael Nicholl (Defender 1975–82) was born in Hamilton, Ontario, Canada.

2001 BECKS LEADS THREE LIONS TO VICTORY

In his second game as the captain of England, United's David Beckham helped the team to a 3–0 win over Spain at Villa Park in an international friendly.

United's Nicky Butt, Andy Cole, Gary Neville (came on as a substitute for his brother), Phil Neville and Paul Scholes also played in the game, which marked Sven Goran Eriksson's first match in charge of England.

29

1972 STYLISH BUCHAN'S ARRIVAL

Three days after drawing with Middlesbrough in the fifth round of the FA Cup at Old Trafford, United visited Ayresome Park and beat Middlesbrough 3–0 in the replay (scorers: Willie Morgan, Bobby Charlton, George Best). Meanwhile, manager Frank O'Farrell made Martin Buchan, the captain of Aberdeen, the club's new record purchase at £125,000.

1996 FERGIE'S THE MAIN MAN

Alex Ferguson was named the Carling Manager of the Month. During the month United won all four of their League games (versus Wimbledon and Bolton Wanderers away and Blackburn Rovers and Everton at home) and also beat Manchester City in the FA Cup fifth round at Old Trafford. He received a trophy, a cheque for £750 and a magnum of champagne.

MARCH

1

Just as Eric Cantona would become in season 1992–93, Joe Cassidy was a crucial mid-season signing in 1892–93, and he also ended up a hero. However, whereas Eric Cantona made history at the top of the table, Joe Cassidy grabbed all the headlines at the other end of the table. Joe was signed by Newton Heath on 1 March 1893 with just six games of their First Division campaign left. However, the Heathens were struggling at the foot of the table and took the decision to sign Cassidy ahead of the dreaded 'Test Match' at the end of the season, which pitted the team lying bottom of Division 1 against the Division 2 champions in a one-off deciding game played at a neutral venue. Only the winner would play Division 1 football the following season. The Heathens finished bottom of Division 1 and faced Small Heath (later Birmingham City) in the Test Match at Stoke with the game ending 1–1 (scorer: Alfred Farman). In the replay, played at Bramall Lane, Sheffield, the Heathens ran out convincing 5–2 winners (scorers: Alfred Farman 3, James Coupar, Cassidy). Cassidy's signing had done the trick, Newton Heath avoided relegation and Cassidy was dispatched north of the border to play for Glasgow Celtic for two months on loan. His loan spell actually lasted two years and he returned to the Heathens in March 1895. His first match on his return to England was quite remarkable with the Heathens annihilating Walsall Town Swifts 14–0 (11 goals were scored in the second half) in Division 2. Cassidy himself netted four but sadly the result did not stand as the Swifts protested about Newton Heath's 'fearfully heavy' Bank Street pitch and a replay was ordered. In the replay the Swifts salvaged some pride by 'only' conceding nine goals this time (eight scored in the second half) to lose the game 9–0. Cassidy scored twice in the win. Over the next five seasons following his return (1895–1900) Cassidy proved himself a powerful and prolific striker for the club, notching 100 goals in 174 appearances for Newton Heath, although 'Test Matches' do not count in official club records. He bagged 90 League goals, nine FA Cup goals and one Test Match goal to make him the first player to score a century of goals for the club. Indeed, his record stood until the legendary Sandy Turnbull reached treble figures in 1914. Cassidy's gift of regularly finding the back of the net made him a valuable asset, a point not lost on Newton Heath's cash-strapped directors when a bid came in from across town. Reluctantly, Cassidy was sold to Manchester City in April 1900 for £250.

CASSIDY, Joseph 'Joe' (Forward 1892–3 and 1895–1900) – debut in the above game. Appearances: FL: 152, goals 90 FAC: 15, goals 9 TOTAL: 167 apps, 99 goals.

1902 THE LAST EVER HEATHEN

Newton Heath 0   Lincoln City 0

James Higson made his Newton Heath debut in a 0–0 draw against Lincoln City at home. Higson was the last League player signed by Newton Heath prior to the club going into bankruptcy and subsequently changing their name to Manchester United.

1949 TOP RAM

United's Johnny Morris left Old Trafford and signed for Derby County for £24,500, a British record transfer fee at the time. In a strange twist of fate, the record fee was beaten when Sheffield Wednesday's Eddie Quigley signed for Preston North End in December 1949 at a cost of £26,500. Quigley was Johnny's uncle.

1953 TIPPING THE TEA LADY TO LAND A LEGEND

Matt Busby was building his second great team at Manchester United in the early 1950s, hoping that they would follow in the footsteps of his first team, which won the 1948 FA Cup and finished Division 1 runners-up on four occasions (1947, 1948, 1949 and 1951). Despite the fast emerging talents of his famous Busby Babes, Matt realised that he lacked an out-and-out goalscorer who would provide that extra ingredient his team needed. So Busby turned his attention to a 21-year-old striker who was playing League football for his home-town club, Tommy Taylor of Barnsley. However, the Yorkshire club were reluctant to let the jewel in their crown move to Old Trafford and Busby had to double United's record transfer purchase (£15,000 for Johnny Berry in August 1951 from Birmingham City) to land the Yorkshire powerhouse, who stood 5ft 11in tall and weighed in at 12st 6lb. However, conscious of the fact that the media would wish to burden his new talent with a £30,000 transfer fee, Busby actually struck a deal with Barnsley's chairman to pay the club £29,999 and to give the other £1 as a tip to the tea lady who looked after the entourage from Manchester United at Oakwell all day.

1980 BAILEY ON SPOT FORM BUT REDS HIT FOR SIX

Ipswich Town 6   Manchester United 0

Gary Bailey saved two penalties in a First Division game away to Ipswich Town at Portman Road but United still lost the game 6–0.

1989 UNITED HELP LOCKERBIE APPEAL

Queen of the South 3   Manchester United 6

Manchester United sent a team to Palmerston Park to play Queen of the South in a friendly to help raise funds for the families who lost loved ones in the tragedy of the Lockerbie Air Disaster. Pan Am Flight 103 exploded above the Scottish town on 21 December 1988, killing all 243 passengers and 16 crew on board.

1997 BUSST CAREER OVER

Manchester United 3   Coventry City 1

David Busst, whose career was ended when he broke his leg at Old Trafford during the 1995–96 season, was welcomed back as a guest for United's home Premiership clash with his former club, Coventry City. United ran out 3–1 winners thanks to two own goals from the Sky Blues and a Karel Poborsky strike.

2

1929 SCORING ON HIS WEDDING DAY

Charlie Ramsden (Forward 1927–31) was married in the morning and then celebrated his marriage in the afternoon by scoring two goals for United's reserve team against Sheffield United Reserves at Old Trafford.

1980 PRESIDENT SIR MATT BUSBY

Sir Matt Busby was elected as the first ever president of Manchester United, and to date he remains the only president in the club's history.

1991 RYAN GIGGS BURSTS ON TO THE SCENE

Manchester United 0   Everton 2

Ryan Giggs made his League debut for Manchester United in this First Division game at Old Trafford, coming on as a 35th-minute substitute for Denis Irwin in a 2–0 home defeat. Darren Ferguson made his Manchester United debut in the same game.

> **FERGUSON, Darren** *(Midfielder 1990–94) – debut in the above game.*
> Appearances: PL: 16 (2), goals 0 FL: 4 (5), goals 0 FLC: 2 (1), goals 0
> TOTAL: 22 (8) apps, 0 goals.
> **GIGGS, Ryan Joseph** *(Forward 1990–present) – debut in the above game.*

1994 UNBEATEN RUN SEQUENCE SET

Sheffield Wednesday 2   Manchester United 4

When Manchester United defeated Sheffield Wednesday 4–2 at Hillsborough in this League (Coca-Cola) Cup semi-final second leg, they set their all-time record of 34 games unbeaten in all competitions. The record began with a 4–2 win over Swindon Town in the Premiership at Old Trafford on 25 September 1993.

3

1934 BILLY THE SCOUT'S ONLY GAME FOR UNITED

Manchester United 2   Bury 1

Billy Behan was the first Irish goalkeeper to play League football for Manchester United and in this, his only senior game for the Reds, he conceded a goal in the first minute. Thankfully, United went on to win the game 2–1 (scorers: John Ball, Stanley Gallimore). Later that month United signed the former England international goalkeeper Jack Crompton and Behan decided to become a scout for United. Billy enjoyed an extremely successful scouting career for the Reds and in September 1983 the club presented him with an inscribed watch to commemorate his 50 years service to Manchester United.

> **BEHAN, William** *(Goalkeeper 1934) – debut in the above game.*
> *Appearances:* FL: 1, goals 0 TOTAL: 1 app, 0 goals.

1967 SMILE, YOU ARE ON CAMERA

Arsenal 1   Manchester United 1

United's 1–1 First Division draw with the Gunners at Highbury (scorer: John Aston Jnr) was the first Division One game to be televised on closed-circuit television.

1999 BECKS REUNION WITH DIEGO

Manchester United 2   Inter Milan 0

Manchester United beat Inter Milan 2–0, both goals scored by Dwight Yorke, in their UEFA Champions League first leg quarter-final encounter at Old Trafford. David Beckham met Diego Simeone for the first time after receiving a red card for kicking out at the Argentinian during the 1998 World Cup in France.

2007 700-UP FOR RYAN

Liverpool 0   Manchester United 1

Ryan Giggs played in his 700th game for Manchester United against Liverpool in a Premiership game at Anfield. United won 1–0 thanks to a dramatic goal in added time from John O'Shea after going down to 10 men following Paul Scholes' dismissal.

4

1972 MASTER CLASS

Tottenham Hotspur 2   Manchester United 0

United's recent acquisition from Aberdeen, Martin Buchan, made his Manchester United debut in a 2–0 defeat at Tottenham Hotspur, the club's seventh successive defeat. Buchan went on to captain United during their revival in the mid-1970s, leading the Reds to the Second Division Championship in 1974–75 and three FA Cup finals (1976, 1977 and 1979). However, his crowning glory has to be the 1977 FA Cup final when United denied a dominant Liverpool side the Treble by beating their bitter rivals 2–1. United's Silver Jubilee Cup success made the stylish Scotsman the first, and to date, only player to have captained an FA Cup-winning team in both England and Scotland (he captained Aberdeen to their 1970 Scottish Cup success, and in 1971 he was voted the Scottish Football Writers' Association Player of the Year). Buchan was once described as having that much class that the London Philharmonic Orchestra should have been in the stands accompanying him when he played. The magnificent Buchan also won 34 international caps for Scotland.

> **BUCHAN, Martin** *(Defender 1972–83) – debut in the above game.*
> *Appearances: FL: 376, goals 4 FAC: 39, goals 0   FLC: 30, goals 0 EUR: 10, goals 0*
> *TOTAL: 456 apps, 4 goals.*

1995 PREMIERSHIP RECORD WIN

Manchester United 9   Ipswich Town 0

United's 9–0 Premier League win over Ipswich Town at Old Trafford set a new Premiership record score in only the third season of the new League, a record that still proudly stands today 13 seasons later. Andy Cole set a Premiership record for scoring most goals in a game, five (subsequently matched by Alan Shearer), while Mark Hughes (2), Paul Ince and Roy Keane added to the Tractor Boys' misery.

1996 ERIC SWOOPS ON MAGPIES

Newcastle United 0   Manchester United 1

A goal from Eric Cantona sealed a dramatic 1–0 victory for the Reds over Newcastle United at St James' Park in a crucial Premiership encounter that would eventually lead to United clinching the FA Premier League title ahead of the Geordies.

5

1949 NEW BOY DOWNIE NOTCHES HIS FIRST

Manchester United 3   Charlton Athletic 2

John Downie celebrated his Manchester United debut with a goal in their 3–2 win over Charlton Athletic. Stan Pearson scored the other two Reds' goals.

> **DOWNIE, John Dennis** *(Forward 1948–53) – debut in the above game.*
> *Appearances:* FL: *110, goals 35*   FAC: *5, goals 1* TOTAL: *116 apps, 37 goals.*

1958 NO MEEK MAN

Manchester United 1   West Bromwich Albion 0

David Meek is a Manchester United legend off the field of play, a highly respected journalist who was a close friend of Sir Matt Busby's and enjoyed an equally amicable relationship with Sir Alex Ferguson during his 37 years writing about the club he loves. David was the *Manchester Evening News'* Manchester United correspondent from 1958 until he finally retired in January 1995, and was a regular columnist in United's official matchday magazine, the *United Review*. His first article for the *United Review* appeared in the match programme for the FA Cup sixth round replay against West Bromwich Albion at Old Trafford on 5 March 1958 under the heading 'United Jottings'. United won the game 1–0 (scorer: Colin Webster).

1986 ROBSON DISLOCATES SHOULDER

West Ham United 1   Manchester United 1

United visited the capital to play West Ham United in an FA Cup fifth round tie. The game ended 1–1 (scorer: Frank Stapleton) but is perhaps remembered more for Bryan Robson crashing to the ground and dislocating his right shoulder than for the football on display. The United and England captain's season was effectively over while the nation would have to wait to see if Captain Marvel would be fit in time to play in the 1986 World Cup finals in Mexico. Robbo eventually made it to Mexico but suffered a similar injury during the tournament.

1994 LISTENERS DISAPPOINTED

Manchester United 0   Chelsea 1

Chelsea were the visitors to Old Trafford for this Premiership game and went back to London with all three points courtesy of a 1–0 win. This win for the Blues was the first time the Reds had lost a game at fortress Old Trafford in 37 games (all competitions). The game was broadcast on Manchester United Radio on the official launch day of the club's new radio station. Fans can now listen to games from Old Trafford on 1413 medium wave.

1997 REDS ISSUE EUROPEAN WARNING

Manchester United 4   FC Porto 0

Manchester United sent a warning to the rest of Europe with this first leg UEFA Champions League quarter-final victory over the team that many football experts regarded as the best club side in the world at the time (scorers: David May, Eric Cantona, Ryan Giggs, Andy Cole).

6

1909 REFEREE HELPS UNITED OUT TWICE

Burnley 1   Manchester United 0 – game abandoned after 72 minutes

United were on their way out of the FA Cup, losing 1–0 to Burnley at Turf Moor in the quarter-final, when, with only 18 minutes of the game remaining, a freak snowstorm resulted in the referee, Herbert Bamlett, abandoning the tie. Four days later United won the replayed match 3–2 (scorers: Jimmy Turnbull 2, Harold Halse) and went on to win the 1909 FA Cup. On 13 April 1927, Herbert Bamlett was appointed manager of Manchester United.

1948 CAUGHT ON CAMERA

Manchester United 3   Sunderland 1

Action pictures appeared in the *United Review* (home game versus Sunderland) for the first time since the war. The pictures were action shots from United's 4–1 FA Cup sixth round victory over Preston North End at Maine Road.

The next *United Review* would not be short of goalmouth action as United beat Sunderland 3–1 in the First Division (scorers: Jimmy Delaney, Charlie Mitten, Jack Rowley).

1949

Martin McLean Buchan (Defender 1972–83) was born in Aberdeen.

7

1933 OUR JACKIE

John 'Jackie' Blanchflower (Half-back 1951–8) was born in Belfast. Although Jackie Blanchflower remained on United's books until 1959, he never played competitive football again following the injuries he sustained in the Munich Air Disaster on 6 February 1958. In the 1957 FA Cup final Blanchflower took over in the Manchester United goal after Ray Wood was carried off the pitch on a stretcher following a collision with Aston Villa's Northern Ireland striker Peter McParland. United lost that final 2–1 (scorer: Tommy Taylor). Sadly, Jackie died on 2 September 1998.

1953 MAGNIFICO DEBUT

Manchester United 5   Preston North End 2

Tommy Taylor made his Manchester United debut in this First Division game following his £29,999 transfer from Barnsley just six days earlier. Taylor marked his United and Old Trafford baptism with two goals to immediately win over the Reds' faithful, while David Pegg (2) and Jack Rowley also scored. Tommy Taylor is regarded by those who saw him play as the greatest centre-forward ever to represent Manchester United and England. He was the finest header of a ball in his era, his control and first-time passing immaculate, his scoring rate for club and country extraordinary. In fact, he was so good that the great Alfredo Di Stefano of Real Madrid dubbed him '*Magnifico*'. The big Yorkshireman's path to Old Trafford was an unusual one in modern terms. At the age of 14 he was working at the Wharncliffe Colliery, a job he left to begin a professional football career with Barnsley FC. At 18 he began two years' national service and on 25 May 1950 duly became Gunner Taylor 22366853, being posted to Oswestry with the Royal Artillery. In 1953, United were coming to the end of an era, with Matt Busby and Jimmy Murphy on the look-out for a new centre-forward. Taylor fitted the bill and once signed he soon justified their faith. In 191 appearances for United he scored 131 goals, giving him a goal ratio of two every three games, a record unsurpassed for four decades (until bettered by Ruud van Nistelrooy). He won championship medals in 1956 (scoring 25 League goals) and 1957 (22 League goals) and also netted an impressive 16 goals in 19 internationals for England, playing for his country in the 1954 World Cup finals in Switzerland. Tragically, on 6 February 1958, along with seven of his team-mates, Tommy lost his life in the Munich Air Disaster. The world at his feet, his future had been snuffed out at the tender age of 26, leaving many to reflect on how good he could have become. But the name of Tommy Taylor among the pantheon of legendary United strikers is assured.

TAYLOR, Tommy (Forward 1953–8) – debut in the above game.
  Appearances: FL: 166, goals 112 FAC: 9, goals 5 EUR: 14, goals 11
  TOTAL: 191 apps, 131 goals.

2007 HENRIK KISSES OLD TRAFFORD GOODBYE

Manchester United 1   LOSC Lille Metropole 0
United beat LOSC Lille Metropole 1–0 in their UEFA Champions League second leg tie at Old Trafford with a goal from Henrik Larsson in what was the Super Swede's last game for the Reds. Ryan Giggs, scorer of United's hotly disputed winning goal in the Stade Felix-Bollaert a fortnight earlier, was booed constantly throughout the game by the French fans. The win guaranteed United a place in the last eight of the UEFA Champions League for the first time since season 2002–03.

8

1922 ROBSON'S TESTIMONIAL FUND

An England Trial match, Possibles versus Probables, was played at Old Trafford on 8 March 1922 to help raise money for the Testimonial Fund that was set up to provide for the family of John Robson (United manager 1914–21) following his death from pneumonia on 11 January 1922.

1941 HITLER SET TO BOMB OLD TRAFFORD

Manchester United 7   Bury 3
This was United's last game at Old Trafford, played three days before the Luftwaffe's bombs severely damaged the stadium (scorers: Johnny Carey 3, Jack Rowley 3, John Smith). It was to be over eight years before League football returned to Old Trafford. United had to rent Maine Road from their City neighbours until the stadium was rebuilt.

1950 PENALTY HAT-TRICK KING

Manchester United 7   Aston Villa 0
Charlie Mitten scored four of United's seven goals in their 7–0 annihilation of Aston Villa at Old Trafford in the First Division. Amazingly, Mitten recorded a unique hat-trick when three of his four came from the penalty spot. The other goalscorers for the Reds were John Downie (2) and Jack Rowley.

1956

Laurence Paul 'Laurie' Cunningham (Forward 1982–3) was born in St Mary's Archway, London.

1975 COPPELL'S DEBUT

Bolton Wanderers 0   Manchester United 1

Steve Coppell made his debut for Manchester United in this 1–0 away win over Bolton Wanderers at Burnden Park in Division Two (scorer: Stuart Pearson). Tommy Docherty paid Tranmere Rovers £60,000 for Coppell in February 1975 and he played in 10 of United's final 11 League games of their 1974–75 Second Division Championship-winning season. Over the following eight seasons he was an automatic starter and along with United's other flying winger, Gordon Hill, he tortured opposing full-backs with his blistering pace and skill. Coppell played in United's three FA Cup finals during the 1970s and their 1983 League Cup final loss to Liverpool. While on England duty in November 1981 he suffered a serious knee injury and over the next two years he had surgery three times. Sadly, in the autumn of 1983 his injury forced him to retire from the game at the age of 28. In all he played 42 times for his country, scoring seven times, and his run of 206 consecutive games for United, between 15 January 1977 and 7 November 1981, is a club record. A former chairman of the PFA and chief executive of the Football League Managers' Association, Steve took Reading into the FA Premier League for the 2006–07 season.

> COPPELL, *Stephen James 'Steve' (Midfielder 1974–83) – debut in the above game.*
> *Appearances:* FL: 320 (2), goals 54   FAC: 36, goals 4   FLC: 25, goals 9
> EUR: 11 (1), goals 3   TOTAL: 393 (3) apps, 70 goals.

1997 LAST VISIT TO ROKER PARK

Sunderland 2   Manchester United 1

Manchester United played Sunderland at their famous Roker Park ground for the last time in this Premier League encounter. Only three days after crushing FC Porto 4–0 in the UEFA Champions League, United were brought back down to earth with a 2–1 defeat (scorer: own goal). In season 1997–98 Sunderland moved to their new purpose-built arena, the Stadium of Light.

2006 GOODBYE TO THE BELFAST BOY

Cracked Flag, a Salford-based band, paid tribute to George Best by releasing a single entitled 'Goodbye to the Belfast Boy'. The song is an upbeat celebration of George's outstanding talent and makes reference to the heart-warming tributes paid by fans from all over the world in acknowledgement of one of the greatest footballers the game has ever seen. The band were invited to play the song live at Old Trafford prior to United's home Premiership game against Newcastle

United on 12 March 2006, at the George Best Memorial Dinner at Old Trafford on 16 March and were also invited to perform the tribute at George's 60th birthday celebration in Belfast on 22 May 2006, organised by the George Best Carryduff Manchester United Supporters Club. Band members Paul Johnston, Dave Mather and Pete Robinson are all life-long Reds who actually worked at Old Trafford during the late 1960s and 1970s as programme sellers and tray boys. The profits from sales of the CD went to the Foundation For Liver Research's George Best Appeal (Reg 268211).

9

1895 RECORD WIN WIPED OFF THE SLATE

Newton Heath 14   Walsall Town Swifts 0
Newton Heath recorded their highest ever score when they beat Walsall Town Swifts 14–0 at Bank Street in Division Two. The 14–0 scoreline would still stand today in English football's League record books had Walsall not lodged a formal complaint with the Football League claiming that the pitch at Bank Street was nothing more than a quagmire. The Football League found in favour of the visitors and ordered a replay, expunging the first result from the records. Walsall fared better in the rearranged game, this time only going down to a 9–0 defeat on 3 April 1895.

1964 THE KING RULES ROKERITES

Manchester United 5   Sunderland 1
Manchester United totally outclassed their opponents, Sunderland, 5–1 in this FA Cup sixth round second replay tie at Leeds Road, Huddersfield. The first meeting, at Old Trafford on 29 February, finished 3–3, while the replay, at Roker Park on 4 March, ended 2–2 after extra time. Denis Law scored a hat-trick in the Reds' 5–1 win, The King's second hat-trick for United in the space of 12 days. Phil Chisnall and David Herd also scored.

1966 BENFICA BESTED

Benfica 1   Manchester United 5
In the first leg of their European Cup quarter-final tie with SL Benfica of Portugal at Old Trafford, United had won 3–2 (scorers: David Herd, Denis Law, Bill Foulkes). Five weeks later United travelled to Lisbon to face the Portuguese champions and 1965 European Cup runners-up in their Stadium of Light ground, which had proved to be a fortress for them in European competition. Prior to the kick-off the fans were buoyed when their hero Eusebio walked out

to the centre of the pitch to be presented with his European Player Of The Year Award. The mainly partisan 75,000 crowd sat back and expected their team to dispose of United, given that a 1–0 win would be good enough to see them into the semi-finals. However, United, and George Best in particular, enjoyed a European glory night that is still being talked about today in Manchester and Lisbon. After just 16 minutes of exhilarating play by the Reds they were 3–0 up and in complete control of the game and the tie. Best scored twice as he ripped through the Portuguese side's defence time and time again. John Connelly added the third. Meanwhile, the newly crowned best player in Europe was having a quiet night while Best stole the limelight from him in his own backyard. Indeed, all six goals in the game were scored by United players as Shay Brennan put the ball past Alex Stepney for Benfica's only goal of the game. United added two more in the last 10 minutes from Paddy Crerand and Bobby Charlton. When the final whistle blew the disgruntled home fans rained cushions on to the pitch in anger at their side's capitulation to the Reds. However, if the truth be told, no team could have lived with United in those 90 minutes such was their superiority in all areas of the field. The legend of El Beatle would soon adorn the sports pages of the newspapers in England and Portugal.

1985 STORMIN' NORMAN

Manchester United 4   West Ham United 2
Norman Whiteside hit a hat-trick for United in their 4–2 FA Cup sixth round victory over West Ham United at Old Trafford. Mark Hughes also scored.

2006 A RICH BOOK WORM

Wayne Rooney signed the largest sports book deal in publishing history with HarperCollins. The £5m deal was for a minimum five books to be published over a 12-year period. His first book under the deal, *Wayne Rooney, The Story So Far, My Autobiography*, was published shortly after the 2006 World Cup finals. Rooney did not achieve a single GCSE at school.

10

1958

Garth Anthony Crooks (Forward 1983–4) was born in Stoke-on-Trent.

1966 THE FIFTH BEATLE

When George Best stepped out of the aircraft upon Manchester United's arrival back in Manchester, after scoring twice the night before in the Reds' scintillating 5–1 European Cup quarter-final win over Benfica in Lisbon's Stadium of Light, he was pictured wearing a huge sombrero-style hat. Fleet Street quickly dubbed him 'El Beatle' and from that moment on he became football's first true superstar. George's life was never quite the same again. Companies flocked to the doorstep of the 'Fifth Beatle' seeking endorsement of their products ranging from clothes to aftershave to sausages and football boots. And George did not let his superstar image down as he drove to and from his three boutiques and his nightclub in his white E-type Jaguar. He even had a luxury bachelor pad built for himself that had all mod-cons, including curtains that were activated by sunlight, hot-air heating pumped underfloor by a large boiler, a TV that disappeared into the chimney, a sunken bath and intercom security. In the 1960s George Best was to football what The Beatles were to pop music – Untouchable!

11

1941 LUFTWAFFE BOMB OLD TRAFFORD

Old Trafford was left virtually a pile of rubble as Luftwaffe bombs targeted the vast Trafford Park industrial complex, one of Britain's key engineering production plants making equipment for the armed forces. The main stand was completely destroyed along with the dressing rooms and offices. Manchester United submitted a claim to the War Damage Commission seeking compensation to help with reconstruction work and they were awarded the sum of £22,278. It would be over eight years before United could open the doors of Old Trafford once more for football matches and so they struck an agreement with neighbours Manchester City to use their Maine Road ground at an annual rent of £5,000 plus a percentage of the gate receipts. The FA assisted United by ensuring that City's home fixture list did not have any dates corresponding with United's home fixture list when season 1941–42 kicked off.

12

1994 SCHMEICHEL SENT OFF

Manchester United 3   Charlton Athletic 1

Peter Schmeichel was sent off in the 44th minute of United's FA Cup quarter-final tie against Charlton Athletic at Old Trafford for handling the ball outside the area. Alex Ferguson immediately withdrew Paul Parker from the field and sent on Les Sealey to play in goal. United won the game 3–1 (scorers: Andrei Kanchelskis 2, Mark Hughes). Schmeichel's dismissal and subsequent suspension cost him his place in the League Cup final against Aston Villa, for which he was replaced by Sealey.

1995 350 FA CUP TIES
Manchester United 2   Queens Park Rangers 0
United's 2–0 win over Queens Park Rangers in the FA Cup sixth round at Old Trafford was the club's 350th FA Cup game. Up until their fourth round encounter in the 1976–77 FA Cup, United had never met the Londoners in the previous 73 years of the competition (QPR were formed in 1904). With this 1995 encounter United had now played QPR six times in the FA Cup in the last 18 years. United won all six games.

2003 YOUNG FLETCHER
Manchester United 1   FC Basle 1
Darren Fletcher made his Manchester United debut in this 1–1 UEFA Champions League draw at home to FC Basle at the age of 19. Gary Neville scored for the Reds.

> FLETCHER, *Darren Barr (Midfielder 2003–present) – debut in the above game.*

13

1925 JOHN MEETS JOHN DOWN UNDER
John Ball (Full-back 1947–9) was born in Ince, Wigan. Ball served in the Royal Navy during the Second World War and played five representative matches in Australia. One of his team-mates was John Aston Snr whom he later teamed up with at United.

1948 SEASIDERS AWAIT
Manchester United 3   Derby County 1
Stan Pearson scored a hat-trick for United against Derby County at Hillsborough to put United into the 1948 FA Cup final where they would face Stanley Matthews' Blackpool.

1974 MAINE ROAD FIGHT NIGHT

Manchester City 0   Manchester United 0

Manchester United's Lou Macari and Manchester City's Mike Doyle received their marching orders in this ill-tempered First Division scoreless derby draw at Maine Road. Paul Bielby made his debut for Manchester United in the match while it was the Reds' seventh 0–0 draw of the season, a club record.

> BIELBY, Paul Anthony *(Forward 1973–4) – debut in the above game.*
> *Appearances: FL: 2 (2), 0 goals TOTAL: 2 (2) apps, 0 goals.*

14

1914 RECORD HOME DEFEAT

Manchester United 0   Aston Villa 6

United suffered their worst ever home defeat when Aston Villa thrashed them 6–0 in this First Division match at Old Trafford. Sixteen years later United were beaten at Old Trafford by the same score in another League game. United's Irish forward Michael Hamill missed the encounter when he played for Ireland against Scotland in the final Home International game of the 1913–14 season.

2007 FONDLY REMEMBERED

Tommy Cavanagh, Manchester United's assistant manager when they won the FA Cup in 1977, died aged 78. Tommy was Tommy Docherty's first appointment when the Doc was named the new Manchester United manager in late 1972. The likeable Cavanagh was on the staff as trainer and then assistant manager for eight years. Born in Liverpool on 29 June 1928, Tommy had an extensive career in the game playing for Preston North End, Stockport County, Huddersfield Town, Doncaster Rovers, Bristol City, Carlisle United and Cheltenham Town. It was at Preston that he first met Docherty, who was also a player at Deepdale. When he hung up his playing boots he got a job as a trainer at Brentford and was later appointed their manager. In 1966 former Manchester United legend Johnny Carey, then manager of Nottingham Forest, brought Tommy to the City Ground as trainer-coach. He was Forest's trainer when they finished runners-up to United in the 1967 First Division title race. Four years later he moved on to Hull City, but was only there for a brief spell before being lured to Old Trafford. After leaving Old Trafford, Tommy served Newcastle United and then Norwegian club Rosenborg Trondheim as assistant manager. He succeeded former Reds captain Martin Buchan as manager at Burnley and was also a coach at Wigan Athletic for a short time. In 2002, Tommy was diagnosed with Alzheimer's disease. United fans and former players will forever remember him with affection for his shock of white hair and his jovial demeanour.

15

1958 TUFF LUCK AT TURF MOOR

Burnley 3   Manchester United 0
Mark Pearson became the first Manchester United player to be sent off in over three years when he was dismissed during United's 3–0 First Division defeat by Burnley at Turf Moor.

1978 HILL SPARES DERBY BLUSHES

Manchester United 2   Manchester City 2
Gordon Hill scored two penalties for United in this 2–2 First Division derby draw with neighbours Manchester City at Old Trafford.

2000 UNITED THWART FLORENTINE THREAT

Manchester United 3   Fiorentina 1
Manchester United rallied after a thunderbolt strike from Gabriel Battistuta fired the Italian side in front, and reached the UEFA Champions League quarter-finals with a magnificent performance. Goals from Andy Cole, Roy Keane and Dwight Yorke guaranteed United's place in the last eight.

16

1949

Alan Edwin Gowling (Forward 1967–72) was born in Stockport.

1994 FOUR WEDNESDAY VICTORIES

Manchester United 5   Sheffield Wednesday 0
Manchester United recorded their biggest win of the 1993–94 Double-winning season with this 5–0 hammering of the Owls at Old Trafford (scorers: Eric Cantona 2, Ryan Giggs, Mark Hughes, Paul Ince). It was United's fourth victory of the season over the Yorkshire team, having already won the corresponding Premiership encounter at Hillsborough and both League Cup semi-final games.

17

1948 UNITED SET RECORD LEAGUE ATTENDANCE

A mammoth post-war crowd of 82,950 filed into Manchester City's Maine Road ground to see United entertain Arsenal in a First Division game. United were still renting their neighbour's ground to stage their home games following the destruction of Old Trafford by German bombs during World War II. The game ended 1–1 with Jack Rowley scoring for United.

18

1899 NINETEENTH-CENTURY FOOTBALL HOOLIGANS

Newton Heath 1   New Brighton Tower 2
When the referee blew the final whistle in this 2–1 (scorer: Joe Cassidy) Division 2 home defeat to New Brighton Tower, a large group of fans ran on to the pitch and surrounded the referee. The fans jostled the startled match official as booing and jeering rained down from the terraces. However, the referee managed to make it back to the changing room without being hurt thanks to the efforts of club officials and several policemen who helped escort him safely off the pitch. The fans were incensed with a number of decisions the referee made during the game that went against the Heathens while the defeat put an end to Newton Heath's hopes of promotion to Division 1. They eventually finished the season fourth in Division 2.

1939

Ron Atkinson (United Manager 1981–6) was born in Liverpool. He was brought up in Birmingham.

1964 UNITED'S WORST EUROPEAN LOSS

Sporting Lisbon 5   Manchester United 0
Manchester United met Sporting Lisbon in the semi-final of the 1963–64 European Cup Winners' Cup. In the home leg at Old Trafford on 26 February 1964, the Reds hammered the Portuguese side 4–1 with a hat-trick from Denis Law and a fourth from Bobby Charlton. Three weeks later the Reds were in the Portuguese capital hoping to secure their first ever appearance in the final of the competition. However, Sporting were awesome on the night and tore the Reds

to shreds, winning 5–0 to progress to the final with a 6–4 aggregate win over the two legs. It was, and remains, United's worst ever defeat in any of the European competitions. To make matters worse, Sporting went on to win the trophy defeating MTK Budapest 1–0 in a replay after they drew 3–3 in the first game.

1967 HERD OUT

Manchester United 5   Leicester City 2
David Herd broke his leg in the act of scoring his 16th goal of the season when Leicester City's Graham Cross slid in to tackle the United striker. The other United goalscorers in this First Division victory at Old Trafford were John Aston, Bobby Charlton, Denis Law and David Sadler. Herd missed the rest of United's Championship-winning season but without question played his part in the success.

19

1994 ERIC SEES RED MIST

Swindon Town 2   Manchester United 2
Eric Cantona was sent off in United's 2–2 (scorers: Paul Ince, Roy Keane) Premier-ship draw with Swindon Town. He was shown the red card for stamping on Swindon's John Moncur. It was United's first-ever visit to Swindon's County Ground and they have not been back since (up to the end of the 2007–08 season).

1995 BRITAIN'S MOST EXPENSIVE SUBSTITUTE

Liverpool 2   Manchester United 0
When Andy Cole replaced Lee Sharpe at half-time in United's 2–0 Premiership defeat to Liverpool at Anfield, he became British football's most expensive sub-stitute at £7m. However, this record has subsequently been beaten on numerous occasions.

1997 FIRST EUROPEAN CUP SEMI-FINALS IN 28 YEARS

FC Porto 0   Manchester United 0
Manchester United visited the Estadio Das Antas with a comfortable 4–0 lead from the first leg of this UEFA Champions League quarter-final tie. Although United were a little nervy in the first 20 minutes of the game, they held on to reach the semi-final stage of the competition for the first time since 1969.

2005 LONG RANGE SMITH

Manchester United 1   Fulham 0

Alan Smith almost bettered David Beckham's 57-yard strike against Wimbledon at Selhurst Park on 17 August 1996 with his own 60-yard attempt against Fulham at Old Trafford. United won this Premiership encounter 1–0 thanks to a goal from Cristiano Ronaldo.

20

1961

Jesper Olsen (Forward 1984–9) was born in Fakse, Denmark.

1982

Tomasz Kuszczak (Goalkeeper 2007–present) was born in Krosno Odrzańskie, Poland.

1985 UNITED PAY EUROPEAN PENALTY

Videoton 1   Manchester United 0

Manchester United lost 1–0 to the Hungarian side Videoton in this second leg of the UEFA Cup quarter-final. However, as United won the home leg by the same score the tie had to be decided by means of a penalty shoot-out. United lost 5–4.

1993 CANTONA BECOMES ENEMY OF THE BLUES

Manchester City 1   Manchester United 1

Eric Cantona scored the first of his many goals against Manchester City in this Premier League match at Maine Road, which was shown live on closed-circuit television at Old Trafford. The game ended 1–1.

21

1959 VIOLLET BLOOMS

Manchester United 4   Leeds United 0

Dennis Viollet netted a hat-trick for United in this 4–0 hammering of Leeds United at Old Trafford in the First Division. Bobby Charlton grabbed the other goal.

1968

Gary Walsh (Goalkeeper 1986–95) was born in Wigan. Exactly 20 years later Gary signed as a professional for United.

1973 POPE MEETS THE DEVIL

SS Lazio 0   Manchester United 0

Prior to their Anglo-Italian Tournament game against SS Lazio in Rome, the Manchester United players and team officials were granted an audience with Pope Paul VI in the Vatican City. Sir Matt Busby, a devout Roman Catholic, was made a Knight Commander of St Gregory, one of the highest civil honours in the Roman Catholic Church. The game ended 0–0.

1984 A MAGICAL EUROPEAN NIGHT

Manchester United 3   FC Barcelona 0

Manchester United went into this European Cup Winners' Cup quarter-final second leg tie trailing Barcelona 2–0 from the first leg. However, on a magical European night that brought back memories of United's European adventures during the 1950s and 1960s, a packed Old Trafford willed United on to victory. The Spanish giants, with Diego Maradona in their line-up, were swept aside 3–0, with goals from skipper Bryan Robson (2) and Frank Stapleton giving the Reds a much deserved 3–2 aggregate victory.

22

1980 THE 100TH MANCHESTER LEAGUE DERBY

Manchester United 1   Manchester City 0

The 100th Manchester League derby was played at Old Trafford. United won the game 1–0 thanks to a Mickey Thomas goal. A bumper crowd of 56,387 was in attendance. On the same day Martin Edwards succeeded his late father Louis Edwards as chairman of Manchester United.

1994 ERIC SENT OFF FOR SECOND TIME IN FOUR DAYS

Arsenal 2   Manchester United 2

Eric Cantona was sent off for the second time in four days in a Premiership game when United visited Highbury. The game ended 2–2 with Lee Sharpe scoring both United goals. Eric's dismissal meant that he became the first Manchester United player to be sent off in consecutive games. It was United's 20th successive game away from home in which they remained unbeaten in all competitions, a club record. Their undefeated run took them to their first Double success at the end of the season.

1995 SPARKY'S FAREWELL GOAL

Manchester United 3   Arsenal 0
Former Old Trafford hero Stewart Houston arrived at Old Trafford as Arsenal's caretaker manager following the sacking of George Graham for allegedly receiving a bung involving a transfer deal. Mark Hughes, Lee Sharpe and Andrei Kanchelskis scored for United. Sparky's goal was his 163rd for the Reds and his last for the club.

23

1957 BOBBY'S DREAM DEBUT

Birmingham City 0   Manchester United 2
Bobby Charlton scored on his FA Cup debut as United beat Birmingham City 2–0 at Hillsborough in the semi-final. Johnny Berry scored the other goal which sent the Reds to Wembley for a showdown with Aston Villa, ironically Birmingham City's local rivals.

1985 SPARKY NETS A HAT-TRICK

Manchester United 4   Aston Villa 0
Mark Hughes scored his second hat-trick for United as they easily beat Aston Villa 4–0 in a Division 1 game at Old Trafford. Norman Whiteside was the other goalscorer.

1989 ROSE COLOUR CHANGE

Gordon Strachan left United and moved across the Pennines to join Leeds United.

1995 FERGIE AWARDED CBE AS CANTONA IS SENTENCED

Alex Ferguson attended Buckingham Palace for his investiture and received the CBE from the Queen. After the ceremony a reporter asked Alex Ferguson for an interview and wanted to talk to him about former Rangers player Davy Cooper, who had died that morning. Alex, a close friend of Davy Cooper's, was too distraught to talk about him. Meanwhile, at Croydon magistrates court, Eric Cantona was sentenced to two weeks' prison for assaulting a Crystal Palace fan in the Selhurst Park crowd on 25 January. He was bailed pending an appeal.

24

1961

Peter Davenport (Forward 1985–9) was born in Birkenhead.

1979 WAR OF THE ROSES HAT-TRICK HERO

Manchester United 4   Leeds United 1

Andy Ritchie scored a superb hat-trick for United in this 4–1 First Division win over Yorkshire rivals Leeds United at Old Trafford. Mickey Thomas also scored for the Reds. Ritchie's hat-trick made him the youngest post-war player to score a League hat-trick; he was aged 18 years 117 days.

1990 LAST OUT, FIRST IN

Manchester United 2   Southampton 0

Immediately after Colin Gibson scored to put United 1–0 up in this First Division game at Old Trafford he was substituted by Alex Ferguson. Late in the game Fergie sent on Mark Robins who scored with his very first touch of the ball.

25

1939 OLD TRAFFORD'S BIGGEST GATE

A huge crowd of 76,962 fans piled into Old Trafford for the 1939 FA Cup semi-final tie between Wolverhampton Wanderers and Grimsby Town.

1940

Norbert Lawton (Half-back 1959–63) was born in Newton Heath, Manchester.

1949

Harold Halse, scorer of 56 goals for United in the early 1900s, died in Colchester aged 63.

1957 BRIGHT NIGHTS ARRIVE AT OLD TRAFFORD

Manchester United 0   Bolton Wanderers 2

With United entering the European Cup competition of 1956–57, against the wishes of the Football Association, meant playing midweek evening games. However, Old Trafford did not have any floodlights and so they decided to erect them at the stadium. In the meantime, United played their first three 'home' European games at nearby Maine Road.

However, the first floodlit game at Old Trafford was a First Division match against Bolton Wanderers, which attracted a crowd of 60,862, the Reds' biggest home gate of the season. But the excitement over the new floodlights could not prevent a dull result for the Reds, a 2–0 defeat.

1967 STALEMATE IN CRUNCH MATCH

Liverpool 0   Manchester United 0
Manchester United visited Anfield for a game that many believed would decide the destination of the First Division Championship despite the fact that nine games still remained to be played. Liverpool, the reigning champions, and United, champions in 1964–65, were both pushing hard in the run-in to the 1966–67 season but neither side could find a way past the other as the game ended 0–0. In the end United won the title comfortably while Liverpool's challenge fell away.

26

1958 YOUNG REDS SECURE CUP FINAL BERTH

Fulham 3   Manchester United 5
Manchester United played Fulham at Arsenal's Highbury Stadium in this FA Cup semi-final replay. Alex Dawson scored a hat-trick for the Reds in their 5–3 victory, which booked their place in the Wembley final against Lancashire rivals Bolton Wanderers, an amazing comeback for the club so soon after the shattering tragedy of Munich. Shay Brennan and Bobby Charlton also scored for United while Dawson's hat-trick made him the youngest post-war player to score a hat-trick, aged 18 years 33 days.

1979

Wesley Michael 'Wes' Brown (Defender 1996–present) was born in Longsight, Manchester.

1983 WEMBLEY'S BABY

Liverpool 2   Manchester United 1 (aet)
Norman Whiteside, Manchester United's Northern Ireland international striker,

scored a superb goal in this 2–1 League Cup (Milk Cup) defeat to Liverpool at Wembley Stadium.

Ronnie Whelan scored for the Merseysiders in extra-time to win the Cup while Whiteside, aged just 17 years 323 days, became the youngest ever player to score a goal in a Wembley Cup final.

27

1897 UNTARNISHED HOME RECORD

Newton Heath 1   Notts County 1
Newton Heath drew 1–1 with Notts County in their final home League game of the 1896–97 season (scorer: William Bryant).

The Heathens went on to end the season as runners-up in the Second Division but failed to secure a place in the top flight after losing out in the end-of-season Test Matches. Newton Heath were undefeated at home in all competitions throughout the season, a total of 22 games (15 League, 5 FA Cup and 2 Test Matches). It was the first time in the history of the club that their home record was untarnished.

1926 BLUES DOUBLE SINKING

Manchester City 3   Manchester United 0
Manchester City prevented United from reaching their second FA Cup final after the Reds lost this semi-final 3–0 to the Blues at Bramall Lane, Sheffield. However, the result had mixed fortunes for both clubs because whereas Manchester United finished ninth in the First Division, their derby rivals were relegated to Division 2 and lost the FA Cup final to Bolton Wanderers.

1968 REDS STEAL BLUES' THUNDER

Manchester United 1   Manchester City 3
In season 1967–68 the two Manchester teams were battling it out head-to-head all season long in the race for the Championship. In this crucial game at Old Trafford the Blues went back across the city with the vital two points. George Best was the United goalscorer. City ended the season as First Division champions with United in the runners-up position but United stole their neighbour's thunder by becoming the first English team to win the European Cup.

1994 TREBLE DREAM BUBBLE BURSTS

Aston Villa 3   Manchester United 1

When United travelled to Wembley Stadium to face Aston Villa in the 1993–94 Coca-Cola (League) Cup final, the Reds were marching towards their second successive Premier League crown and in 17 days would be back at Wembley to play Oldham Athletic in the FA Cup semi-final. United were attempting to do something no other club in the history of English football had ever done, win the domestic Treble. On the day, United lacked their usual fizz and soon found themselves trailing 2–0 and their Treble dreams slowly evaporating. However, a goal from Mark Hughes with eight minutes left breathed new life into the Reds (they were actually wearing their Newton Heath green and yellow shirts at the time) before disaster struck. United's flying Russian winger, Andrei Kanchelskis, found himself in his own area defending a Villa attack in the last minute of the game only to handle a shot on the line. He was sent off and Dean Saunders converted the spot kick to give Villa the Cup. Two statistical oddities arose in this game: first, it was the second time in three years that United lost the League Cup final to a side managed by their former manager, Ron Atkinson (Sheffield Wednesday in 1991), and second, it was goalkeeper Les Sealey's third game in three years for United. Sealey had replaced the suspended Peter Schmeichel; his previous games were United's sixth-round FA Cup win over Charlton Athletic sixteen days earlier and United's glory night in the 1991 European Cup Winners' Cup final when they beat Barcelona 2–1. After the Villa final the critics had a field day with many claiming that United 'lacked the bottle for a fight' but the players responded by winning the club's first Double at Wembley in May 1994 after beating Chelsea 4–0 in the final.

28

1949

Frank Kopel (Full-back 1967–9) was born in Falkirk.

1988 WHITE HART HEAT

Tottenham Hotspur 2   Manchester United 3

This game was played at White Hart Lane as a testimonial match for the ex-Spurs player Danny Thomas. United did not do the home side any favours, winning the game 3–2.

29

1906 PEDDIE OUTFOXES THE FOXES

Leicester City 2   Manchester United 5
Jack Peddie scored a hat-trick for United in their 5–2 Second Division away win at Leicester City. John Picken and Charles Sagar also scored for United.

2008 BACK HEEL SETS UP ROUT

Manchested United 4   Aston Villa 0
Cristiano Ronaldo's cheeky back heel set United on the way to a spectacular 4–0 triumph over Aston Villa, who had not won at Old Trafford since 1983. With Wayne Rooney scoring twice and Carlos Tevez also on target it, ended up a comfortable win in the rain.

30

1889 COMBINATION FAREWELL

Newton Heath 0   South Shore 1
Newton Heath's last game in the Football Combination was a 1–0 home loss to South Shore on 30 March 1889.

1960 VIOLLET SMELLS OF ROSES

Sheffield Wednesday 4   Manchester United 2
Bobby Charlton and Dennis Viollet scored for United in this 4–2 First Division defeat by the Owls at Hillsborough. It was Viollet's 32nd and last League goal of the 1959–60 season, making him both United's and the First Division's top goalscorer from 36 games. Viollet's 32-goal collection remains a club record in the League.

1972 CZECH MATE

Karel Poborsky (Forward 1996–7) was born in Tøeboò, Czechoslovakia. Poborsky is the Czech Republic's all-time leader in appearances for his country, 118 games and 18 goals.

1994 OVER THE MILLION MARK

Manchester United 1   Liverpool 0

United's biggest home attendance of the season, 44,751, watched United beat Liverpool thanks to a Paul Ince goal. In total 1,218,426 fans passed through Old Trafford's turnstiles during the 1993–94 season (average 43,515) to watch 21 Premier League, one FA Cup, four League Cup and two European Cup games.

31

1906 AN EARLY TESTIMONIAL

Manchester United 5   Barnsley 1

Although this was a Second Division home game (played at United's Clayton ground), it was awarded as a benefit match to United's Alfred Schofield and James Hayes (scorers: Charles Sagar 3, Alexander Bell, John Picken).

1973 WHEN SIX COMES OUT TOP

Manchester United 2   Southampton 0

During the 1972–73 season goals were increasingly hard to come by for United's players. When Bobby Charlton found the back of the net in this 2–0 home win over Southampton in the First Division, it was not only his sixth and last League goal of the season, but it also made him United's top League goalscorer for the entire season. Jim Holton scored the other goal in the 2–0 victory. United found the back of the net just 44 times in their 42 League games to finish the season in 18th place, just one place above relegation to Division Two. Sadly, this was the shape of things to come. United went down the following season, having scored just 38 League goals.

1995 ERIC'S POETIC JUSTICE

A relieved Eric Cantona appeared at a press conference shortly after he successfully appealed against a two-week prison sentence, subsequently reduced to 120 hours' community service. The reporters with their microphones at the ready waited to hear what the enigmatic United superstar, who was no friend of the media given the constant intrusions on his personal life, had to say. Eric did not disappoint them and famously said: 'When the seagulls follow the trawler it is because they think that sardines will be thrown into the sea.' Eric pushed back his chair, stood up, and walked out of the room without uttering another word. Typical Ericness from the man who could do no wrong in the eyes of all United fans.

1996 DOUBLE CARLING AWARD GOES TO OLD TRAFFORD

Manchester United 2   Chelsea 1

A day of celebration for Manchester United. First Alex Ferguson was named the Carling Manager of the Month for March and Eric Cantona won the Carling Player of the Month award. Then in the FA Cup semi-final at Villa Park, United beat Chelsea 2–1 to book an encounter with Liverpool in the FA Cup final at Wembley thanks to goals from Andy Cole and David Beckham.

2007 FILLED TO THE RAFTERS

Manchester United 4   Blackburn Rovers 1

United's 4–1 thumping of Lancashire rivals Blackburn Rovers en route to winning the 2006–07 Premier League title was watched by a crowd of 76,098. The attendance is United's record attendance at Old Trafford and it is also the highest ever crowd for a Premiership game. United trailed 1–0 at half-time but in a truly magnificent second-half performance the Red Devils scored four times (scorers: Paul Scholes, Michael Carrick, Ji-Sung Park, Ole Gunnar Solskjaer). During the game Nemanja Vidic suffered a broken collarbone after falling awkwardly and was immediately stretchered off the field. He returned to action at the beginning of May for the Champions League semi-final second leg against AC Milan.

APRIL

1

1905 ROBERTS BECOMES UNITED'S FIRST THREE LIONS STAR

Charlie Roberts, the captain of Manchester United, became the first United player to win an international cap for England when he took part in their 1–0 win over Scotland in a Home International game played at the Crystal Palace, London.

1935

William 'Liam' Whelan (Forward 1954–8) was born in Dublin.

1954 MERLIN'S ARRIVAL

Gordon Alexander Hill (Forward 1975–8) was born in Sunbury-on-Thames. The United fans nicknamed Gordon 'Merlin' due to his magical left foot and mercurial wing play.

1978 SIX TIMES THREE

Arsenal 3   Manchester United 1
Manchester United conceded three goals at Highbury for the sixth consecutive season when they lost this First Division game 3–1 (scorer: Joe Jordan). However, it was actually the seventh successive game against the Gunners in which they let three past them, six League games and one League Cup tie.

2000 STIRRING THE SLEEPY DEVIL

Manchester United 7   West Ham United 1
Manchester United found themselves a goal down to West Ham United after just 11 minutes of play in this Premiership game at Old Trafford. However, the goal merely awakened the Reds as they ripped into the hapless Hammers defence, scoring seven times without further reply from the shell-shocked visitors.

Paul Scholes bagged a hat-trick while Denis Irwin, Andy Cole, David Beckham and Ole Gunnar Solskjaer also scored.

2008 FERGIE LANDMARK

AS Roma 0   Manchester United 2

For the second year in succession, United were drawn against Roma in the UEFA Champions League quarter-finals. This was the ninth time under Sir Alex that United had reached this stage of the tournament, and it was also his 1,200th game in charge. United won with goals from Cristiano Ronaldo and Wayne Rooney. A 1–0 win in the second leg (scorer: Carlos Tevez) saw United through to the semi-final against Barcelona.

2

1915 MATCH-FIXING SCANDAL ROCKS UNITED

Manchester United 2   Liverpool 0

Following this First Division 2–0 (scorer: George Anderson 2) win for United against Liverpool at Old Trafford, allegations of match fixing were made against several players on both teams. The Football Association acted swiftly and after investigating the allegations they handed out lifetime bans to a number of players including United's Sandy Turnbull, Enoch West and Arthur Whalley. However, after the end of the First World War all of the bans were annulled by the FA as a result of the players' contributions during the war but sadly Turnbull was killed in action in Arras, France on 3 May 1917.

1966 SUPER TED ARRIVES

Edward Paul 'Teddy' Sheringham (Forward 1997–2001) was born in Walthamstow.

1995 BECKS MAKES HIS LEAGUE DEBUT

Manchester United 0   Leeds United 0

Although David Beckham made his Manchester United debut in a League Cup tie for the Reds in September 1992, it wasn't until the end of the 1994–95 season that he was given his League baptism in this 0–0 Premiership draw with Leeds United at Old Trafford.

2002 FIESTA TIME

Deportivo La Coruna 0   Manchester United 2

Manchester United's 2–0 away victory at Deportivo La Coruna was their first away win against a Spanish club in European competition in 13 attempts dating back 46 years.

3

1886 MANCHESTER COUNTY FA SENIOR CUP WINNERS

Newton Heath 2   Manchester City 1
After losing the inaugural Manchester County FA Senior Cup final the previous season, the Heathens won the Cup defeating neighbours Manchester City 2–1.

1896 CAPTAIN OF THE HEATHENS AND DEVILS

Newton Heath 4   Darwen 0
William Kennedy hit a hat-trick for the Heathens in this 4–0 Second Division win over Darwen (James McNaught also scored). The game marked the debut of Harry Stafford who would go on to captain the Heathens. When the club changed its name to Manchester United in 1902, Stafford became the first and only player to have captained both Newton Heath and Manchester United.

> STAFFORD, Harry *(Full-back 1896–1903) – debut in the above game.*
> *Appearances: FL: 183, goals 0 FAC: 17, goals 1 TOTAL: 200 apps, 1 goal.*

1965 BOBBY'S HAT-TRICK

Blackburn Rovers 0   Manchester United 5
Bobby Charlton scored his only hat-trick of the 1964–65 First Division Championship-winning season in United's 5–0 win at Blackburn Rovers. David Herd and John Connelly also scored.

1983

Ben Foster (Goalkeeper 2005–present) was born in Leamington Spa.

4

1953 DUNCAN EDWARDS MAKES HIS DEBUT

Manchester United 1   Cardiff City 4
One of the greatest of the famous Busby Babes, Duncan Edwards was born in Dudley in 1936. When he was only 11 years old he played in the Dudley Boys team whose players had an average age of 15. Matt Busby travelled to Dudley and signed the young Edwards just two hours into his 16th birthday. The rest is history. Duncan made his United debut aged 16 years 185 days and made his full

England debut aged 18 years 183 days (in which England beat Scotland 7–2). With the Reds, Duncan won three FA Youth Cup winners' medals, two Championship medals (1956 and 1957) and appeared in the 1957 FA Cup final loss to Aston Villa. Tragically, he lost his life in the Munich Air Disaster when he was only 21.

1959 CENTURION REDS

Manchester United 3   Bolton Wanderers 0

Albert Scanlon scored United's second goal of the game in their 3–0 win (Bobby Charlton and Dennis Viollet also scored) over Lancashire rivals Bolton Wanderers to record United's 100th League goal of the 1958–59 season. Despite 103 League goals (including two own goals) the Reds finished the season as First Division runners-up to Wolverhampton Wanderers.

1964

Paul Andrew Parker (Defender 1991–5) was born in West Ham, London.

1973 DALY ARRIVAL

Gerry Daly joined the Reds in a £20,000 move from the Dublin-based club Bohemians.

1979 GREENHOFF BOOKS UNITED'S FA CUP FINAL PLACE

Manchester United 1   Liverpool 0

Jimmy Greenhoff scored United's winner against Liverpool in their FA Cup semi-final replay at Goodison Park. The Reds now faced Arsenal at Wembley Stadium in the final.

1988 NORMAN THE CONQUEROR

Liverpool 3   Manchester United 3

United took the lead in this Easter Monday battle with a goal from skipper Bryan Robson. However, the Merseysiders fought back and led 3–1 early in the second half. In the 54th minute Alex Ferguson sent on his two substitutes (Norman Whiteside and Jesper Olsen for Mike Duxbury and Clayton Blackmore) for an all-out attack. The new arrivals helped United assert themselves in the match and when Colin Gibson was sent off on the hour mark all seemed lost. However, in the final 30 minutes United staged a remarkable comeback: they scored again through Robson and then with just 13 minutes left on the clock Peter Davenport put Gordon Strachan through for United's equaliser. The main turning point was United's domination of the midfield thanks to Whiteside's determination and aggressive tackles on Liverpool's Steve McMahon who was no match for the young Irishman in the heat of battle.

1994 THE THEATRE OF NIGHTMARES

Manchester United 3   Oldham Athletic 0
United's 3–0 win over Oldham Athletic in their Premier League game meant that Oldham had not beaten United at Old Trafford for 60 years. Oldham are still waiting to taste victory at the Theatre of Dreams. Dion Dublin, Ryan Giggs and Paul Ince all scored for the Reds.

2007 UNITED FANS ATTACKED BY POLICE

AS Roma 2   Manchester United 1
Manchester United travelled to Italy for the first leg of their UEFA Champions League quarter-final encounter against AS Roma in the Stadio Olimpico, Rome. Crowd trouble flared before and during the game, despite warnings from United to fans making the trip that the Italian capital was a dangerous place for away supporters. Roma won the game 2–1 with Wayne Rooney scoring for the Reds, the club's 100th goal of the 2006–07 season.

5

1889 LEAGUE WOUND UP

In 1889 Newton Heath became the first 'unofficial' winners of the newly created Football Combination, which lasted just one season and was wound up on 5 April 1889. The balance of the funds from the league was donated to an orphanage in Derby. Newton Heath together with many other teams from the Football Combination then became founder members of the Football Alliance in 1889.

1941 UNITED LOSE OPENING GAME AT THEIR ADOPTED HOME

Manchester United 2   Blackpool 3
Severe bomb damage to Old Trafford on the night of 11 March 1941 resulted in United having to rent the Maine Road ground of their neighbours Manchester City until 24 August 1949. In this first League game at their temporary home the Seasiders won 3–2.

1975 UNITED BOUNCE STRAIGHT BACK INTO THE TOP FLIGHT

Southampton 0   Manchester United 1

Manchester United beat Southampton 1–0 at The Dell to ensure their return to the First Division. Lou Macari scored the vital goal.

2003 SCOUSE BUSTERS

Manchester United 4   Liverpool 0

The Red Devils hammered their bitter rivals in this crucial game for United who were seeking to reclaim the Premiership crown. Ruud van Nistelrooy (2), Ryan Giggs and Ole Gunnar Solskjaer scored for United to keep them on course for the title.

6

1883

Charles Roberts (Half-back 1903–13) was born in Darlington.

1930

David 'Dave' Sexton (United manager 1977–81) was born in Islington, London.

1938

Frederick Charles 'Fred' Erentz (Full-back 1892–1902) was is born in Dundee. Fred's brother Henry also played for United.

1960

Colin Gibson (Defender 1985–90) was born in Bridport, Dorset.

2006 ALEX IS GOD

Manchester United announced the biggest shirt sponsorship deal in UK football by signing a record-breaking four-year £56.5m agreement with the US insurance and financial services company American International Group, Inc. (AIG). The deal meant that the brand of the leading international insurance organisation would appear on the famous red Manchester United shirt from the start of the 2006–07 season. Meanwhile, the T-shirt sellers in and around Old Trafford were quick to seize another sale by printing T-shirts emblazoned with AIG on the front of them with the words 'Alex Is God' appearing beneath the logo.

2008 750 FOR GIGGS

Middlesbrough 2   Manchester United 2
Ryan Giggs became the second United player ever to play 750 times for the club.
Only Bobby Charlton, with 759 has played more. Cristiano Ronaldo, with his
37th of the season, and Wayne Rooney were United's scorers.

7

1890 BROTHERS SCORE

Newton Heath 9   Small Heath 1
Roger and Jack Doughty both found the net in Newton Heath's 9–1 home win
over Small Heath (later Birmingham City) in this Football Alliance encounter.
This game is historic in that despite the fact that five sets of brothers have played
for the club (Buchan, Doughty, Erentz, Greenhoff and Neville) this game marked
the first and only time that two brothers scored for the club in the same game.

1928 HAT-TRICK FOR RAWLINGS

Manchester United 4   Burnley 3
Bill Rawlings netted a hat-trick for the Reds in their 4–3 First Division win over
Lancashire rivals Burnley at Old Trafford. David Williams also scored.

1948 LOWRIE'S DERBY DEBUT

Manchester United 1   Manchester City 1
Thomas Lowrie joined United after impressing United's Scottish international,
Jimmy Delaney, in a charity match while he was on holiday in Ireland. Lowrie
made his United debut in this First Division draw at Maine Road with Rowley
scoring for the Reds.
> LOWRIE, **Thomas** *(Half-back 1947–50) – debut in the above game.*
> *Appearances:* FL: *13, goals 0* FAC: *1, goals 0* TOTAL: *14 apps, 0 goals.*

1956 BUSBY BABES CLINCH THEIR FIRST TITLE

Manchester United 2   Blackpool 1
In front of their biggest crowd of the season, 62,277, United beat Blackpool 2–1
(scorers: Johnny Berry, Tommy Taylor) at Old Trafford to win the First Division
Championship for the fourth time in the club's history. United's superb League
form at the turn of the year was instrumental in their Championship success. In
the second half of the season the Reds lost just once in their final 17 League
games, a 3–1 defeat away to Preston North End.

8

1893 HEATHENS FACE THE DROP

Newton Heath 3   Accrington 3

This 3–3 draw (scorers: Robert Donaldson, Thomas Fitzsimmons, William Stewart) in the final game of the Heathens' first season in the Football League, meant that they finished at the bottom of Division 1 (16th place). They now faced a Test Match (a play-off between the team that finished bottom of Division 1 and the winners of Division 2) against Birmingham City to determine which team would play in Division 1 the following season. It was also the last time that Newton Heath (or Manchester United) met Accrington in a League game.

1970 BAGGIES BAGGED

Manchester United 7   West Bromwich Albion 0

Three Manchester United players (Bobby Charlton, John Fitzpatrick, Alan Gowling) scored two goals each in the Reds' impressive 7–0 drubbing of West Bromwich Albion at Old Trafford in this First Division game. United's other scorer was George Best.

1990 FA CUP SEMI-FINAL THRILLER

Manchester United 3   Oldham Athletic 3

This was the second of a live television FA Cup semi-final double-header, Crystal Palace having already booked their Wembley appearance earlier in the day with a dramatic 4–3 extra-time win over Liverpool. The game, played at Maine Road, didn't disappoint the fans who were lucky enough to obtain a ticket nor the millions of armchair viewers. Oldham took the lead following a mistake by United's keeper Jim Leighton, but goals from Bryan Robson and Neil Webb put the Reds ahead. Oldham levelled at 2–2 and forced extra-time. Once again United went ahead, with a goal from Danny Wallace, but Oldham's Roger Palmer forced a replay with his side's third goal of the game.

9

1892 THE END OF LANCASHIRE & YORKSHIRE RAILWAY

Newton Heath 3   Birmingham St George's 0

Newton Heath Lancashire & Yorkshire Railway Football Club played three seasons in the Football Alliance, finishing eighth in 1889–90, ninth in 1890–91 and runners-up in 1891–92. The Heathens' last game in the Alliance was a 3–0 home win against Birmingham St George's (scorers: Robert Donaldson 2, William Hood). For the 1892–93 season the club made the decision to drop the 'Lancashire & Yorkshire Railway' from their name, becoming known as Newton Heath Football Club. Therefore the 3–0 win was the club's last-ever game as Newton Heath Lancashire & Yorkshire Railway Football Club.

1966 HOME RECORD FALLS

Manchester United 1   Leicester City 2

Leicester City became the only side to win at Old Trafford during season 1965–66, taking away both points in this First Division encounter (scorer: John Connelly).

1969 WILF MCGUINNESS TO BE NEXT UNITED MANAGER

Manchester United announced that Wilf McGuinness, a former Busby Babe, had been appointed the club's chief coach, a move made in expectation of Sir Matt Busby's retirement at the end of the 1968–69 season. On 1 June 1969, McGuinness became the 10th manager of Manchester United but things did not quite work out for him and in December 1970 he was forced to step down. Wilf reverted to trainer-coach of United's reserve team.

10

1891

Frank Barson (Half-back 1922–8) was born in Grimethorpe, Sheffield.

1926 UNITED SUFFER THEIR WORST EVER AWAY DEFEAT

Blackburn Rovers 7   Manchester United 0

Blackburn Rovers hammered Manchester United 7–0 at Ewood Park in this First

Division game, the Reds' worst away defeat. The 7–0 reversal has happened three times in the club's history, the others being at Aston Villa in 1930 and at Wolverhampton Wanderers in 1931.

1970 FA CUP THIRD PLACE PLAY-OFF
Manchester United 2   Watford 0
Brian Kidd scored both goals for United in the competition's third place play-off at Highbury.

1993 BRUCE DOUBLE STRIKE LATE IN INJURY TIME SEALS VICTORY
Manchester United 2   Sheffield Wednesday 1
This win was unquestionably the one victory that propelled Manchester United to their first Championship success in 26 years. Trailing 1–0 to the visitors in this Premiership game at Old Trafford, the game went into injury time. Steve Bruce scored two headers for the Reds in seven minutes of injury time, the second of which resulted in Alex Ferguson and Brian Kidd running excitedly on to the Old Trafford pitch amid scenes of jubilation on the terraces.

1994 SPARKY STRIKE SAVES DOUBLE
Manchester United 1   Oldham Athletic 1
At the end of 90 minutes followed by the first extra period of 15 minutes, this FA Cup semi-final was scoreless. However, in the opening minute of the second period of extra-time Neil Pointon scored for the Latics and, whereas the season looked so promising for United a number of weeks ago, they now seemed to be heading out of the Cup, having already lost out in the League Cup final to Aston Villa. But with just 60 seconds left on the clock, barely visible in the fading light, Brian McClair headed the ball into the Oldham box and Mark Hughes smacked it on the turn with a terrific volley that flew into the net. The game ended 1–1, much to United's relief, and in the replay the Latics never even came close, losing 4–1 at Maine Road. United went on to win the Cup and retain their Premiership crown to claim the coveted Double for the first time in the club's history.

2000 SCHOLES CRACKER
Middlesbrough 3   Manchester United 4
Paul Scholes scored a magnificent goal from the edge of the Boro box to help United to a 4–3 Premier League win over their North East opponents at the Riverside Stadium. Andy Cole, Quinton Fortune and Ryan Giggs also found the Middlesbrough net.

2007 DEMOLITION NIGHT AT THE THEATRE OF DREAMS

Manchester United 7   AS Roma 1

'Be afraid, be very afraid' was the message United sent to the rest of Europe following their 7–1 demolition of AS Roma at Old Trafford in the second leg of their UEFA Champions League quarter-final encounter. United, trailing 2–1 from the first leg, blasted their way through the Italians' defence to reach the semi-finals with goals from Michael Carrick (2), Cristiano Ronaldo (2 – his first goals in 27 Champions League games), Alan Smith, Wayne Rooney and Patrice Evra. United went into the game slightly under-strength with injury victims Gary Neville, Nemanja Vidic, Louis Saha and Ji-Sung Park all ruled out along with the suspended Paul Scholes. Remarkably, Smith was given only his fourth start of the campaign, partnering Wayne Rooney in attack. It was the first time United had managed to overturn a first-leg deficit in a European tie since they beat FC Barcelona 3–0 in the 1983–84 European Cup Winners' Cup quarter-final at Old Trafford.

11

1951

James Allan 'Jim' Holton (Half-back 1972–5) was born in Lesmahagow, Lanarkshire.

1953 FIVE DIFFERENT GOALKEEPERS

Newcastle United 1   Manchester United 2

Dennis Viollet made his United debut in this 2–1 First Division win over Newcastle United at St James' Park (scorer: Tommy Taylor 2).

For the game the Reds used their fifth goalkeeper of the season, Les Olive, after Ray Wood, Jack Crompton, Reg Allen and Johnny Carey had all appeared in the green jersey (Carey was an outfield player but played in an emergency away to Sunderland).

> OLIVE, **Robert Leslie** (*Goalkeeper 1952–3*) – *debut in the above game.*
> Appearances: FL: 2, goals 0 TOTAL: 2 apps, 0 goals.
> Les Olive is remembered more for the 30 years he spent at United as the club's secretary than for his two League games. He joined the Reds ground staff from school in 1942 and played in almost every position for all five of United's teams. In 1988 he was made a director of the club.
> VIOLLET, **Dennis Sydney** (*Forward 1952–62*) – *debut in the above game.*
> Appearances: FL: 259, goals 159 FAC: 18, goals 5 FLC: 2, goals 1 EUR: 12, goals 13 TOTAL: 293 apps, 179 goals.
> Dennis Viollet is one of the most prolific goalscorers in the history of the club. A product of United's youth team, he formed a deadly striking partnership with Tommy Taylor

until Taylor lost his life in the Munich Air Disaster. Dennis Viollet survived the crash and in season 1959–60 scored 32 League goals in just 36 games, a club record. In January 1962 he was sold to Stoke City for £25,000, a move that surprised many at the time.

1957 UNITED'S RECORD ATTENDANCE

Real Madrid 3   Manchester United 1
A crowd of 135,000 attended this European Cup semi-final first leg game at Real Madrid's Estadio Santiago Bernabeu. It is the largest crowd that United have ever played in front of.

1990 UNITED REACH FIRST CUP FINAL UNDER FERGUSON

Manchester United 2   Oldham Athletic 1
Three days after their 3–3 draw, United were on their way to Wembley with a 2–1 win over Oldham Athletic after extra time in their FA Cup semi-final replay at Maine Road. Brian McClair and Mark Robins scored the vital goals. Amazingly, it was the first game of the 1989–90 FA Cup that United hadn't played on a Sunday.

1998 PELE PERFORMS AT OLD TRAFFORD

Manchester United's new £4m three-floor museum complex was opened by Brazilian World Cup legend Pele. The museum took seven months to build and features a number of interactive rooms with the latest computer technology.

12

1965 HISTORY-MAKING ASTONS

Manchester United 1   Leicester City 0
John Aston Jnr made his Manchester United debut in their 1–0 win over Leicester City (scorer: David Herd) at Old Trafford in the First Division. It was United's 36th League game of the season and Aston's debut came as a result of Denis Law's absence. John's father, John Aston Snr, served United from 1944–54 as a full-back. United went on to win the 1964–65 First Division Championship but Aston did not collect a winners' medal as this was his one and only League performance of the season.

However, in season 1966–67 John Jnr played his part in United winning their second First Division title in three years and this time won a League Championship winners' medal. John Snr and John Jnr are the only father and son pair to have won English First Division Championship winners' medals with the same club, John Snr in 1951–52 and John Jnr in 1966–67.

ASTON, John (Jnr) (Forward 1965–72 – debut in the above game.
Appearances: FL: 139 (16), goals 25 FAC: 5 (2), goals 1 FLC: 12 (3), goals 0
EUR: 8, goals 1 TOTAL: 166 (21) apps, 27 goals.

1972 MARTIN BUCHAN SCORES HIS FIRST GOAL FOR THE CLUB
Manchester United 1 Manchester City 3
Martin Buchan's first goal for club wasn't enough to send the United fans home
happy as City won this second derby game of the season (the first Manchester
derby game ended 3–3 back in November). He would score only three more in
a career of 455 appearances for the club.

1988 McCLAIR TIPS HAT TO BEST
Manchester United 3 Luton Town 0
Brian McClair became the first Manchester United player since George Best,
during season 1967–68, to score 20 goals in a season for the club. McClair scored
in the 3–0 home win over Luton Town and went on to finish the 1987–88 season
with 24 League goals and a total of 31 in all competitions. Peter Davenport and
Bryan Robson also scored against the Hatters.

1992 THIRD TIME LUCKY LEAGUE CUP
Manchester United 1 Nottingham Forest 0
In season 1991–92 Manchester United were fighting on two main fronts, the race
to win the last ever First Division Championship and the League (Rumbelows)
Cup. The Reds reached their third League Cup final in 1991–92 having lost their
first to Liverpool in 1982–83 and their second to Sheffield Wednesday in 1990–
91. Their opponents for the 1992 League Cup final were Nottingham Forest, not
quite the force they were a decade earlier when they won the First Division and
two European Cups, but any side managed by Brian Clough was hard to beat.
United finally won the only domestic trophy to have eluded them thanks to a
goal from Brian McClair in the 14th minute of the final at Wembley Stadium.
    Manchester United: Schmeichel, Parker, Irwin, Bruce, Phelan, Pallister,
Kanchelskis (Sharpe), Ince, McClair, Hughes, Giggs.

1995 FIERY KEANO GIVEN EARLY BATH
Crystal Palace 0 Manchester United 2
Roy Keane became the fifth Manchester United player to be sent off during the
1994–95 season following a stamping incident, after which both he and Crystal
Palace's Darren Patterson angrily exchanged punches. Patterson was also shown
the red card. The crowd of only 17,987 for this replay was the lowest FA Cup
semi-final crowd since the Second World War. The original tie, three days earlier,
had attracted over 38,000.

1997 ERIC'S LAST COMPETITIVE GOAL FOR UNITED

Blackburn Rovers 2   Manchester United 3

Despite missing an early penalty Eric Cantona inspired Manchester United to victory over their Lancashire rivals. The game lived up to its billing – between them United and Rovers had won the first four Premier League titles – and featured plenty of open attacking play. However, the scoreline somewhat flattered the home side as United totally outplayed them, much to the annoyance of many of the home fans who had accepted defeat and were on their way home when their team scored a late second goal. The United goalscorers were Andy Cole, Paul Scholes and Cantona. Eric's 11th goal of the season was his last competitive goal for the club. His penalty miss was only the second he missed for United in four and a half years.

2003 MAGPIES LEAVE NEST

Newcastle United 2 Manchester United 6

Manchester United totally outplayed Newcastle United at St James' Park and led 5–1 at half-time. Many of the Toon Army walked out rather than have to sit and watch their team ravaged by a rampant Manchester United side on course to reclaim their Premiership crown. Paul Scholes hit a superb hat-trick with goals from Ole Gunnar Solskjaer, Ryan Giggs and Ruud van Nistelrooy completing the rout.

13

1927 BAMLETT TAKES CHARGE

Herbert Bamlett succeeded Clarence Hilditch as the manager of Manchester United with six League games of the season remaining. Louis Rocca was appointed assistant manager. When Bamlett arrived at Old Trafford United were a club in crisis and finished the season 15th in Division One. However, United's fortune didn't improve under Bamlett and he left the club four years later. Prior to becoming a manager, Bamlett had been one of England's leading referees and in 1914, aged 32, he became the youngest man to referee an FA Cup final (Burnley v Liverpool). Before his time in charge of United he also managed Oldham Athletic, Wigan Borough and Middlesbrough.

1977 NOT SEEING EYE TO EYE WITH THE DOC

Gerry Daly left United to join Derby County in a £175,000 transfer. Daly fell out with United's manager Tommy Docherty, who ironically followed Daly to Derby a few years later.

1988

Anderson Luis de Abreu Oliveira (Midfielder 2007–present) was born in Porto Alegre, Brazil.

1994 ROBSON'S LAST FA CUP GAME FOR UNITED

Manchester United 4   Oldham Athletic 1

Bryan Robson helped Manchester United to their fourth FA Cup final since his arrival at the club with a goal in this semi-final replay, played at Maine Road. The other United goalscorers were Denis Irwin, Andrei Kanchelskis and Ryan Giggs. It was Robbo's 33rd FA Cup game for the Reds and his 10th goal in the competition for United. Robson was dropped for the final and lost his chance of winning a record fourth FA Cup winners' medal.

1996 GREY DAYS FOR UNITED

Southampton 3   Manchester United 1

When Manchester United travelled to The Dell for their Premiership game with Southampton they wore their infamous grey kit for the fifth and as it turned out final time. Ryan Giggs was the last player to score in the unlucky kit in which United drew one game and lost the other four. David Beckham and Eric Cantona were the only other players to score wearing it.

2007 RONALDO SIGNS A NEW FIVE-YEAR DEAL

Cristiano Ronaldo signed a new five-year contract with United which keeps him at Old Trafford until 2012. Ronaldo joined United from Sporting Lisbon in August 2003 for £12m on a five-year contract which he extended by a further two years in November 2005. By the end of the 2006–07 season, he had scored 50 goals in 190 appearances, with 23 of them in that season alone. His reported £120,000 a week deal made him the highest paid player in United's history.

14

1894 NEWTON HEATH DEAD LAST

Newton Heath 1   Preston North End 3

This result meant that the Heathens now faced a Test Match against Liverpool to determine which of the two teams would have the privilege of playing in the First Division the following season, 1894–95. It was a disappointing season for the Heathens with the team winning only six of their 30 League games, five of them being at home.

1941 REDS INFLICT BLUES' HEAVIEST HOME DEFEAT

Manchester City 1   Manchester United 7

In a North Regional League Second Competition game the Reds beat Derby rivals City 7–1 (scorers: Jack Rowley 4, Stan Pearson 2, John Smith) at Maine Road. It was Manchester City's heaviest defeat at Maine Road since the ground was first opened in 1923.

1997 BECKHAM VOTED PFA YOUNG PLAYER OF THE YEAR

David Beckham was voted the PFA Young Player of the Year for 1996–97. He followed in the footsteps of former team-mate Mark Hughes and current team-mate Ryan Giggs, both of whom also won the award while with United. In the overall award for the PFA's Player of the Year, Beckham finished second to Alan Shearer of Newcastle United.

1999 GIGGSY SCORES UNITED'S GREATEST EVER GOAL

Manchester United 2   Arsenal 1

After their 0–0 draw three days earlier, United and Arsenal were back at Villa Park to decide who would appear in the 1999 FA Cup final against Newcastle United. This game was the last ever FA Cup semi-final replay and what an epic encounter it turned out to be. David Beckham gave the Treble-seeking United the lead with a superb long-range shot that totally outfoxed David Seaman in the Gunners net. Arsenal, still on course to claim the Double, pulled themselves level thanks to Dennis Bergkamp, and then the Reds were reduced to 10 men when Roy Keane was shown the red card. United's Treble dream looked to be over when Phil Neville gave away a penalty in the last minute but Peter Schmeichel pulled off a wonder save to keep the Reds in the game.

No one who saw the game will ever forget what happened in extra-time when Patrick Vieira sloppily gave the ball away in the middle of the park. Ryan Giggs latched on to the errant pass and set off on a mazy run to the Arsenal goal leaving five Gunners in his wake as he crashed a vicious shot high up into the roof of the net from the left-hand side of the box. As the ball flew past Seaman, Giggsy went on a celebratory run that included removing his shirt and waving it frantically in the air. United held on and won the game 2–1, and so the Treble dream lived on.

Giggsy's goal was later voted the Greatest Ever Manchester United Goal in a poll conducted by the club, an excellent choice by the United faithful because if Mark Hughes's leveller against Oldham Athletic in the 1994 FA Cup semi-final was 'the goal that inspired the Double' then Giggsy's goal was surely 'the goal that fired the Treble'.

2001 SKY BLUE TRIPLE DELIGHT

Manchester United 4   Coventry City 2

A midday 4–2 win over Coventry City at Old Trafford (scorers: Dwight Yorke 2, Andy Cole, Ryan Giggs) was good enough to clinch United's third consecutive Premiership crown, seventh overall, as their nearest challengers, Arsenal, lost 3–0 to Middlesbrough later the same day.

2007 UNITED SECURE NEW WEMBLEY FA CUP FINAL APPEARANCE

Manchester United 4   Watford 1

After just six minutes of their FA Cup semi-final tie with Watford at Villa Park, Wayne Rooney fired home a brilliant 20-yard drive; he later added a second, with Ronaldo and Kieran Richardson also scoring. It was United's 25th FA Cup semi-final appearance, equalling Arsenal's record, and their 11th FA Cup semi-final at Villa Park (W7, D4). Incredibly, United had not lost a game at Villa Park since their 3–1 opening day defeat by Aston Villa in season 1995–96 (P18, W15, D3).

15

1934

David George Herd (Forward 1961–8) was born in Hamilton, Lanarkshire.

1944 REDS BATTER BURNLEY

Manchester United 9   Burnley 0

Manchester United beat Burnley 9–0 in a wartime regional fixture with a hat-trick from John Smith and two goals each for Brook, William Bryant and Jack Rowley.

1950 BABY BABE

Manchester United 0   Portsmouth 2

Portsmouth came away from Old Trafford with this 2–0 victory in the First Division, a game that marked the first senior appearance of Jeffrey Whitefoot. Matt Busby gave the young half-back, aged just 16 years 105 days, his debut making him United's youngest post-war League player. Ironically, exactly one week later his place in the team would be taken by United's oldest ever post-war League player, Jack Warner.

1968 JIMMY'S DOUBLE

Manchester United 3   Fulham 0

Jimmy Rimmer replaced Alex Stepney in goal for this First Division game against Fulham at Old Trafford. It was Rimmer's debut appearance for the Reds and he kept a clean sheet in United's 3–0 win (scorers: John Aston Jnr, George Best, Bobby Charlton). Rimmer was United's unused substitute in the 1968 European Cup final. After he left United, Rimmer played for Arsenal (1974–7) and Aston Villa (1977–83). In 1981 he won a First Division winners' medal with the Villans and in 1982 he helped Villa to the European Cup final against Bayern Munich. In the final Rimmer had to be substituted after just nine minutes of play through injury but his replacement, Nigel Spink, helped Villa to a 1–0 win. Amazingly, Rimmer is the only English player to have won a European Cup winners' medal at two different clubs despite the fact that he played for just nine minutes in the two finals.

> RIMMER, John James 'Jimmy' *(Goalkeeper 1967–73) – debut in the above game.*
> *Appearances: FL: 34, goals 0   FAC: 3, goals 0   FLC: 6, goals 0   EUR: 2 (1), goals 0*
> *TOTAL: 45 (1) apps, 0 goals.*

1995 DOUBLE CENTURY

Leicester City 0   Manchester United 4

When Manchester United scored their first goal against Leicester City at Filbert Street in this Premiership game it was their 100th goal of the season in all competitions – and their last goal in the 4–0 rout was their 100th away goal in the Premier League. Andy Cole (2), Paul Ince and Lee Sharpe all found the back of the Foxes' net. Paul Ince's goal was his last for the club as he left for Inter Milan in the summer.

1997 CHOCCY TRIBUTE

Manchester United 1   Celtic 2

A crowd of 43,743 came to Old Trafford to pay tribute to a true Manchester United legend, Brian 'Choccy' McClair, in this his testimonial match. Choccy joined United from Celtic in the summer of 1987 and was instrumental in the club's success during the 1990s. He scored the winning goal in both the 1991 European Super Cup final and the 1992 Rumbelows League Cup final and in 1988 became the first player since George Best to score 20 League goals in a season. United's opponents on Brian's big night were, fittingly, his former club, Celtic, whose fans also showed their appreciation for one of their old heroes. The Hoops won 2–1.

16

1921 MEREDITH'S DOUBLE TRIPLE CENTURY

Manchester United 0   Middlesbrough 1
Billy Meredith played his 300th League game for United in this 1–0 home defeat
to Middlesbrough in the First Division. He is the only player in history to have
played more than 300 League games for both Manchester-based clubs, 303 for
United and 366 for City.

1963 LAW HAT-TRICK NOT ENOUGH

Leicester City 4   Manchester United 3
Despite a hat-trick from The King, United were beaten 4–3 at Filbert Street. It
was the same score as the corresponding fixture the previous season.

2003 TITLE DECIDER

Arsenal 2   Manchester United 2
With only five games of the 2002–03 season to go Manchester United visited
Highbury for a crucial game against the defending champions. Billed as a title
decider, this game seesawed with both sides taking the lead, but the Reds came
away with a 2–2 draw (scorers: Ryan Giggs, Ruud van Nistelrooy) and a firm
grasp on the Premiership crown.

17

1985 QUE SERA SERA

Manchester United 2   Liverpool 1
In their FA Cup semi-final replay against Liverpool at Maine Road, United beat
their bitter rivals 2–1 to reach their second FA Cup final in three years thanks to
goals from Bryan Robson and Mark Hughes.

1988 UNITED FALL SHORT IN CENTENARY SOCCER SHOW

United were beaten 2–1 by Sheffield Wednesday in the semi-final of the Mer-
cantile Credit Football League Centenary Festival, a two-day extravaganza at
Wembley. Knock-out games of 20 minutes each way, many decided by penalty
shoot-outs, ultimately produced a winning side, Nottingham Forest.

18

1958 THE BOSS COMES HOME

Matt Busby, who had spent the previous 71 days in the Rechts der Isar Hospital in Munich, Germany, recovering from the injuries he sustained in the fateful Munich Air Disaster on 6 February 1958, was welcomed back to his home in Kings Road, Chorlton by thousands of United fans who were delighted to see him.

1970 A MUDDY AFFAIR

In Northern Ireland's 1–0 defeat by Scotland at Windsor Park, Belfast, George Best was sent off for throwing mud at the referee.

1995 ERIC IN THE COMMUNITY

Eric Cantona began his community service for his 'kung-fu' attack on a fan at Selhurst Park in January.

19

1957 WHELAN GRABS A HATFUL

Burnley 1   Manchester United 3
Liam Whelan scored a hat-trick for United in their 3–1 win over Burnley at Turf Moor in this First Division encounter.

1958 UNITED LEGEND DIES

Billy Meredith, who played for Manchester United from 1906–21, died in Withington, Manchester, aged 83. After helping the Reds win the First Division Championship in 1908 and 1911 and the FA Cup in 1909, Meredith was given a free transfer at the age of 47 and rejoined Manchester City. Billy Meredith's place in the history of the club is assured.

1997 PALLISTER HEADS FOR PREMIERSHIP GLORY

Liverpool 1   Manchester United 3
Manchester United visited Anfield knowing that a win over Liverpool would virtually assure them of winning their fourth Premiership crown in five seasons.

In a pulsating game the Reds didn't disappoint Fergie's travelling Red and White Army, playing with the authority of champions and winning the game 3–1. Gary Pallister scored two bullet-like headers direct from corner kicks and Andy Cole sealed victory with United's third goal. David James had a nightmare of a game in the Liverpool goal.

2003 AN EVENTFUL DEBUT

Manchester United 3   Blackburn Rovers 1

When Fabien Barthez left the field injured, United's summer signing Ricardo Lopez Felipe made his debut for the Reds and celebrated it by bringing down a former United hero, Andy Cole, for a penalty. However, Ricardo redeemed himself by saving David Dunn's spot kick and United ran out 3–1 winners (scorers: Paul Scholes 2, Ruud van Nistelrooy).

20

1957 UNITED RETAIN THE CHAMPIONSHIP

Manchester United 4   Sunderland 0

Manchester United beat Sunderland 4–0 (scorers: Liam Whelan 2, Duncan Edwards, Tommy Taylor) to clinch the First Division Championship for the second year running.

1966 PADDY'S EARLY BATH

Manchester United 1   Partizan Belgrade 0

Paddy Crerand received his marching orders along with Mihaslovic during United's second leg European Cup semi-final 1–0 win over Partizan Belgrade at Old Trafford. However, the victory was not good enough to put the Reds into the final having lost the away leg 2–0.

1992 FOREST FRUSTRATE REDS' TITLE HOPES

Manchester United 1   Nottingham Forest 2

United's biggest home gate of the season, 47,576, saw them lose 2–1 (scorer: McClair) to Nottingham Forest. It was a crushing blow for United's title aspirations as Leeds United took full advantage of the slip-up by winning their game later that evening. In total 944,678 fans attended First Division games at Old Trafford throughout the season, an average of 44,985 per match.

21

1906 UNITED'S OLYMPIC GOLD MEDAL WINNER

Harold Hardman, Manchester United forward in 1908 (4 games, 0 goals) and the club's chairman from 1951–65, was a member of the Everton side that beat Newcastle United 1–0 in the 1906 FA Cup final played at the Crystal Palace Stadium. Hardman, who was an amateur footballer, won a gold medal with Great Britain's football team at the 1908 Olympic Games held in London.

1925 DOUBLE HAT-TRICK

Manchester United 5   Sunderland 1
Christopher Taylor scored a hat-trick for the Reds in their 5–1 First Division win over Sunderland at Old Trafford (Harry Thomas and Thomas Smith also scored). Ten days later he held on to his second match ball after netting another hat-trick in United's 3–2 win over West Bromwich Albion in their final League game of the season. Taylor made 28 League appearances for United from 1925–30 and scored six times, his two hat-tricks.

1956 BABES WIN TITLE

Manchester United 1   Portsmouth 0
On the final day of the 1955–56 season United, crowned First Division champions two weeks earlier, beat Portsmouth 1–0 at Old Trafford thanks to Dennis Viollet's 20th League goal of the campaign. The Reds won the title by 11 points from Blackpool to equal the record winning margin set in the late 1800s by the infamous trio of Preston North End, Sunderland and Aston Villa. Amazingly, the United team had an average age of just 22. The Busby Babes had truly made their mark in English football.

1975

Benjamin 'Ben' Thornley (Midfielder 1993–8) was born in Bury.

1991 ATKINSON EXACTS REVENGE ON UNITED

Manchester United 0   Sheffield Wednesday 1
Sheffield Wednesday, managed by former Manchester United manager Ron Atkinson, beat Manchester United in the final of the Rumbelows League Cup. It was the second time that a club from a lower division had beaten the Reds in a Wembley final (Southampton won the 1976 FA Cup final 1–0).

1993 SPARKY'S DOUBLE TEN

Crystal Palace 0   Manchester United 2

Manchester United beat Crystal Palace 2–0 (scorers: Mark Hughes, Paul Ince) at Selhurst Park to edge them closer to their first Championship success in 26 years. Mark Hughes's goal was his 100th for United making him only the 10th Manchester United player to score 100 League goals for the club. Ironically, Sparky wore the Reds' famous No.10 shirt for most of his Old Trafford career.

1999 KEANO MAGNIFICO

Juventus 2   Manchester United 3

Manchester United beat Juventus 3–2 in the Stadio Delle Alpi in the second leg of their UEFA Champions League semi-final clash and progressed to their first European Cup final since 1968, following the 1–1 draw at Old Trafford in the first leg a fortnight earlier. The all-important goals were scored by Roy Keane, Dwight Yorke and Andy Cole while Keano's booking in the game meant that he would miss the Nou Camp showdown with Bayern Munich. Despite his booking Keano played his heart out for United in a game that many Manchester United fans believe to be Keano's finest ever game for the club.

22

1893 HEATHENS FACE TEST MATCH TO STAY UP

Newton Heath 1   Small Heath 1

In 1892 the Football League decided that at the end of the 1892–93 season, the three bottom clubs in the new First Division would play the first three placed teams in the Second Division to determine which club would be playing First Division football the following season. Two weeks after finishing bottom of the First Division, Newton Heath played Small Heath in a Test Match at Stoke. The winners would play First Division football during season 1893–94 while the losers would have to settle for Second Division football. Alfred Farman was the Newton Heath goalscorer in this first of two play-off games.

1911 LIVERPOOL HAND UNITED THE TITLE

Aston Villa 4   Manchester United 2

When Manchester United lost 4–2 (scorer: Harold Halse 2) at Aston Villa on 22 April 1911 the First Division Championship was delicately poised. Villa's victory put them level on points with United, 50, and they had a game in hand. Villa drew their game in hand at Blackburn Rovers two days later to put them one point clear at the top of the table with only one game remaining. On the final

Saturday of the season Villa travelled to Liverpool while United were at home to Sunderland. Villa lost 3–1 while United beat Sunderland 5–1. United thus finished one point ahead of Villa and were crowned champions for the second time in three years.

1925 CLUB'S TIGHTEST EVER DEFENCE

Manchester United 1   Southampton 1

Southampton's goal in this 1–1 draw (scorer: Albert Pape) at Old Trafford was the 23rd and last goal United leaked during the 1924–25 season, a club record. The extremely mean Manchester United defence helped them finish second in the Second Division behind Leicester City and secure promotion to the top flight.

1950 UNITED'S GENERATION GAME

Newcastle United 1   Manchester United 1

When Manchester United drew 1–1 (scorer: John Downie) with Newcastle United at St James' Park in this First Division game, Jack Warner, aged 38, became United's oldest post-war League player. Jack was named in the Reds starting line-up, replacing the injured Jeff Whitefoot, who ironically had become United's youngest post-war League player just seven days earlier.

1957 BUSBY THE INNOVATOR

Manchester United 2   Burnley 0

Matt Busby was probably the first football manager to realise that his first-choice players needed rest between important games and for this game against Burnley at Old Trafford the legendary United manager refused to play nine of the team that had beaten Sunderland 4–0 at Old Trafford just two days earlier (scorers: Liam Whelan 2, Duncan Edwards and Tommy Taylor). However, Busby's makeshift United beat Burnley 2–0 on their way to retaining the First Division Championship (scorers: Alex Dawson, Colin Webster).

The tactically astute Busby rested his first team in preparation for their European Cup semi-final second leg tie with Real Madrid at Old Trafford three days later.

DAWSON, *Alexander Downie (Forward 1956–61) – debut in the above game.*
Appearances: FL: 80, goals 45 FAC: 10, goals 8 FLC: 3, goals 1 TOTAL: 93 apps, 54 goals.
Alex Dawson scored on his League, FA Cup and League Cup debuts for the Reds. Dawson was as strong as a bull and a prolific scorer for the club, with an average of more than a goal every two games. When David Herd arrived at Old Trafford in the summer of 1961 it effectively signalled the end of Dawson's United career and in October 1961 he was sold to Preston North End for £18,000.

1963
Scott McGarvey (Forward 1981–3) was born in Glasgow.

1969
Dion Dublin (Forward 1992–3) was born in Leicester.

1992 DISGRACEFUL HAMMERS
West Ham United 1   Manchester United 0
Despite already being relegated West Ham United produced their best display of the season to beat Manchester United 1–0 at Upton Park. United's hopes of securing their first Championship in 25 years was practically at an end following this defeat to the Hammers. After the game Alex Ferguson described the West Ham performance a disgrace.

1996 KEEGAN CRACKS UNDER FERGIE PRESSURE
Just a few nights after Manchester United had beaten Leeds United 1–0 (scorer: Roy Keane) in the Premiership at Old Trafford, an emotional Kevin Keegan, the Newcastle United manager, went before the Sky TV cameras and hit back at Alex Ferguson's comments that he didn't think Leeds would try as hard against Newcastle, saying: 'I'll tell you honestly, I will love it if we beat them, love it.'

2000 DEVILS RIP SAINTS APART
Southampton 0   Manchester United 3
Manchester United clinched the 1999–2000 Premiership title in record time with a 3–0 win over Southampton at The Dell (scorers: David Beckham, Ole Gunnar Solskjaer, o.g.). United went on to win their remaining four Premier League games to land the title by a mammoth 18 points over Arsenal.

2007 RONALDO WINS PFA AWARDS DOUBLE
Manchester United's Cristiano Ronaldo was named the Player of the Year and the Young Player of the Year by the Professional Footballers' Association.

He is the first player to win both awards in the same season since Andy Gray (Aston Villa) in 1977. Chelsea's Didier Drogba came second with Ronaldo's United team-mate Paul Scholes third in the senior award. Ryan Giggs also made the shortlist. Sir Alex Ferguson commented: 'I think he is the best player in the world and his season has been incredible.' On an incredible night for Manchester United Sir Alex was honoured with the PFA Special Merit Award while eight United players made it into the PFA Team of the Year. *PFA Premier League Team of the Year:* Edwin van der Sar, Gary Neville, Nemanja Vidic, Rio Ferdinand, Patrice Evra, Ryan Giggs, Paul Scholes,

Cristiano Ronaldo (all Man Utd), Steven Gerrard (Liverpool), Didier Drogba (Chelsea), Dimitar Berbatov (Tottenham).

23

1902 LAST LEAGUE GAME OF LAST SEASON AS THE HEATHENS
Newton Heath 2   Chesterfield 0
1901–02 was Newton Heath's final season. They finished the season in 15th place in the Second Division and won the Manchester Senior Cup. The Heathens' final League game took place on 23 April 1902 at Bank Street. They won 2–0 against Chesterfield with goals from James Coupar and Stephen Preston.

1966 FIFTH SEMI-FINAL ON THE TROT
Everton 1   Manchester United 0
The Reds reached their fifth successive FA Cup semi-final but were beaten 1–0 by Everton at Burnden Park, Bolton. Everton went on to beat Sheffield Wednesday 3–2 in the final.

1969 TEN MEN OF MANCHESTER FAIL IN MILAN
AC Milan 2   Manchester United 0
John Fitzpatrick received his marching orders as the Italian champions beat United 2–0 in this European Cup semi-final first leg at the San Siro. The game was beamed live to Old Trafford from Milan on closed-circuit television. United now faced a tough return leg to retain the trophy they won the previous May at Wembley.

1973 GUARD OF HONOUR
Manchester United 1   Sheffield United 2
Sheffield United were the visitors for United's penultimate League game of the 1972–73 season, their final home game of the campaign. The players with the exception of one took to the pitch together, the odd man out being Bobby Charlton who had announced his retirement and was playing his last ever game at his spiritual home, Old Trafford. As Bobby Charlton walked out on to the pitch for the 758th time in United's colours both teams formed a guard of honour for the Manchester United and England legend. However, it was not to be a winning finale for Bobby as the Blades won 2–1 (scorer: Brian Kidd) before a crowd of 57,280. While the game celebrated the end of Charlton's Old Trafford career it marked the start of Arnold Sidebottom's when he made his Manchester United debut in the First Division encounter. Sidebottom was born in Barnsley

and as well as being a professional footballer he was a medium fast bowler who represented Yorkshire at county level and was a member of the England team that played Australia in 1985.

SIDEBOTTOM, Arnold (Half-back 1972–5) – debut in the above game.
Appearances: FL: 16, goals 0 FAC: 2, goals 0 FLC: 2, goals 0 TOTAL: 20 apps, 0 goals.

1997 GERMAN BLOCKADE

Manchester United 0   Borussia Dortmund 1
Manchester United's hopes of reaching the European Cup final for the first time since 1968 came to an abrupt end at Old Trafford following this 1–0 defeat to Borussia Dortmund. Despite enjoying most of the possession and creating several good chances, the Reds just could not force a way past a well-disciplined German defence. It was United's third defeat at Old Trafford in the 1996–97 UEFA Champions League, having previously gone 40 years without ever losing a home European tie.

2001 FERGIE GETS RUUD

Almost exactly one year after he nearly signed Ruud van Nistelrooy, Sir Alex Ferguson finally got his man when Manchester United paid PSV Eindhoven a new British record fee of £19m. In his first season at Old Trafford the Dutch striker scored 23 goals in 32 League games (plus 10 in the UEFA Champions League), including scoring in a record eight consecutive Premier League games, and was fittingly named the 2001–02 PFA Player of the Year.

2003 REAL CLASS ACT

Manchester United 4   Real Madrid 3
Manchester United were totally outclassed in every department by Real Madrid in the second leg of this UEFA Champions League quarter-final tie at Old Trafford. United had lost the first leg 3–1 (scorer: Ruud van Nistelrooy) in the Estadio Santiago Bernabeu 17 days earlier. Two goals from David Beckham, who came on as a substitute in the game, a Ruud van Nistelrooy goal and an own goal were not enough to see United past the Spanish giants. Ronaldo, Madrid's Brazilian striker, scored a superb hat-trick for Real Madrid and when he was substituted he was given a standing ovation from the downbeat, but appreciative, United fans.

2008 FERGIE MATCHES SIR MATT IN EUROPE

Barcelona 0   Manchester United 0
Manchester United's 0–0 draw with FC Barcelona in their first leg UEFA Champions League semi-final encounter at Camp Nou was the tenth time the Reds had reached the last four of the competition. It was also the fifth time Sir Alex

Ferguson had guided United into the semi-finals, while Sir Matt Busby took the Reds to their first five. It was also the first time United had played at Camp Nou since lifting the trophy in 1999, a game that Paul Scholes had missed. This tie was his 100th in the Champions League, the second United player after Ryan Giggs to reach the landmark.

24

1909 FA CUP LOVE AFFAIR BEGINS

Manchester United 1   Bristol City 0
In 1909 Manchester United reached their first-ever FA Cup final, which in the pre-Wembley Stadium days was hosted at the Crystal Palace, London. Thousands of Reds made the train journey down to the capital, swelling the crowd to 71,401, and went home happy thanks to a Sandy Turnbull goal in the 22nd minute, which gave United the Cup. Prior to the final the FA ordered both teams, who each wore red shirts, to change their kit for the match. United ran out wearing a white shirt with a large cherry red 'V' on the front. Billy Meredith, United's Welsh Wizard, was the man of the match, claiming his second FA Cup winners' medal (his first was won with Manchester City in 1904) while Charlie Roberts became the first United captain to hold aloft the prestigious trophy.

Manchester United: Moger, Stacey, Hayes, Duckworth, Roberts, Bell, Meredith, Halse, Turnbull J, Turnbull A, Wall.

1929 DOC MEETS THE DOC

Tommy Docherty (United manager 1972–7) was born in the Gorbals district of Glasgow.

1937 REDS DROP INTO DIVISION 2

West Bromwich Albion 1   Manchester United 0
Having won the Second Division Championship during season 1935–36, United were relegated again after only one season back in the top flight. The Reds finished second from bottom (21st) in the table with just 10 wins from their 42 League matches.

1948 BUSBY CLAIMS FIRST UNITED SUCCESS

Manchester United 4   Blackpool 2
The 1948 FA Cup final was the club's second appearance in the showcase event and their first visit to the Twin Towers. Just three years after taking charge at Old Trafford Matt Busby guided the Red Devils to their second FA Cup victory, his

first trophy success as the manager of Manchester United. The Blackpool side contained England greats Stanley Matthews and Stan Mortensen but they were no match for the side captained by Johnny Carey. Jack Rowley (2), John Anderson and Stan Pearson fired the goals for the Reds as Carey became the first Manchester United player to climb the famous Wembley steps up to the Royal Box where he was presented with the trophy by King George VI.

Manchester United: Crompton, Carey, Aston, Anderson, Chilton, Cockburn, Delaney, Morris, Rowley, Pearson, Mitten.

2007 UNITED TAME MILANESE

Manchester United 3 AC Milan 2
Wayne Rooney scored twice, including an injury-time winner, to give United a 3–2 victory over AC Milan in the first leg of their UEFA Champions League semi-final tie. United, seriously weakened at the back with key players injured, started energetically against their Italian opponents just as they had against AS Roma in the quarter-final and were ahead within five minutes. Milan's keeper Dida palmed a Ronaldo header into his own net in the fifth minute to send the crowd crazy only to see Milan's Brazilian Kaka put the visitors 2–1 in front at half-time with two superbly taken individual goals. Then in the second half Rooney scored just before the hour mark to level the game at 2–2 before he struck again in injury time to send the United faithful delirious with delight.

25

1903 MANAGER OF HEATHENS AND DEVILS

Barnsley 0 Manchester United 0
Manchester United drew 0–0 with Barnsley at Oakwell in the final game of the 1902–03 season, their first as Manchester United, to finish fifth in the First Division. It was manager James West's last game in charge of the club, the only man ever to have managed both Newton Heath (1900–02) and Manchester United (1902–03).

1908 CHAMPIONS FOR THE FIRST TIME

Manchester United 2 Preston North End 1
On the last day of the 1907–08 season Manchester United beat Preston North End 2–1 (scorers: Harold Halse, Rodway o.g.) to clinch the First Division Championship for the first time in the club's history. In winning the Championship, United set a record for the most League points at that time, 52, following 23 wins and 6 draws from their 42 League games played.

1909 CIVIC RECEPTION FOR CUP HEROES

Manchester United returned to Manchester the day after they had won the 1909 FA Cup, the first FA Cup win in the club's history. Hundreds of thousands of fans welcomed the team home when they arrived at Manchester Central Station. A horsedrawn carriage took the players and the Cup to the Town Hall where the Lord Mayor held a civic reception for the team.

1957 FIRST EUROPEAN TIE AT OLD TRAFFORD

Manchester United 2   Real Madrid 2
Manchester United played their first European tie at Old Trafford under floodlights when Real Madrid held them to a 2–2 draw (scorers: Tommy Taylor, Bobby Charlton). However, it was the Spanish champions who went through to the final having already beaten United 3–1 in the first leg (scorer: Tommy Taylor). All of United's previous home games in the European Cup had been played at Maine Road. United's floodlight system cost the club £40,000. Four 160ft steel towers were erected with each tower containing 54 floodlights.

1959 TON-UP AGAIN

Leicester City 2   Manchester United 1
Warren Bradley's goal in this 2–1 defeat to Leicester City at Filbert Street in the First Division was the Reds' 103rd League goal of the season, equalling the club record. Despite scoring a century of goals, United also leaked them at the back, conceding 66, and finished runners-up to the champions, Wolverhampton Wanderers.

1964 DENIS LAW HITS 46

Manchester United 3   Nottingham Forest 1
Denis Law scored twice in United's final League game of the 1963–64 season with Nottingham Forest on the receiving end of a 3–1 defeat at Old Trafford. Law's goals were his 45th and 46th of the season, a United record that still proudly stands today (30 League, 10 FA Cup, 6 ECWC). Graham Moore also scored for United.

1981 SEXTON'S LAST GAME IN CHARGE OF UNITED

Manchester United 1   Norwich City 0
This 1–0 (scorer: Joe Jordan) home win over Norwich City on the final day of the 1980–81 First Division season proved to be Dave Sexton's last game as the manager of Manchester United despite the Reds winning their last seven League matches. Ironically, it was United's best ever finish to a season, which was subsequently equalled in season 1992–93. The Reds finished eighth in the

First Division, drawing 18 of their 42 League games, 11 of them at Old Trafford.

2007 MORE SILVERWARE FOR RONNIE

Cristiano Ronaldo was named the PFA Fans' Player of the Year, an annual award presented to the Premier League's most outstanding player and voted for by football fans from all over the United Kingdom.

26

1890 HEATHENS' FIRST STEPS

Newton Heath 1   Sheffield Wednesday 2
Newton Heath finished their first season of existence in eighth position in the Football Alliance, losing 2–1 at home to Sheffield Wednesday.

1902 HEATHENS' FINAL FAREWELL

Newton Heath 2   Manchester City 1
Newton Heath beat local rivals Manchester City 2–1 in the final of the Manchester Cup in their last ever game under the banner of Newton Heath. After the game an emergency meeting of the club was held at Islington Public Hall, Ancoats. Harry Stafford addressed the audience and announced that he and John H. Davies had a plan to save the club. Davies and three other local businessmen pledged to invest £500 each thus guaranteeing the existence of the club. At the meeting the club changed its name to Manchester United and John H. Davies was appointed as the club's new chairman.

1915 CASUALTY OF WAR

Manchester United 1   Aston Villa 0
Manchester United played their last League game before the First World War forced the Football Association to abandon League football for the duration of hostilities. The Reds beat Aston Villa 1–0 in this First Division game played at Old Trafford (scorer: George Anderson).

1952 GUNNERS OUTGUNNED

Manchester United 6   Arsenal 1
Manchester United hammered Arsenal, the only team who stood a chance of catching them in the race for the First Division title, 6–1 in the final game of the season to clinch the Championship for the first time since 1911 (their third

overall). Jack Rowley grabbed a hat-trick while Stan Pearson (2) and Roger Byrne also scored for the champions. Arsenal went into the game knowing that only a 7–0 win over United would guarantee them the title but even the Gunners must have known that this was out of the question.

1958 THE MAN OF STEEL

Chelsea 2   Manchester United 1
Bill Foulkes played in his 42nd game of the 1957–58 season despite the fact that he was involved in the Munich Air Disaster on 6 February 1958. He was the only Manchester United player to have played in all 42 League games. Remarkably, Foulkes also played in all eight of United's FA Cup games during the season, including the loss to Bolton Wanderers in the final. In fact, the practically indestructible United right-back also played in all eight of United's European Cup games in season 1957–58.

The 2–1 away defeat to Chelsea (scorer: Ernie Taylor) was United's 58th fixture of the season and because of the postponement of games in the aftermath of the Munich Air Disaster it was also their ninth First Division game of the month. United ended the season in ninth place. Dennis Viollet was the only other United player to have appeared in both the opening and last League games of the season.

1960 DUNNE DEAL

Tony Dunne joined United from the Irish side Shelbourne for a modest £5,000.

1965 SIX PACK FOR THE REDS

Manchester United 3   Arsenal 1
Manchester United's 3–1 home win over Arsenal (scorers: Denis Law 2, George Best) was good enough to crown the Reds champions of England with one game of the season (away to Aston Villa) still to play. A resurgent Leeds United under the astute guidance of Don Revie had pushed the Red Devils all season long in a ding-dong Battle of the Roses but in the end United took the spoils, albeit narrowly winning the title on a slender goal average (as opposed to today's goal difference system) of 0.686. Law, who netted twice, almost did not play in the game as he had stitches in a knee wound but Matt Busby told him he was needed and sent him into battle. And as for the last game, alas the party celebrations proved too much, United losing 2–1 (scorer: Charlton). It was United's sixth First Division Championship crown, Matt Busby's fourth as manager.

1975 SECOND, SECOND DIVISION CHAMPIONSHIP

Manchester United 4   Blackpool 0
Manchester United effectively led the League all season long and returned to the First Division at the first attempt, clinching the Second Division title with this

comprehensive 4–0 win over Blackpool on the final day of the season. Stuart Pearson (2), Jimmy Greenhoff and Lou Macari were all on target for the champions. In a strange twist of fate Aston Villa finished second to United while Norwich City finished third. When United won their next League Championship, the inaugural FA Premier League in season 1992–93, Aston Villa finished runners-up and Norwich City finished third.

27

1893 NEWTON HEATH HOLD ON TO THEIR FIRST DIVISION STATUS

Newton Heath 5   Small Heath 2
The Heathens won their Test Match replay 5–2 (scorers: Alfred Farman 3, Joe Cassidy, James Coupar) against Small Heath (later renamed Birmingham City) at Bramall Lane, Sheffield, thereby guaranteeing them First Division football for season 1893–94.

1897 FISH AND CHIPS ALL ROUND

Sunderland 2   Newton Heath 0
Manchester United lost out in their four-game series of Test Matches to earn the right to play First Division football in season 1897–98, losing their fourth game 2–0 away to Sunderland. Earlier the Heathens had lost to Burnley away, beaten Burnley at home and drawn with Sunderland at home. As a reward for all their hard work during the season the cash-strapped directors treated the players to a fish and chip supper.

1908 UNITED PARTICIPATE IN THE FIRST EVER FA CHARITY SHIELD

Manchester United 1   Queens Park Rangers 1
Manchester United, the Northern League champions, took on Queens Park Rangers, the Southern League title holders, in the first ever FA Charity Shield. The game was played at Stamford Bridge and ended 1–1 (scorer: Billy Meredith). The replay did not take place until 29 August 1908.

1928

Robert Leslie Olive (Goalkeeper 1952–3) was born in Salford.

1958 EURO INVITE

The day after the 1957–58 campaign ended, UEFA invited Manchester United to participate in the European Cup during the 1958–59 season along with Wolverhampton Wanderers, the newly crowned First Division champions. The Reds had finished ninth in the League but, out of respect for the United players who lost their lives in the Munich Air Disaster two months earlier, UEFA decided to issue the invitation. However, the Football Association refused United permission to play in European football in 1958–59. Two years earlier Matt Busby had defied the FA by pioneering European football for English clubs, so perhaps this was the FA's revenge.

1963 UNITED'S GOOD CUP FORM CONTINUES

Manchester United 1   Southampton 0

Despite a disappointing League campaign the Reds made it to Wembley for the FA Cup final after beating Southampton 1–0 at Villa Park in their semi-final tie. Denis Law scored the goal that booked the Reds their fifth FA Cup final appearance, their fourth at Wembley Stadium.

1974 LAW'S BACK-HEELED GOAL HELPS RELEGATE UNITED

Manchester United 0   Manchester City 1

On the last Saturday of the 1973–74 season United faced neighbours City in a game that could have decided whether or not the Reds would be playing Second Division football the following season. Denis Law, who was making his last Football League appearance, was warmly welcomed by both sets of supporters, but little did they know what lay in store for them. City had also made Law their captain for the day. Defeat for the Reds would almost certainly mean Second Division football while a draw might be enough to stay up. The game came to life with only eight minutes remaining and the score standing at 0–0. Colin Bell and Francis Lee combined well to find Law in the Manchester United penalty area. With his back to the goal Law casually back-heeled the ball and then watched in amazement as it slipped past Stepney and into the net. Law realised what he had done and didn't even celebrate his goal as the Manchester United fans invaded the pitch. It turned out to be his last kick in League Football because when the game restarted three minutes later, Hanson had replaced Law in the game. A second invasion of the pitch and a fire in the Stretford End resulted in the referee, David Smith, abandoning the game. The Football League ordered the result to stand and United were relegated. As it turned out United would still have gone down even if they had beaten City, as the results on the final day of the season did not go in their favour.

1996 SIR MATT BUSBY STATUE

A bronze statue of Sir Matt Busby was unveiled at the Scoreboard End of Old Trafford as Manchester United remembered the man who is considered by many to be 'The Father of Manchester United'.

1998 YIP JAAP STAM

Manchester United and PSV Eindhoven finally agreed a £10m fee for the Dutch side's 25-year-old international defender, Jaap Stam. Stam had always made it known that he wanted to join the Reds and is said to have waived his 10% cut of the transfer fee to help ease the deal through. Alex Ferguson was delighted with his latest capture and claimed that he tried to sign Stam in the summer of 1997 but PSV were not prepared to sell him then.

2002 SEVEN FOR THE RECORD

Ipswich Town 0 Manchester United 1
When Manchester United beat Ipswich Town 1–0 away (scorer: Ruud van Nistelrooy) in the Premier League, they set a new club record of seven consecutive away wins.

2008 RONNIE'S DOUBLE PFA SCOOP

Christiano Ronaldo was named the Professional Footballers' Association Player of the Year for the successive season, only the second player ever to have done so. 'I feel very happy. It is a great moment; it is an honour, a pleasure,' said the 23-year-old Portuguese star. Meanwhile, Arsenal's Cesc Fabregas denied Ronaldo a unique double when the Spanish star pipped him to the Young Player of the Year Award, Ronaldo having won it in season 2006–07. The 2007–08 PFA Premier League Team of the Year saw two of Ronaldo's team-mates join him. Rio Ferdinand and Nemanja Vidic.

28

1900 GOAL-A-GAME HOLT

Manchester United 2 Chesterfield 1
Edward Holt made his one and only appearance for the club, and scored in a 2–1 home win over Chesterfield (other scorer: John Grundy).

1902 MANCHESTER UNITED ARE BORN

Midway through the 1901–02 season Newton Heath were in severe financial trouble with things coming to a dramatic head at the end of the season. The

Heathens finished 15th in the Second Division out of 18 clubs and could muster only 11 wins from their 34 League matches played. Fans, the lifeblood of the club, were beginning to stay away from games as crowds dipped to as little as 500 on one occasion. The directors announced that the club was in the red (literally) to the tune of £2,670, a huge sum of money at the turn of the 20th century. But with the season over, and the injection of the promised £500 cash each from four wealthy benefactors, the club wanted to start afresh and a meeting was called at Islington Public Hall to decide the club's future. The decision was taken to continue but with a change of name, and the local newspaper, the *Manchester Guardian*, announced: 'The Newton Heath combination will now be renamed Manchester United.' However, the new name was not the first choice of many and was only chosen after others, including Manchester Central and Manchester Celtic, were unanimously rejected. It was Louis Rocca who suggested the name Manchester United. Mr John Henry Davies was elected the new chairman and the club captain of the Heathens, Harry Stafford, linked up with the current manager, James West, to handle the day-to-day running of the new club.

1906 PROMOTION TO DIVISION 1

Manchester United 6   Burton United 0
With this 6–0 victory (scorers: John Picken 2, Charles Sagar 2, John Peddie, George Wall) over Burton United the Reds finished runners-up in the Second Division behind champions Bristol City to win promotion to the top flight, thus bringing to an end a 12-year absence from the First Division.

1951 HUDDERSFIELD HAMMERED AGAIN

Manchester United 6   Huddersfield Town 0
For the second consecutive season Manchester United hammered Huddersfield Town 6–0 at Old Trafford in the First Division (scorers: John Aston 2, Henry 'Harry' McShane 2, John Downie, Jack Rowley). Rowley was the only player to score in both games.

1953

Brian Greenhoff (Defender 1973–9) was born in Barnsley.

1965 FANS CELEBRATE DESPITE DEFEAT

Aston Villa 2   Manchester United 1
Bobby Charlton scored Manchester United's last goal of the 1964–65 season in their 2–1 loss to Aston Villa at Villa Park in the First Division. However, the players and fans of United still celebrated, having clinched the title two days earlier with a 3–1 home win over Arsenal (scorers: Denis Law 2, George Best).

Amazingly, United had used only 18 players in the League and 19 different players in all competitions during the season.

1973 BOBBY'S FAREWELL AT THE BRIDGE

Chelsea 1   Manchester United 0

After arriving at Old Trafford in January 1953 aged just 15, Bobby Charlton made his 606th and final League appearance in a Manchester United shirt. The Chelsea players and his United team-mates formed a guard of honour as the United legend took to the Stamford Bridge pitch. Bobby made a record 759 appearances (two of them as a substitute) for the club and scored a record 249 goals after making his scoring debut on 6 October 1956.

2007 UNITED ESCAPE FROM STICKY TOFFEE

Everton 2   Manchester United 4

United visited Goodison Park for a crucial must-win FA Premier League encounter, their game kicking off at the same time as Chelsea's match against Bolton Wanderers at Stamford Bridge. Things started badly for the two title contenders with both Everton and Bolton taking early leads. Chelsea fought back to lead 2–1 as United trailed 2–0. Bolton then equalised while in the last 30 minutes of the game at Goodison, United scored four times through John O'Shea, Phil Neville (o.g.), Wayne Rooney and Chris Eagles for a 4–2 victory. Chelsea's game finished 2–2 in what proved to be Sam Allardyce's last game in charge of the Trotters.

29

1911 CHAMPIONS AGAIN

Manchester United 5   Sunderland 1

Manchester United beat Sunderland 5–1 (scorers: Harold Halse 2, Sandy Turnbull, Enoch West, Milton o.g.) at Old Trafford on the last day of the 1910–11 season to clinch the First Division Championship title. United were neck and neck with Aston Villa going into the last day of the campaign but the Villans lost 3–1 to Liverpool at Anfield. Amazingly, after winning their second First Division Championship in three years, two world wars would be fought before United would be crowned champions of England again.

1912 MANGNALL FIRST AND LAST

Manchester United 3   Blackburn Rovers 1

Goals from Michael Hamill, Billy Meredith and Enoch West ensured that Ernest

Mangnall's last ever game in charge of United ended in victory.

Mangnall guided Manchester United to two First Division titles (1908 and 1911) and the FA Cup in 1909. When he left Old Trafford he took up the position as manager of Manchester City. He is the only man ever to have managed both Manchester clubs.

1936 DIVISION 2 CHAMPIONS

Bury 2   Manchester United 3
With a 3–2 away win at Bury (scorers: Thomas Manley 2, George Mutch) United clinched the Second Division title.

1949

Brian Kidd (Forward 1967–74) was born in Collyhurst, Manchester.

1950 BOGOTA BANDIT'S LAST GAME FOR UNITED

Manchester United 3   Fulham 0
Manchester United beat Fulham 3–0 (scorers: Jack Rowley 2, Henry Cockburn) on the last day of the 1949–50 First Division season, finishing fourth in the table. It was Charlie Mitten's 161st and final game for United scoring 61 times, including 17 penalties from 17 attempts. Mitten was unhappy with the maximum wage for footballers at the time and, like many players, he decided to ply his trade in Colombia where he joined Santa Fe. FIFA did not recognise the Colombian league competition at the time, so the overseas stars who played there were depicted as 'mercenaries' and 'rebels'. He returned after a year in South America, the promise of huge sums of money not materialising, but was snubbed by United and the football authorities before finally managing to sign for Fulham.

1956

Kevin Bernard Moran (Defender 1978–88) was born in Dublin.

1957 BUSBY BABES WIN SECOND CHAMPIONSHIP RUNNING

Manchester United 1   West Bromwich Albion 1
Alex Dawson scored for United in their 1–1 draw with West Bromwich Albion at Old Trafford on the last day of the 1956–57 First Division season. The new champions paraded the trophy before a meagre crowd of just 20,357 at Old Trafford. It was the Reds' third title in the past five seasons. United had actually won the Championship nine days earlier with a 4–0 home win over Sunderland (scorers: Liam Whelan 2, Duncan Edwards, Tommy Taylor) before a packed house of 58,725. Sadly, all three players would subsequently lose their lives in the Munich Air Disaster nine months later. During the season the rampant Reds

scored 103 League goals, a club record for the most League goals in a season (equalled by United in 1958–59), and in all competitions they managed to find the back of the net 143 times.

1972 BEST TOP OF THE TOPS

Manchester United 3   Stoke City 0

George Best, Bobby Charlton and Ian Storey-Moore scored the goals that gave Manchester United a 3–0 win over Stoke City in their final home game of the 1971–72 season. The Reds finished eighth in the First Division, 10 points behind the champions Derby County. Best's goal was his 18th League goal of the season, making the Irishman the Reds' top scorer in all competitions (26 goals) and the club's leading First Division goalscorer for the fifth successive season, a record that still stands today.

1974 UNITED SINK INTO DIVISION TWO

Stoke City 1   Manchester United 0

Having lost the penultimate League game of the season 1–0 to Manchester City at Old Trafford, courtesy of the now infamous Denis Law back-heel, United went into their final game of the 1973–74 season knowing already that Divison Two football awaited them in season 1974–75 following relegation after the Derby-day defeat.

However, United lost 1–0 at Stoke City while others around them managed results good enough for safety, thereby sending United down. During the 42-game League campaign the Reds managed only 10 wins, the club's post-war record low. Meanwhile the 20 League defeats they suffered amounted to a post-war record high. United scored just 38 League goals and remarkably every Red numbered 1 to 12 scored during the season.

2006 METATARSAL NIGHTMARES

Chelsea 3   Manchester United 0

When Wayne Rooney broke the fourth metatarsal in his right foot in the 3–0 defeat by Chelsea at Stamford Bridge, it not only spelt the end of Manchester United's hopes of reclaiming the FA Premier League but also placed in jeopardy Rooney's chances of making the World Cup finals in Germany.

2008 REDS MOSCOW BOUND

Manchester United 1   Barcelona 0

Paul Scholes's 14th minute 25-yard thunderbolt goal against FC Barcelona at Old Trafford in their UEFA Champions League semi-final second leg tie was enough to see the Reds reach the final in Moscow on 21 May going through 1–0 on aggregate. The win was United's 12th consecutive home victory in the

Champions League, a tournament record. The win was Sir Alex's 700th in charge of the Reds (in 1207 games).

30

1906 MEREDITH'S SUSPENSION ENDS

In August 1905, while a Manchester City player, Billy Meredith was suspended by the Football Association for allegedly offering an Aston Villa player a bribe of £10 to lose a game. He was suspended until 30 April 1906. After a long Football Association enquiry he joined Manchester United, having been put on the transfer list by Manchester City.

1954 DALY BABY ARRIVAL

Gerard Anthony 'Gerry' Daly (Midfielder 1973–7) was born in Cabra, Dublin.

1955 DOUBLE OVER THE CHAMPIONS

Manchester United 2   Chelsea 1
Manchester United completed a First Division double over Chelsea by beating them 2–1 at Old Trafford on the final day of the 1954–55 season (scorers: Albert Scanlon, Tommy Taylor). The Reds finished fifth in the table while Chelsea were crowned champions.

1960 REDS FINISH ON A HIGH

Manchester United 5   Everton 0
United rounded off the 1959–60 season in fine style, defeating Everton 5–0 at Old Trafford (scorers: Alex Dawson 3, Warren Bradley, Albert Quixall). The Reds finished seventh in the First Division.

1979 FIRST FOR MORAN

Southampton 1   Manchester United 1
Kevin Moran made his Manchester United debut in this 1–1 First Division draw at The Dell (scorer: Andy Ritchie). Moran joined United in February 1978 after making his name in Gaelic Football. One of the bravest players ever to wear a United shirt, he would put his head where other players wouldn't risk their foot. Moran became the first player to be sent off in an FA Cup final when he was dismissed at Wembley in 1985 in United's 1–0 win over Everton. He also won an FA Cup winners' medal in 1983.

MORAN, Kevin (Defender 1978–88) – debut in the above game.
Appearances: FL: 228 (3), goals 21 FAC: 18, goals 1 FLC: 24 (1), goals 2
EUR: 13 (1), goals 0 TOTAL: 284 (5) apps, 24 goals.

1981 SEXTON SACKED

Five days after the end of the 1980–81 Dave Sexton was sacked by Manchester United. On the same day, John O'Shea (Defender/Midfielder 1999–present) was born in Waterford, Ireland.

1994 TOP OF THE POPS

United were flying high in season 1993–94 both on and off the pitch. By the end of the season they had retained the FA Premier League, won the FA Cup to claim the first Double in the club's history and narrowly missed out on claiming an unprecedented domestic Treble after losing to Aston Villa in the League Cup final. Off the pitch the all-conquering Red Devils released a single entitled *Come On You Reds* (PolyGram Records), which went to No.1, resulting in a guest appearance for the United team on *Top of the Pops*. The song spent an amazing 15 weeks in the UK singles charts.

MAY

1

1948 LEAKY HOME DEFENCE

Manchester United 4   Blackburn Rovers 1
Manchester United won their final First Division home game of the season, a 4–1 hammering of Blackburn Rovers (scorers: Stan Pearson 3, Jimmy Delaney). Amazingly, United had conceded more goals at home 27 than they conceded on the road, 21. However, in truth all 48 were conceded 'away' as United played their home games at Maine Road during the 1947–48 season while Old Trafford was still being repaired.

1976 UNDERDOGS SPOIL UNITED'S CUP DREAM

Southampton 1   Manchester United 0
At the end of their first season back in the top flight, Manchester United made it to Wembley for the FA Cup final. United were firm favourites to lift the Cup for the fourth time in history but it was the team from the lower division who took the Cup back to the South Coast with a goal late in the game from Bobby Stokes. It was the first time the Reds were beaten at Wembley by a team from a lower division.

1986 MUSEUM OPENED AT OLD TRAFFORD

Manchester United's Museum was opened at Old Trafford by the club's chairman, Martin Edwards.

1991 THE RED, RED DEVIL

Andrei Kanchelskis joined Manchester United from the Ukranian side Shakhtar Donetsk in a £1m deal.

2000 BEST

The movie *Best* was released in UK cinemas. The Manchester United legend was played by *Sliding Doors* star John Lynch (who also wrote the screenplay) and the movie focused on George's life following the death of Sir Matt Busby in 1994.

Sir Matt was played by the late Ian Bannen. Other famous Manchester United players in the movie were played by Jerome Flynn (Bobby Charlton), Roger Daltrey (Denis Law) and Ian Hart (Nobby Stiles).

2

1931 UNITED ARE RELEGATED

Manchester United 4   Middlesbrough 4
This was Manchester United's last League game of the 1930–31 season but, despite scoring four times (scorers: Tom Reid 2, Ray Bennion, Stanley Gallimore), they could not save themselves from relegation to Division Two after ending the season bottom of the table with a miserable 22 points from a possible 84. United lost 27 League games, nine at home and 18 away. Those nine home defeats remain the highest number of home losses in a single season, and the 18 away defeats are also an unwanted club record for a single season. Not surprisingly, Herbert Bamlett resigned his managerial position and was replaced by Walter Crickmer, who also acted as club secretary.

1936 CHAMPIONS OF DIVISION TWO

Hull City 1   Manchester United 1
In the last game of their 1935–36 Second Division Championship-winning season, the Reds drew 1–1 (scorer: Thomas Bamford) away to Hull City, finishing a point clear of Charlton Athletic.

1950

George Buchan (Defender 1973–4) was born in Aberdeen. George played alongside his older brother Martin in the Manchester United team.

1973 BOBBY CHARLTON'S *ARRIVEDERCI*

Verona 1   Manchester United 4
This game marked Manchester United legend Bobby Charlton's last ever game for his beloved Red Devils. Fittingly, he scored twice in the Reds' 4–1 win over Verona in a Group One Anglo-Italian Cup match. The other goals were scored by Willie Morgan and Peter Fletcher.

1975

David Robert Joseph Beckham (Midfielder 1992–2003) was born in Leytonstone.

1993 FIRST IN MORE THAN A QUARTER OF A CENTURY

When Aston Villa, managed by former Manchester United boss Ron Atkinson, lost 1–0 to relegation-threatened Oldham Athletic at Villa Park, the champagne corks were uncorked at Old Trafford to celebrate United winning the inaugural FA Premier League, the Reds' first Championship success in 26 years.

2007 SECOND TREBLE DREAM OVER

AC Milan 3   Manchester United 0 (Aggregate: 5–3)
Manchester United's dreams of completing a second Treble in eight years were brought back down to earth following a 3–0 defeat to AC Milan in the San Siro. United led 3–2 from the first leg of their semi-final tie but, amid thunderstorms and incessant rain during the first half of the return leg in Milan, it was the Italians who lit up the night with a breathtaking performance. It was the third time (1958 and 1969) that AC Milan had defeated United at the semi-final stage of Europe's premier club trophy. Yet it might never have happened had AC Milan, who were thrown out of the UEFA Champions League in July 2006 after the probe into match-fixing in Serie A, not been granted permission to participate in the 2006–07 competition after lodging an appeal.

3

1917 KILLED IN ACTION

Alexander 'Sandy' Turnbull, who scored the only goal of the 1909 FA Cup final to give United a 1–0 win over Bristol City at the Crystal Palace, was killed in action in Arras, France, where he was serving his country in the Great War.

1958 FA CUP FINAL DEFEAT FOR THE SECOND YEAR RUNNING

Bolton Wanderers 2   Manchester United 0
In the wake of the Munich Air Disaster, the Reds, against all the odds, made it to Wembley for the 1958 FA Cup final. However, their makeshift, rebuilt side was not good enough on the day to beat Nat Lofthouse and his Bolton team-mates. Manchester United became the first team in the 20th century to lose consecutive FA Cup finals and also had their goalkeeper injured for the second year running. None of the Bolton side that beat United had previously played for another club, the first time this ever happened in an FA Cup final.

1993 INAUGURAL FA PREMIER LEAGUE CHAMPIONS

Manchester United 3   Blackburn Rovers 1

Twenty-six years after clinching their last First Division Championship, United celebrated winning the inaugural FA Carling Premier League following this 3–1 win over Blackburn Rovers at Old Trafford in the penultimate League game of the season (scorers: Ryan Giggs, Paul Ince, Gary Pallister). Bryan Robson and Steve Bruce held the trophy aloft before the 40,447 fans who were privileged to be inside Old Trafford as 'We Are The Champions' by Queen was played repeatedly and unashamedly on the stadium's PA system. Pallister's goal came direct from a free-kick in the final minutes of the game to avoid his blushes – prior to his goal he was the only outfield player not to have scored all season long. Meanwhile, the inspiration behind the title success, Eric Cantona, completed a unique hat-trick of Championships.

In 1991, Eric won the French First Division, *Le Championnat*, with Olympique Marseille and in 1992 he won the last First Division Championship with Leeds United. United's 1993 Premiership win gave him an unusual hat-trick of success and of course he made it four titles in a row the following season when United won the coveted Double for the first time in the club's history.

2003 RUUD'S TRIPLE TRIPLE

Manchester United 4   Charlton Athletic 1

Ruud van Nistelrooy's third hat-trick of the season in their penultimate game of the 2002–03 campaign put the icing on Manchester United's Championship celebration cake, leaving only the candles to be lit in the last game away to Everton. David Beckham also scored in what proved to be his last game for Manchester United at Old Trafford.

4

1946 LAST WARTIME LEAGUE GAME

Manchester United 2   Stoke City 1

On the last day of the final wartime League, Manchester United beat Stoke City 2–1 at Maine Road (scorers: Edward Buckle, Stan Pearson) to finish fourth in the Football League North.

1957 DOUBLE ELUDES THE BABES IN FA CUP FINAL

Aston Villa 2   Manchester United 1

The Busby Babes arrived at Wembley Stadium with only Aston Villa in the way of Manchester United winning their third FA Cup and thereby becoming the first team in the 20th century to lift the coveted Double, having wrapped up the 1956–57 First Division Championship five days earlier. However, whereas the Reds were seeking history, the Villans were out to preserve history, as Aston Villa were the last team to do the Double. With only six minutes of the game gone United were down to 10 men when Villa's Northern Ireland striker, Peter McParland, was involved in a collision with Ray Wood. The United goalkeeper had to be stretchered off and another Irishman, Jackie Blanchflower, moved from his half-back slot into the nets – at the time substitutes were not yet permitted. After 10 minutes Wood came back on with a fractured cheekbone. Blanchflower remained in goal while Wood found himself in alien territory, out on the wing. Despite the shake-up, the Babes slotted back into their smooth rhythm and at the interval the score remained 0–0, though United looked the more likely to lift the Cup. However, in the second half the history books did not have to be rewritten when McParland netted twice for the Midlands club. Tommy Taylor pulled a goal back for the Reds and when Wood went back in goal for the last 10 minutes of the game an equaliser looked on the cards. The Babes probed at the Villa defence, which somehow thwarted a swarming United attack, including a disallowed goal scored by the Reds, to take the FA Cup home to Birmingham.

1976 UNITED RETAIN BRAGGING RIGHTS AS CURTAIN DROPS ON SEASON

Manchester United 2   Manchester City 0
Manchester United beat neighbours City 2–0 on the last day of the 1975–76 season to finish third in Division One in their first season back in the top flight (scorers: Gordon Hill, Sammy McIlroy). Michael Docherty, the son of United's manager Tommy, was in the City team.

1992 WHEN THE END CAME DOWN

Manchester United's famous Stretford End was demolished and building work immediately began on a new structure, the West Stand.

5

1934 UNITED STARE DIVISION THREE IN THE FACE

Millwall 0   Manchester United 2
The significance of this Second Division win cannot be emphasised enough in the long and proud history of Manchester United. It was the final day of the 1933–34 season with United lying second from bottom of the table on 32 points, one place above Lincoln City, already doomed to Division Three for the following

season, and one place below Millwall who had 33 points. The London side just needed a point from this home game to avoid the drop while United knew they had to win or face Division Three football for the first time in the club's 56-year history. United tried a number of different things towards the end of the season to arrest their poor form – 13 wins from 41 games – and for this all-important game they changed their kit for luck, opting for a white shirt with a cherry coloured hoop. Either the United players handled their nerves better than their opponents or the shirt swap worked with United winning 2–0 (scorers: Thomas Manley, John Cape). The win sent Millwall down with Lincoln while United recorded the lowest ever League position in the club's history, 20th in Division Two. We may never know just how vital this win was.

1971 WINNING SEND-OFF FOR SIR MATT

Manchester City 3   Manchester United 4
This last game of the 1970–71 season was Sir Matt Busby's final game in charge of the club in his second spell as manager. Fittingly, his team gave him a winning send-off, defeating their Blue neighbours 4–3 at Maine Road in the First Division (scorers: George Best 2, Bobby Charlton, Denis Law). Just before the kick-off Sir Matt was surprised by Eamonn Andrews, the host of *This Is Your Life*, on the pitch.

1992 GIGGS AND THE BOYS WIN FA YOUTH CUP

Manchester United 3   Crystal Palace 2
Manchester United's youth team went into the second leg of their 1992 FA Youth Cup final with a comfortable 3–1 away victory in the first leg. In the second leg, played at Old Trafford, United's kids won 3–2 for an aggregate 6–3 victory. The youth team captain, Ryan Giggs, proudly collected the trophy at a packed Old Trafford. Among Giggsy's team-mates were future United stars Gary Neville, David Beckham, Nicky Butt, Ben Thornley and Keith Gillespie. It was the club's sixth success in the competition although remarkably their first FA Youth Cup win since 1957.

1996 DOWN TO THE WIRE IN THE NORTH EAST

Middlesbrough 0   Manchester United 3
The outcome of the 1995–96 Premier League title came down to a battle between the two Uniteds on the last day of the season. Newcastle United, managed by Kevin Keegan, had set the early pace but showed signs of cracking after United went to St James' Park in March and came away with a 1–0 win (scorer: Eric Cantona) and, more importantly, the three points. The Geordies had to beat Tottenham Hotspur at St James' Park and hope that their North East neighbours, Middlesbrough, could end their season on a high with a win over United, which

would give the Toon Army a party to remember. However, Manchester United seized the moment and beat Boro 3–0 at the Riverside Stadium (scorers: David May, Andy Cole, Ryan Giggs) while the Geordies could manage only a draw. Viewers of *Match of the Day* could see Newcastle United staff take away some hoardings printed with the words 'Premier League Champions 1995–96' as news of United's dominance at Boro filtered through. It was United's third Premiership crown in four years and put them on course for a record second Double with the small matter of an FA Cup final against Liverpool to come the following weekend.

1997 THRILLER IN THE RAIN

Manchester United 3   Middlesbrough 3

At a rain-soaked Old Trafford the visitors, Middlesbrough, shocked the Reds by taking a 3–1 lead. However, Manchester United staged a second-half fightback against the team in relegation trouble and rescued a valuable point in their quest for a fourth Premiership title in five seasons. The United goalscorers were Roy Keane, Gary Neville and Ole Gunnar Solskjaer. Neville's goal was his first for the club.

2007 UNITED CLOSE IN ON TITLE

Manchester City 0   Manchester United 1

United beat neighbours City 1–0 at Eastlands in the Manchester derby thanks to a penalty strike from Cristiano Ronaldo (34 minutes). It was Ronaldo's 23rd goal of the season for the Reds and his 50th goal for United. The win put United eight points ahead of their nearest challengers, the current champions Chelsea, who had three games still to play. Edwin van der Sar saved a penalty from Darius Vassell in the 79th minute to move the Reds within touching distance of winning their ninth FA Premier League crown, their 16th top flight Championship success.

6

1922 UNITED ARE RELEGATED FOR THE SECOND TIME

Cardiff City 3   Manchester United 1

In a season which saw John Chapman replace John Robson as manager, Manchester United were relegated, finishing in 22nd and last place in the First Division after winning just eight games all season.

1937

Seamus Anthony 'Shay' Brennan (Full-back 1957–70) was born in Manchester.

1967 UNITED CLINCH THEIR SEVENTH FIRST DIVISION TITLE

West Ham United 1   Manchester United 6
Although Manchester United experienced early exits in both the FA and League
Cups, their League form during 1966–67 was outstanding. The Reds remained
unbeaten in their last 20 games and they won the Championship on the pen-
ultimate Saturday of the season by thrashing West Ham United 6–1 at Upton
Park (scorers: Denis Law 2, George Best, Bobby Charlton, Paddy Crerand, Bill
Foulkes).

1989 IRISH PAIR BOW OUT

Southampton 2   Manchester United 1
This defeat at The Dell proved to be both Paul McGrath's and Norman Whiteside's last game for the Reds. At the end of the 1988–89 season both players were
allowed to leave Old Trafford. In August 1989 McGrath joined Aston Villa in a
£450,000 transfer while Whiteside joined Everton in a £750,000 deal.

1991 CHAMPIONS PUT UNITED TO THE SWORD

Arsenal 3   Manchester United 1
Arsenal, the newly crowned Barclay's League Division 1 champions, beat United
3–1 at Highbury thanks to a hat-trick from their in-form striker, Alan Smith.
Steve Bruce scored a 90th-minute consolation goal for United from the penalty
spot, his 11th penalty success of the season and his 19th goal of the 1990–91
campaign, a record for a United defender.

2007 UNITED WIN THEIR NINTH PREMIERSHIP CROWN

Manchester United clinched their ninth FA Premier League title, and their first
since 2003, when Chelsea failed to beat Arsenal at the Emirates Stadium. Chelsea's
1–1 draw left the Reds seven points clear at the top of the table with just two
games remaining. United's season tally of 28 wins equalled their Premier League
record set in 1999–2000. It was Sir Alex Ferguson's 18th major trophy at United,
extending his lead as English football's most successful manager of all time over
Bob Paisley (13 trophies). Ryan Giggs set a new record in becoming the first
player ever to have won nine League titles, beating Alan Hansen and Phil Neal.

7

1921 OLD TRAFFORD HIGH AND LOW

Manchester United 3   Derby County 0

The date, 7 May 1921, will always be remembered for two important events that occurred at Old Trafford. The legendary and incomparable Billy Meredith played his 335th and final game for Manchester United after joining the club from local rivals Manchester City in October 1906. A crowd of 10,000 turned out to watch the Welsh Wizard wear the red of United for his 303rd League appearance as he helped United to a 3–0 win over Derby County (scorers: Joseph Spence 2, George Sapsford). At the time of the game Meredith was 48 years 285 days old and his name is enshrined in the annals of Manchester United as one of the greatest players ever to play for the club. When he left Old Trafford he moved back across the city to rejoin Manchester City and in 1924 he helped them reach the FA Cup semi-final, making him the oldest player to have played in the competition. Earlier in the day a crowd of just 13 people are believed to have paid to come into Old Trafford to see Stockport County play Leicester City in a Second Division game. County's ground was closed at the time as a result of an FA suspension.

1938 PROMOTION TO FIRST DIVISION CLINCHED

Manchester United 2   Bury 0

Manchester United finished in runners-up spot in the Second Division and clinched promotion to the First Division on the goal average rule over Sheffield United with this 2–0 win against Bury at Old Trafford (scorers: William McKay, John Smith).

1949 UNITED PLAY THEIR LAST HOME LEAGUE GAME AT MAINE ROAD

Manchester United 3   Portsmouth 2

After eight years of 'home' games at Maine Road, Manchester United played their last 'home' League game at their neighbour's ground and beat champions Portsmouth 3–2 on the final day of the 1948–49 season (scorers: Jack Rowley 2, Charlie Mitten). Although this was United's last home League game at Maine Road, they still needed the use of City's ground for European ties during the 1950s as Old Trafford did not have any floodlights.

1965

Norman Whiteside (Midfielder/Forward 1981–9) was born in Belfast.

1995 NEVILLE BROTHERS UNITED

Manchester United 1   Sheffield Wednesday 0

Phil Neville replaced David May as a 24th minute substitute in Manchester United's 1–0 home Premiership win over Sheffield Wednesday. With older brother Gary already on the field at right-back, the Nevilles become the fifth pair of brothers to play in the same Manchester United side. Incidentally, David May scored the only goal of the game. Meanwhile, the crowd of 43,868 was Old Trafford's highest attendance of the season. In total 1,190,638 fans poured through the Old Trafford turnstiles during the 1994–95 season: 21 League, 3 FA Cup, 2 Coca-Cola Cup and 3 European Cup games, an average of 42,523 per game.

1997 PREMIER LEAGUE TITLE HANDED TO UNITED

Manchester United were champions for the fourth time in five seasons when their nearest rivals, Liverpool and Newcastle United, both failed to win. Liverpool lost at Wimbledon while the Geordies could only manage a draw at West Ham United. The Reds were Premier League champions with two games to spare.

8

1958 EUROPEAN CUP SEMI-FINAL

Manchester United 2   AC Milan 1

Manchester United minus Bobby Charlton beat Italian champions AC Milan 2–1 at Old Trafford in the first leg of their European Cup semi-final. Charlton missed the tie because he was named in the England squad for a friendly against Portugal at Wembley.

1976 MANCHESTER UNITED THE SINGLE

Manchester United entered the UK singles chart for the first time with a song entitled, appropriately enough, *Manchester United* (Decca Records). The song debuted at No.50 but lasted just one week on the British pop scene.

1994 ON THE ROAD TO THE FIRST DOUBLE

Manchester United 0   Coventry City 0

Following this 0–0 draw with Coventry City at Old Trafford, Manchester United were crowned Premier League champions for the second successive year, their ninth top-flight title. The game marked a first and a last for the Manchester

United fans packed into Old Trafford – Gary Neville made his debut while Bryan Robson played his last game for United after 13 years' loyal service.

NEVILLE, Gary (Defender 1992–present) – debut in the above game.

9

1983 REDS EQUAL CLUB RECORD FOR SEASON

Manchester United 3   Luton Town 0

Two goals from Paul McGrath and one from his Republic of Ireland team-mate Frank Stapleton, gave United a 3–0 victory over Luton Town at Old Trafford on the final day of the 1982–83 season. The Reds claimed third place in the First Division, good enough for a UEFA Cup slot for season 1983–84, but more importantly they were unbeaten at Old Trafford for the entire season in all competitions: 21 League, 2 FA Cup, 5 League Cup and 1 UEFA Cup. The impregnability of Old Trafford for visiting sides mirrored similar seasons in 1896–97 and 1955–56.

1988 REDS FINISH RUNNERS-UP

Manchester United 2   Wimbledon 1

At the end of Alex Ferguson's first full season in charge, Manchester United finished runners-up in the First Division, nine points behind Liverpool. Brian McClair scored both goals for the Reds.

1993 REDS CELEBRATE FIRST CHAMPIONSHIP IN 26 YEARS

Wimbledon 1   Manchester United 2

Manchester United beat Wimbledon 2–1 at their rented Selhurst Park home to record their seventh successive FA Premier League victory (scorers: Paul Ince, Bryan Robson). The victory, in the last game of the 1992–93 season, equalled the Reds' best ever finish to a season, first set in 1980–81.

United were crowned the inaugural FA Premier League champions by a margin of 10 points over their nearest challengers, Aston Villa.

2006 KEANO TRIBUTE

Manchester United 1   Celtic 0

In a packed Old Trafford, 69,591 fans paid tribute to one of the greatest players ever to have worn the red shirt of Manchester United when Glasgow Celtic, Roy Keane's current club, visited the Theatre of Dreams in honour of his testimonial game. The United legend, and Irish midfield hero, played the first half of the game for his beloved Manchester United, and the second 45 minutes in the green and white hoops of the Bhoys. United won the game 1–0. The principal benefactor was the Guide Dogs for the Blind Association, Keano's favoured charity. The crowd of 69,591 remains to this day a record for an English testimonial match.

10

1995 SCHMEICHEL FINALLY BREACHED

Manchester United 2 Southampton 1
Manchester United beat Southampton 2–1 at Old Trafford in their final home game of the 1994–95 season (scorers: Andy Cole, Brian McClair). Amazingly, it was the first FA Premier League goal conceded by Peter Schmeichel at home all season. Manchester United actually conceded four home Premiership goals but Gary Walsh was in goal at the time and not their Danish international custodian.

11

1968 BAD LUCK FROM BLACK CATS

Manchester United 1 Sunderland 2
Going into the final League game of the 1967–68 season Manchester United, the reigning First Division champions, and local rivals Manchester City were level on 56 points each. Both clubs faced North East competition on the last day, United welcoming Sunderland to Old Trafford while City had a tricky away visit to Newcastle United. United were favourites to lift their third Championship title in three years but fate had other plans in store for the Blue and Red halves of Manchester. United lost 2–1 (scorer: George Best) while City came away from St James' Park with both points after a 4–3 win and the League title was theirs.

1987 LIGHTS TAKEN OUT AT OLD TRAFFORD

Manchester United demolished the floodlight towers surrounding Old Trafford and replaced them with a new floodlighting system, which was housed along the roof of the stadium. The original floodlight towers had stood as an Old Trafford landmark for 30 years.

1991 RUSSIAN FLYING MACHINE TAKES OFF

Crystal Palace 3   Manchester United 0

Crystal Palace confirmed third place in the table with this emphatic win over United, who would end up in sixth place.

> **KANCHELSKIS, Andrei** *(Forward 1991–5) – debut in the above game.*
> *Appearances: FL: 96 (27), goals 28   FAC: 11 (1), goals 4   FLC: 15 (1), goals 3*
> *EUR: 7, goals 1   TOTAL: 132 (29) apps, 36 goals.*

1996 THE DOUBLE DOUBLE

Manchester United 1   Liverpool 0

Manchester United's 1–0 win over Liverpool in the 1996 FA Cup final, thanks to a late Eric Cantona goal, made the Red Devils the first club in the history of the game to win English football's domestic Double twice. The achievement was all the sweeter for the Manchester United faithful as it was completed against Liverpool, whom United had prevented from winning the Double at Wembley in 1977. Amazingly, their second Double came just two years after their first and was completed in a season that many felt would be a bedding-in period for United's youngsters after Paul Ince, Andrei Kanchelskis and Mark Hughes all left Old Trafford prior to the start. However, the young and inexperienced United players, about whom Alan Hansen famously quipped, 'You can't win anything with kids,' after United's 3–1 reversal at Villa Park on the opening day of the Premier League season, proved the former Liverpool captain wrong.

   Manchester United: Schmeichel, Irwin, Neville P., May, Pallister, Beckham (Neville G.), Keane, Butt, Giggs, Cantona, Cole (Scholes).

1997 THE END OF AN ERA

Manchester United 2   West Ham United 0

In the final game of the 1996–97 season Manchester United beat West Ham United 2–0 (scorers: Jordi Cruyff, Ole Gunnar Solskjaer) at Old Trafford to claim their fourth Premier League title in five seasons. Prior to the game, the 55,249 fans packed inside the stadium witnessed a remarkable achievement as United's three other teams walked out on to the Old Trafford pitch and paraded the trophies they had won during the season – the Pontins League Premier Division, the Lancashire League Division 1 and Lancashire League Division 2 titles. It was the club's first ever clean sweep of championships. Meanwhile, a fifth cup was displayed when Ken Doherty, the newly crowned World Professional Snooker champion and a Manchester United fanatic, walked out to the centre circle parading the trophy he had won the previous week. The win over West Ham United proved to be Eric Cantona's last competitive game for United as he announced his retirement the next day. Fans still sing his name at Old Trafford today, such is the esteem he is held in by all Reds.

2003 BECKS' LAST GAME FOR UNITED

Everton 1   Manchester United 2
David Beckham scored a superb free-kick in what was his last game for the club he adored as a young boy. Despite the disappointment of Becks' imminent departure to Real Madrid, the Reds were in celebratory mood at Goodison Park after being presented with the Premiership trophy, their eighth Premier League crown. Ruud van Nistelrooy also scored in United's win.

12

1951 FESTIVAL OF BRITAIN

Manchester United 1   Red Star Belgrade 1
Red Star Belgrade became the first foreign side to play at Old Trafford when they provided the competition for Manchester United in a Festival of Britain game.

1979 LATE SUNDERLAND WINNER DENIES UNITED AT WEMBLEY

Arsenal 3   Manchester United 2
Arsenal took the lead in this FA Cup final when Brian Talbot put them ahead after only 12 minutes. Then just before the interval Frank Stapleton scored to put the Gunners 2–0 up. As the second half dragged on the Reds were still 2–0 down with only four minutes remaining and then a remarkable sequence of events unfolded. Gordon McQueen pulled a goal back for the Reds and it merely seemed a consolation goal until Sammy McIlroy weaved his way through the Arsenal defence to place his shot past Pat Jennings and bring the two sides level with less than a minute to go. But victory was snatched from United's grasp when Alan Sunderland scored for Arsenal in the dying seconds of the game.

1990 EAGLES HOLD DEVILS

Manchester United 3   Crystal Palace 3 (aet)
Manchester United and their London opponents, Crystal Palace, played out a 3–3 thriller at Wembley in the 1990 FA Cup final. It was Alex Ferguson's first Cup final with United while the opposing manager was the former Manchester United hero Steve Coppell. The game was also the first time the two sides had met each other in the FA Cup. United had just about squeezed past Oldham Athletic in the semi-final while the Eagles were flying high, having taken the scalp of Liverpool. Palace took the lead in the 18th minute thanks to a goal from Gary O'Reilly but United skipper Bryan Robson drew the Reds level in the 35th minute. Seventeen minutes into the second half Mark Hughes twisted his body before unleashing an unstoppable shot into the Palace net. Coppell decided it

was time to introduce Ian Wright to the action and he scored within three minutes of coming on. The final whistle sounded at 2–2 and that meant extra-time was needed to decide the winner. Wright scored again two minutes into extra-time, giving Jim Leighton in the United goal no hope of saving his shot. An upset looked on the cards until Sparky scored his second goal of the game in the 117th minute with yet another stunning shot. The game ended 3–3 with the two sides leaving Wembley to prepare for the replay five days later.

Manchester United: Leighton, Ince, Martin (Blackmore), Bruce, Phelan, Pallister (Robins), Robson, Webb, McClair, Hughes, Wallace.

1997 ERIC'S ADIEU

The day after Manchester United were presented with the 1996–97 Premier League trophy at Old Trafford, United fans everywhere were in a state of shock when a press conference was held at Old Trafford to announce that Eric Cantona had retired. *Le Roi* had helped United to become the most dominant force in English football during the 1990s while he personally won four Premiership titles, two FA Cups (including the Double, *twice*) and three Charity Shields during his four and a half years at Old Trafford.

13

1961

Ralph Milne (Forward 1988–90) was born in Dundee.

1967 CHAMPIONS END SEASON UNBEATEN AT HOME

Manchester United 0   Stoke City 0
Manchester United, the new First Division champions, drew their final game of the 1966–67 season with Stoke City. The impressive Reds finished the campaign unbeaten at Old Trafford in the League (21 games) before an average home gate of 53,800.

2007 RONALDO CLEANS UP AWARDS

Manchester United 0   West Ham United 1
Prior to United's last game of the season, against West Ham United at Old Trafford, Cristiano Ronaldo received two more awards, this time from the club itself, the Sir Matt Busby Player of the Year Award, and the Fans' Player of the Year Award. Then a crowd of 75,927 saw United celebrate their ninth Premier League title triumph, where the already crowned champions lost to a Carlos Tevez goal that kept the Hammers in the top division. It meant that a staggering

1,440,694 fans attended Manchester United games at Old Trafford during 2006–07, the highest ever for a single season in the history of the club.

14

1958 UNITED'S DREAM OF EUROPEAN CUP SUCCESS ENDS

AC Milan 4 Manchester United 0 ·

Manchester United missed out on a place in the 1958 European Cup final, crashing out of the competition 4–0 in the San Siro Stadium. The Reds lost their semi-final encounter 5–2 on aggregate. Having missed the first leg because of international duties, Bobby Charlton was absent again because he was in the England squad for their game against Yugoslavia in Belgrade.

1988 FERGIE GETS HIS OLD No.1 BACK

Alex Ferguson paid his former club Aberdeen a British record fee for a goalkeeper when he splashed out £750,000 for Jim Leighton.

1994 UNITED WIN FIRST DOUBLE

Manchester United 4 Chelsea 0

Manchester United faced Glenn Hoddle's Chelsea at Wembley Stadium seeking a place in the history books. After retaining their Premier League crown, an FA Cup final victory for the Reds would make them only the sixth team in English football to win the coveted Double. However, Alex Ferguson knew his side had a game on their hands after Chelsea had won both League encounters during the season. But United were in no mood for complacency and swept aside the Blues in the pouring rain. After the first half ended 0–0 Eric Cantona scored two second-half penalties while Mark Hughes and Brian McClair also found the net to hand the Reds a comfortable 4–0 win. It was United's eighth FA Cup victory and their first Double.

Manchester United: Schmeichel, Parker, Bruce, Pallister, Irwin (Sharpe), Kanchelskis (McClair), Ince, Keane, Giggs, Cantona, Hughes.

1995 SO NEAR YET SO FAR

West Ham United 1 Manchester United 1

On the final day of the 1994–95 season Manchester United lost their Premiership crown when they failed to beat West Ham United at Upton Park. The Reds' closest rivals, Blackburn Rovers, lost 2–1 at Liverpool but still clinched the Championship by a single point. Brian McClair scored United's goal.

15

1969 LAST EUROPEAN ADVENTURE FOR BUSBY AND FOULKES

Manchester United 1   AC Milan 0

When Manchester United, the defending European Cup holders, beat the Italian giants AC Milan 1–0 at Old Trafford (scorer: Bobby Charlton) it marked Sir Matt Busby's 56th and last ever European game in charge of his beloved team. Meanwhile, Bill Foulkes also played his last game in European competition for United when they exited the European Cup in the semi-final second leg stage of the competition. Bobby Charlton's goal was United's 100th in European competition. Foulkes's appearance was his 52nd for United in Europe, a club record at the time. Trailing 2–0 from the first leg, United had a mountain to climb but with 13 minutes of the game remaining the Reds thought that they had brought the aggregate scores level when Pat Crerand's cross appeared to cross the line. However, the goal was not given, which resulted in a section of the Stretford End throwing missiles on to the pitch. AC Milan's Cudicini was hit by a stone. Following the stone-throwing incident, UEFA ordered United to erect screens behind the goals at Old Trafford for future European games. Ironically it was eight years before the Reds qualified for European football again.

1982 STORMIN' NORMAN AND BAILEY THE ROCK

Manchester United 2   Stoke City 0

Norman Whiteside scored along with Bryan Robson in this final First Division game of the 1981–82 season in which Manchester United finished in third place. The young Irish striker's goal made him, at 17 years and 8 days, the youngest ever scorer in the history of Manchester United. United's goalkeeper Gary Bailey won the inaugural Golden Gloves Trophy after the Reds' No.1 conceded just 23 goals in the 39 League games he played (Paddy Roche was in the United goal for the other three League games and let in six goals).

1991 EUROPEAN CUP-WINNERS' CUP WINNERS

Manchester United 2   Barcelona 1

Manchester United had a European night to remember in Rotterdam on 15 May 1991 when they beat the Spanish giants FC Barcelona 2–1 in the European Cup-Winners' Cup final. Mark Hughes, labelled a flop by the Spanish media during his unsuccessful time with the Catalan club, sent the Spaniards back to the Nou Camp to rue their words as he scored both of United's goals. The win meant that United became the first English club to win both the European Cup and the

European Cup-Winners' Cup. Alex Ferguson also became the first manager to win the trophy with two different British sides, having guided Aberdeen to Cup-Winners' Cup glory over Real Madrid in Gothenburg in 1983.

Manchester United: Sealey, Irwin, Bruce, Pallister, Blackmore, Phelan, Robson, Ince, Sharpe, McClair, Hughes.

1981

Patrice Evra (Full-back 2006–present) was born in Dakar, Senegal.

16

1906 ONCE BLUES ALWAYS REDS

Following a bribes and illegal payments scandal, which resulted in Manchester City's Jimmy Bannister, Herbert Burgess, Billy Meredith and Sandy Turnbull receiving lengthy suspensions from the Football Association, the talented quartet crossed the city and signed for Manchester United.

1977 TOMMY DOCHERTY'S LAST LEAGUE GAME IN CHARGE OF UNITED

West Ham United 4   Manchester United 2
Gordon Hill and Stuart Pearson scored for Manchester United in this 4–2 defeat to West Ham United at Upton Park, which resulted in United finishing sixth in the First Division. The game was Tommy Docherty's last League game in charge of the Reds.

1984 OLD NEW ROUTINE

Nottingham Forest 2   Manchester United 0
Manchester United lost their last League game of the 1983–84 season 2–0 at the City Ground, Nottingham and finished fourth in the First Division. Viv Anderson, who later signed for United, and Garry Birtles, who United sold back to Forest, scored the goals.

> **BLACKMORE, Clayton Graham** *(Midfielder 1983–94) – debut in the above game.*
> *Appearances: FL/PL: 150 (36), goals 19 FAC: 15 (6), goals 1*
> *FLC: 23 (2), goals 3 EUR: 12, goals 2 TOTAL: 201 (44) apps, 26 goals.*

1999 ONE DOWN, TWO TO GO

Manchester United 2   Tottenham Hotspur 1
Manchester United faced Tottenham Hotspur at Old Trafford in the final Premier

League game of the 1998–99 season needing a win to guarantee them the title over Arsenal, who had been hanging on their coat tails for most of the season. United were anxious to wrap up the first leg of an unprecedented Treble haul of silverware, having reached both the FA Cup final and the UEFA Champions League final. Arsenal fans up and down the country claimed allegiance to their North London rivals – well, for 90 minutes. United began the game nervously and gave the Arsenal fans hope when they fell behind to a looped shot from Les Ferdinand that somehow bounced over Peter Schmeichel and hit the underside of the roof of the United net. The United fans among the 55,189 crammed into Old Trafford fell silent before a huge roar came up from the United faithful to spur the Reds on. United answered the rallying call and David Beckham sent the teams in level at half-time with a superb strike from the edge of the box that flew past Ian Walker and into the Tottenham net. Andy Cole came on for Spurs old boy Teddy Sheringham in the second half and netted the winner, an exquisite lob over Walker, to give United their fifth Premiership crown and the first leg of the Treble. The Gunners finished runners-up, one point adrift of the Reds.

17

1969 SIR MATT BUSBY'S FIRST FAREWELL

Manchester United 3   Leicester City 2

This 3–2 First Division win over Leicester City at Old Trafford was Sir Matt Busby's final game in charge of his beloved Manchester United before he handed over the reins to Wilf McGuinness. George Best, Denis Law and Willie Morgan scored for the Reds to give Sir Matt a winning send-off. Busby subsequently had to return to United to take charge after McGuinness was forced to step down.

1990 7–UP IN THE CUP FOR UNITED

Manchester United 1   Crystal Palace 0

Manchester United disposed of Crystal Palace at the second attempt thanks to a superb strike from their left-back Lee Martin, which gave United their magnificent seventh FA Cup win, Alex Ferguson's first trophy success with United. Martin's pile driver at Wembley was only his second goal for the club. Prior to the game the United boss caused a stir on the back pages by dropping Jim Leighton for the replay, opting instead to start the game with their on-loan goalkeeper Les Sealey. Ironically, it was Sealey's FA Cup debut for United and the first time an on-loan player played in an FA Cup final. The Cup win meant that Alex Ferguson became the only manager since the Second World War to win both the FA Cup and the Scottish Cup (he won the latter with Aberdeen in 1982, 1983, 1984 and 1986). Jimmy Cochrane guided Kilmarnock to Scottish

Cup success in 1929 and was the manager of Sunderland when they won the FA Cup in 1937.

Manchester United: Sealey, Ince, Bruce, Pallister, Martin, Phelan, Robson, Webb, Wallace, McClair, Hughes.

18

1985 UNITED UNSTICK TOFFEES' TREBLE HOPES

Manchester United 1   Everton 0 (aet)
Manchester United faced Everton in the 1985 FA Cup final at Wembley with the Merseyside team aiming to complete a unique Treble. They had been crowned First Division champions a week earlier and four days before the Cup final they lifted the European Cup-Winners' Cup. However, just as United had ended Liverpool's dreams of a Treble in 1977, they also ended Everton's dreams with a superbly taken goal from Norman Whiteside in extra-time after being reduced to 10 men. Despite Whiteside's marvellous curled shot past Neville Southall, the game will probably be remembered more for Kevin Moran's sending off. The Irish defender became the first player to be sent off in an FA Cup final when the referee, Peter Willis, a retired police inspector, showed him the red card following a late tackle on Peter Reid. Moran was devastated, perhaps unable to take in the enormity of what had just happened to him, and it took a while to get him off the pitch. As Moran sat weeping on the sidelines his team-mates fought on bravely against the Toffees, who made excellent use of the extra man. The game ended 0–0 and went into extra-time. In the 110th minute Whiteside scored the goal that won United the Cup but Moran was not given his winners' medal after the game and had to wait a few days before the FA agreed that he could have it.

Manchester United: Bailey, Gidman, McGrath, Moran, Albiston (Duxbury), Strachan, Robson, Whiteside, Olsen, Hughes, Stapleton.

2007 RONALDO'S TREBLE AWARD

Cristiano Ronaldo won the Football Writers' Association Player of the Year Award to claim a unique treble having already been named PFA Player of the Year Award and the PFA Young Player of the Year. The treble made him the first player to claim a clean sweep of English football's most prestigious individual awards. He was also named the Portuguese Player of the Year for 2007.

19

1945 LEAGUE NORTH CUP FINAL

Bolton Wanderers 1   Manchester United 0
Manchester United lost the first leg of the League North Cup final 1–0 to Bolton Wanderers at Burnden Park.

1957 PEGG FIRST AND LAST

Manchester United's David Pegg won his first and only full international cap for England in their 1–1 World Cup qualifying draw with the Republic of Ireland at Dalymount Park, Dublin. United's Roger Byrne, Duncan Edwards and Tommy Taylor also played for England.

2001 CHAMPIONS BEATEN

Tottenham Hotspur 3   Manchester United 1
Manchester United went into the final Premiership game of the 2000–01 season with their third consecutive Premiership crown safely in the bag, their seventh in total. Paul Scholes scored in this 3–1 loss to Spurs at White Hart Lane and then the team headed back to Manchester to celebrate their Championship success in style. United lost six games on their way to retaining the title and amazingly half of them came in the last three games of the season.

2007 WEMBLEY RETURN

Manchester United 0   Chelsea 1 (aet)
After one of the most hard-fought title races in recent years, United and Chelsea seemed the perfect sides to contest the first FA Cup final at the new Wembley. However, the game itself failed to live up to expectations as two tired sides struggled to raise themselves for one last effort, cancelling each other out for much of the game. United hopes were raised when Ryan Giggs appeared to bundle the ball and Chelsea goalkeeper Petr Cech over the line, but the goal wasn't given. In the end, it was Didier Drogba who scored a goal late in extra-time to secure the trophy for the Blues and so prevent United from achieving their fourth domestic Double. Ryan Giggs equalled Roy Keane's modern-day record of appearing in seven FA Cup finals (1994, 1995, 1996, 1999, 2004, 2005, 2007).

20

1963 LOWEST LEAGUE POSITION UNDER MATT BUSBY

Nottingham Forest 3   Manchester United 2

David Herd and Johnny Giles scored for Manchester United in this 3–2 defeat to Nottingham Forest at the City Ground in the final League game of the 1962–63 season. United ended the season in 19th place in the First Division, their lowest ever League placing under the management of Sir Matt Busby. The Red Devils lost nine of their 21 home games in the League, another unwanted record, equalling their nine losses at Old Trafford during the 1930–31 season (finished bottom of Division One). The Forest game also marked the debut of Dennis Walker who became the first black player to play for United's first team. However, it was Walker's only game for United and he was sold to York City in April 1964.

1991 BLUES OUTSHINE REDS

Manchester United 1   Tottenham Hotspur 1

On the final day of the 1990–91 Barclay's First Division season Manchester United drew 1–1 (scorer: Paul Ince) with Tottenham Hotspur at Old Trafford. The Reds finished the League campaign in sixth place in the table, three points and one place behind rivals Manchester City. It was the last time the Blues ended a season higher than the Reds.

1995 DEFEAT IN THE FA CUP FINAL

Everton 1   Manchester United 0

Only six days after losing the 1994–95 Premier League on the last day of the season at West Ham United, the Reds had to try to pick themselves up off the floor for the 1995 FA Cup final against Everton. Manchester United, the Cup holders, went into the final without Eric Cantona, who was halfway through his nine-month ban, while Andy Cole was Cup-tied after having played for Newcastle United in an earlier round. A goal from Paul Rideout won the Cup for Everton.

21

1977 DOC'S TIGERS END LIVERPOOL'S TREBLE DREAM BY LIFTING FA CUP

Manchester United 2   Liverpool 1

Manchester United met Liverpool, the newly crowned First Division champions, in the 1977 FA Cup final at Wembley Stadium. The Merseyside club was hoping to emulate Arsenal's Double-winning team from the 1970–71 season with First Division Championship and FA Cup success. Liverpool had also reached the final of the European Cup.

But this Manchester United team was out to prove that the previous year's defeat in the FA Cup final to Southampton was just a minor blip. While Arthur Albiston was making his FA Cup debut, Liverpool's Kevin Keegan was playing his last game for the club before his move to SV Hamburg in West Germany. In the first half Liverpool played their possession game but they could not break down a solid United defence, marshalled superbly by their captain Martin Buchan. The game came to life in a five-minute period in the second half that brought three goals. Stuart Pearson fired United into the lead only for Jimmy Case to level for the Merseysiders. However, thanks to a deflected goal off Jimmy Greenhoff from Lou Macari's shot, United won the Cup. Tommy Docherty's promise to the Manchester United fans in May 1976 that United would be back at Wembley the following year to win the Cup was well and truly kept. Brian and Jimmy Greenhoff became the first pair of brothers to play in an FA Cup-winning team. Sadly for many Manchester United fans, this was Tommy Docherty's last game in charge of the Reds as he was sacked six weeks later by the club over an affair that he was having with Mary Brown, the wife of the club physio Lawrie Brown.

Manchester United: Stepney, Nicholl, Greenhoff (B.), Buchan, Albiston, Coppell, McIlroy, Macari, Hill (McCreery), Greenhoff (J.), Pearson.

1983 SEAGULLS SWOOP ON DEVILS

Brighton & Hove Albion 2   Manchester United 2 (aet)

Manchester United were the red-hot favourites to win the 1983 FA Cup final. Ron Atkinson's men had finished third in the 1982–83 First Division title race while their opponents had been relegated to Division Two after propping up the table in last place. All the top football pundits agreed that United would win comfortably. However, the Seagulls were no pushovers, having dumped Liverpool out of the Cup by winning at Anfield in one of the greatest FA Cup shocks of all time. Indeed, the underdogs showed the same hunger they displayed at

Anfield and took a shock lead with a headed goal from Gordon Smith to go in at the interval 1–0 up.

Frank Stapleton's goal to level the scores gave the Irishman a piece of FA Cup history, by becoming the first player to have played, and scored, in two Wembley Cup finals for two different teams (Big Frank scored for Arsenal against United in the 1979 FA Cup final). The game looked destined for a 1–1 finish until Ray Wilkins scored a superb 30-yard curler with only eight minutes left on the clock. But the tiger-like Seagulls summoned all their willpower and strength in the closing stages of the game and were rewarded for their bravery when Gary Stevens scored an equaliser to force the game into extra-time.

The additional 30 minutes of play were uneventful until the 120th minute when Gordon Smith looked certain to score only to watch in dismay as Gary Bailey pulled off a miraculous save to earn United another bite at the coveted cherry.

Manchester United: Bailey, Duxbury, Moran, McQueen, Albiston, Davies, Wilkins, Robson, Muhren, Stapleton, Whiteside.

2005 A HISTORIC FA CUP FINAL

Arsenal 0   Manchester United 0 (aet; Arsenal won 5–4 on penalties)
Despite United totally outplaying their London opponents in the 2005 FA Cup final at the Millennium Stadium in Cardiff, Arsenal somehow took home the trophy. The game ended 0–0 after extra-time resulting in a penalty shoot-out, which United lost 5–4. It was the first time in the 134-year history of the competition that the winner was decided by a penalty shoot-out. Sadly, it was Paul Scholes, who had a superb game, who missed the all-important penalty that gave the Gunners the Cup. Arsenal's Jose Antonio Reyes was sent off after being shown two yellow cards. The United skipper, Roy Keane, set a modern-day record by playing in his seventh FA Cup final: after appearing in the 1991 showpiece game for Nottingham Forest he also played for Manchester United in the finals of 1994, 1995, 1996, 1999 and 2004. Lord Kinnaird played in nine of the first 11 FA Cup finals from 1872–82.

2007 OWEN SET TO JOIN UNITED

Bayern Munich issued a statement confirming that they had agreed to sell their England midfielder Owen Hargreaves. The Bundesliga club's president, Franz Beckenbauer, told German TV: 'Owen is leaving. That was the player's wish. It's a good match and it's also a good deal financially.' Manchester United, who had been chasing Hargreaves since the 2006 World Cup finals, subsequently signed the 26-year-old for a fee in the region of £17m.

22

1946

George Best (Forward 1963–74) was born in Belfast.

1999 TWO DOWN, ONE TO GO

Manchester United 2   Newcastle United 0
One week after securing the Premier League title, their fifth, Manchester United were at Wembley to face Newcastle United in the 1999 FA Cup final hoping to become the first team to win the Double three times. It was the second game in an all-important 10-day period for the Reds, with the team leaving London the following day to jet off to Spain to play Bayern Munich in the 1999 UEFA Champions League final four days later. United clinched their hat-trick of Doubles thanks to goals from Teddy Sheringham and Paul Scholes. It was United's 10th FA Cup win.

   Manchester United: Schmeichel, Neville G., May, Johnsen, Neville P., Beckham, Scholes (Stam), Keane (Sheringham), Giggs, Cole (Yorke), Solskjaer.

2004 UNITED THE LION TAMERS

Manchester United 3   Millwall 0
The 2004 FA Cup final saw Manchester United face the Championship side Millwall, with former Chelsea captain Dennis Wise as their player-manager. However, it proved to be exactly what it was on paper, a total mismatch, as the Reds outclassed their London opponents in Cardiff to win the Cup for a record 11th time. United ran out 3–0 winners in the one-sided affair at the Millennium Stadium (scorers: Ruud van Nistelrooy 2, Cristiano Ronaldo).

   Manchester United: Howard (Carroll), Neville G., Brown, Silvestre, O'Shea, Ronaldo (Solskjaer), Fletcher (Butt), Keane, Scholes, Giggs, Van Nistelrooy.

23

1996 NEVILLE BROTHERS LIONS TOGETHER

Phil Neville made his international debut and joined older brother Gary in the England team that beat China in Beijing. The Nevilles became the first pair of brothers to represent England in the same team since Bobby and Jackie Charlton. They are also only the sixth pair of brothers to have played for England.

24

1966

Eric Cantona (Forward 1992–7) was born in Marseille, France.

1997 SCHOLES THE LION CUB

England 2   South Africa 1
Paul Scholes made his international debut for England as Old Trafford played host to the first ever meeting between England and South Africa. England won 2–1 in front of 52,676 fans in this Green Flag international.

25

1928 BIRTH OF UNITED'S BUCCANEER

Malcolm Irving Glazer was born in Rochester, New York, USA. In 2005, Malcolm Glazer, owner of the Tampa Bay Buccaneers in the NFL, purchased Manchester United for £790m.

1963 DEVILS OUTFOX CITY

Manchester United 3   Leicester City 1
Manchester United's League form in season 1962–63 was poor. They won just 12 of their 42 First Division games to finish in a precarious 19th place, just one place and one point away from Second Division football. However, although fighting to avoid relegation in the League, United's FA Cup form was a completely different story. The Red Devils disposed of Huddersfield Town, Aston Villa, Chelsea, Coventry City and Southampton to book their final appearance at Wembley Stadium against Leicester City. The Foxes, who finished fourth in the First Division, were the clear favourites to win their first ever FA Cup while United were looking for their third success in the competition. In the 29th minute Denis Law gave United the lead when he turned and shot past the England goalkeeper, Gordon Banks.

The score remained 1–0 to United at the interval and then in the 57th minute David Herd put the Reds 2–0 up. Herd's father had played alongside Matt Busby for Manchester City in the 1933 and 1934 FA Cup finals. In the 85th minute a goal from Ken Keyworth breathed life into the Foxes but moments later Herd scored his second and United's third to make sure the Cup went back to Old Trafford for the first time since 1948.

Manchester United: Gaskell, Dunne, Cantwell, Crerand, Foulkes, Setters, Giles, Quixall, Herd, Law, Charlton.

2001 THREE HISTORY-MAKING LIONS

This game was the first time in history that three Manchester United players scored in the same game for England – David Beckham, Paul Scholes and Teddy Sheringham all scored in England's 4–0 win over Mexico City (Liverpool's Robbie Fowler was the other goalscorer). The game was played at Derby County's Pride Park Stadium.

26

1909

Alexander Matthew 'Matt' Busby (Manager 1945–69 and 1970–71) was born in Orbiston, near Bellshill, Scotland.

1947 REDS FINISH SECOND IN DIVISION 1

Manchester United 6   Sheffield United 2

Manchester United finished runners-up just one point behind Liverpool in the 1946–47 First Division Championship, in what was the latest finish to any League season for United. Jack Rowley scored his second hat-trick of the campaign to confirm his place as the club's top scorer that season with 28. Johnny Morris (2) and Stan Pearson got the other goals.

1981

Clayton Blackmore signed on as a trainee for Manchester United.

1983 FA CUP FINAL REPLAY JOY

Manchester United 4   Brighton & Hove Albion 0

Sir Matt Busby celebrated his 74th birthday by travelling to Wembley Stadium to watch his beloved Manchester United, the team he had guided to European Cup glory at the famous old stadium in 1968. United beat Brighton & Hove Albion 4–0 to win the FA Cup for the fifth time in the club's history. Two goals in the space of four minutes midway through the first half effectively ended the game as a contest. Bryan Robson opened the scoring for the Reds and a few minutes later Norman Whiteside scored to become the youngest goalscorer in an FA Cup final (aged 18 years 18 days) and the only player to have scored in both the League Cup final and FA Cup final in the same season. Just before the interval Robbo scored again to put the Reds 3–0 up. In the second half Arnold Muhren added a fourth for United from the penalty spot to give United a resounding 4–0 victory, a scoreline equalled in the 1994 final against Chelsea.

Manchester United: Bailey, Duxbury, Moran, McQueen, Albiston, Davies, Wilkins, Robson, Muhren, Stapleton, Whiteside.

1999 UNITED CLAIM HISTORIC TREBLE

Manchester United 2   Bayern Munich 1

After clinching the Premier League and the FA Cup in the previous nine days, Manchester United faced Bayern Munich in the 1999 UEFA Champions League final in what was their third consecutive game with a trophy up for grabs. The Reds were out to do what no other European team had ever managed to achieve, the unique Treble of domestic League, domestic Cup and the European Cup. However, their German opponents were on the same historic path, having already won their 15th Bundesliga title with the DFB-Pokal (German Cup) final against SV Werder Bremen still to be played. Tens of thousands of United fans invaded the Spanish city of Barcelona for the final at the famous Nou Camp stadium.

Things did not go to plan for United when they fell behind to a Mario Basler goal direct from a free-kick. The Reds went in 1–0 down at half-time and in the second half rode their luck, with the Germans striking the crossbar as Peter Schmeichel could only look on. However, two substitutes embedded United's names in the history books. Alex Ferguson sent on Teddy Sheringham and Ole Gunnar Solskjaer for Andy Cole and Jesper Blomqvist. Cole and Yorke had banged in the goals all year but on a balmy night in Barcelona they simply never looked likely to score. The game went into injury time and the officials had already tied the ribbons in Bayern's colours onto the famous two handles of European club football's most coveted and prestigious prize. But, amazingly, United drew level from a corner, with Schmeichel sent forward to cause mayhem in the box – Teddy Sheringham scored from close range after swivelling on to a shot from Ryan Giggs. The Germans could not believe it, seconds from victory and now extra-time was looming. However, a rejuvenated United went up the pitch again after the re-start and won another corner. David Beckham floated the corner in and it was flicked on by Sheringham and Solskjaer stuck out his right boot to steer the ball into the roof of the German net. Match referee Pierluigi Collina described the game as the most memorable he ever took charge of.

Manchester United: Schmeichel, Neville G., Johnsen, Stam, Irwin, Beckham, Butt, Giggs, Blomqvist (Sheringham 67), Cole (Solskjaer 81), Yorke.

27

1942 WARTIME CHAMPIONS

Manchester United 3   Manchester City 1

This 3–1 'home' derby win (scorers: Harold Worrall 2, Herbert Whalley) over Manchester City at Maine Road meant Manchester United were crowned champions of the Football League Northern Section (Second Championship). During the Second World War the League was divided into two Championships, one covering August to December (United finished fourth) and a second from January to May.

1971

Lee Stuart Sharpe (Forward 1988–96) was born in Halesowen, West Midlands.

28

1976 RAY WILKINS AND GORDON HILL ARE CAPPED

Gordon Hill made his England debut against Italy in New York in a tour game. Ray Wilkins, then of Chelsea, also made his international debut for England.

1984 HENSHAW'S BLIND INSTITUTION BENEFIT MATCH

Manchester City 3   Manchester United 2

Rivals City beat United 3–2 at Maine Road in a benefit game for Henshaw's Blind Institution.

29

1949

Brian Kidd (Forward 1967–74) was born in Collyhurst, Manchester.

1968 EUROPEAN CUP FINAL AT WEMBLEY STADIUM

Manchester United 4   SL Benfica 1 (aet)

Ten years after the Munich Air Disaster, Matt Busby saw his dream fulfilled when his Manchester United side were crowned Kings of Europe. The 100,000 fans inside Wembley watched United beat the champions of Portugal, Benfica, 4–1 after extra-time. The first half was largely disappointing, but early in the second half Bobby Charlton put United in the lead with a rare headed goal. However, the team could not hold on to their advantage and Graca equalised. With only moments to full-time, Benfica's star player, Eusebio, bore down on Alex Stepney's goal, but the keeper made the most crucial save in his 539-game career for United to take the game into extra-time. On a very warm evening, with the energy-sapping turf draining the players, George Best came into his own and scored the second goal. After that, birthday boy Brian Kidd and Bobby Charlton added further goals to secure a comfortable result in the end, which ensured that United became the first English club ever to win the European Cup. Interestingly, it was the third different Cup that captain Bobby Charlton had won at Wembley following his FA Cup win with Manchester United in 1963 and the World Cup with England in 1966.

Manchester United: Stepney, Brennan, Dunne, Crerand, Foulkes, Stiles, Best, Kidd, Charlton, Sadler, Aston.

1980

Mark Hughes signed apprentice forms for Manchester United.

1999 UNITED HIT RECORD

Following immediately after their Treble success, United once again proved themselves the best in a surprising way. Their single 'Lift It High (All About Belief)' went into the charts, reaching No. 11. It was the club's eighth single to chart, six of which have reached the Top 20, something no other club can match.

30

1899 THE ALL-ROUND KEEPER

Leonard Langford (Goalkeeper 1934–6) was born in Sheffield. Langford was an all-round sportsman in the army, winning a middleweight boxing championship of the Household Brigade along with the championship of Aldershot Command. He also played cricket (wicket-keeper) and won several medals for high-jumping.

1968 EUROPEAN CUP HEROES ARE HONOURED

A civic reception was held in Manchester for United's successful European Cup-winning team. However, earlier in the day, the Manchester United team and their manager Matt Busby visited the hospital where Denis Law was recovering following his knee operation, and brought the trophy for him to see.

2007 DEVIL ENDS HIS CAREER AS A DRAGON

Ryan Giggs announced his retirement from international football with Wales after 16 years in the spotlight. Giggs, capped 63 times, said he would make his final appearance for his country in their Euro 2008 qualifier against the Czech Republic in the Millennium Stadium, Cardiff on 2 June 2007. Giggs never managed to make it to a major Championship with Wales. The Welsh last played in such an event at the 1958 World Cup finals in Sweden. The 33-year-old Manchester United star made his debut for Wales against West Germany in Nuremberg in October 1991.

31

1965 HUNGARIAN RHAPSODY

Manchester United 3   Ferencvaros 2
Manchester United beat Ferencvaros 3–2 at Old Trafford (scorers: David Herd 2, Denis Law) in the first leg of their Inter-Cities Fairs Cup semi-final tie. This was United's last game at Old Trafford in the Fairs Cup because the next time they qualified for the competition it had changed its name to the UEFA Cup.

1974 BOBBY THE FIRST

Bobby Charlton was the first recipient of the Professional Footballers' Association Merit Award.

1975 DENIS THE SECOND

For the second year running the PFA's Merit Award went to a former Old Trafford hero, this time Denis Law. Sir Matt Busby was also honoured at the 1980 ceremony.

1985 SPARKY'S AWARD

Mark Hughes won the Professional Footballers' Association Young Player of the Year Award. It was the first time that a Manchester United player had won the award. Lee Sharpe followed in his footsteps by winning the title in 1991 while Ryan Giggs was the winner in 1992 and 1993. Wayne Rooney and Cristiano Ronaldo were similarly honoured in 2006 and 2007 respectively.

1989 HUGHESIE FIRST RED TO WIN PFA PLAYER OF THE YEAR

Mark Hughes became the first Manchester United player to win the Professional Footballers' Association Player of the Year Award. Sparky was the winner again in 1991.

1993 PFA AWARDS

Ryan Giggs won the Professional Footballers' Association Young Player of the Year for the second year running. The PFA's Merit Award was presented to Manchester United's 1968 European Cup-winning team a few days after the 25th anniversary of their triumph.

1994 ROBBO BIDS FAREWELL TO UNITED

Shortly after winning his second FA Premier League winners' medal, Captain Marvel himself, Bryan Robson, took the decision to retire and hung up his boots in search of a new career in football management. He left Old Trafford after almost 13 years at United but he did not wait long for a new job as Middlesbrough came knocking on his door and Robbo accepted.

1995 SPARKY BRINGS CURTAIN DOWN AT UNITED

Mark Hughes finally brought down the curtain on his Manchester United career after spending 10 years at Old Trafford spread over two periods with the club, 1983–86 and 1988–95.

1996 UNITED WINNERS

Alex Ferguson was voted the Carling Manager of the Season and Eric Cantona won the Carling Player of the Season.

2007 UNITED'S TREBLE SIGNING

Manchester United signed Anderson, FC Porto's 19-year-old Brazilian, and Sporting Lisbon's Nani, a 20-year-old Portuguese winger. The nine-times Premiership champions also confirmed that Owen Hargreaves would be joining them from Bayern Munich on 1 July 2007.

JUNE

1

1926 BIRTH OF A BABE

John James Berry (Forward 1951–8) was born in Aldershot. Johnny Berry's total of 273 appearances for the Reds would have been practically doubled had he not been forced to quit playing football as a result of the injuries he sustained in the Munich Air Disaster on 6 February 1958.

1969 WILF MCGUINNESS IS THE NEW UNITED MANAGER

Wilf McGuinness had the unenviable task of following in the footsteps of Sir Matt, and to increase the pressure on him he was now in charge of a squad of ageing players, including his former team-mate Bobby Charlton. McGuinness was a Busby Babe, appearing in three FA Youth Cup finals in the 1950s, and he also captained the England Youth team. He made his debut for Manchester United against Wolverhampton Wanderers in October 1955 aged 16. McGuinness missed the trip to Belgrade in 1958 as he was recovering from a cartilage operation and then tragedy struck again when he broke his leg during a Central League game in December 1959. He didn't play again but United rewarded his loyalty by giving him a coaching job. In April 1969, aged 31, he was named by the United board as Sir Matt's successor. On 1 June 1969 Wilf became the new manager of Manchester United. To say things didn't go well for him would be an understatement and in December 1970 the Manchester United board stepped in. Sir Matt resumed charge temporarily and McGuinness returned to a coaching job.

1978 BIG AL GOES TRANSATLANTIC

After serving the club for 11 years Alex Stepney left Old Trafford and joined the North American Soccer League (NASL) revolution, signing for the Dallas Tornados.

1980 SPARKY DEAL

Mark Hughes, aged 16, signed professional forms with Manchester United.

1988 A SHARPE SIGNING

Alex Ferguson brought Lee Sharpe to Manchester United from Torquay United. The fee of £185,000 plus the proceeds from a friendly between the two clubs in September 1989 proved to be an absolute bargain.

1994 PHIL TURNS PRO

Phil Neville signed professional forms for Manchester United.

1996 BRUCEY LEAVES

After eight seasons at Old Trafford in which he helped United win a League Cup, the European Cup Winners' Cup, the European Super Cup, three FA Cups and three Premier League titles, Steve Bruce left Manchester United and joined Birmingham City.

2

1894 THE BIRTH OF UNITED'S FIRST AND ONLY PLAYER-MANAGER

Clarence George 'Lal' Hilditch (Half-back 1919–32) was born in Hartford, Cheshire. In October 1926 when John Chapman, United's manager, was suspended by the FA for what they called financial irregularities and subsequently sacked, Hilditch stepped into the breach to take charge of the team until a suitable successor could be found. Hilditch was a player at United at the time and therefore became the first and only player-manager in the history of Manchester United. Hilditch had signed for the Reds during the First World War (January 1916) from local side Altrincham and played 16 seasons for the club. He made a total of 322 appearances for United and scored seven goals. At the end of the 1926–27 season Hilditch gladly handed over control of the team to Herbert Bamlett and resumed his playing career at Old Trafford until he announced his retirement from the game in 1932.

1951

Arnoldus Johannus Hyacinthus 'Arnold' Muhren (Midfielder 1982–5) was born in Volendam, Holland.

3

1898

Charles William 'Charlie' Moore (Full-back 1919–30) was born in Cheslyn Hay, Staffordshire.

1982 ROBBO SCORES

Bryan Robson scored twice for England in a 1982 World Cup warm-up game against Finland in Helsinki. England won the match 4–1.

1995 NEVILLE THE LION

Gary Neville made his international debut for England against Japan.

4

1949

Luigi 'Lou' Macari (Forward 1972–84) was born in Edinburgh, Scotland.

1950 TWELVE-GOAL THRILLER

Atlas Club Mexico 6   Manchester United 6
Manchester United shared a 12-goal thriller with Atlas Club Mexico in the Gilmore Stadium, Los Angeles during their 1950 tour of the USA.

1997 SCHOLES MAKES HIS MARK WITH ENGLAND

Paul Scholes scored his first goal for England in their win over Italy in *Le Tournoi*, played in France, and Andy Cole won his second cap for his country under two different managers. Terry Venables awarded Andy his first cap versus Uruguay in March 1995 and Glenn Hoddle capped him for the Italy game. Remarkably, Andy's next two caps were also awarded by different managers – Howard Wilkinson and Kevin Keegan.

5

1925

Joseph 'Joe' Walton (Full-back 1945–8) was born in Manchester.

1963 TRIPLE RED LION

Bobby Charlton scored a hat-trick for England in their 8–1 mauling of Switzerland in Zurich. He was the first Manchester United player to score a hat-trick for England.

1981 THOMAS DOES A RUNNER

The Manchester United team assembled at Heathrow Airport to set off on a 1981 pre-season tour of Kuala Lumpur. Mickey Thomas was teased that much by his team-mates about the type of food he would have to eat for the next two weeks that he walked out of Heathrow with £50 in his pocket and his bags on the plane.

1999 SCHOLES'S UNWANTED PIECE OF HISTORY

Paul Scholes became the first England player to be sent off on home soil when he was shown the red card during England's 0–0 draw with Sweden at Wembley in a 2000 European Championship qualifying game.

6

1950 A DEAR PAIR OF GLOVES

Manchester United paid Queens Park Rangers a British record transfer fee for a goalkeeper when they handed over £11,000 for Reg Allen.

1960

Colin John Gibson (Defender 1985–90) was born in Bridport, Dorset.

1965 COIN TOSS LOSS

Ferencvaros 1   Manchester United 0
Manchester United lost 1–0 in Hungary in the second leg of their Fairs Cup semi-final tie with Ferencvaros. United's Crerand and Ferencvaros's Orosz were

both sent off in a very hot-tempered affair. With the aggregate score at 3–3 over the two legs a play-off game was required as the away goals rule was not yet in force for European ties. The Reds lost the coin-toss for choice of venue for the play-off match and had to return to Hungary 10 days later.

2007 NANI PASSED FIT

Nani, the 20-year-old Sporting Lisbon and Portugal winger, passed his medical at Old Trafford and all that needed to be done then for United to clinch his transfer was to await his international clearance. He joined United's other new recruit, the 19-year-old Brazilian midfielder Anderson Luis de Abreu Oliveira of FC Porto, at Old Trafford for the new Premiership campaign, which kicked off in August 2007. Nani, whose full name is Luis Carlos Almeida da Cunha, played 29 times for Sporting in season 2006–07 and scored five goals. He had also played five times for Portugal, scoring once.

7

1938 SWAN TURNS INTO A DEVIL

Just two months after scoring a superb headed goal for his club, Swansea City, in a 2–2 draw against Manchester United, John 'Jack' Warner became a Manchester United player.

1989

William George Roughton (Full-back 1936–9) died in Southampton aged 79.

2006 UNITED OUTRANK THE FA

Three days before England's opening game against Paraguay in the 2006 World Cup finals, United's Wayne Rooney underwent an MRI scan on the fourth metatarsal bone of his right foot at a BUPA hospital in Manchester. The good news for England fans was that Rooney's foot had healed and he could join the squad in Germany.

8

1870

James Rankin McNaught (Half-back 1893–8) was born in Dumbarton, Scotland.

1990 IRWIN JOINS UNITED

Denis Irwin joined Manchester United from Oldham Athletic in a £625,000 transfer. He would go on to play for United for 12 years and make a total of 529 appearances for the club, one of only nine players to top the 500 mark – four of whom (also Ryan Giggs, Paul Scholes and Gary Neville) played their entire careers under the management of Sir Alex Ferguson.

9

1981 BIG RON BREEZES IN

Having had a flamboyant manager in Tommy Docherty, who was then replaced with a thoughtful manager in Dave Sexton, Manchester United decided to go for a little sparkle again in their choice of Sexton's replacement. That sparkle was in the shape of Ron Atkinson. In his playing days Big Ron was instrumental in Oxford United's rise from non-league football to Division Two. Then as a manager he first cut his teeth at Cambridge United, guiding them from the depths of the Football League towards the Second Division. West Bromwich Albion tempted him away from Cambridge with the offer of First Division football and he proved a major success at The Hawthorns. Atkinson made an unfashionable West Brom side into serious Championship contenders with young players such as Bryan Robson, Remi Moses, Laurie Cunningham, Brendon Batson and Cyrille Regis. So it was no surprise when United went after him following the sacking of Dave Sexton. At the press conference officially announcing his appointment Atkinson said: 'When I was offered the job I was both thrilled and flattered, but I could not help feeling that Manchester United and Ron Atkinson were made for each other. It doesn't bother me that I was not the first choice. I prefer to think that I was offered the job in front of the best manager in the country – Brian Clough. I will not be just United's manager, I'll be an ardent fan. If the team bores me, it will be boring to the supporters who hero-worship the players. I will not allow these people to be betrayed.' Strong closing words from a man with a strong character.

In his years at Old Trafford Atkinson spent heavily (£8m) but he also recouped a lot of money (£6m) with the sale of players such as Ray Wilkins and Mark Hughes. Atkinson brought the glory years back to United, with the side winning two FA Cups in his five years in charge, during which time they never finished lower than fourth in the League. Despite this record, which most football fans would gladly accept for their own club, it wasn't good enough for Manchester United. Atkinson was sacked in November 1986 with United languishing fourth from bottom of Division One after only one win in their opening nine League games and a 4–1 League Cup defeat by Southampton. But it was his failure to land the First Division title that undoubtedly brought Big Ron's United reign at Old Trafford to an end.

1993 ENGLAND'S FIRST BLACK CAPTAIN

Manchester United's Paul Ince became the first black player to captain England in a full international when he led his country to a 2–0 win over the USA in Boston. United's Gary Pallister and Lee Sharpe also played in the game.

10

1957

Peter Simon Barnes (Forward 1985–7) was born in Manchester.

1969

Ronny Johnsen (Defender 1996–2002) was born in Sandefjord, Norway.

1994 DIFFERENT SHAPED BALLS

Manchester United signed David Fevre to replace Jim McGregor as the club's physiotherapist. Fevre was the physio to Rugby League side Wigan at the time and had performed the same role for the Great Britain Rugby League team on 28 occasions.

2007 CHASING CARLOS

According to reports in the *Sun* Sir Alex Ferguson had set his sights on bringing West Ham United's Argentinian striker Carlos Tevez to Old Trafford. Manchester United had already spent £30m over the summer on Nani and Anderson with another £17m expected to be paid out on 1 July for Owen Hargreaves. Sir Alex eventually got his man.

11

1916

Ernest 'Dick' Pegg (Forward 1902–4) died in Leicester aged 37 years.

1977 THE GREEN RED FORWARD LINE

When Northern Ireland was beaten 1–0 by Iceland in Reykjavik, the entire Irish forward line was made up of past and present Manchester United players: 7 T. Jackson (United), 8 S. McIlroy (United), 9 C. McGrath (United), 10 D. McCreery (United), 11 T. Anderson (Swindon Town). Trevor Anderson was at United from 1973–4. Also playing for Northern Ireland, at No. 4, was United's Jimmy Nicholl. The game marked Tommy Jackson's 35th and last cap for his country.

1994 ARISE SIR BOBBY

Busby Babe Bobby Charlton received a knighthood for his long and distinguished service to football but immediately said: 'I will never be able to replace Sir Matt.'

2004 UNITED SNARE HEINZE

Manchester United completed the signing of the 26-year-old Argentinian defender Gabriel Heinze from Paris St Germain for a fee of £6.9m. A delighted Sir Alex Ferguson said: 'We've been monitoring Gabriel for a long time and he demonstrates all the qualities of the top Argentinian defenders – strength, speed and excellent technical ability.' Before joining PSG, the versatile Heinze, who can play at left-back or centre-half, played in Spain for Valladolid and in Portugal for Sporting Lisbon.

12

1885

Richard 'Dick' Holden (Full-back 1904–13) was born in Middleton, Lancashire.

2004 UNITED PAST, PRESENT AND FUTURE

When England met France in Estadio da Luz, Lisbon, Portugal, in the World Cup finals on 13 June 2004, one incident had a big Manchester United involvement. England were awarded a penalty kick. Manchester United's Mikael Silvestre brought down Wayne Rooney (signed for Manchester United after the finals) and David Beckham (ex-Manchester United then at Real Madrid) took the spot kick. Beckham's penalty was saved by the ex-Manchester United goalkeeper Fabien Barthez (then at Olympique de Marseille).

13

1897

Albert Arthur Pape (Forward 1924–6) was born in Elsecar, near Wath-on-Dearne, Yorkshire.

1997 UNITED REFUSE TO BREAK THE BANK

Manchester United's chairman Martin Edwards issued a statement stating that the club would not pay foreign imports higher wages than current stars such as Roy Keane and club captain Peter Schmeichel. United were linked with £10m bids for Juninho and Marcel Desailly, which were both rejected, while their offer of £5m to Bayern Munich for their German defender Markus Babbel was accepted but United opted out when they discovered that Babbel wanted £1.4m per year wages. Had United met his wage demands it would have resulted in disharmony among the current players. Babbel went on to sign for Liverpool.

2003 FABS TO STAY PUT

Following newspaper reports that Manchester United were keen to sign the USA goalkeeper Tim Howard or Leeds United's Paul Robinson to replace Fabien Barthez, United's French star claimed the stories were nonsense. Fabs, who cost the Reds £7.8m, was dropped for the final three matches of United's 2002–03 Premiership-winning season.

14

1970 A LION'S FAREWELL

Bobby Charlton's England career was brought to an end when he was substituted by Sir Alf Ramsey in the 1970 World Cup quarter-final versus West Germany in Leon, Mexico. It was Charlton's 106th cap for his country (49 goals), the most for any United player. England lost the match 3–2 in extra-time.

2007 ROYAL VISITORS

The Premier League released the fixture list for the 2007–08 season with Manchester United, the reigning Premiership champions, beginning the defence of their crown at home against Reading on 11 August 2007. The Royals are managed by former Manchester United hero Steve Coppell.

15

1933

Mark Jones (Half-back 1950–8) was born in Barnsley.

1959

Alan Bernard Brazil (Forward 1984–6) was born in Simshill, Glasgow.

2007 GIGGSY AWARDED OBE

Ryan Giggs was awarded an OBE for his services to football in the Queen's Birthday Honours List. It marked a special year for Giggsy, who won a record ninth League title and became only the second player in United's history to pass the 700 appearances mark. However, the only downside to the year was the announcement of his retirement from international football for Wales after winning 64 caps over 16 years for his country. Sir Bobby Charlton, himself a former recipient of the honour before receiving a knighthood and United's record appearance holder, paid tribute to the 33-year-old winger on United's official website ManUtd.com, saying: 'I couldn't have been more pleased if he was a close relative. Ryan is a fantastic member of Manchester United and the ultimate professional. Added to that his marvellous skills and his services to football make him a pleasure to watch. If only he'd have played for England!' As well as Giggsy and Sir Bobby, three other Manchester United greats have been previously honoured with an OBE: Bryan Robson, Mark Hughes and David Beckham. Former United hero Teddy Sheringham was also honoured in the 2007 awards, receiving an MBE.

16

1965 INTER-CITIES FAIRS CUP SEMI-FINAL PLAY-OFF GAME

Ferencvaros 2   Manchester United 1
Manchester United failed in their bid to make it to the 1965 Fairs Cup final, going down 2–1 in Hungary to Ferencvaros in their play-off game (scorer: John Connelly). It was the first time in the club's history that they lost in successive

European games to the same side. Borussia Dortmund repeated the feat in both legs of their Champions League semi-final clash with United in season 1996–97.

2007 TWO UNITED PLAYERS TIE THE KNOT

Gary Neville married his girlfriend Emma Hadfield at Manchester Cathedral while his Old Trafford team-mate Michael Carrick tied the knot with Lisa Roughhead at St Peter's Church in Wymondham, Leicestershire. Several hundred Reds converged outside Manchester Cathedral waiting to cheer the United captain and his bride out of the Cathedral. Wayne Rooney, Ryan Giggs and Paul Scholes all attended the ceremony but David Beckham missed his best mate's big day as he was preparing to play his final League game with Real Madrid the following day.

17

1964

Graeme Hogg (Defender 1984–8) was born in Aberdeen.

2003 MADRID BOUND

Manchester United made an agreement with Real Madrid for the transfer of David Beckham to the Spanish giants for a fee of €35m (£25m), with the final paperwork due to be signed in early July. Becks also agreed personal terms to link up with Madrid's Galacticos. In response to the transfer Sir Alex Ferguson said: 'I've known David since he was 11 years of age, and it's been a pleasure to see him grow and develop into the player he has become. David has been an integral part of all the successes that Manchester United have achieved in the last decade. I would like to wish him and his family every success in the future, and thank him for his service to the club.' However, United did not receive the entire transfer fee in one lump sum; €7.5m was paid upon completion of the sale, and €17.5m over the following four years in equal instalments. The remaining €10m was conditional upon Real Madrid's performances in the UEFA Champions League.

2007 A MEDAL AT LAST

Exactly four years after he agreed to sign for Real Madrid from United, David Beckham finally received his first winners' medal in Spanish football when Real Madrid won the Primera Division of La Liga for 2006–07, their 30th League title, on the final day of the season with a 3–1 win over Mallorca at the Bernabeu.

Beckham, playing his last game for Madrid, had to go off in the second half with an injury but managed to hop around in celebration after the game. It was his seventh League winners' medal, adding to the six he won with United. Ex-Old Trafford favourite Ruud van Nistelrooy also won a La Liga winners' medal in his first season with the Spanish giants.

18

1994 IRISH HISTORY

United's Roy Keane helped the Republic of Ireland to a historic 1–0 win over Italy in New York at the 1994 World Cup finals in the USA.

2007 RUUD FALLS SHORT

Ruud van Nistelrooy, the former Manchester United striker, came second in the race for the 2006–07 European Golden Boot Award, which was won by Francesco Totti of AS Roma. The 30-year-old Italian striker scored 26 League goals in Serie A for his club while van Nistelrooy scored 25 times for Real Madrid on their way to winning the Spanish title. 'I feel sorry for Van Nistelrooy. I can imagine how bitter he must have felt, but he is still a great player and deserves full respect for fighting until the end,' said Totti, who has been a one-club player since he became a professional in 1993.

19

1946

James 'Jimmy' Greenhoff (Forward 1976–81) was born in Barnsley.

1993 UNITED (WE LOVE YOU)

To celebrate winning the inaugural FA Premier League, United's first Championship success in 26 years, the club released a single entitled, *United (We Love You)* (Living Beat Records). It entered the British singles chart and spent just two weeks on the pop scene, reaching a highest position of No.37.

20

1981

George Vose (Half-back 1933–40) died in Wigan aged 69.

1994 HE WILL RETURN

Mike Phelan left Old Trafford and joined West Bromwich Albion on a free transfer, after making 146 appearances for United since 1989. He would later return to the club to become first-team coach.

2003 ADIOS BECKS

David Beckham released a statement regarding his transfer to Real Madrid: 'I would like to publicly thank Sir Alex Ferguson for making me the player I am today. I will always hold precious memories of my time at Manchester United and Old Trafford as well as the players, who I regard as part of my family, and the brilliant fans who have given me so much support over the years and continue to do so. I recognise this is an amazing opportunity for me at this stage in my career and a unique and exciting experience for my family. I know that I would always regret it later in life if I turned down the chance to play at another great club like Real Madrid that also has world-class players. I would like to thank other clubs who were interested in signing me, including Barcelona, and I wish them every success in the future. But I really want to play in the Champions League. I wish Manchester United the best of luck and led by such an inspirational captain like Roy Keane I am sure they will continue to go from strength to strength.'

21

1949

James Stuart Pearson (Forward 1974–9) was born in Hull.

1995 INCE JOINS INTER MILAN

Paul Ince left Old Trafford in a £7m transfer deal that took him to Inter Milan. At the time the sum was a Manchester United record fee received for a player. In his career at United, the self-styled 'Guvnor' won two Premier League titles, two FA Cups, a League Cup, European Cup-Winners' Cup and a Super Cup.

INCE, *Paul Emerson Carlyle* (*Midfielder 1989–95*)
Appearances: *FL/PL: 203 (3), goals 25 FAC: 26 (1), goals 1 FLC: 23 (1), goals 2 EUR: 21, goals 0 TOTAL: 276 (5) apps, 25 goals.*

22

1901

Richard Iddon (Forward 1925–7) was born in Tarleton, Lancashire.

1948

Colin Waldron (Defender 1976–7) was born in Bristol.

2005 UNITED DELISTED

Malcolm Glazer delisted Manchester United shares from the Stock Exchange, bringing to an end to a 14-year listing on the financial market. Six days later the American tycoon secured 98% of shares – and total control of the club.

23

1988 WELSH DRAGON RETURNS HOME

After what some described as an unsuccessful period at Barcelona, Mark 'Sparky' Hughes rejoined Manchester United. During his period at the Nou Camp, Sparky had also had a spell on loan to Bayern Munich in West Germany.

1995 SPARKY LEAVES UNITED

Exactly seven years after returning to Old Trafford, Manchester United legend Mark Hughes joined Chelsea in a £1.5m deal. His final goals tally of 163 puts him in seventh place in United's all-time list, with only Brian McClair having scored more than his 16 goals in the League Cup.

2007 FOUR REDS TURN BLUE IN LAS VEGAS

Manchester United's Wes Brown, Rio Ferdinand, John O'Shea and Wayne Rooney were all in Las Vegas, Nevada to cheer on Manchester-born Ricky Hatton in his IBO World Light-Welterweight Championship fight against Jose Luis

Castillo from Mexico. Hatton entered the ring wearing a sombrero and a poncho in the colours of Manchester City behind Rooney and Mexican boxing legend Marco Antonio Barrera, who were carrying The Hitman's two World Championship belts (IBF and IBO Light-Welterweight) for him. Hatton knocked the Mexican challenger out in the fourth round.

24

1902

George Lydon (Half-back 1930–32) was born in Newton Heath, Manchester.

1970

David May (Defender 1994–2003) was born in Oldham.

25

1982 YOUNG STORMIN' NORMAN

Less than five weeks after making his Manchester United debut, Norman Whiteside became the youngest player to have appeared in a World Cup finals game when he played for Northern Ireland at the 1982 tournament, helping his country to a famous 1–0 win over the host nation Spain, in Valencia.

2006 BECKHAM THE HISTORIC LION

David Beckham scored the only goal of the game when England beat Ecuador 1–0 during the 2006 World Cup finals in Germany. The former United (then at Real Madrid) star's goal enshrined Becks' name in the history books by making him the only England player to score in three different World Cup finals; he had previously scored against Colombia in 1998 and Argentina in 2002. Manchester United's Rio Ferdinand and Wayne Rooney also played in the game.

26

1952

Gordon McQueen (Defender 1978–85) was born in Kilbirnie, Ayrshire.

1996 VAN DER GOUW ARRIVES AT UNITED

Raimond van der Gouw joined Manchester United from Vitesse Arnhem in a £500,000 transfer. He would make 60 appearances in goal before leaving the club in 2001.

2003 CARLOS JOINS BECKS IN MADRID

Less than two months after helping to secure the club's eighth Premier League title, Sir Alex Ferguson's assistant Carlos Queiroz packed his bags in Manchester and followed David Beckham to the sunny climate of Spain, where he took up his position as the new head coach of Real Madrid. Queiroz became the fourth assistant the Boss had lost in his 17 years in charge of United following the departures of Archie Knox (Rangers, 1991), Brian Kidd (Blackburn Rovers, 1998) and Steve McClaren (Middlesbrough, 2001). Sir Alex was disappointed to let his Portuguese right-hand man go but wished him well and thanked him for all he had done with the players: 'This is a wonderful opportunity, too big a chance for him to turn down. He brought modern ideas, and also an ability to speak four languages. He was able to get his message across to everyone.'

27

1967 LAW'S OZ FINE

Western Australia 0   Manchester United 7
Denis Law swore at the referee during Manchester United's 7–0 win over Western Australia in Perth and was fined 50 Australian dollars (£20) by the Australian Football Federation.

28

1947

John Aston Jnr (Forward 1964–72) was born in Manchester.

1996 CANTONA LOVED BY THE FANS

In a poll conducted among Manchester United fans, Eric Cantona won the Fans' Player of the Year Award with 81% of the votes going to the mercurial Frenchman. Peter Schmeichel was second with 9% of the votes. In a separate vote to determine the Best Newcomer, David Beckham topped the voting with 43% closely followed by Gary Neville with 38%.

2007 A No.10 APPOINTMENT FOR ROONEY

Manchester United announced that Wayne Rooney would wear the club's famous No.10 shirt in season 2007–08. Rooney, aged 21, wore the No.8 shirt in his first three seasons at Old Trafford but could hardly contain his pride at being allocated the iconic No.10 shirt most famously worn by Manchester United legend Denis Law. 'When I was offered the chance to wear the number 10 shirt I jumped at it. Some of the greatest players have become legends wearing number 10 – none more so than Denis Law. He was crowned King of the Stretford End during his time at the club and it is a great honour for me to wear a shirt that has such history behind it,' said Rooney, who was presented with his new No.10 shirt by The King himself, Denis Law, at United's Carrington training HQ.

29

1990 KEANE AND IRWIN MEET THE POPE

The day before their quarter-final encounter with host nation Italy during the 1990 World Cup finals, the Republic of Ireland team met Pope John Paul II in the Vatican. Despite receiving a papal blessing, the Irish lost 1–0 to the Italians.

2007 PERMISSION TO GO TO WORK

Manchester United received a much-awaited work permit for 19-year-old Anderson, their £18m Brazilian midfielder. United's original application was refused on the grounds that he did not have enough international caps but United won their Home Office appeal. A club statement read: 'Manchester United is pleased to confirm that the club has been successful in its application for a work permit for Anderson.' Just 24 hours earlier, Anderson had made his full international debut for Brazil in their Copa America 2–0 defeat to Mexico played in Venezuela.

30

1943

Ian Moir (Forward 1960–65) was born in Aberdeen.

1965

Gary Andrew Pallister (Defender 1989–98) was born in Ramsgate, Kent.

1990 ROVING DUXBURY

Mike Duxbury left Old Trafford and joined Blackburn Rovers in a free transfer. The defender had been with United for a decade, making a total of 378 appearances in that time, scoring seven goals. He was an FA Cup winner in 1983.

1991 ON THEIR WAY

Les Sealey and Ralph Milne were allowed to leave Old Trafford on free transfers. Mark Bosnich's registration at Old Trafford was cancelled.

1994 ROBBO LEAVES UNITED IN OLD TRAFFORD CLEAROUT

Bryan Robson left Old Trafford after 13 years at the club to take up his appointment as player-manager of Middlesbrough. Les Sealey was handed a free transfer – his second by United. Mike Phelan and Russell Beardsmore were also given free transfers. Robson was one of United's greatest midfielders, and captained the side for most of his time at the club.

2007 LET'S WIN EVERYTHING

Manchester United's new England midfielder, Owen Hargreaves, said his farewells to his Bayern Munich team-mates and thanked the Bundesliga club for giving him his start in professional football. The Canadian-born 26-year-old won four Bundesliga titles with Bayern as well as the 2001 Champions League and Intercontinental Cup (Club World Championship). Hargreaves looked ahead to his new career, which is about to begin with United, saying: 'I set lots of targets over the last decade and I have also fulfilled them. I expect that to continue. A new era is starting for me now and I hope to achieve even more. I don't have any concrete aims, but you have got to win everything at Manchester United.'

JULY

1

1961 THE SHEPHERD CAPTURES HERD

Although born in Hamilton, Lanarkshire, David Herd grew up locally in Moss Side and joined his father, a former Manchester City player, at Stockport County as an amateur in 1949. In May 1951 the 15-year-old Herd made his League debut playing alongside his 39-year-old father in the Stockport County side. In 1954, David joined Arsenal where he scored an impressive 99 goals in 166 matches for the Gunners. After ending the 1960–61 season as the First Division's second leading goalscorer, after the prolific Jimmy Greaves, Arsenal's David Herd had a huge admirer in Matt Busby. On 1 July 1961, Matt paid the Gunners £40,000 for the services of his fellow Scot and took the young striker to Old Trafford. Herd did not disappoint the United manager, scoring on his United debuts in the FA Cup, the League Cup and all three European competitions, and on his third League outing for the Reds he bagged a brace to take his Football League goals tally to 100. Herd ended his first season at Old Trafford with 14 goals from 27 starts and scored twice in the 3–1 FA Cup final victory over Leicester City in 1963, before helping United finish second in the League the following season, when his partnership with Denis Law reached 50 goals. United were crowned champions a year later, and in the following season, 1965–66, Herd found the back of the net 32 times. More title glory followed in 1967, but success was tinged with sadness for Herd, who suffered a broken leg in November 1966, shortly after scoring a hat-trick against three different goalkeepers in a 5–0 win over Sunderland. The injury would ultimately limit his first-team chances. Although he missed the 1968 European Cup final, he was awarded a winners' medal for his part in United's triumphant campaign, but two months later he moved to Stoke City. He later turned his hand to management and enjoyed spells with Waterford and Lincoln City. In seven years at Old Trafford, he scored 145 times in 265 appearances, an average of 1.8 games per goal.

1976

Rutgerus Johannes Martinius 'Ruud' van Nistelrooy (Forward 2001–6) was born in Oss, North Brabant, The Netherlands.

1984 LOU'S FAREWELL

Lou Macari said farewell to Old Trafford after 11 memorable years despite the fact that he almost ended up a Liverpool player. In January 1973, the Celtic and Scotland striker was courted by Liverpool boss Bill Shankly, and was a guest visitor on 13 January 1973 when Liverpool took on Burnley in a third round FA Cup tie. Coincidentally, United's assistant manager Pat Crerand, himself an ex-Celtic player, was sat close by, learned of Liverpool's intentions and persuaded Macari to have talks with United instead. Five days later Macari moved to Old Trafford for £200,000, leaving Shankly to claim that the striker would only have been a substitute at Anfield! In addition to United and Liverpool a number of other clubs wanted Macari who, in six years with the Glasgow giants, won two League Championships and two Scottish Cups, and played in three Scottish League Cup finals. His fee raised a few eyebrows, but he quickly endeared himself to the United faithful by scoring on his debut, in a 2–2 draw with West Ham United at Old Trafford, a game that also marked the debut of his fellow Scot Jim Holton. Macari helped United to the Second Division Championship title in 1974–75 (finishing second in the scoring charts with 11), and he landed an FA Cup winners' medal in 1977 and runners-up medals in 1976 and 1979. He was never an overly prolific striker, and in the late 1970s Tommy Docherty moved him into a midfield role. The switch greatly improved Macari's game, but his United career took a turn for the worse when Ron Atkinson replaced Dave Sexton in 1982. The Scot spent the majority of the next two seasons on the United bench, and he left on 1 July 1984 to turn his hand to management. Macari's first role was as player-manager of Swindon Town, followed by spells at West Ham United, Birmingham City, Stoke City (twice) and Celtic. He also worked as a scout for the Republic of Ireland, and today he is a regular pundit on MUTV.

1987 CHOCCY ARRIVES AT OLD TRAFFORD

Alex Ferguson's search for an out-and-out goalscorer came to an end when Brian McClair arrived at Old Trafford from Celtic.

1989 FERGIE BUSY IN TRANSFER MARKET

Alex Ferguson signed Mike Phelan from Norwich City and Neil Webb from Nottingham Forest. Webb's transfer fee was subsequently to be decided by a Football Transfer Tribunal.

1990 YOUNG FERGUSON TURNS PRO

Darren Ferguson, the son of United boss Alex Ferguson, signed professional forms for Manchester United.

1994 MAY AT OLD TRAFFORD IN JULY

David May joined Manchester United from Blackburn Rovers on the same day that Terry Cooke signed professional forms for the club. Blackburn Rovers went on to win the Premier League in season 1994–95. On another busy day of transfer activity, Raimond van der Gouw completed his move from Vitesse Arnhem to Old Trafford.

1998 IN THE MONEY

Gary Pallister left Manchester United and signed for Premiership new boys Middlesbrough in a deal worth £2.5m. Manchester United bought the silky defender from Middlesbrough in August 1989 for £2.3m, a £200,000 profit for United from the sale! When United signed Pally they paid a club record transfer fee for his services. Pally's former Old Trafford team-mate and skipper, Bryan Robson, now the manager of Boro, brought the Ramsgate-born Pallister back to his spiritual North East home. Brian McClair also brought the curtain down on his Old Trafford career.

2004 QUEIROZ RETURNS

Carlos Queiroz was appointed as Sir Alex Ferguson's assistant in his second spell with Manchester United.

2007 THE WORST-KEPT SECRET IN FOOTBALL

Owen Hargreaves completed his move to Manchester United from Bayern Munich, putting pen to paper on a four-year contract with the champions. In an exclusive interview with ManUtd.com a clearly relieved Hargreaves said: 'It's been a long time coming. It was probably the worst-kept secret in football, but it's great to be here.'

2

1973 LAW RETURNS TO CITY

Denis Law put pen to paper to sign for Manchester City, his second spell at Maine Road. The Lawman left City in 1961 for Torino before joining United in July 1963. 'I am a very lucky player to be able to come here,' said the man dubbed The King by the Stretford End faithful. I have left one great club for another and they're both in Manchester, which I love. If City hadn't come along, I would have packed in the game.'

2 JULY

2003 BECKS OFF TO MADRID

Having spent a decade in the red of his beloved United, David Beckham left Old Trafford and signed for Spanish giants Real Madrid in a transfer deal worth £25m. In 1991, Beckham, a boyhood fan of the Reds, moved north from Leytonstone to sign apprentice forms for the club he loved, and quickly formed part of the Class of 1992, along with Nicky Butt, Paul Scholes and the Neville brothers. Dubbed 'Fergie's Fledglings', they won the FA Youth Cup that year, but Beckham had to wait a few years for his League debut, at home to Leeds United on 2 April 1995. The departure of Andrei Kanchelskis during the summer of 1995 freed up a place on the right of midfield, and Beckham made it his own. He scored the winner in United's 2–1 win over Chelsea in the FA Cup semi-final at Villa Park and ended his first full season in the side helping United win a second Double. He began the 1996–97 Premiership campaign with a 57-yard strike against Wimbledon at Selhurst Park and a month later began his England journey with a debut against Moldova. That season also brought another Premiership medal. After his sending off in the 1998 World Cup, Beckham responded by scoring a free-kick against Leicester City in the first Premiership game of the season and went on to enjoy a campaign that would have been beyond his or any other Red's wildest dreams by playing a major role in United's unprecedented Treble-winning season. The following term brought his fourth Premiership winners' medal and Beckham was voted second best player in Europe and the World with Rivaldo of FC Barcelona and Brazil pipping him to both awards. The 2000–01 season was his third consecutive and fifth overall Premiership-winning campaign and to top things off he was handed the England captaincy by Peter Taylor. Beckham repaid the faith placed in him by almost single-handedly booking England's place in the 2002 World Cup finals with an incredible match-winning performance against Greece at Old Trafford, when he scored the all-important goal, a trademark free-kick, in the last seconds of the game. Always in the media spotlight along with his wife, and former Spice Girl, Victoria, Beckham introduced the world to the term metatarsal injury when he broke his foot in a UEFA Champions League match against Deportivo La Coruna but recovered in time to score a redemptive penalty against Argentina in the World Cup finals in Japan and Korea in 2002. The 2002–03 season proved to be his last at Old Trafford. After months of speculation, Beckham made the switch to Real Madrid but not before picking up his sixth Premiership medal and signing off in style with a final free-kick goal in his last game, against Everton at Goodison Park.

BECKHAM David Robert Joseph (Midfielder 1993–2003)
Appearances: PL: 237 (28), goals 62 FAC: 22 (2), goals 6 FLC: 10 (2), goals 1 EUR: 79 (4), goals 155 TOTAL: 356 (38) apps, 85 goals.

2007 TRIO'S MOVES SEALED

Manchester United's new signings Nani and Anderson both put pen to paper on five-year deals with the club. Nani, the 20-year-old Portuguese winger, and Anderson, a 19-year-old Brazilian midfielder, cost a combined £30m when joining from Sporting Lisbon and FC Porto respectively. Meanwhile, United's Polish keeper Tomasz Kuszczak made his season-long loan from West Bromwich Albion into a permanent move. Kuszczak joined United on loan from West Brom in August 2006 to act as an understudy to Old Trafford No.1 Edwin van der Sar and made six Premier League and five FA Cup starts during the 2006–07 season.

3

1921

Joseph 'Joe' Dale (Forward 1947–8) was born in Northwich, Cheshire.

1977

Michael Clegg (Defender 1996–2002) was born in Tameside.

2006 ROONEY LEFT GOBSMACKED

Manchester United's Wayne Rooney said he was totally 'gobsmacked' to be sent off after he stamped on Chelsea's Portuguese defender Ricardo Carvalho in England's World Cup quarter-final against Portugal just two days ago. However, he did make it abundantly clear that he had no problem with his club colleague Cristiano Ronaldo's actions leading up to him being sent off

4

1977 THE DOC IS SACKED

Tommy Docherty was called before the Manchester United board a few weeks after his affair with Mary Brown, the wife of the club's physio, was splashed across the newspapers. The meeting was held at the home of Louis Edwards in Alderley Edge. The club's directors asked The Doc for his resignation and after he refused, he was sacked.

2005 DR LAW I PRESUME

Denis Law was awarded an honorary Doctorate from the University of Aberdeen, the city of his birth.

2007 HAIR-BRAINED IDEA

Cristiano Ronaldo told Sir Alex Fergsuon: 'I'll shave my hair off if I don't score 20 Premier League goals – you shave your hair off if I do.' The Portuguese winger's latest bet with Sir Alex followed the bet the pair made at the start of the 2006–07 season when the United No.7 won a £400 bet after scoring 17 times, beating the target of 15 they set in their bet. He was to become the first player in 2007–08 to reach 20 Premiership goals when he scored two goals at St James' Park in United's 5–1 victory over Newcastle on 23 February.

5

1891

James Hodge (Defender 1910–20) was born in Stenhousemuir, Scotland.

1971 THE QUIET MAN

After leading Leicester City to the Second Division title and promotion to the top flight, Frank O'Farrell resigned his position as manager of the Foxes and became the new Manchester United manager, replacing Sir Matt Busby, who retired for a second time. However, the soft-spoken Irishman would last only 18 months in the hot seat at Old Trafford before being sacked himself with three and a half years still left on his contract.

1993 TWO TRAINEES

Michael Clegg and Phil Neville signed on as trainees for Manchester United.

2005 HEINZE SCOOPS FANS' AWARD

Gabriel Heinze, United's 27-year-old Argentinian full-back, won the Manchester United Fans' Player of the Year Award. Heinze played 39 games for United in his debut season of 2004–05 and became the first non-European to win the fans' award.

6

1993 THOMAS SENT TO JAIL

Former Manchester United winger Mickey Thomas was given an 18-month jail sentence at Warrington Crown Court for passing counterfeit £10 notes on to Wrexham Youth Training Scheme players.

2007 TEVEZ TO SIGN FOR THE REDS

According to media reports quoting agent Kia Joorabchian's lawyers, the West Ham United striker Carlos Tevez agreed personal terms with Manchester United.

7

1954

Michael Reginald 'Mickey' Thomas (Midfielder 1978–81) was born in Mochdre, near Colwyn Bay, Wales.

> *Appearances: FL: 90, goals 11 FAC: 13, goals 2 FLC: 5, goals 2 EUR: 2, goals 0*
> *TOTAL: 110 apps, 15 goals.*

1974 AA SIGNS ON

Arthur Albiston, aged 16, signed professional forms with Manchester United. The young Scot arrived at Old Trafford as an apprentice in July 1972.

2006 RONALDO PIPPED TO AWARD

Lukas Podolski, Germany's exciting young striker, won the 2006 FIFA Young Player of the World Cup award, beating off competition from United's Portuguese star winger Cristiano Ronaldo.

8

1991 BIG TV DEAL SEALED

Manchester United signed a lucrative contract with ITV granting the television network the exclusive rights to screen all of the Reds' European home ties for the forthcoming defence of their European Cup Winners' Cup trophy in season 1991–92.

1991 FERGIE'S FLEDGLINGS NEST

David Beckham, Nicky Butt, Gary Neville and Paul Scholes began life at Old Trafford by signing as trainees for Manchester United.

9

1955

Stephen James 'Steve' Coppell (Forward/Midfielder 1974–83) was born in Norris Green, Liverpool.

1958 REDS ANNOUNCE RECORD PROFIT

Manchester United became the first British club to announce a six-figure profit for a season, £100,000 for 1957–58.

1969 UNITED IN THE DOCK

Following trouble in United's European Cup semi-final 1–0 victory over AC Milan, during which the Italians' goalkeeper Fabio Cudicini was hit by a stone and knocked out, United appeared before a UEFA disciplinary court in Geneva and the club was ordered to erect screens behind the goals at Old Trafford for future European games.

10

1956

Frank Anthony Stapleton (Forward 1981–7) was born in Dublin.

> *Appearances: FL: 204 (19), goals 60 FAC: 21, goals 7 FLC: 26 (1), goals 6
> EUR: 14 (1), goals 5 TOTAL: 267 (21) apps, 78 goals.*

1993 STRETFORD END RECEIVES A FACE LIFT

The building work to Manchester United's famous Stretford End (now called the West Stand) was finally completed at a cost of £10.3m. The original cantilever stand had cost the club £350,000 when it was completed during the summer of 1964.

11

1966 ANIMALS

The England manager Alf Ramsey described the Argentinian team as 'animals' following a bad-tempered 0–0 draw between the two sides at Wembley Stadium during the 1966 World Cup finals. The South American team's captain, Antonio Rattin, was sent off and when the final whistle blew Ramsey ran on to the pitch and prevented George Cohen from swapping shirts with Alberto Gonzalez. Manchester United's Bobby Charlton, John Connelly and Nobby Stiles all played in the stormy clash.

12

1962 THE KING ARRIVES AT OLD TRAFFORD

Denis Law joined Manchester United from the Italian side AS Torino for a new British record transfer fee of £115,000. Manchester United became the first British club to pay a six-figure sum for a player.

1967 AIR TURNED BLUE

Manchester United's 1963 FA Cup-winning captain, Noel Cantwell, was fined £5 at Sheffield Magistrates' Court after he pleaded guilty by mail of using insulting language during United's 2–2 draw (scorer: Bobby Charlton 2) with Sheffield Wednesday at Hillsborough on 10 April 1967. Cantwell apologised profusely for his actions in his letter to the court.

1991 MONEY BAGS

Manchester United's pre-season ticket sales for the 1991–92 season raked in a mammoth £4.5m with over 20,000 season tickets and box seats sold.

2001 SEBA'S RECORD-BUSTING TRANSFER

Juan Sebastian Veron arrived at Old Trafford from SS Lazio for a Manchester United club record transfer fee of £28m.

2005 HEINZE SCOOPS DOUBLE AWARD

Gabriel Heinze, United's 27-year-old Argentinian full-back, added Manchester United's Players' Player of the Year Award to his United fans' award. The likeable Heinze just edged out Wayne Rooney with Cristiano Ronaldo occupying third place. 'I really value and appreciate their decision, especially when you think it is my first season here,' Heinze told Manchester United's official magazine.

2006 RONALDO GOING NOWHERE

In the aftermath of Wayne Rooney's dismissal against Portugal at the 2006 World Cup finals in Germany, Manchester United released a statement saying, 'The club can confirm there is no possibility of Cristiano being sold. Cristiano recently signed a new contract until 2010 and the club fully expects him to honour that contract. The club will not listen to any offers for Cristiano.' United issued the statement to quell rumours that their star winger, who was accused of persuading the referee to send his United team-mate off, was about to join Real Madrid.

13

1966 WORLD CUP VENUE

Old Trafford hosted the 1966 World Cup group game between Portugal and Hungary. The Portuguese won 3–1.

1994 ERIC IN CUFFS

Eric Cantona was placed in handcuffs in Los Angeles prior to the USA '94 World Cup semi-final clash between Brazil and Sweden. Eric, who was co-commentating for French television, was alleged to have been involved in a Press Box punch-up. Eric was released by police after the intervention of Guido Tognini, the World Cup Press Officer.

14

1957

Arthur Richard Albiston (Defender 1974–88) was born in Edinburgh, Scotland.

1971 THE LOYAL SERVANT

Jack Crompton left Manchester United after 27 years' loyal service as both a player and a member of the coaching staff.

1977 DAVE SEXTON REPLACES THE DOC

Just 10 days after the sacking of Tommy Docherty, Dave Sexton became the new Manchester United manager. Sexton's record before he arrived at Old Trafford was impressive. He guided Chelsea to FA Cup success and a European Cup Winners' Cup final. After his time at Chelsea he moved on to Queens Park Rangers and took them to within a whisker of the First Division title. He was a quiet, considerate and articulate man, quite the opposite of his predecessor. In his four years in charge of United he took them to Wembley in 1979 and FA Cup defeat at the hands of Arsenal. Sexton's United, which included players such as Gordon McQueen, Ray Wilkins, Joe Jordan and Garry Birtles, finished First Division runners-up in season 1979–80 but a disastrous 1980–81 effectively spelt the end for Sexton. He was sacked in April 1981 despite the fact that United had won their last eight consecutive games.

15

1927 WHEN OLD TRAFFORD'S PITCH BECAME A COURT

During the 1920s C. B. Cochran was a well-known West End producer whose plays sold out in London. However, the famous impresario moved away from the theatre during the summer of 1927 and set his sights on a bigger stage, Old Trafford. Cochran persuaded the six-times Wimbledon Ladies Singles champion Suzanne Lenglen and Bill Tilden, twice Men's Singles champion at Wimbledon, to play in a tournament at United's home. However, despite the celebrated status of both Lenglen and Tilden the event was a flop.

1989 LAURIE CUNNINGHAM DIES

The football world mourned the loss of Laurie Cunningham who lost his life in a car crash near Madrid aged 33. In March 1983, Laurie joined Manchester United on loan from Real Madrid and scored two goals in only three games for the club. In 1988 he won an FA Cup winners' medal with Wimbledon in their shock 1–0 victory over Liverpool. Laurie made his name at West Bromwich Albion as a speedy and skilful winger under the watchful eye of Ron Atkinson and then moved on to Real Madrid in June 1979.

2006 VIDIC TIES THE KNOT

Manchester United's no-nonsense centre-half Nemanja Vidic married his girl-friend Ana Ivanovic, an Economics student studying at the University of Belgrade. The couple have a son, Luka.

16

1971 FA CLOSE OLD TRAFFORD

As a result of a knife-throwing incident during a League game at Old Trafford against Newcastle United on 27 February 1971, the Football Association announced that Old Trafford would be closed for the Reds' opening two home games of the 1971–72 season.

2007 PARK OUT

Manchester United announced that Park Ji-Sung might be sidelined until January because of a knee injury. The 26-year-old South Korean midfielder had an operation in the USA in April 2007 after damaging his knee in United's 4–0 Premiership win over Blackburn Rovers at Old Trafford on 31 March 2007, a game in which he scored.

17

1924 UNITED PLAYER MOVES TO THE LINES

Joseph 'Jack' Quinn played two games for Manchester United from 1909–10. In July 1924 he was appointed as a linesman for the Scottish League.

1991 LEAGUE BREAKAWAY

Manchester United were one of a number of First Division clubs to sign a 'Founder Member Document' pledging to play in the new Premier League from season 1992–93.

2007 UNITED KICK OFF THEIR 2007 TOUR OF ASIA

Manchester United began their 2007 pre-season tour of Asia with a 2–2 draw against the reigning Japanese J-League champions, the Urawa Diamonds, in the Saitama City Cup played in the Saitama Stadium, Saitama, Japan. United's goals came from Darren Fletcher and Cristiano Ronaldo. United were lined up to play the Urawa Diamonds at Old Trafford in the 2004 Vodafone Cup before the game was cancelled due to a huge electrical storm in the Manchester area. The Saitama Stadium was purposely built for the 2002 World Cup finals co-hosted by Japan and South Korea.

18

2000 FAB SIGNING

Manchester United paid a British transfer record fee for a goalkeeper when they signed AS Monaco's Fabien Barthez for £7.8m.

2007 UNITED CALL IN FIFA OVER TEVEZ DISPUTE

David Gill, Manchester United's chief executive, stated that the club had asked FIFA to intervene in the Carlos Tevez dispute with West Ham United. Tevez was at Old Trafford but the Hammers refused the 23-year-old Argentina international striker permission to have a medical with United. Gill said the case would be rushed through by FIFA so that it could be dealt with as soon as possible while the Hammers also requested the world governing body's intervention to bring the dispute to an amicable ending.

19

1993 UNITED BREAK THE BANK TO LAND KEANO

Following their relegation from the Premier League, Nottingham Forest agreed a £4m transfer fee with Blackburn Rovers to sell their dynamic and energetic young Irish midfield general Roy Keane to Manchester United's Lancashire rivals, rejuvenated under Kenny Dalglish's management and Sir Jack Walker's financial backing. However, the day before the final paperwork was due to be signed Alex Ferguson telephoned Keane and asked him whether he would like to join United rather than Rovers. The rest is history with Keane going on to become one of the greatest ever players United has had. Roy Keane joined Manchester United in a deal worth £3.75m, a new British record transfer fee.

2007 VAN DER SAR UNCERTAIN ABOUT HIS UNITED FUTURE

Edwin van der Sar, United's 36-year-old No.1, announced that season 2007–08 may be his final season with Manchester United. Van der Sar openly admitted that he felt he did not perform well in 2006–07 despite helping the Reds to their ninth Premiership crown. His current Old Trafford contract expires in June 2008.

20

1957 A NOSEY BAN

Following an operation on his nose, Roger Byrne was issued with a strict 'ban' by the Manchester United club doctor not to head a football for four weeks until his nose had fully recovered from the surgery.

2007 FERGIE OBJECTS TO HEINZE JOINING ARCH RIVALS

Rafael Benitez, the Liverpool manager, stated that the club's lawyers were working on forcing through a £6.8m deal for Gabriel Heinze from Manchester United while Sir Alex is set against his 29-year-old Argentina international defender moving to Anfield. The last Manchester United player to make the switch from Old Trafford to Anfield was Phil Chisnall in April 1964. In the end, Heinze joined his former United team-mate Ruud van Nistelrooy at Real Madrid.

21

1969 CELEBRATION TIME

George Best and Bobby Charlton played in the Rest of the United Kingdom XI that beat the Football Association of Wales team 1–0 at Ninian Park. The match was part of the celebrations held to mark the investiture of Prince Charles as the Prince of Wales.

1995 A RED LEAVES THE REDS

Manchester United's flying Russian winger Andrei Kanchelskis left Old Trafford and joined Everton in a deal worth £5m.

22

1989 TRIBUNAL CASE

A Football League Tribunal ordered Manchester United to pay Nottingham Forest the sum of £1.5m for Neil Webb. It was the first time a tribunal had ordered a club to pay in excess of £1m for a player.

1993 GIGGSY PUTS THE BOOT IN

Ryan Giggs signed a lucrative three-year sponsorship deal, worth an estimated £300,000, to wear Reebok football boots.

2002 RIO THE RECORD MAKER

Rio Ferdinand joined Manchester United from Leeds United in a five-year deal to become the most expensive British footballer in history at £31m.

23

1951 PLAYERS GO ON STRIKE

When the Manchester United players turned up at Old Trafford to commence pre-season training none of them had signed a contract with the club for the 1951–52 season. All professional players were contacted by their union, who wanted contracts to run from August to July. The dispute was eventually settled and United were crowned First Division champions at the end of the 1951–52 season.

2007 NANI MAKES ACROBATIC DEBUT

Shenzhen FC 0   Manchester United 6
Nani made an impressive debut for Manchester United in their 6–0 win over Shenzhen FC in the Macau Stadium, Macau, to win the Venetian Cup. He was always an attacking threat in the game and thrilled the crowd when he scored, performing his trademark acrobatic celebration. The other United goals were scored by Chris Eagles, Ryan Giggs, John O'Shea, Cristiano Ronaldo and Wayne Rooney.

24

1941 SIR MATT'S UNSUNG HERO

Anthony 'Tony' Peter Dunne was born on 24 July 1941 in Dublin. On 1 April 1960, Matt Busby signed the young Irish full-back from Shelbourne and he went on to serve the club for 14 years making 535 appearances for the club, scoring 2 goals. Dunne was signed as cover for Noel Cantwell or Shay Brennan and his big chance came when he replaced Brennan in the line-up for the 1963 FA Cup final victory over Leicester City at Wembley. A brave, speedy defender, he went on to cement a place in the first team following that success and missed only six League games over the next four seasons. The Irish international also helped United to win the First Division Championship title in 1965 and 1967 and the European Cup in 1968. On 1 August 1973, Dunne left Old Trafford and joined Bolton Wanderers on a free transfer. Yet, far from nearing the end of his career, aged 32, he went on to play more than 200 matches for the Trotters, contributing to over 700 career League appearances in total. He won 33 caps for the Republic of Ireland in an international career spanning 14 years and was the Irish Footballer of the Year in 1969, a rare personal award for such a team player. Dunne will always be remembered as the unsung hero of Sir Matt Busby's trailblazing side of the 1960s and is one of the greatest full-backs in the club's history.

1945 EDWARDS ARRIVES

Martin Edwards was born in Adlington, Cheshire. The son of Louis Edwards, Manchester United's chairman, he was elected to the Manchester United board in March 1970 and, following the death of his father of a heart attack in 1979, he was appointed the club's chairman in March 1980. Edwards later also became the chief executive, resigning from his position as CEO in 2000 after selling the vast majority of his shares in the club. He remains the club's life honorary president.

1958

James 'Jim' Leighton (Goalkeeper 1988–90) was born in Johnstone, Renfrewshire.

25

1993 ROBBO OFF

Bryan Robson was shown his marching orders in a pre-season friendly against Arsenal.

1995 FERGIE IN HOT WATER

Following the publication of *A Year In The Life* by Alex Ferguson, Leeds United contacted Manchester United to complain officially about a comment made by the United boss in his book when he said: 'I almost want Leeds to be relegated because of their fans. You can feel the hatred and animosity.' The United boss later sent a letter of apology to the chairman of the Elland Road club, stating that he had not actually meant what he said and that his comments had been written at an emotional time.

26

1966 CHARLTON SECURES ENGLAND A WORLD CUP FINAL APPEARANCE

Two goals from Bobby Charlton at Wembley Stadium in England's 2–1 win over Portugal saw England through to the 1966 World Cup final.

2000 CARRINGTON OPENS ITS DOORS

Manchester United's new purpose-built training complex situated at Carrington was officially opened by Ryan Giggs and Stephen Clegg, the youngest player on United's books at the time.

27

1932 UNITED ATTRACT THE LADIES

After finishing the 1931–32 season in 12th place in the English First Division with dwindling attendances at Old Trafford, Manchester United announced the prices of season tickets for the 1932–33 season. The cost of a season ticket was frozen at £1, with half-price admission for juniors, while a ladies' season ticket would cost a mere 10 shillings.

1956

Garry Birtles (Forward 1980–82) was born in Nottingham.

1968 A DINNER FIT FOR CHAMPIONS

A celebratory banquet was held in the Midland Hotel, Manchester, to commemorate Manchester United beating SL Benfica 4–1 (aet) in the 1968 European Cup final at Wembley Stadium just two months earlier.

28

1981

Michael Adrian Carrick (Midfielder 2006–present) was born in Wallsend, Tyne & Wear.

2006 RUUD MOVE

Real Madrid completed the signing of Ruud van Nistelrooy after Manchester United's 30-year-old Dutch striker passed a medical. Ruud was paraded before the Spanish press and the fans at the Estadio Santiago Bernabeu. He reportedly cost the Spanish giants £10.2m. Ruud scored scored 150 goals in 219 appearances for United after arriving at Old Trafford from PSV Eindhoven for £19m in 2001.

29

1996 OLE ARRIVES

Manchester United signed Ole Gunnar Solskjaer from Norwegian side Molde for the modest fee of £1.5m. Over the next 11 years he would make 366 appearances for United, a record 150 of them as substitute, and score 126 goals, most memorably the one in extra-time that secured the Champions League trophy for the Reds in 1999.

2004 BYE-BYE BUTT

Nicky Butt made a £2.5m move to Newcastle United, ending 13 years at Old Trafford.

30

1874 A LEGEND IS BORN

William 'Billy' Meredith was born in Chirk, North Wales. Manchester United signed the mercurial winger from neighbours City in May 1906 following a bribes and illegal payments scandal at Maine Road that ultimately resulted in Meredith and a few of his team-mates receiving suspensions from the Football

Association. After joining United, Billy went on to establish himself as a legend, one of the greatest players in the history of the club. Billy helped United to their first Championship success in 1908 and a second in 1911 and was a key player in the club winning the FA Cup for the first time in 1909.

1966 NOBBY PRAYS FOR HELP

History will show that England famously beat West Germany 4–2 after extra time to win the 1966 World Cup final at Wembley Stadium. On the morning of the epic final Manchester United's Nobby Stiles, a key member of Alf Ramsey's Wingless Wonders, took a stroll from the England team hotel in Golders Green, London, and attended Mass. Nobby's prayers were certainly answered and although Geoff Hurst's hat-trick deservedly grabbed all the headlines, few who were inside the stadium or the millions watching on television will ever forget little Nobby's victory jig on the Wembley turf.

1994 SEALED WITH A KISS

Manchester United were in Dublin for a friendly and during the game a young girl ran on to the pitch just as Ryan Giggs was about to take a corner. She wrapped her arms around the United pin-up and kissed him.

31

1971 NO MORE WATNEY'S

Halifax Town beat Manchester United 2–1 at The Shay in the first round of the Watney Cup (scorer: George Best). It was the Reds' final appearance in the competition.

1995 FA UNHAPPY WITH SHUT DOORS

The FA informed Manchester United that they were not permitted to play the suspended Eric Cantona in games behind closed doors at their Cliff training ground. The FA said that Eric's suspension included all games including those played away from the public gaze.

2006 CARRICK BECOMES A DEVIL

Tottenham Hotspur and England midfielder Michael Carrick completed his move to Manchester United in a deal that could be worth up to £18.6m. Sir Alex Ferguson said that Carrick would wear the number 16 shirt, which was formerly worn by United's inspirational captain Roy Keane.

2006 WHEN RONNY MET ROONEY

Cristiano Ronaldo met up with Wayne Rooney for the first time since their World Cup quarter-final clash in Germany when the Portuguese winger reported for pre-season training with Manchester United at their Carrington base. Ronaldo returned to training later than the other members of the squad after being given an extended break following Portugal's World Cup campaign. Portugal's final game was the third-place play-off loss to the hosts Germany on 8 July. United brought in additional security to cope with any adverse reaction Ronaldo might attract from disgruntled fans.

AUGUST

1

1934 SILCOCK'S DEPARTURE

After spending 18 seasons (1916–34) at Old Trafford John 'Jack' Silcock left United and joined Oldham Athletic. Although not an instantly recognisable name to many United fans, John Silcock's place in the annals of the history of Manchester United is guaranteed.

During his 15 seasons playing as a professional with the club between the wars he was a loyal and highly dependable full-back. For most men of his generation, football was rare as a first-class profession and the Wigan-born (15 January 1898) Jack began his working life as a miner at Aspull Colliery. His football talents were spotted with local outfit Aspull juniors, and he signed for the Lancashire Combination club Atherton FC. In 1916 John Robson, the manager of Manchester United, spotted Silcock, still just 18 years old, on a scouting trip and snapped him up on amateur terms. It was a lucky break for Jack as the United manager had actually gone to the game with his eye on another full-back named Lucas who ended up at Liverpool. Jack played for United in the wartime league (Lancashire Section/Principal Tournament), and after making his debut in a 1–1 draw with Derby County at the Baseball Ground on 30 August 1919 (scorer: Wilfred Woodcock) he became a permanent fixture in the United back-line. Another future United legend, Clarence 'Lal' Hilditch, also made his United debut in the same game. Jack, a strong, technically gifted full-back with excellent distribution skills, went on to make 449 first-team appearances (2 goals) in a decade and a half with United. Although his sterling performances alongside his defensive partner Charlie Moore didn't deliver any silverware, they earned him three full England caps. He was the fifth United player to wear the Three Lions of England. He also played three times for the Football League representative side. When he moved to Oldham Athletic he could not force his way into the starting XI and after spending half a season in the reserves at Boundary Park, he moved to non-league Droylsden in March 1935. He coupled his playing days for the Lancashire Combination side with running the Rob Roy Hotel in Stretford.

1973 DUNNE MOVES ON

Tony Dunne left Manchester United and joined Bolton Wanderers on a free transfer, bringing to an end 14 years at Old Trafford.

1988 ALBISTON'S CAREER AT UNITED COMES TO AN END

After signing for Manchester United as an apprentice in July 1972, Arthur Albiston brought the curtain down on his 16-year career (485 appearances, 7 goals) at Old Trafford by moving on to West Bromwich Albion, managed by his old United boss Ron Atkinson. Only nine players have made more appearances for Manchester United than the reliable, consistent Scottish left-back who, for the best part of a decade, was a permanent fixture in the Reds' starting line-up. Six days after his debut for United in the 1974–75 League Cup (a 1–0 home win over Manchester City) he was given his League debut at home to Portsmouth but, despite United not conceding in either game, the young Scot had to wait until 1976–77 for his big breakthrough as a first-team regular. His opportunity arrived in dramatic circumstances: following an injury to his fellow countryman Stewart Houston, Albiston was called into the team by manager Tommy Docherty as a replacement for the unfortunate Houston to face Liverpool in the 1977 FA Cup final. Very few players make their FA Cup debuts in the final at Wembley but the 19-year-old Albiston put in an impressive performance at left-back to help United to a 2–1 victory. After collecting his winners' medal Albiston then admirably offered it to Houston who politely refused the generous gift. After his Cup-final display, Albiston spent the next few seasons battling it out with Houston for the left-back berth, including four months out of the game in season 1978–79 following a cartilage operation. However, he eventually made the No.3 shirt his own to keep, appearing in four FA Cup finals, collecting three winners' medals, a club record at that time. One big disappointment for Albiston in his illustrious career must have surely been the fact that he was capped just 14 times by his country, making his debut versus Northern Ireland in 1982.

1999 EARLY START

Manchester United 1   Arsenal 2
Manchester United lost 2–1 to Arsenal in the FA Charity Shield at Wembley (scorer: Dwight Yorke). It is the earliest official start to the season in United's history.

2

1954

Samuel Baxter 'Sammy' McIlroy (Midfielder 1971–82) was born in Belfast.

1957

Augustine Ashley Grimes (Midfielder 1977–83) was born in Dublin.

2007 UNITED SIGN NINE-YEAR-OLD WONDERKID

Manchester United confirmed that they had signed a nine-year-old boy named Rhain Davis. Rhain's grandfather sent United a DVD highlighting the wonder-kid's skill with a football while many pundits claimed he is the next Wayne Rooney. It was believed that more than 3 million viewers watched video footage of him on YouTube.com. Rhain, who was born in England but lived in Australia since he was four, played for an under-10 side in Brisbane. 'He's a member of our academy and we don't comment on individual members,' said a United spokesman when contacted by Reuters. Journalists were seeking young Rhain's whereabouts after it was learned that he had moved back to England to live with his father near United's Carrington training ground.

2007 SMITH TO THE MAGPIES

United agreed a deal with Newcastle United to allow Alan Smith to join the Geordies. Smith, aged 26, had been unsettled about his future at Old Trafford for some time and with speculation that Carlos Tevez was about to become a Red, 'Smudger' felt it was time for a new challenge.

3

1892 HEATHENS' FIRST CHANGE OF NAME

Newton Heath Lancashire & Yorkshire Railway Football Club dropped the 'Lancashire & Yorkshire Railway' from the club's name prior to the start of the 1892–93 season, their inaugural campaign in the Football League.

1996 MOVE, MOVE, MOVE (THE RED TRIBE)

Manchester United's 1996 FA Cup final song, *Move, Move, Move (The Red Tribe)* re-entered the British singles chart three months after it was originally released and reached No.50, spending four weeks in the UK singles chart. It had reached its highest position of No.6 after eleven weeks in the charts when first released.

1997 BECKS DROPS HIS 'H'

Manchester United 1 Chelsea 1 (United won 4–2 on penalties)
Manchester United drew 1–1 (scorer: Ronny Johnsen) with Chelsea in the FA Charity Shield at Wembley and went on to lift the Shield, defeating the Londoners

4–2 in the penalty shoot-out. Former United legend Mark Hughes scored for Chelsea. The reverse of David Beckham's shirt actually read BECKAM.

4

1970 SAYING FAREWELL TO SHAY

Seamus 'Shay' Brennan left Manchester United after 14 years' loyal service and was appointed the player-manager of Waterford in Ireland. The Irish international made his debut for United in the club's first game after the Munich Air Disaster and was a member of the team that helped secure a third consecutive FA Youth Cup triumph in 1955. Shay began life at United as an inside-forward, scoring twice in United's 3–0 FA Cup fifth round win over Sheffield Wednesday on 19 February 1958. After making his debut he was unluckily forced to take a back seat for the remainder of the season (although he scored in the FA Cup semi-final replay against Fulham) as more senior players returned to action, resulting in him missing out on appearing in the 1958 FA Cup final. It wasn't until the 1959–60 season that Brennan returned to the fold at right-back, and although he missed the 1963 FA Cup final win over Leicester City, having played in the first four games, he went on to collect First Division Championship winners' medals in 1964–65 (playing in all 42 League games) and 1967–68, a season that climaxed with glory against Benfica in the European Cup final at Wembley.

5

1970 ENGLISH FOOTBALL'S FIRST PENALTY SHOOT-OUT

Hull City 1   Manchester United 1
Manchester United visited Boothferry Park to play Hull City in the semi-final of the 1970 Watney Mann Invitation Cup (the Watney Cup). The game ended 1–1 (scorer: Denis Law) and is best remembered as the first in England to be decided on penalties. United won English football's first ever penalty shoot-out to book their place in the final against Derby County. George Best was the first penalty taker under this format while, amazingly, Denis Law was the first to miss.

1995 STICKY TRANSFER

Manchester United announced that Andrei Kanchelskis's proposed move to Everton was off because the Toffees had failed to cough up the £1.1m fee built into the flying winger's contract. The money was due to be paid to Shakhtar Donetsk, the club from which he had joined United.

2007 VAN DER SAR HAT-TRICK WINS SHIELD FOR UNITED

Manchester United 1   Chelsea 1 (United won 3–0 on penalties)
The 2007 game celebrated the 99-year history of the FA Community Shield (previously the FA Charity Shield), with United winning the inaugural competition in 1908. Manchester United had now played in 24 of them, winning 16 (12 outright and 4 shared). Ryan Giggs was making his 10th appearance in the Shield, winning his sixth in 2007 to equal Ray Clemence's record (5 with Liverpool and 1 with Tottenham Hotspur). However, it was United's Edwin van der Sar who proved the United hero after the game finished 1–1 after 90 minutes. Giggsy opened the scoring in the 35th minute and Chelsea's new French striker, Florent Malouda, equalised 10 minutes later. The big Dutch goalkeeper made a hat-trick of penalty saves from Chelsea's first three spot kicks while Rio Ferdinand, Michael Carrick and finally Wayne Rooney successfully converted United's opening three penalties to win the Shield 3–0 on penalties. It was the eighth time van der Sar had been involved in a penalty shoot-out with his record now won 3 lost 5. Meanwhile Giggs was making his 16th appearance at Wembley Stadium, old and new, 10 Shields, 5 FA Cup finals and 1 England Schoolboys appearance. His goal was his first for United at either Wembley.

6

1982 FIRST SPONSORSHIP DEAL

Manchester United signed their first ever sponsorship contract, linking up with the Japanese electrical appliance manufacturer Sharp in a deal worth £250,000 over three seasons.

1994 ERIC'S RED MIST

Eric Cantona was sent off in United's pre-season friendly game against Glasgow Rangers at Ibrox Stadium after receiving two yellow cards. Alex Ferguson was so incensed that he said Manchester United would never return to Ibrox for a friendly with the SPL side. To date, the United boss has been true to his word.

7

1978 CENTENARY GAME

Manchester United 4   Real Madrid 0
Manchester United celebrated the club's Centenary with a high-profile glamour friendly against the Spanish giants Real Madrid at Old Trafford.

1993 KEANO LIFTS TROPHY IN HIS FIRST GAME

Manchester United 1   Arsenal 1 (United won 5–4 on penalties)
Mark Hughes scored for Manchester United who went on to win the FA Charity Shield 5–4 on penalties with Peter Schmeichel scoring against his opposite number in the Arsenal goal, David Seaman. The game also marked Roy Keane's debut for United.

8

1970 THE INAUGURAL WATNEY CUP FINAL

Derby County 4   Manchester United 1
Derby County beat Manchester United 4–1 (scorer: George Best) in the first ever Watney Cup final played at Derby's Baseball Ground in front of 32,049 fans. The Watney Mann Invitation Cup (the Watney Cup) was a pre-season knockout tournament that began in 1970 but only lasted until 1973. Eight teams took part in the invitational tournament, the top two leading goalscorers in each of the four Divisions of the English Football League who had not won a European place or promotion to the division above them. The competition was a straight knock-out format without replays while the venue for the final would be the home ground of one of the eight teams taking part. The competition was one of the first in Britain to receive sponsorship with the Watney Mann brewery as the financial backer. Colchester United won the 1971 Watney Cup, Bristol Rovers in 1972 and Stoke City in 1973.

1978

Louis Laurent Saha (Forward 2004–present) was born in Paris.

1984 UEFA SETTLE STRACHAN TRANSFER DISPUTE

UEFA settled the dispute involving Aberdeen, FC Cologne and Manchester United surrounding the transfer of Scottish international midfielder Gordon Strachan. FC Cologne lodged a formal complaint with UEFA, claiming that the Scottish side had reached an agreement with them for Strachan only to lose out when he signed for United. Strachan's transfer to Old Trafford was given the green light by UEFA but they ordered Aberdeen to pay the Bundesliga club £100,000 in compensation.

2004 GUNNED DOWN

Arsenal 3   Manchester United 1
In the traditional curtain-raiser to a new season Arsenal's 2003–04 Double-winning side beat Manchester United at the Millennium Stadium, Cardiff, to lift the first piece of silverware for the 2004–05 season, the FA Community Shield. It was clear from the outset that the two teams still disliked one another, with some flying tackles punctuating the early stages of what proved to be an entertaining game of football. But in the end Arsenal's combination of young talent and a sprinkling of old heads was enough to see them celebrate the win. United's goal was scored by their new summer acquisition from Leeds United, Alan Smith.

9

1933

Albert Quixall (Forward 1958–64) was born in Sheffield.

1958

Gary Richard Bailey (Goalkeeper 1978–86) was born in Ipswich.

1977

Mikael Silvestre (Defender 1999–present) was born in Chambray-les-Tours, France.

1998 NO CHARITY FOR UNITED

Arsenal 3   Manchester United 0
United lost 3–0 to 1997–98 Double winners Arsenal in the FA Charity Shield at Wembley Stadium. Jaap Stam made his debut in the game and would go on to make 127 appearances for the Reds.

10 AUGUST

2005 PARK ON THE PITCH

Manchester United beat Debreceni 3–0 in their UEFA Champions League qualifying round, first leg encounter at Old Trafford. The scorers were Rooney, van Nistelrooy and Ronaldo. Ji-Sung Park made his debut in the game as a second-half substitute for Roy Keane. This game was the earliest start to a European season in United's history.

10

1971 THERE'S ONLY ONE KEANO!

Roy Maurice Keane was born in Mayfield Cork. Keano began his career with Cobh Ramblers after failing to gain an apprenticeship in English football. However, Brian Clough liked what he saw in the fiery young Irishman and brought him to Nottingham Forest before he completed a then-record £3.75m move to Manchester United in the summer of 1993 after he snubbed both Arsenal and Blackburn Rovers. He made his debut in United's FA Charity Shield penalty shoot-out win over Arsenal at Wembley Stadium and scored twice on his home debut, a 3–0 win over Sheffield United. At the end of his first season with United the gladiatorial Keane won the first of seven Premiership medals, adding a European Cup, Intercontinental Cup and four FA Cup winners' medals along the way. When Eric Cantona made his shock decision to retire after United won the 1996–97 Premiership crown, Keane was handed the captain's armband by Alex Ferguson. However, his first season as United skipper was cut short by a cruciate knee ligament injury sustained in a tackle with Leeds United's Alf-Inge Haaland at Elland Road in September 1997. The 1998–99 season was one of mixed fortunes for Keane. On his way to leading United to their historic Treble, a sending-off in the FA Cup semi-final replay victory over Arsenal was followed by a yellow card during arguably his greatest display in a red shirt, United's 3–2 UEFA Champions League second leg semi-final win over Juventus in the Stadio delle Alpi, which put United in the final for the first time since 1968. United were trailing 2–0 in Turin when up stepped Keano to score a header from a corner before rallying his comrades to one of the greatest victories in the club's long and proud history. During the game Keano knew his booking would rule him out of the final but where most men would be crestfallen, Keano played magnificently, a Julius Caesar controlling the midfield. Aside from his influential displays for United, Keane won the coveted Footballer of the Year and Players' Player of the Year awards in 2000 and he proved an inspiration to his country, winning close on 70 caps for the Republic of Ireland. Keane broke a metatarsal bone in his foot in United's Premiership match against Liverpool at Anfield on 18 September 2005, a match that was to prove his last for the club. He was still out of action on 19 November when a shock announcement to rival Eric's in 1997 was made. Manchester United issued a statement through ManUtd.com declaring that Keane's Old Trafford career was over. The Reds had reached agreement with Keano to end his contract immediately, enabling him to join Celtic. Keano helped Celtic to the SPL title and Scottish League Cup in 2005–06 and then took up the position of Sunderland manager shortly after the 2006–07 season began and guided the Black Cats to Coca-Cola Championship success and promotion to the Premiership.

1985 STICKY START AGAINST THE TOFFEES

Manchester United 0   Everton 2
Despite this disappointing result in the Charity Shield, overturning the outcome of the FA Cup final three months previously, United followed up by winning the first 10 League games of the season – their best-ever start to a campaign.

2003 HOWARD'S DAY

Manchester United 1   Arsenal 1 (United won 4–3 on penalties)
Mikael Silvestre scored for Manchester United in a game that ended 1–1 between the winners of the last eight FA Premier League campaigns, United 6 and Arsenal 2. Francis Jeffers was sent off for Arsenal 17 minutes from time after Silvestre's opening goal had been cancelled out by a long-range free-kick from Thierry Henry. Tim Howard, United's new American goalkeeper, made his debut in the game and saved two penalties in the penalty shoot-out, from Giovanni van Bronckhorst and Robert Pires, to help the Reds win the Shield 4–3 on spot kicks.

2006 A POLE BETWEEN THE POLES

Manchester United signed West Bromwich Albion's Polish international goal-keeper Tomasz Kuszczack on a one-year loan deal with a view to making the switch permanent in July 2007. The deal involved United's Under-18 goalkeeper Luke Steele and defender Paul McShane moving in the opposite direction.

2007 COME IN NO.32 – TEVEZ SIGNS

The Reds finally completed the transfer of Carlos Tevez after the Premier League registered the striker as a Manchester United player. United also announced their squad numbers for the 2007–08 season: Owen Hargreaves took over the unsettled Gabriel Heinze's No.4 shirt, Anderson was given the No.8 shirt vacated by Wayne Rooney who moved to No.10 and Nani was given the No.17 shirt. Meanwhile, Carlos Tevez took the No.32 shirt, the same number he wore at West Ham United.

11

1996 UNITED RED HOT AGAINST TOON

Manchester United 4   Newcastle United 0
Manchester United, Double winners in 1995–96, faced Newcastle United, Premiership runners-up, in the 1996 FA Charity Shield at Wembley Stadium. The Geordies were no match for the red-hot United who strolled to a 4–0 win under the famous Twin Towers (scorers: David Beckham, Nicky Butt, Eric Cantona, Roy Keane).

1998 REDS HIT THE SILVER SCREEN

Manchester United launched their very own TV station, MUTV.

12

1967 GOALIE SCORES AGAINST HIS OPPOSITE NUMBER

Manchester United 3   Tottenham Hotspur 3
Manchester United, the First Division Champions, entertained Tottenham Hotspur, the FA Cup holders, at Old Trafford on a hot summer's day for the 1967 FA Charity Shield. In the curtain raiser to the 1967–68 season the two sides played out an entertaining 3–3 draw with Bobby Charlton scoring twice and Denis Law once to share the trophy equally for six months. The Spurs goals were scored by Robertson and Saul and an incredible effort from their goalkeeper, Pat Jennings. The Northern Ireland international booted a massive left-footed clearance deep into Manchester United's half. The ball landed on the rock-hard Old Trafford surface, took one huge bounce and caught Alex Stepney in the United goal completely by surprise as it sailed over his head and into the back of the net. The crowd of 54,106 could not believe what they had seen.

2001 RUUD'S SCORING DEBUT

Liverpool 2   Manchester United 1
Ruud van Nistelrooy made his long-awaited Manchester United debut in the 2001 FA Charity Shield played at the Millennium Stadium, Cardiff. As the stadium roof was closed, this was British football's first ever top-flight game played indoors. However, despite Ruud scoring, United went down 2–1. A prolific goal-getter, Ruud van Nistelrooy's scoring exploits at Old Trafford have

safeguarded his place in the Manchester United history books. The Dutch front-man scored over 100 goals in his first three seasons at Old Trafford, and he took over United legend Denis Law's title as the club's all-time top scorer in European competition in only his fourth season with the Reds; by the end of his fifth season he had racked up an incredible 150 goals in 219 games. Ruud was born on 1 July 1976 in Oss, North Brabant, Holland and on his 22nd birthday he signed for PSV Eindhoven from Heerenveen for £4.2m, a record fee between Dutch clubs at the time. In two seasons Ruud scored 60 goals for PSV, alerting Europe's top clubs, including United and Real Madrid. United initially had to be patient to get their man, but Sir Alex was so determined to sign van Nistelrooy that he kept in contact with the player for a year as Ruud recovered from the cruciate knee ligament injury suffered while training with PSV. The setback came days after failing a medical with United in April 2000. After a remarkable recovery, he finally signed for the Reds on 23 April 2001 for £19m. Ruud netted 36 goals in his debut season, a frightening achievement that, incredibly, was eclipsed in the 2002–03 season as he scored 44 times to inspire United to their eighth Prem-iership title. Another 30 goals followed in his third season but in season 2004–05 injury ruined his campaign, although he still scored 16 goals in 27 appearances and finished top scorer in the UEFA Champions League with eight goals. The 2005–06 campaign was also tempered with disappointment – 10 goals in 12 games meant Ruud got off to a flyer, and by December he had scored 17 goals from 26 starts. But the return to form and fitness of Louis Saha resulted in van Nistelrooy being edged out of the side. A disgruntled van Nistelrooy left Old Trafford in the summer of 2006 and headed to Spain to join Real Madrid, winning the La Liga title with them in his first season, as well as winning the coveted Pichichi, the trophy awarded by Spanish sports newspaper *Marca* to the season's top goalscorer. Ruud scored 25 goals in La Liga for Madrid.

VAN NISTELROOY, **Ruud** *(Forward 2001–6) – debut in the above game.*
Appearances: PL: 137 (13), goals 95 FAC: 11 (3), goals 14 FLC: 5 (1), goals 2
EUR: 45 (2), goals 38 TOTAL: 200 (19) apps, 150 goals.

2007 A ROYAL PERFORMANCE

Manchester United 0   Reading 0
Manchester United's defence of the Premier League did not go to plan on the opening day of the season when they played out a 0–0 draw with Reading at Old Trafford despite the visitors going down to 10 men. However, the biggest downside to the gloomy day was the loss of Wayne Rooney at the half-time interval after the England striker fractured his foot following an innocuous challenge by the Royals' Michael Duberry. It was the first time in Premier League history that United had started the season with a 0–0 draw.

13

1977 SCORELESS SHIELD

Manchester United 0   Liverpool 0
After their goalless encounter before a Charity Shield record crowd of 82,000, both sides shared the trophy for six months each. Since their meeting in the FA Cup final three months before, Liverpool had been crowned European champions for the first time.

1985 WINNING HEARTS AND MINDS

Manchester United officially opened their new L Stand at Old Trafford, a dedicated 1,500-seater family enclosure.

14

1965 FA CHARITY SHIELD AT OLD TRAFFORD

Manchester United 2   Liverpool 2
George Best and David Herd scored for Manchester United in front of 48,502 fans and the rivals shared the trophy for six months each.

1979 CLUB RECORD BUTCH DEAL

Manchester United broke into the Old Trafford coffers to pay a club record £825,000 to lure the Chelsea captain Ray 'Butch' Wilkins to United. Dave Sexton was the Manchester United manager at the time, and was also Wilkins's manager at Stamford Bridge when he signed the then 15-year-old for Chelsea.

1983 JESPER UNDOES UNITED

Ajax Amsterdam 1   Manchester United 0
Jesper Olsen scored the only goal of the game to give the Dutch champions a 1–0 win over Manchester United in a friendly. The Reds were so impressed with the young Danish star's dazzling performance that they signed him within the year. However, the game was marred by Gordon McQueen's sending off for clattering the Liverpool-bound Jan Molby, ironically another talented Dane.

1994 DOUBLE DOUBLE SHIELD

Manchester United 2   Blackburn Rovers 0

An Eric Cantona penalty and a goal from Paul Ince gave the 1993–94 Double-winning Manchester United a 2–0 victory over the 1993–94 Premier League runners-up at Wembley Stadium. It was United's second successive Charity Shield triumph, equalling the feat they first achieved in 1956 and 1957.

15

1978 SIR STANLEY GUEST OF HONOUR AT UNITED

As part of the club's Centenary celebrations Manchester United held a gala dinner at the Piccadilly Hotel in Manchester. Among the guests was Sir Stanley Rous, the former President of FIFA, who paid tribute to the many legends who had played for United since their creation as Newton Heath Lancashire & Yorkshire Railway in 1878.

1987 NORMAN AT THE DOUBLE

Southampton 2   Manchester United 2

United visited The Dell for a First Division game and drew 2–2 (scorer: Norman Whiteside 2). Viv Anderson and Brian McClair made their Manchester United debuts in the game.

> **McCLAIR, Brian** *(Forward 1987–98) – debut in the above game.*
> *Appearances: FL/PL: 296 (59), goals 88 FAC: 38 (7), goals 14 FLC: 44 (1), goals 19 EUR: 18 (6), goals 6 TOTAL: 398 (73) apps, 127 goals.*

> **ANDERSON, Vivian Alexander** *(Full-back 1987–91) – debut in the above game.*
> *Appearances: FL: 50 (4), goals 2 FAC: 7, goals 1 FLC: 6 (1), goals 1 TOTAL: 64 (5) apps, 4 goals.*

2007 TEVEZ DEBUT AS RONALDO SEES RED

Portsmouth 1   Manchester United 1

Carlos Tevez made his Manchester United debut in this Premiership encounter at Fratton Park, which ended 1–1 (scorer: Paul Scholes). Both sides finished the game with 10 men. United took the lead after 15 minutes when Tevez set up Paul Scholes who rifled home a superb drive from 25 yards. However, the home side drew level when Benjani guided a well-taken header past Edwin van der Sar. Portsmouth's Sulley Muntari got his marching orders from referee Steve Bennett following a second yellow card, earned for a late tackle on Michael Carrick, while Cristiano Ronaldo was given a straight red after pushing his forehead on to Richard Hughes's forehead. It was United's second successive draw in their opening two games of the 2007–08 season. Scholes's goal was his 96th in the Premier League, making him United's all-time leading Premier League scorer (Ruud van Nistelrooy scored 95). Ryan Giggs was on 93 Premier League goals and just two short of a century of League goals.

16

1991 UNITED HAND IN RESIGNATION

Manchester United wrote to the Football League to announce their resignation from English football's top flight. However, the Reds were not alone in their action since the other 21 members of the First Division all tendered their resignations just as the 1991–92 campaign, which was the last season prior to the creation of the FA Premier League, was about to begin without a Committee to oversee the League.

1994 EDWARDS ATTACKS PFA

Gordon Taylor, the chief executive of the Professional Footballers Association, came under fire from United's chief executive Martin Edwards, after Taylor's claim that the plethora of foreign players in the English game was detrimental to national interests.

17

1963 FA CHARITY SHIELD AT GOODISON PARK

Everton 4   Manchester United 0
This was United's worst-ever defeat in a match with a major trophy at stake.

1983 BUCHAN'S TESTIMONIAL

Manchester United 2   Aberdeen 2
Aberdeen visited Old Trafford to provide the competition for Manchester United in Martin Buchan's testimonial match. The game ended in an entertaining 2–2 draw. For a decade Martin Buchan was unquestionably Manchester United's most influential player. A cool and cultured centre-half with a real presence both on and off the pitch, he was captain for six years during the 1970s, leading United to the Second Division title in 1974–75, FA Cup runners-up in 1975–76 and FA Cup glory in 1976–77. The stylish Buchan began his career at Aberdeen as a schoolboy before signing as a professional in August 1966. His progress at

Pittodrie was rapid and, aged just 20, he was handed the captain's armband. As the Dons' captain he led the team to victory in the 1970 Scottish Cup final, the youngest player ever to do so. On 29 February 1972 Frank O'Farrell signed Buchan for £125,000, the club's record signing at the time. However, United were already heading in the wrong direction when the young Scot arrived and were relegated to Division Two at the end of the 1973–74 season. 'I wasn't happy about relegation, but I decided to stay and help the club back into the First Division,' he later explained. United walked away with the Division Two title in 1974–75 and when he captained United to a 2–1 FA Cup final win over Liverpool at Wembley in 1977 he became the first man to captain a side to both English and Scottish FA Cup success. In addition to his 456 appearances for United over 11 years, scoring four goals, he played 34 times for Scotland, including two World Cup final tournaments in 1974 and 1978. He was without doubt one of the classiest and most gifted defenders Old Trafford has ever seen. His brother George also played for United.

1996 BECKHAM'S LONG DISTANCE STRIKE

Wimbledon 0   Manchester United 3
Manchester United, the reigning champions, and double Double winners, began the 1996–97 season in fine form with a 3–0 win over Wimbledon at Selhurst Park, the London club's rented home. David Beckham scored a sensational goal from his own half, a 57-yard wonder strike. Eric Cantona and Denis Irwin also scored. It was the longest goal in FA Premier League history at the time.

18

1962 HAIL THE KING

Manchester United 2   West Bromwich Albion 2
As soon as Matt Busby learned that the former Huddersfield Town and Manchester City striker Denis Law was unsettled in Italy he had no hesitation in setting a new Manchester United record transfer fee by splashing out £115,000 on AS Torino's Scottish international striker. It was the first time a British club had paid a six-figure sum for a player. Law made an immediate impact, scoring on his debut for the Reds in a 2–2 First Division draw with West Bromwich Albion at Old Trafford (David Herd also scored). This was the first of 237 goals The King scored in the red of United, followed by his famous trademark goal celebration of arm raised in the air, hand clutching the cuff of his jersey, finger pointing at the sky. It was a celebration copied up and down the country by thousands of would-be footballers in their school playgrounds.

Law's journey to Old Trafford followed a long and winding road. He began his career at Huddersfield in 1955 under manager Bill Shankly and became the Yorkshire club's youngest League debutant aged 16 on 24 December 1956 in their 2–0 Second Division win over Notts County. He signed for Manchester City for a British record fee of £55,000 in 1960 and 15 months later became the first £100,000 footballer when Torino secured his precious goalscoring ability. However, his Italian honeymoon lasted only a year before he returned to English football with United. When he arrived at Old Trafford on 12 July 1962, Law was already an established international for Scotland. Indeed, he was first capped by his country at the age of 18 by the then Scotland boss Matt Busby.

In his first season with United he helped the club to their third FA Cup success, scoring in the final, a 3–1 win over Leicester City. The following season, 1963–64, he scored 46 goals in 41 games and was named European Player of the Year in May 1964. He was United's top scorer again as the Reds won League titles in 1965 and 1967 but, devastatingly, injury deprived him of a place in the 1968 European Cup final side. Law was recuperating in a Manchester hospital following an operation on his injured knee as his mate George Best was running rings around Benfica on that historic night at Wembley. The following day, Matt Busby and the United team visited him in hospital with the coveted trophy. After the 1967–68 season the great United side of the 1960s was gradually beginning to break up and no longer capable of achieving its former highs. After Sir Matt Busby stepped down as manager things started to go wrong for United on and off the pitch. Wilf McGuinness, Frank O'Farrell and Tommy Docherty all followed the great man into the United manager's hot seat but none was capable of replacing him. Law was still at United after the other two members of their Holy Trinity, George Best and Bobby Charlton, had left.

During the summer of 1973 Denis was on holiday, visiting family in Aberdeen, when he learned that Docherty no longer wanted him at the club and so he rejoined Manchester City on a free transfer in July of that year. The final goal of his career came towards the end of the infamous Manchester derby match at Old Trafford on 27 April 1974 when his back-heeled shot gave Manchester City victory and effectively sealed United's relegation to the Second Division. This touch was his final one in League football as he asked to be substituted immediately, cutting a forlorn figure as he left the field, mobbed by invading Reds. Denis later spoke about this incident, admitting, 'I have seldom felt so depressed as I did that weekend.' He retired from football after the 1974 World Cup finals in West Germany where he made the last of his 55 appearances for Scotland, having scored a record 30 goals, an achievement he shares with Kenny Dalglish. He also held the record for the most FA Cup goals, 40, before it was passed by Ian Rush in 1996. His great friend George Best described him as: 'Up there with the all-time greats. Electric. As a bloke and as a pal he's different class.' Thousands of United fans will echo those sentiments. Fittingly, a statue of Denis stands on the Stretford End concourse as a lasting monument to his impact on Old Trafford, a deserved tribute to one of United's true living legends. The ultimate goalscorer, his flair, spirit and genuine love for the game made him a hero of a generation and he revelled in the nickname 'The King'. His Old Trafford reign lasted for 13 years and he is the club's second highest goalscorer behind Bobby Charlton.

LAW, Denis (Forward 1962–73) – debut in the above game.
Appearances: FL: 305 (4), goals 171 FAC: 44 (2), goals 34 FLC: 11, goals 3
EUR: 33, goals 28 TOTAL: 398 (6) apps, 237 goals.

1989 EDWARDS SELLS UNITED FOR £20M

A statement was released to the London Stock Exchange stating that Manchester United Football Club had been sold for £20m in what was the biggest ever takeover deal in British football history. After 25 years of the Edwards family being in charge of United, chairman Martin Edwards agreed to sell his majority share in the club for a reported £10m although he would remain at Old Trafford as chief executive. Mr Edwards had previously refused to entertain a £10m bid for the club from the newspaper magnate Robert Maxwell. The statement confirmed that the new man at the helm of the world's most famous football club was Michael Knighton, a property tycoon based on the Isle of Man. Martin Edwards had assumed control of Manchester United following the death of his father on 26 February 1980. The new plans for the club included a cash injection of £10m by Mr Knighton to improve facilities at Old Trafford, second only in capacity in England to Wembley Stadium. Mr Knighton's proposed takeover of United subsequently collapsed and he ended up purchasing Carlisle United.

19

1950 ALLEN CLEAN SHEET

Manchester United 1   Fulham 0
Manchester United signed Reg Allen from Queens Park Rangers in June 1950 and their new goalkeeper made his United debut in their 1–0 win over Fulham (scorer: Stan Pearson) on the opening day of the 1950–51 season.

ALLEN, Reginald Arthur 'Reg' (Goalkeeper 1950–52) – debut in the above game.
Appearances: FL: 75, goals 0 FAC: 5, goals 0 TOTAL: 80 apps, 0 goals.

1989 WEBB'S SCORING DEBUT

Manchester United 4   Arsenal 1
Manchester United hammered the reigning First Division champions Arsenal on the opening day of the 1989–90 season. Goals from Steve Bruce, Mark Hughes, Brian McClair and their new debutant Neil Webb gave the Reds a comfortable 4–1 victory over the Gunners at Old Trafford. Webb scored only 11 goals for

United in 110 appearances (5 as substitute) following his high-profile transfer from Nottingham Forest, but, quite remarkably, he scored on his debut in every competition he played in for United, including the FA Cup, League Cup and European Cup-Winners' Cup.

1990 SIX MONTHS EACH FOR BITTER RIVALS

Manchester United 1   Liverpool 1

Manchester United and Liverpool shared the Charity Shield for six months each. Clayton Blackmore scored United's goal in front of a crowd of 66,558 at Wembley. Denis Irwin, a summer signing from Oldham Athletic, made the first of his 529 appearances for the Reds in this game.

1995 'YOU CAN'T WIN ANYTHING WITH KIDS'

Aston Villa 3   Manchester United 1

During the summer of 1995 the knives were out for Alex Ferguson after he was personally and heavily criticised for 'allowing' three of Manchester United's star players to leave without splashing out in the transfer market to strengthen what many pundits considered to be a depleted squad. Blackburn Rovers had pipped United to the 1994–95 Premiership title on the final day of the season; needing a win to secure their third consecutive Championship crown, the Reds drew 1–1 away to West Ham United while Blackburn went down 2–1 to Liverpool at Anfield. But it was Kenny Dalglish, back at the ground where he helped Liverpool dominate English and European football during the 1970s, who was left smiling as he held aloft the trophy. United had also lost the 1995 FA Cup final, 1–0 to Everton. Many United fans had no doubt that what proved to be a trophy-less season would have seen United win the Premiership and retain the FA Cup had Eric Cantona not been given a nine-month ban in January 1995. Paul Ince was the first through the Old Trafford exit and joined Inter Milan for £7.5m. Mark Hughes followed Ince out the door; many fans were shocked when Sparky was sold to Chelsea for a bargain £1.5m after it had emerged that he had not signed the contract he had been offered by the club in January 1995. Two key players, linchpins of United's first Premiership success in 1993 and the Double in 1994, had now departed with no players lined up by United to replace them. Within days, Andrei Kanchelskis was sold to Everton and, while many fans were left scratching their heads wondering if United were about to implode, the one man who did not panic as his empire appeared to be crumbling bit-by-bit before his own eyes was Alex Ferguson.

Along with Brian Kidd and the United youth team coaches, Ferguson knew he had a crop of young players, nicknamed 'Fergie's Fledglings', who could all make it as top professionals and now he had to let his young charges loose to express themselves. The youngsters included Gary Neville, Phil Neville, David Beckham, Paul Scholes and Nicky Butt, while the equally youthful and talented

Ryan Giggs was already an established first-team player. On the opening day of the 1995–96 season United travelled to Villa Park and were soundly beaten 3–1 (scorer: David Beckham). The media had a field day at Fergie's expense and took great pleasure in mocking him. When highlights of the game were shown that Saturday evening on BBC's *Match of the Day* the show's anchorman, Des Lynam, remarked: 'United were scarcely recognisable from the team we've known over the past couple of seasons. What's going on do you feel?' Alan Hansen famously replied: 'You can't win anything with kids … he's got to buy players, it's as simple as that.' How wrong the eight-times First Division winner was. Fergie's Fledglings won their next five matches and, although they found themselves 14 points behind runaway leaders Newcastle United in early 1996, that good run of wins, inspired by the talismanic French genius of Eric Cantona (he returned from suspension on 1 October 1995), continued when United beat the Geordies 1–0 at St James' Park (scorer: Cantona). The Reds marched on to win the Premiership, confirmation coming on the final day of the season thanks to a 3–0 away win (scorers: David May, Andy Cole, Ryan Giggs) over former United hero Bryan Robson's Middlesbrough. Six days later the 'kids' ran out at Wembley to face Liverpool in the 1996 FA Cup final and sealed the club's second Double in three years with a 1–0 win, the goal coming from – well, who else? – Cantona. 'Are you watching, Alan Hansen?' echoed around Wembley Stadium while many other football pundits had their critical comments about Fergie well and truly rammed back down their throats.

2007 OL' BLUE EYES IS BACK IN TOWN

Manchester City 1   Manchester United 0
Sven Goran Eriksson tasted success in his first ever Manchester derby when his City side beat United 1–0 at the City of Manchester Stadium. United completely dominated possession but could not find their way past the City defence or Caspar Schmeichel, son of the legendary Peter Schmeichel, in the Blues' goal. It was the 148th competitive Manchester Derby, (the 21st in the Premier League). United went into the game without the injured Wayne Rooney and the suspended Cristiano Ronaldo, the first time they had started a competitive game without either player in the team. United have won three times as many Manchester Premier League derbies as City while Sir Alex Ferguson's record in his 31 Manchester derbies is won 16, drawn 9 and lost 6.

The game marked Owen Hargreaves's competitive debut for his new club, and was United's worst start to the season since August 1992.

20

1966 CRUISE CONTROL

Manchester United 5   West Bromwich Albion 3
After 22 minutes of this First Division game at Old Trafford, Manchester United were in cruise control leading the bewildered Baggies 5–0 with goals from Denis Law (2), George Best, David Herd and Nobby Stiles. United then took their foot off the accelerator and the visitors pulled three goals back to make the score an acceptable 5–3 in United's favour.

1971 HOME SIDE BEATS ARSENAL AWAY

Manchester United 3   Arsenal 1
Manchester United's first home game of the 1971–72 season was a First Division match against Arsenal. However, because the FA had ordered United to close Old Trafford for their opening two 'home' games of the 1971–72 season, the Reds had to entertain the Gunners at Anfield, Liverpool. United won 3–1 with goals from Bobby Charlton, Alan Gowling and Brian Kidd. The gates to Old Trafford were locked following a knife-throwing incident during United's 1–0 home win (scorer: Brian Kidd) over Newcastle United on 27 February 1971.

1977 LOU GIVES BLUES THE BLUES

Birmingham City 1   Manchester United 4
On the opening day of the 1977–78 season Lou Macari scored a hat-trick for Manchester United in a 4–1 win over Birmingham City at St Andrews. Gordon Hill also scored for the Reds.

1983 ROBBO BRACE LANDS SHIELD AT LAST

Manchester United 2   Liverpool 0
Two goals by Bryan Robson secured United's first outright victory in the Charity Shield since 1957. Arthur Graham made his debut for United in this game, and would make 52 appearances in total, scoring 7 goals.

2006 AN EVER-GROWING OLD TRAFFORD

Manchester United 5   Fulham 1
On the opening day of the 2006–07 Premiership season Manchester United hammered Fulham 5–1 at Old Trafford with goals from Wayne Rooney (2), Cristiano Ronaldo, Louis Saha and an own goal courtesy of Ian Pearce. The

game marked the first time that Ronaldo and Rooney teamed up since Portugal knocked England out of the 2006 World Cup finals in Germany, and their rapport on the pitch answered all those critics who had said they would never be able to play together. With United's new Quadrants fully open, the crowd of 75,115 set a new all-time Premier League record at the time, which only Manchester United themselves can better since the second largest Premiership stadium, Arsenal's Emirates, has a maximum capacity of 60,432.

21

1968 RYAN'S A WINNER

Manchester United 1   Coventry City 0
Jimmy Ryan was the unlikely goalscorer in this early season contest at Old Trafford. He was unable to establish himself in United's star-studded line-up of the time, making just 27 appearances in five seasons. This was his last goal for the club.

1999 IT'S ALL ABOUT BELIEF, AGAIN

Manchester United's 1999 FA Cup final song, *Lift It High (All About Belief)*, re-entered the British singles chart almost three months after it was originally released and reached No.75, spending a solitary week in the singles chart. It had achieved its highest position of No.11 after six weeks in the UK singles charts when first released.

22

1999 THE TWELVE SECONDS MAN

Arsenal 1   Manchester United 2
Nick Culkin made his debut in goal for Manchester United in a 2–1 away win over Arsenal (scorer: Roy Keane 2) in the FA Premier League. When the final whistle blew a spotless Culkin did not require a shower as he had only been on the field for 12 seconds. He never played for Manchester United again and thus holds the record for the shortest ever career for a United player.

2007 HEINZE'S REAL DEAL

Manchester United's Gabriel Heinze agreed to join Real Madrid. The Argentinian international defender was bought to replace the veteran Brazilian left-back

Roberto Carlos, and would join former United team-mate Ruud van Nistelrooy at Estadio Santiago Bernabeu. Meanwhile, United teenager Darron Gibson became the third Red in 12 months to win an international cap before starting a Premier League game for United when he played for the Republic of Ireland in their 4–0 win over Denmark. Gibson came on at half-time for Andy Reid. In September 2006, Jonny Evans played in Northern Ireland's memorable 3–2 win over Spain at Windsor Park, while goalkeeper Ben Foster made his England bow (also against Spain) in February 2007.

Evans and Foster had never tasted any first-team action prior to being capped by their country, while Gibson had made his United debut as a 76th-minute substitute in United's 2005 Carling Cup tie against Barnet.

23

1966 CENTURION LAWMAN

Everton 1   Manchester United 2
Denis Law scored twice for Manchester United to reach 100 goals for the club. His two strikes helped United beat Everton 2–1 at Goodison Park in the First Division in front of 60,657 fans. Amazingly, it had taken The King just 139 games to reach his century for the Reds. The goals were also his third and fourth in the opening two games of the new season.

2006 CARRICK PULLS ON A RED SHIRT

Charlton Athletic 0   Manchester United 3
Following his transfer from Tottenham Hotspur, Michael Carrick made his official debut for Manchester United, coming on as a substitute in their 3–0 Premiership win over Charlton Athletic at The Valley (scorers: Darren Fletcher, Louis Saha, Ole Gunnar Solskjaer). Carrick had played for the Reds in the pre-season Amsterdam Tournament. A player with superb vision, lightning quick feet and a broad-ranging repertoire of passes, Michael Carrick settled well into the heart of the United midfield and proved himself to be the ideal partner to play alongside Paul Scholes following the loss of Roy Keane. Carrick even accepted Sir Alex's offer to take over the No.16 shirt so famously worn by the Irish midfield general for 13 years. Carrick's and Scholes's playmaking talents were key to the free-flowing football that won United a ninth Premiership title. Carrick began his career at West Ham United, winning an FA Youth Cup winners' medal with them in 1999, but when the Hammers failed to win promotion to the Premiership at the end of the 2003–04 season he moved across London to join Tottenham Hotspur for £2.75m. At White Hart Lane the young English midfielder blossomed playing Spurs' traditional free-

flowing football, and after spending two seasons with Tottenham (2 goals from 64 games), Sir Alex persuaded him to join United in a deal worth £14m (although this subsequently rose to £18.6m).

24

1949 WELCOME HOME

Manchester United 3 Bolton Wanderers 1

Having rented Manchester City's Maine Road ground for the previous eight seasons, Manchester United finally welcomed football back to Old Trafford for their opening home game of the 1949–50 season. Lancashire rivals Bolton Wanderers provided the opposition and United sent the crowd of 41,748 away happy with a 3–1 win (scorers: Charlie Mitten, Jack Rowley, o.g.). The game was United's first Division One game at Old Trafford in almost 10 years.

1984 WE'LL MEET AGAIN

Manchester United 1 Watford 1

Gordon Strachan, Ron Atkinson's recent acquisition from Alex Ferguson's all-conquering Aberdeen side, made a scoring debut for Manchester United in this 1–1 First Division draw at Old Trafford. Atkinson brought Strachan to United for £600,000 to replace the outgoing Ray Wilkins, who joined AC Milan for £1.5m. The Scottish international was still at United when Alex Ferguson replaced Atkinson in November 1986.

> STRACHAN, Gordon David *(Midfielder 1984–9) – debut in the above game.*
> *Appearances: FL: 155 (5), goals 33 FAC: 22, goals 2 FLC: 12 (1), goals 1 EUR: 6, goals 2 TOTAL: 195 (6) apps, 38 goals.*

25

1996 OLE, OLE, OLE

Manchester United 2 Blackburn Rovers 2

Ole Gunnar Solskjaer made his debut for United and scored within six minutes of coming on as a substitute, the other scorer being Jordi Cruyff. The United faithful took the young Norwegian, affectionately nicknamed 'The Baby Faced Assassin', immediately to their hearts and his exploits in the red of United will be forever remembered. Solskjaer found the net 17 more times in the Premiership in his first season at Old Trafford, helping United reclaim the Premiership title, their third in four years.

SOLSKJAER, Ole Gunner (Forward 1996–2007) – debut in the above game.
Appearances: PL: 151 (84), goals 91 FAC: 15 (15), goals 8 FLC: 8 (3), goals 7
EUR: 37 (45), goals 20 TOTAL: 216 (150) apps, 126 goals.

26

1961 ROVERS HIT FOR SIX

Manchester United 6   Blackburn Rovers 1
United had their best win of the season against local rivals Blackburn, putting six past the unlucky keeper. The scorers on the day were Herd (2), Quixall (2), Charlton and Setters. New signing David Herd took his total to three goals in three games and would end the season as United's top scorer (a feat he would repeat in 1965–66) with 17.

2007 HARGREAVES AND TEVEZ MAKE THEIR OLD TRAFFORD BOW

Manchester United 1   Tottenham Hotspur 0
Manchester United claimed their first win of the 2007–08 Premier League campaign in yet another game wrapped in controversy against their London opponents. Owen Hargreaves and Carlos Tevez made their United Old Trafford debuts. The visitors, with one win at Old Trafford in the previous 30 years, had two penalty appeals turned down. However, Nani won the game for the Reds with a lightning strike from 25 yards that seemed to shave Carlos Tevez on the way past as Paul Robinson in the Spurs goal was well beaten.

27

1921 TOFFEES GIVE UNITED PLENTY TO CHEW ON

Everton 5   Manchester United 0
Manchester United lost 5–0 to Everton at Goodison Park on the opening day of the 1921–22 season, the club's worst-ever opening-day defeat.

1938 LAST SEASON BEFORE WWII

Middlesbrough 3   Manchester United 1
Manchester United lost the opening game of their 1938–39 season 3–1 away to Middlesbrough at Ayresome Park (scorer: John Smith). Charles Craven made

his debut in the game, the last season of regular football prior to the outbreak of World War II.

CRAVEN, Charles 'Charlie' (Forward 1938–9) – debut in the above game. Appearances: FL: 11, goals 2 TOTAL: 11 apps, 2 goals.

1960 ONLY ABANDONED DERBY

With the score at 2–2 (scorers: Alex Dawson, Dennis Viollet) the referee abandoned the game due to a waterlogged pitch at Maine Road, the only Manchester derby to be abandoned. Denis Law scored one of the City goals. When the game was replayed on 4 March 1961, United won 3–1 with Alex Dawson among the scorers again.

28

1982 A HISTORIC SHIRT

Manchester United 3   Birmingham City 0
Not only was this the opening game of the 1982–83 First Division season but it was also the first time Manchester United took to the pitch for a League game with a sponsorship logo adorning their shirts, namely that of the consumer electronics company Sharp. Goals from Steve Coppell, Kevin Moran and Frank Stapleton gave the new-look United a comfortable 3–0 victory over the Blues at Old Trafford.

2007 OLE HANGS UP HIS BOOTS

Ole Gunnar Solskjaer's father announced that the Manchester United legend had decided to retire from football. Ole, already assured of his legendary status in United's history books after netting the winner in the 1999 UEFA Champions League final, joined the Reds from Molde in 1996 for a modest £1.5m. During his Old Trafford career he won six Premier League Championship winners' medals and two FA Cup winners' medals plus the UEFA Champions League. Despite battling a niggling knee injury for the past four seasons, the 34-year-old helped United reclaim the Premiership crown in 2006–07, scoring 11 times. The former Norwegian international striker made 366 appearances for United, scoring 126 times including a goal on his debut as a substitute against Blackburn Rovers. Ole's final game for the Reds was the 2007 FA Cup final defeat to Chelsea on 19 May when he came on as substitute in extra-time at the new Wembley. In 2006 he was appointed an Ambassador for United and helped coach the youth team.

29

1908 INAUGURAL SHIELD WINNERS

Manchester United 4   Queens Park Rangers 0
Almost four months after the two sides had drawn 1–1 at the same venue, Manchester United put their name in the history books by winning the inaugural FA Charity Shield with this comprehensive 4–0 victory in the capital at Stamford Bridge (scorers: Sandy Turnbull 3, George Wall). In 1909 the Shield was contested between the Northern League champions, Manchester United, and the Southern League champions, Queens Park Rangers, in contrast to the Premiership champions versus the FA Cup winners, which is the custom today.

1956 BLOOMING VIOLLET

Manchester United 3   Preston North End 2
Dennis Viollet scored a hat-trick in Manchester United's 3–2 First Division home win over Preston North End.

1981 BIG RON WOE

Coventry City 2   Manchester United 1
Ron Atkinson's first season in charge of United got off to a bad start when his side went down 2–1 at Highfield Road to Coventry City on the opening day of the 1981–82 season (scorer: Lou Macari).

30

1919 DEBUT FOR REDS' ONLY EVER PLAYER-MANAGER

Derby County 1   Manchester United 1
Clarence George 'Lal' Hilditch, John 'Jack' Silcock and Joseph 'Joe' Waters Spence all made their United debuts in a 1–1 draw away at Derby County (scorer: Wilfred Woodcock) in the First Division. The trio would go on to become United legends and loyal servants, Hilditch (1919–32) making 322 appearances, Silcock (1919–34) making 449 appearances and Spence (1919–33) making 510 appearances. Hilditch holds the unique distinction of being the only player-manager in the history of Manchester United, October 1926–April 1927. Sadly, despite their commitment, dedication and professionalism, none of them won any silverware during their Old Trafford careers.

HILDITCH, Clarence George 'Lal' (Half-back 1919–32) – debut in the above game.
  Appearances: FL: 301, goals 7 FAC: 21, goals 0 TOTAL: 322 apps, 7 goals.
SILCOCK, John 'Jack' (Full-back 1919–34) – debut in the above game.
  Appearances: FL: 423, goals 2 FAC: 26, goals 0 TOTAL: 449 apps, 2 goals.
SPENCE, Joseph Waters 'Joe' (Forward 1919–33) – debut in the above game.
  Appearances: FL: 481, goals 158 FAC: 29, goals 10 TOTAL: 510 apps, 168 goals.

1941 LUCKY 13 FOR WARTIME REDS

Manchester United 13   New Brighton Tower 1

Manchester United completely annihilated New Brighton Tower on the opening day of the Football League Northern Section (First Championship) season. United's prolific striker with the thunderbolt left-foot shot, Jack 'Gunner' Rowley, hit 7 of United's haul of 13 goals with John Smith adding a hat-trick along with strikes from Billy Bryant (2) and Charlie Mitten. It was United's biggest ever wartime league victory while at the end of the First Championship they finished fourth in the division.

31

1946 DELANEY AND MITTEN MAKE UNITED DEBUTS

Manchester United 2   Grimsby Town 1

Matt Busby's first signing, Jimmy Delaney from Glasgow Celtic, made his Football League debut for Manchester United in this 2–1 First Division win over Grimsby Town at Maine Road. The goals were scored by Jack Rowley and another player who was making his Manchester United debut in the game, Charlie Mitten. The game marked the opening day of the 1946–47 season, the first League football played since the end of the 1938–39 season.

DELANEY, James 'Jimmy' (Forward 1946–51) – debut in the above game.
  Appearances: FL: 164, goals 25 FAC: 19, goals 3 TOTAL: 184 apps, 28 goals.
MITTEN, Charles 'Charlie' (Forward 1946–50) – debut in the above game.
  Appearances: FL: 142, goals 50 FAC: 19, goals 11 TOTAL: 162 apps, 61 goals.

1985 BARNES ON TARGET

Nottingham Forest 1   Manchester United 3

Peter Barnes made it a Manchester United debut to remember, scoring for the Reds in their 3–1 First Division win over Nottingham Forest at the City Ground. Mark Hughes and Frank Stapleton also found the net for United.

BARNES, Simon Peter (Forward 1985–7) – debut in the above game.
  Appearances: FL: 19 (1), goals 2 FLC: 5, goals 2 TOTAL: 24 (1) apps, 4 goals.

SEPTEMBER

1

1900 ALF SCHOFIELD'S DEBUT

Glossop North End 1   Newton Heath 0

Alf Schofield made his Newton Heath debut on the opening day of the 1900–01 season in this 1–0 Division Two loss away to Glossop. Schofield was signed by the Heathens from Everton as a replacement for Billy Bryant and stayed with the club, through their name change to Manchester United in 1902, for seven years although he knew he would lose his place at inside-right when the legendary Billy Meredith arrived on New Year's Day 1907. He retired shortly after Meredith's arrival, having made just 10 appearances during his final season at the club, 1906–07. During his time with the Heathens/United, Schofield lived in Liverpool and played cricket in Blackburn.

> SCHOFIELD, Alfred John 'Alf' (*Forward 1900–07*) – *debut in the above game.*
> *Appearances: FL: 157, goals 30 FAC: 22, goals 5   TOTAL: 179 apps, 35 goals.*

1902 WHEN GREEN AND GOLD TURNED RED

When Newton Heath became Manchester United on 26 April 1902 the name was not the only thing they changed. They also changed the colour of their kit from the shirts with green and gold halves and white shorts to red shirts with white shorts, the colours they still use today. They wore their new kit for the first time in a friendly against Preston North End five days before the start of the 1902–03 First Division season.

1959

Michael 'Mike' Duxbury (Full-back 1980–90) was born in Accrington, Lancashire.

1966 STEPNEY MAKES SWITCH

Alex Stepney joined Chelsea from Millwall for £52,000 in June 1966 but after only three months at Stamford Bridge he made the switch to Old Trafford, Matt Busby paying a then world-record fee for a goalkeeper of £55,000.

2

1893 HEATHENS CHUCKED OFF HOLY LAND

Newton Heath 3   Burnley 2

Newton Heath opened their 1893–94 First Division campaign with a 3–2 home win over Burnley thanks to a hat-trick from Alfred Farman. However, whereas they played their inaugural season in the Football League (1892–93) at their North Road home, this campaign was played at a new home, Bank Street. The ground at North Road was owned by the Manchester Cathedral authorities and midway through season 1892–93 the Executive Board of the Church group issued a decision declaring that the Heathens would no longer be allowed to charge the general public to visit Church property. Since admission charges to home games were essential to the future of the club, the Heathens objected and were served with a notice to quit. The directors of Newton Heath found a piece of muddy land at Bank Street where they laid a pitch and built temporary fencing just in time for the beginning of the 1893–94 season.

1905 SAGAR OFF TO A FLIER

Manchester United 5   Bristol City 1

Charles Sagar became the first man to score a hat-trick for United on his debut, a feat that was not repeated for 99 years until Wayne Rooney did so in 2004. In his shortlived career, Sagar scored 24 goals in 33 games, including another hat-trick later that season.

1907 PLAYING LIKE CHAMPIONS

Aston Villa 1   Manchester United 4

Manchester United began the 1907–08 First Division season in sparkling form beating Aston Villa 4–1 (scorers: Billy Meredith 2, James Bannister, George Wall) in their opening game played at Villa Park. Their good form continued all season long and United clinched their first ever Championship title at the end of the League campaign. Ironically, Aston Villa finished runners-up.

1912 LIKE FATHER LIKE SON

Woolwich Arsenal 0   Manchester United 0

Manchester United signed Robert Beale from Norwich City in May 1912 for £275 after having placed two of their goalkeepers, Henry Moger and Hugh Edmonds, on the transfer list in May 1912. Beale made his United debut in this 0–0 First Division draw with Woolwich Arsenal at their then home, the Manor

Ground, Plumstead. In May 1938 United signed Robert's son, Walter, from Tunbridge Wells Rangers who like his father was a goalkeeper. However, Beale Jnr stayed at Old Trafford for a only single season without ever making a first team appearance.

BEALE, Robert Hughes (Goalkeeper 1912–15) – debut in the above game.
Appearances: FL: 105, goals 0 FAC: 7, goals 0 TOTAL: 112 apps, 0 goals.

1931 THE LOWEST GATE

Manchester United 2   Southampton 3
In the opening home game of their 1931–32 Division Two campaign, Manchester United lost 3–2 to Southampton at Old Trafford (scorers: John Ferguson, William Johnston). Only 3,507 bothered to attend the game, United's lowest Old Trafford gate.

1939 IT'S WAR

Charlton Athletic 2   Manchester United 0
Manchester United lost 2–0 to Charlton Athletic in their third game of the 1939–40 season with Beaumont Asquith and Allenby Chilton both making their debuts for the Reds. However, it proved to be Asquith's only game for United because when the team arrived back in Manchester from London the following day, Britain had declared war on Hitler's Germany. Chilton on the other hand went on to serve the club until 1955. He arrived at Old Trafford in November 1938 from Liverpool after they agreed to cancel his amateur contract at Anfield. When war was declared Chilton enlisted in the Durham Light Infantry (he was born in County Durham) and was twice wounded, during the Normandy D-Day landings and in the battle for Caen. Amazingly, in April 1944, just two months before that battle begun, Chilton had helped Charlton Athletic win the League Cup South final, and Charlton were the only team he had played against competitively for Manchester United up to that time.

ASQUITH, Beaumont (Forward 1939–40) – debut in the above game.
Appearances: FL: 1, goals 0 TOTAL: 1 app, 0 goals.
CHILTON, Allenby (Half-back 1939–55) – debut in the above game.
Appearances: FL: 352, goals 3 FAC: 37, goals 0 TOTAL: 391 apps, 3 goals.

1992 BAD BREAK FOR DUBLIN

Manchester United 1   Crystal Palace 0
This game marked Dion Dublin's full Old Trafford debut but unluckily for the new recruit from Cambridge United, he broke his leg in Manchester United's 1–0 victory (scorer: Mark Hughes).

1998 BUSBY BABE LOSES HIS BATTLE AGAINST CANCER

Former Busby Babe and a survivor of the 1958 Munich Air Disaster, Jackie Blanchflower, died at the age of 65 after a long battle against cancer. Jackie was born in Belfast on 7 March 1933 and made his debut for United away to Liverpool on 24 November 1951. In 1954 he made the first of his 12 appearances for Northern Ireland, making his debut alongside his famous brother, the Tottenham Hotspur and Northern Ireland captain Danny Blanchflower. He won two League titles, scoring 25 goals, with United before the plane crash brought his football career to a premature end (rib cage damage). Jackie was affectionately nicknamed 'Twiggy' by his fellow Busby Babes, eight of whom sadly lost their lives in Munich.

3

1892 BAPTISMAL FIRE

Blackburn Rovers 4   Newton Heath 3
This game was the Heathens' first in the Football League but unfortunately their arrival was not greeted with a win, as they went down 4–3 to Blackburn Rovers at Rover's Ewood Park home. James Coupar, Robert Donaldson and Alfred Farman scored in this First Division game.

1921

John Aston Senior (Full-back 1946–54) was born in Prestwich, Manchester.

1963 TRACTOR BOYS PLOUGHED DOWN

Ipswich Town 2   Manchester United 7
Manchester United ran riot at Portman Road, beating Ipswich Town 7–2 in this First Division encounter. Denis Law scored a hat-trick with United's other goals coming from Phil Chisnall, Ian Moir, David Sadler and Maurice Setters.

1983 A GRAND DAY OUT

Stoke City 0   Manchester United 1
The most significant aspect of this 1–0 Division One win over Stoke City at the Victoria Ground was that Arnold Muhren's winning goal gave United their 1,000th victory in the top flight.

1992 AN EXPENSIVE MEDAL

The winners' medal Johnny Carey received when he captained Manchester United to FA Cup final glory in 1948 was sold at Christie's for £10,575.

4

1897 IMPS NO MATCH FOR HEATHENS
Newton Heath 5   Lincoln City 0
On the opening day of the 1897–98 Division Two season, Newton Heath hammered Lincoln City 5–0. Henry Boyd scored a hat-trick against the visiting Imps while William Bryant and Joe Cassidy also found the net.

1957 BABES PULL IN THE CROWDS
Everton 3   Manchester United 3
Manchester United drew 3–3 with Everton at Goodison Park in this First Division game, which attracted a crowd of 72,077, United's biggest post-war away League crowd and a record League attendance for a midweek game at the time. Johnny Berry, Dennis Viollet and Liam Whelan scored for the Busby Babes.

1960 THE BEST CUPPA
When 14-year-old George Best arrived at Old Trafford he was not allowed to sign for Manchester United as an apprentice due to Irish and Scottish League rules at the time. The two Football Associations had officially lodged a complaint with the English Football Association, claiming that the big clubs in England were poaching their best talent. So, George had to sign as an amateur and was only permitted to train with the club two days per week. On the other three week days the young Best worked as a clerk at the Manchester Ship Canal where his duties included making tea and carrying out various errands. George soon got fed-up in Manchester and packed his bags at Mrs Fullaway's house in Aycliffe Avenue, Chorlton-cum-Hardy, where he was in digs, and returned home to Belfast claiming he was homesick. Thankfully for United fans, Matt Busby persuaded George to return to Manchester a short time later. The rest, as they say, is history.

5

1903 THREE-QUARTERS OF A GOALKEEPER
Manchester United 2   Bristol City 2
Manchester United opened their 1902–03 League Division Two campaign with a home 2–2 draw against Bristol City (scorer: William Griffiths 2). The game

marked the debut of United's new goalkeeper, John Sutcliffe. Amazingly, Sutcliffe began his sporting life in Rugby Union and was good enough to play for England at three-quarter back against the New Zealand Maoris in 1889. However, when his club side Heckmondwike was suspended for alleged professionalism, Sutcliffe turned his attention to football and began his career as a centre-forward. Bolton switched him to goalkeeper after one particular game he played for their Reserves side. The opposing goalkeeper came out to clobber Sutcliffe only to run into a brick wall. The goalkeeper came off worse in the head-on collision as Sutcliffe picked him up off the pitch and threw him into the back of his net. After making 332 League appearances for the Trotters and playing in the 1894 FA Cup final (lost 4–1 to Notts County), he moved to Millwall Athletic in April 1902 aged 35 before joining United in May 1903. He left United in January 1905 but played on until he was 44 years old.

SUTCLIFFE, John William (Goalkeeper 1903–5) – debut in the above game.
Appearances: FL: 21, goals 0 FAC: 7, goals 0 TOTAL: 28 apps, 0 goals.

1956 WHELAN'S SUPER EIGHT

Chelsea 1   Manchester United 2
Manchester United, the reigning First Division champions, beat Chelsea 2–1 at Stamford Bridge with goals from Tommy Taylor and Liam Whelan. Whelan's goal sparked a golden run for the Irishman as he scored again in each of United's next seven League games, ending with his eighth goal in successive games in the 5–2 home loss to Everton on 20 October 1956. Whelan's other six goals came against Newcastle United (1–1 away), Sheffield Wednesday (4–1 home win), Manchester City (2–0 home win), Arsenal (2–1 away win), Charlton Athletic (4–2 home win) and Sunderland (3–1 away win). The hot streak was a club record that lasted almost half a century until bettered by Ruud van Nistelrooy.

6

1902 UNITED'S FIRST EVER GAME

Gainsborough Trinity 0   Manchester United 1
This game went down in the club's history as their first game under their new name, Manchester United, as they beat Gainsborough Trinity 1–0 away in Division Two. And Chas Richards firmly etched his name into the history books by becoming the first player to score a League goal for Manchester United, doing so on his debut for the club. This was his first and last League goal for United. Daniel Hurst and John Peddie also made their Manchester United debuts in the 1–0 win.

HURST, Daniel (Forward 1902–3) – debut in the above game.
Appearances: FL: 16, goals 4 FAC: 5, goals 0 TOTAL: 21 apps, 4 goals.
PEDDIE, John Hope 'Jack' (Forward 1902–3, 1904–7) – debut in the above game.
Appearances: FL: 112, goals 52 FAC: 9, goals 6 TOTAL: 121 apps, 58 goals.
RICHARDS, Chas (Forward 1902–3) – debut in the above game.
Appearances: FL: 8, goals 1 FAC: 3, goals 1 TOTAL: 11 apps, 2 goals.

1992 WHITE ROSE WILTING

Manchester United 2   Leeds United 0
Having lost out on the title in 1991–92, United were eager to make amends in the following campaign, and this early season victory over champions Leeds seemed to suggest they were on the right track, thanks to goals from Steve Bruce and Andrei Kanchelskis.

7

1907 REDS SOAR TO TOP

Manchester United 4   Liverpool 0
After beating Aston Villa away (4–1) in their opening game of the 1907–08 season Manchester United soundly beat Liverpool 4–0 at Clayton. Sandy Turnbull's first of four hat-tricks for the club and a goal from George Wall sent United to the top of the table.

1996 ERIC SLIPS UP

Leeds United 0   Manchester United 4
Eric Cantona uncharacteristically missed a penalty for Manchester United and it could not have given the opposing fans more pleasure as his spot-kick miss came against his former club Leeds United. However, the Reds still went on to hammer Leeds 4–0 at their Elland Road home thanks to an own goal and goals from Nicky Butt, Karel Poborsky and, of course, Eric himself. The next day Leeds United sacked their manager Howard Wilkinson, the man who signed Eric for Leeds and sold him to United. Wilkinson had guided the Yorkshire club to the last ever First Division Championship crown (1991–92, when Manchester United finished runners-up) and so remains the last English manager to win the title.

2007 MR AND MRS GIGGS

Ryan Giggs married his long-time partner Stacey Cooke at a private ceremony in Manchester, which was attended by close family and friends. The couple's two children, Liberty aged four and Zach aged one, were also present.

8

1934 MUTCH LUCK WITH 7

Manchester United 4   Barnsley 1

After going a goal down inside six minutes to Barnsley at Old Trafford in this Second Division encounter, United were inspired to victory by George Mutch. The former Scottish schoolboy international, signed by United from Arbroath in May 1934 for £800, scored a hat-trick in just seven minutes, finding the Barnsley net in the 24th, 26th and 30th minutes. Thomas Manley added United's fourth early in the second half.

1951 GUNNER'S HAT-TRICK OF HAT-TRICKS

Manchester United 4   Stoke City 2

Jack 'Gunner' Rowley scored his third hat-trick in 22 days in United's 4–2 home win over Stoke City played at Maine Road. Stan Pearson scored the other goal to notch-up United's 16th consecutive victory. Rowley's first hat-trick of the run came against West Bromwich Albion in a 3–3 draw on the opening day of the season, 18 August at The Hawthorns. His second was scored against Middlesbrough at home (Maine Road) in a 4–2 win (Stan Pearson also scored) on 22 August. The prolific striker also scored a goal against Newcastle United away, two away to Boro and two at home (Maine Road) against Stoke City in between. At his peak Rowley, like his equally prolific brother Arthur, was one of the most feared strikers in the country, great in the air and on the ground with a thunderbolt of a shot from his left foot. United signed Rowley for £3,000 in October 1937 from Bournemouth & Boscombe Athletic, where he scored 10 goals in 11 appearances. In his first full season at Old Trafford he helped United to a Second Division runners-up spot and a first return to Division One since 1931. He fought for his country during World War II and when a full League programme recommenced in 1946, Rowley resumed his career with United. He was a mainstay of the 1948 FA Cup-winning side (scoring twice in the final), one of Matt Busby's 'Famous Five' forward line alongside Jimmy Delaney, Johnny Morris, Stan Pearson and Charlie Mitten. In 1952 Gunner struck up a terrific alliance with the diminutive veteran Scotsman Jimmy Delaney and his 30 League goals helped Manchester United win the First Division Championship for the first time since 1911. In February 1955 he left United as Matt Busby was building his second great side at Old Trafford, the famous Busby Babes. Rowley also won six England caps, averaging a goal a game for his country.

1973 THE FIRST OF THE GREENHOFF BROTHERS

Ipswich Town 2   Manchester United 1

Brian Greenhoff joined Manchester United straight from school and made steady progress through the junior ranks at Old Trafford up until his debut in this 2–1 First Division loss to Ipswich Town at Portman Road (scorer: Trevor Anderson). He went on to win a Second Division Championship winners' medal with United in 1974–75, FA Cup runners-up medals in 1976 and 1979 plus an FA Cup winners' medal in 1977. In August 1979 Dave Sexton sold the versatile Greenhoff to Leeds United for £350,000. However, things did not work out for Brian at Elland Road as a series of injuries restricted his appearances. A loan spell in Hong Kong was followed by a move to Rochdale in December 1983 where his brother Jimmy, a former team-mate at Old Trafford, was manager.

> *GREENHOFF, Brian (Defender 1973–9) – debut in the above game.*
> *Appearances: FL: 218 (3), goals 13 FAC: 24, goals 2 FLC: 19, goals 2 EUR: 6, goals 0*
> *TOTAL: 268 (3) apps, 17 goals.*

9

1922 THE HARDEST OF THE HARDMEN

Wolverhampton Wanderers 0   Manchester United 1

Frank Barson was Manchester United's first hardman and is widely considered to be the hardest player who ever played the game. He was born in the Sheffield steel belt of Grimesthorpe on 10 April 1891 and after working as a blacksmith he began his football career at Barnsley (1911–19). During his time at Oakwell he served a two-month suspension as a result of an incident in a friendly against Birmingham. Then while playing for the Yorkshire club in an FA Cup tie at Everton, Barson had to be smuggled out of Goodison Park as a mob waited outside for him, unhappy with the roughhouse treatment he dished out to several of the Toffees players during the game. Barson joined Aston Villa in October 1919 for £2,700, the highest ever transfer fee at the time. However, above all else he was a leader and when an opposing player kicked lumps out of any of his team-mates this was the signal Barson needed to roll up his sleeves and exact revenge on the culprits. Legend has it that prior to the 1920 FA Cup final he was warned by the referee, Jack Howcroft, in the Villa dressing room that he would be keeping a close eye on his behaviour. 'The first wrong move you make Barson, off you go,' said Howcroft. Villa beat Huddersfield Town 1–0 after extra-time. In August 1922 Barson signed for United for what was then the massive fee of £5,000 (Villa actually tried to hold out for £6,000). The United fans took him to their hearts immediately and worshipped Barson's no-nonsense aggressive style of play.

In the 1926 FA Cup semi-final between United and Manchester City played at Bramall Lane, Sheffield, it was alleged that Barson knocked out cold the City centre-half Sam Cowan. Although the referee did not see the incident, and therefore did not send Barson off, a subsequent FA hearing suspended him for two months. He helped United regain promotion to Division One in 1925 and was rewarded by the United board when they gave him the keys to his own hotel in Ardwick Green, Manchester. However, when he opened for business for the first time the hotel was swamped with United fans who turned up to wish him well. After just 15 minutes Barson threw the keys to his head waiter, gifting him the establishment, and walked out the front door never to return. After leaving United in May 1928 Barson moved on to a number of clubs including Watford, Hartlepools United, Wigan Borough and Rhyl Athletic. Finally, perhaps the greatest of all the stories told about Frank Barson concerns the one when his football career was almost at an end. Aggrieved that he was not being paid his worth, Barson met his manager to discuss a pay rise and placed a loaded gun on the desk. Barson got his pay increase.

BARSON, Frank (Half-back 1922–8) – debut in the above game.
Appearances: FL: 140, goals 4 FAC: 12, goals 0 TOTAL: 152 apps, 4 goals.

1959 ROSES MASSACRE

Manchester United 6   Leeds United 0
Manchester United were in scintillating form in this First Division game at Old Trafford. Leeds United were sent back across the Pennines on the back of a 6–0 whitewash thanks to goals from Warren Bradley (2), Bobby Charlton (2), Albert Scanlon and Dennis Viollet.

10

1892 FOOTBALL ARRIVES IN MANCHESTER

Newton Heath 1   Burnley 1
This was the first-ever Football League game to be played in the City of Manchester. Newton Heath drew 1–1 with Burnley in the First Division with the Heathens' Robert Donaldson on the score sheet.

Newton Heath: James Warner, Andrew Mitchell, James Brown, George Perrins, William Stewart, Fred Erentz, William Hood, Robert Donaldson, James Coupar, Adam Carson, William Mathieson.

1898 MENAGERIE AT BANK STREET

Newton Heath 3   Manchester City 0
With dwindling crowds coming to watch the Heathens' home games the club

advertised their opening Division Two game of the 1898–99 season by putting up posters in the Manchester area inviting the general public to come and see their mascot Billy the Goat, and hear the dulcet tones of the Bank Street canary. A massive 20,000 turned up to watch the Heathens beat local rivals Manchester City with goals from Henry Boyd, Joe Cassidy and James Collinson. Meanwhile, the canary turned out to be a ruse, while the goat was housed in a pen in a corner of the ground awaiting its fate as the players' Christmas dinner. Indeed the goat was owned by one of the players and was a regular post-match attraction at the local pub where it would be plied with ale before collapsing drunk.

1927 GEORDIE HAMMERING

Manchester United 1   Newcastle United 7
The Geordies hammered Manchester United 7–1 in this First Division encounter at Old Trafford. Joe Spence scored United's only goal. Amazingly, United have conceded seven goals in a League game at home only twice and both times to Newcastle United (Manchester United 4 Newcastle United 7 on 13 September 1930).

2007 SIR ALEX ATTACKED AT RAILWAY STATION

Sir Alex Ferguson was in London to attend a function but got more than he bargained for when a man punched him in the groin before lashing out at a police community support officer at Euston railway station. The man pleaded guilty to the assault two days later and was formally charged with actual bodily harm, assault and two public order offences.

11

1897 FIRST PLAYER TO TWENTY GOALS

Burton Swifts 0   Newton Heath 4
Henry Boyd scored his second successive hat-trick for Newton Heath in their second game of the 1897–98 Second Division season, a 4–0 away victory over Burton Swifts. The other scorer was Joe Cassidy. At the end of the 1897–98 season the prolific Boyd, who had scored on his debut for the Heathens back in February 1897, became the first Newton Heath player to score 20 goals in a season for the club. During his final season with the Heathens, 1898–99, a number of disciplinary problems blotted his copybook. First of all he missed pre-season training and was suspended for seven days, then he went missing again after learning that the club had suspended him and even sent a telegram from Glasgow requesting leave. However, the club did not take too kindly to the telegram and

suspended him for a further 14 days and placed him on the transfer list. In August 1899 he joined Falkirk and scored for them on his debut.

1937 A TALE OF WOES

Manchester United 4   Barnsley 1
Although Thomas Bamford scored a hat-trick for Manchester United (the other scorer was Thomas Manley), the game will probably best be remembered for the ill-fortune The Tykes suffered at Old Trafford. Manley's 25th minute shot, which resulted in a goal, was hit so ferociously that it broke two of Barnsley goalkeeper Binns's fingers and he was taken to a nearby hospital. Shortly afterwards one of their defenders, Ives, had to leave the field after breaking his ribs. The only piece of luck for the visitors came by way of their goal, a last-minute penalty scored by the former Manchester United striker Ernest Hine.

1946 REDS NO MATCH FOR REDS

Manchester United 5   Liverpool 0
A hat-trick from Stan Pearson and goals from Charlie Mitten and Jack Rowley helped United send Liverpool packing from Maine Road following a 5–0 trouncing in this First Division game. It was United's fourth consecutive victory of the 1946–47 season and the fourth consecutive game in which Rowley scored.

1993 RECORD FALLS AT THE BRIDGE

Chelsea 1   Manchester United 0
When Chelsea beat Manchester United 1–0 in this Premier League game at Stamford Bridge it was the first time in 17 Premiership games the Reds had tasted defeat.

12

1908 CHAMPIONS HIT SIX

Manchester United 6   Middlesbrough 3
James Turnbull scored four times for Manchester United as they smacked Middlesbrough for six. Harold Halse and George Wall also scored for the reigning First Division champions in their 6–3 victory.

1925 WELCOME TO MAINE ROAD

Manchester City 1   Manchester United 1
This was the first derby game played by the Blue and Red halves of Manchester

at City's Maine Road ground. Clatworthy Rennox scored United's first ever derby goal there in this 1–1 First Division draw.

1936 BUMPER DERBY CROWD

Manchester United 3   Manchester City 2

Manchester United beat local rivals Manchester City 3–2 in this First Division game played at Old Trafford (scorers: Thomas Bamford, William Bryant, Thomas Manley). City went on to clinch the First Division Championship for the first time in their history at the end of the 1936–37 season. Meanwhile, the crowd of 68,796 stood as a record derby day attendance at Old Trafford until it was surpassed 70 years later in season 2006–07.

1956 UNITED PIONEER EUROPE

RSC Anderlecht 0   Manchester United 2

The inaugural European Cup took place in season 1955–56 at the suggestion of French sports journalist and editor of *L'Equipe*, Gabriel Hanot, and was contested between the winners of Europe's national leagues. Chelsea, the 1954–55 First Division champions, were barred from participating by the Football Association, who viewed the competition as a distraction from their own domestic Championship. United, First Division champions in 1955–56, defied FA orders and entered Europe's premier club competition the following season, 1956–57. Their inaugural game was against Belgian League champions, RSC Anderlecht. The Red Devils won their preliminary round first leg away 2–0 thanks to goals from Dennis Viollet and Tommy Taylor in front of 35,000 people.

1973 GOALKEEPER TURNED POACHER

Manchester United 1   Leicester City 2

In season 1973–74 United's goalkeeper Alex Stepney was the club's nominated penalty taker after Willie Morgan, the usual spot-kick taker, was ruled out with injury. Stepney scored from the spot, his first ever senior goal for United, in this home First Division loss to Leicester City. The United manager Tommy Docherty had been impressed with Stepney's penalty taking during their pre-season tour of Spain. Stepney scored from the spot again in United's 1–0 home win over Birmingham City in Division One on 20 October 1973.

13

1902 FIRST AT HOME AS UNITED

Manchester United 1 Burton United 0
This was Manchester United's first home game since changing their name from Newton Heath at the end of the previous season. Daniel Hurst scored the only goal of the game in a 1–0 win for United in Division Two.

1930 IT'S RAINING GOALS

Manchester United 4 Newcastle United 7
Manchester United conceded 13 goals in the space of only four days by losing 6–0 to Huddersfield Town on 10 September 1930 and 7–4 to Newcastle United. Both games were played at Old Trafford and they marked United's fourth and fifth defeats respectively of the 1930–31 season.

1957

Malachy 'Mal' Martin Donaghy (Defender 1988–92) was born in Belfast.
> *Appearances: FL: 76 (13), goals 0 FAC: 10, goals 0 FLC: 9 (5), goals 0 EUR: 2 (3), goals 0 TOTAL: 98 (21) apps, 0 goals.*

1980 BIG NIKKI

Manchester City 5 Leicester City 0
Manchester United beat Leicester City 5–0 at Old Trafford in this First Division game with goals from Nikola Jovanovic (2), Steve Coppell, Ashley Grimes and Lou Macari. Jovanovic was the first Eastern European to play for the club.

2006 BRITISH GIANTS SERVE UP THRILLER

Manchester United 3 Celtic 2
Louis Saha scored twice and Ole Gunnar Solskjaer once to give United a 3–2 UEFA Champions League win against Celtic at Old Trafford. Jan Vennegoor of Hesselink put Celtic ahead, Saha equalised and then put United 2–1 up. A free-kick from Shunsuke Nakamura levelled the score at 2–2 before Ole grabbed United's winner. Amazingly, this was the first time these two British giants had met in a competitive fixture. Meanwhile, the Manchester United shirt worn by George Best when he scored six goals against Northampton Town in an FA Cup tie on 7 February 1970 was sold in an auction at Christie's for a staggering £24,000.

14

1956 A BUTCH PLAYER

Raymond Colin 'Butch' Wilkins was born in Hillingdon, Middlesex. Butch made his name with Chelsea during the 1970s, leading to United signing the stylish midfielder for £825,000 in 1979. Dave Sexton, the United manager, hoped that Wilkins would prove the catalyst to bring the long-awaited First Division Championship back to Old Trafford. Many United fans disliked Wilkins's style of play, criticising the England international for being over defensive and opting on many occasions to play the ball off squarely rather than drive up midfield or attempt a defence-splitting pass. Indeed some United fans nicknamed him 'Squareball Wilkins' and 'The Crab' because of his lack of adventure. In 1983 he played in United's losing League Cup final side against Liverpool at Wembley Stadium but the same season he helped United to FA Cup glory at Wembley over Brighton & Hove Albion. Wilkins scored in the first game, which ended 2–2. At the end of the 1983–84 season he joined AC Milan for £1.5m and later in his career had stints at Paris Saint-Germain, Glasgow Rangers, QPR and Millwall. He has also been the manager of QPR and Fulham. Wilkins captained England on several occasions and won 84 caps for his country, playing in the World Cup finals of 1982 and 1986.

1960 HAMMERS HAMMERED

Manchester United 6   West Ham United 1
Manchester United were at their best when West Ham United visited Old Trafford for this First Division game. The Hammers were on the end of a hammering, going down 6–1 to goals from Bobby Charlton (2), Dennis Viollet (2), Albert Scanlon and Albert Quixall.

1963 BEST'S DEBUT

Manchester United 1   West Bromwich Albion 0
The 50,413 spectators inside Old Trafford this day, when Manchester United beat West Bromwich Albion, have the privilege of saying: 'I was there when Bestie made his debut for United.' A goal from David Sadler gave United a 1–0 win in a match that included the 17-year-old Belfast Boy for the first time. A skinny teenager from Belfast's Cregagh Estate, Best was spotted by the Manchester United scout Bob Bishop, who famously sent a telegram to Matt Busby that simply read: 'Boss, I think I've found you a genius.' How right Bob Bishop's words were because George Best truly was a genius. Having fought off initial

homesickness, Best turned professional on his 17th birthday, 22 May 1963, and scored on his second appearance (in a 5–1 home win over Burnley on 28 December 1963) while a first cap for Northern Ireland soon followed for the dashingly handsome young Irishman. In 1964–65, playing alongside Denis Law, Bobby Charlton and David Herd, Best was a key figure in the Reds' first title triumph since the pre-Munich era (champions in 1956–57). The following season he almost single-handedly destroyed SL Benfica in the European Cup quarter-final in their own back yard, scoring twice in a 5–1 win to inflict the Lisbon giants' first home defeat in Europe. The next day the newspapers dubbed him 'El Beatle'. A second First Division Championship success followed in 1966–67 and Best proved the scourge of Benfica again a year later in the 1968 European Cup final, giving the Reds a 2–1 extra-time lead en route to a 4–1 victory. Best's 28 goals that season made him United's top scorer, a position he retained over the next four campaigns. In season 1967–68 he was also named the PFA, FWA and European Footballer of the Year. As the Busby era ended and an ageing side was dismantled, Best struggled with the personal demons that would dog him until his death on 25 November 2005. He famously 'retired' to Marbella in 1972, before coming back again and eventually leaving for good on 2 January 1974 for a globe-trotting series of destinations taking in, among others, the rather unlikely surroundings of Brisbane Lions, Cork Celtic, Dunstable Town, Fulham, Hibernian, Los Angeles Aztecs, Stockport County and the Jewish Guild of South Africa.

'If I'd been born ugly, you'd never have heard of Pelé.' Many a true word is spoken in jest, and few would argue that George Best was the most naturally gifted footballer Britain has ever produced. Speed, balance, vision, superb close control, the ability to create chances and score from seemingly impossible situations only tell half the story. The other half was an uncontainable zest for the game as it should be played, a ceaseless trickery and joy. Pelé, for his part, dubbed Best 'the greatest player in the world' and no one disagreed. Prior to his death, George asked that he be remembered for what he did on the football pitch and not what was reported on the front pages of newspapers. There is not a single Manchester United fan who would deny Bestie his wish and what glorious memories they are. George still holds the post-war record for the most goals scored by a United player in a single match, his double hat-trick against Northampton Town in an 8–2 FA Cup fifth-round mauling on 7 February 1970. George was capped 37 times for Northern Ireland and scored nine times although this would have been 10 had his famous 'goal that was not a goal' against England at Windsor Park on 15 May 1971 not been disallowed by the referee, even though he had his back turned to the play. George received an Honorary Doctorate from Queens University of Belfast in 2001, and in 2002 he was made a Freeman of Castlereagh (his birthplace) and was an inaugural inductee to the Football Hall of Fame. In 2006 George was posthumously presented with a PFA Special Merit Award for his services to football. The Belfast Boy is a United legend.

BEST, George (Forward 1963–74) – debut in the above game.
Appearances: FL: 361, goals 137 FAC: 46, goals 21 FLC: 25, goals 9 EUR: 34, goals 11
TOTAL: 470 apps, 179 goals.

1966 LEAGUE CUP NIGHTMARE

Blackpool 5   Manchester United 1
This 5–1 defeat (scorer: David Herd) at Bloomfield Road in the second round
of the 1966–67 competition is United's worst result in the League Cup. Whereas
United began to field lesser sides in the competition from the mid 1990s onwards,
this 1966 side featured nine international players!

1977 BREAD WARS

AS Saint-Étienne 1   Manchester United 1
United drew this European Cup Winners' Cup first round, first leg tie 1–1 (scorer:
Gordon Hill) at the Stade Geoffroy-Guichard. A large contingent of Reds made
the trip across the English Channel, carrying their scarves and an enormous
amount of bread. There was a bread strike on in France at the time but rather
than hand out some *bon ami* the United fans teased the home fans by throwing
slices of bread at them. When the match report reached UEFA's HQ they were
rather unimpressed with the behaviour of the English fans towards their French
hosts and banned United from staging the second leg at Old Trafford. In fact
UEFA went so far as to say that the return leg should be played at least 300 miles
from Manchester. Home Park, Plymouth was the chosen venue.

15

1930 UNITED HIT FOR NINE IN FIVE DAYS

Huddersfield Town 3   Manchester United 0
Five days after crashing six goals past United at Old Trafford, Huddersfield Town
made it nine goals in two league games. With this defeat United had lost their
first seven League games.

1976 FIRST UEFA CUP GAME

Ajax Amsterdam 1   Manchester United 0
For Manchester United's first ever game in the UEFA Cup they were drawn away
to Ajax Amsterdam. United lost 1–0 in the Olympisch Stadion (Ajax did not
move to the Amsterdam ArenA until 1996).

1993 OLD ACQUAINTANCE RENEWED

Kispest Honved 2   Manchester United 3
This game marked Manchester United's first European Cup game in almost 25 years. Two goals from Roy Keane and one from Eric Cantona gave United a 3–2 victory.

16

1918

Allenby Chilton (Half-back 1939–55) was born in South Hylton, County Durham.

1957

David McCreery (Midfielder 1975–9) was born in Belfast.

1989 SPARKY TAMES THE LIONS

Manchester United 5   Millwall 1
Mark Hughes scored a hat-trick for Manchester United in their 5–1 demolition of Millwall in this First Division game at Old Trafford. Bryan Robson and Lee Sharpe also scored.

17

1958 SCANLON HAT-TRICK HITS HAMMERS

Manchester United 4   West Ham United 1
Albert Scanlon played arguably his greatest game in a Manchester United shirt, scoring a superb hat-trick in their 4–1 win over West Ham United in this First Division game at Old Trafford. The scorer of the fourth goal was Colin Webster. Just nine days earlier United lost 3–2 to the Hammers at Upton Park (scorers: Wilf McGuinness, Colin Webster).

1966 CLEAN DERBY FOR DEBUTANT GOALIE

Manchester United 1   Manchester City 0
After signing for the Reds 16 days earlier, Alex Stepney made his Manchester United debut in the Manchester derby, keeping a clean sheet in United's 1–0 win over City at Old Trafford thanks to a goal from Denis Law. It was the day before

Alex's 24th birthday. United went on to win the First Division Championship in his first season at the club. In fact, such was his contribution that Matt Busby described signing him as 'the single most important factor behind our championship win in 1967'. Stepney began his career as a trainee at Millwall, before moving on to Chelsea in June 1966 where he stayed just three months before Matt Busby took him to Old Trafford. Alex Stepney earned Old Trafford immortality the night Manchester United became European champions in 1968. On that balmy May evening at Wembley, with United and Benfica drawing 1–1, Stepney held on to a ferocious shot from Eusebio to ensure the game would go into extra-time. The additional half-hour was illuminated by goals from George Best, Bobby Charlton (scoring his second) and Brian Kidd, as the Reds ran out 4–1 winners, but the importance of Stepney's save was lost on no one. Indeed, many believe Stepney's crucial save to be more important than any of United's four goals in the final. For more than a decade Stepney proved a reliable, steady and efficient goalkeeper. He had excellent positional skills and during the club's ill-fated 1973–74 campaign was even employed as penalty taker, scoring twice. 'Big Al', as he was affectionately nicknamed, remains United's all-time top-scoring goalkeeper. In all he won one First Division winners' medal, an FA Cup winners' medal (1977), one Second Division winners' medal (1974–75), as well as the European Cup. He joined the NASL revolution in June 1978 when he signed for Dallas Tornado, and later had spells as a goalkeeping coach at Southampton, Exeter City and Manchester City.

STEPNEY, Alex (Goalkeeper 1966–78) – debut in the above game.
Appearances: FL: 433, goals 2 FAC: 44, goals 0 FLC:35, goals 0 EUR:23, goals 0
TOTAL: 539 apps, 2 goals.

18

1942
Alexander Cyril 'Alex' Stepney (Goalkeeper 1966–78) was born in Mitcham, Surrey.

1946 ASTON SNR MAKES HIS UNITED BOW
Manchester United 1   Chelsea 1
John Aston Snr made his Manchester United debut in their 1–1 First Division draw with Chelsea at Maine Road. Allenby Chilton scored for United.

ASTON, John (Snr) (Full-back 1946–54) – debut in the above game.
Appearances: FL: 253, goals 29 FAC: 29, goals 1 TOTAL: 284 apps, 30 goals.

1965 A HAT-TRICK FIT FOR A KING

Manchester United 4   Chelsea 1

Manchester United beat Chelsea 4–1 at Old Trafford in this one-sided First Division game with a hat-trick from The King, Denis Law, and a Bobby Charlton goal.

1968 BLUES AND REDS ALL OVER EUROPE

Waterford 1   Manchester United 3

Manchester United began the defence of their 1968 European Cup triumph with this 3–1 away win over Irish champions Waterford (scorer: Denis Law 3). The first round of the 1968–69 competition marked the first and only time that two English teams from the same city have participated in the competition in the same season (excludes the UEFA Champions League format). Manchester City, First Division champions in season 1967–68, earned the right to play in Europe's premier club competition for the only time in the club's history. However, whereas United made it all the way to the semi-finals for the second consecutive year, City fell at the first hurdle, going down 2–1 on aggregate to Turkey's Fenerbahce.

1971 MAGICAL BEST

Manchester United 4   West Ham United 2

George Best was at his magical best scoring a hat-trick for Manchester United in their 4–2 First Division win over West Ham United at Old Trafford. Bobby Charlton scored United's other goal.

1972 BOBBY'S RECORD TRIBUTE

Manchester United entertained Celtic in a game played for Bobby Charlton's testimonial. However, all was not well within the club and George Best refused to play in the game, saying, 'To do so would be hypocritical.' Despite the fact that Manchester United had not won a game in season 1972–73 (drawn 4, lost 5), a crowd of 60,538 poured into Old Trafford to pay tribute to the United legend who had been at the club since putting pen to paper as an amateur in January 1953. The crowd stood as a record number for a testimonial until 2004 when Ryan Giggs's testimonial surpassed it.

19

1908 UNITED'S HARDMAN

Manchester City 1   Manchester United 2

Harold Hardman made his Manchester United debut in this 2–1 away win over local rivals Manchester City. Harold Halse and Sandy Turnbull scored the goals that gave the reigning First Division champions a 2–1 win over their bitter rivals. Although this was the first of only four games Hardman played for United, he won four England amateur international caps and an Olympic gold medal with the Great Britain football team when London hosted the Games in 1908. When he retired from football, Hardman served as a Manchester United director for more than half a century.

HARDMAN, Harold (Forward 1908) – debut in the above game.
Appearances: FL: 4, goals 0 TOTAL: 4 apps, 0 goals.

1981 £100,000 PER GOAL

Manchester United 1 Swansea City 0
After his headline-making £1.25m transfer from Nottingham Forest to Manchester United in October 1980 Garry Birtles finally scored his first League goal for United in their 1–0 win over Swansea City at Old Trafford in the First Division. Birtles, who could not stop finding the back of the net for Forest, took 30 League games to register his account for United. When he was off-loaded back to Forest in September 1982 for a bargain basement £250,000, he had scored just 11 League goals and one FA Cup goal for United in 64 total appearances, working out at £104,167 per goal.

2007 EUROPEAN CENTURY FOR UNITED

Sporting Lisbon 0 Manchester United 1
Cristiano Ronaldo and Nani made a return to their former club for the first time since both players left Sporting to join Manchester United, Ronaldo in 2003 and Nani in 2007. And it was a second-half header (61 minutes) from Ronaldo that gave United a 1–0 victory in their opening Group game of the 2007–08 UEFA Champions League. However, his goal celebration was slightly muted before his former admirers who graciously applauded his goal. When Carlos Tevez replaced Ronaldo after 86 minutes the home crowd gave the United winger a standing ovation. Meanwhile, Wayne Rooney made his comeback after breaking his foot in United's opening game of the season. The victory was United's 100th win in the European Cup/Champions League.

20

1924 WILLIE TO THE RESCUE

Oldham Athletic 0 Manchester United 3
William Henderson scored a hat-trick for United in their 3–0 Second Division win over Oldham Athletic at Boundary Park.

1933

Dennis Sydney Viollet (Forward 1952–62) was born in Manchester.

1935

David Pegg (Forward 1952–62) was born in Doncaster.

1947 CITY'S BIGGEST DERBY DAY CROWD

Manchester City 0   Manchester United 0

Although both teams were using Maine Road for their home games in season 1947–48, this was City's home First Division game against the Reds. A record derby crowd (since surpassed) of 71,364 watched the two sides play out a drab 0–0 draw. However, the attendance still ranks as the Blues' highest derby home attendance.

21

1912

George Mutch (Forward 1934–8) was born in Aberdeen.

1994 SCHOLES'S BIG NIGHT

Port Vale 1   Manchester United 2

Paul Scholes scored twice on his debut for Manchester United in this 2–1 win over Port Vale in the League Cup. Scholesy became the first Manchester United player to find the back of the net twice on his debut since Bobby Charlton's brace in a 4–2 home win over Charlton Athletic on 6 October 1956. Paul Scholes began life at Old Trafford as a trainee on 8 July 1991 and turned professional on 23 July 1993. The young ginger-haired midfield dynamo won an FA Youth Cup winners' medal in 1992 and a runners-up medal in the same competition the following year. In 1993, he was also a member of the England Under-18 team, which won the 1993 European Championship. His full Manchester United League debut came against Ipswich Town on 24 September 1994, when he again found the net twice, but this time the Reds lost 3–2. It wasn't until Eric Cantona was handed an eight-month suspension in January 1995 that Scholes was able to command a regular place in the team. In May 1995 he picked-up an FA Cup runners-up medal after coming on as a substitute in the 1–0 defeat to Everton at Wembley. However, in season 1995–96, following the exit of Mark Hughes, Paul Ince and Andrei Kanchelskis, Scholesy and the rest of 'Fergie's Fledglings' came to the fore. The youthful United side, featuring players such as Ryan Giggs, David

Beckham, Nicky Butt and Gary Neville, completely dominated the domestic scene, winning the Premier League title and FA Cup. Paul made his international debut for England in a friendly against South Africa at Old Trafford on 24 May 1997 coming on as a substitute for Teddy Sheringham (then at Tottenham Hotspur). Then, in his second game for his country, his first start, he scored in England's 2–0 win over Italy in a friendly played in Nantes, France. At the 1998 World Cup finals in France he scored in England's opening match against Tunisia and started all four of their games in the tournament.

Scholes is a big-game player and similar in many ways to two former United legends, Bobby Charlton and Bryan Robson: he has a superb football brain, is an excellent passer of the ball and tenacious in the tackle, and has the handy knack of being able to make late runs from deep positions. His lightning reflexes and quick feet have helped him score many goals from the tightest of situations. In Europe during the 1998–99 season he scored vital goals against Bayern Munich, Barcelona and perhaps most importantly the deciding equaliser in a 1–1 draw with Inter Milan at the San Siro. However, a suspension ruled him out of United's glory night at the Nou Camp in the 1999 UEFA Champions League final. He also scored United's second goal in the 1999 FA Cup final against Newcastle United and collected his third Premiership winners' medal in the Reds' Treble-winning season. In season 1999–2000 Scholes won his fourth Premiership winners' medal and a fifth followed in 2000–01. When United bought Juan Sebastian Veron in the summer of 2001 Scholesy was given a new position in the team by Sir Alex Ferguson, a support striker to Andy Cole and Teddy Sheringham. In 2002 he played alongside his United team-mates David Beckham and Nicky Butt in the England midfield during the World Cup finals in Japan and South Korea. His 20 goals during the 2002–03 season helped United reclaim the Premiership title, his sixth Championship winners' medal. A third FA Cup winners' medal came his way in 2004 and in season 2006–07 he was instrumental in United winning their ninth Premiership crown after an eye problem had kept him out of action for many months, his seventh Premier League winners' medal.

22

1956 REDS ON THEIR WAY TO THE TITLE

Manchester United 2   Manchester City 0
On their way to clinching the First Division Championship in season 1956–57, the Busby Babes beat local rivals Manchester City 2–0 in the first derby game of the season, played at Old Trafford. Dennis Viollet and Liam Whelan scored. City ended the season in 18th place (out of 22 teams).

1993 UNITED RESERVES?

Stoke City 2   Manchester United 1

Following this 2–1 Coca-Cola Cup second round, first leg defeat (scorer: Dion Dublin) by Stoke City, Manchester United were accused by the Football League of fielding a reserve team for the game. However, the Reds won the second leg 2–0 (scorers: Brian McClair, Lee Sharpe) and went all the way to the final where they lost 3–1 to Aston Villa at Wembley Stadium. It was the only domestic trophy United failed to win in season 1993–94.

2004 MUNICH TRIBUTE UNVEILED

Sir Alex Ferguson and Manchester United director Sir Bobby Charlton were among a club delegation to visit Munich, Germany. Charlton, a former Busby Babe and survivor of the fateful 1958 Munich Air Disaster, choked back tears as he helped unveil a memorial to the 23 people (8 of whom were former team-mates) who lost their lives in the fateful crash on 6 February 1958.

23

1964 HERD FIRST IN INTER-CITIES FAIRS CUP

David Herd scored United's goal in a 1–1 away draw with Swedish side Djur-gardens IF in the first leg of this Inter-Cities Fairs Cup first round tie. It was United's first ever game in the competition, which subsequently became known as the UEFA Cup. Herd's goal made him the first Manchester United player to score in all three major European competitions.

Clayton Graham Blackmore (Midfielder 1983–94) was born in Neath, Wales.

1989 MAINE ROAD MASSACRE

Manchester City 5   Manchester United 1

City, newly promoted from Division Two, went into this Division One derby game at Maine Road having won just one game in their opening six back in English football's top flight, and after suffering an embarrassing exit from the League Cup at the hands of Brentford a few days earlier. On the other hand, United had defeated reigning League champions Arsenal at Old Trafford on the opening day of the season, although the club was still largely overshadowed by speculation about Michael Knighton's proposed takeover. But United still went to Maine Road in decent form, having beaten both Millwall at home and Ports-mouth away (League Cup) in the previous week. Both sides had key players missing but it was the absence of the inspirational Bryan Robson in the red of United that would prove the biggest loss. The game was halted early on following crowd trouble, but when play resumed David Oldfield, Trevor Morley and Ian Bishop scored to send City in 3–0 up at half-time. Whatever Alex Ferguson said in the interval in the dressing rooms paid instant dividends when United came out and pulled a goal back thanks to a superb acrobatic scissors-kick from Mark Hughes, which crashed on to the underside of the crossbar and over the line. But then David Oldfield scored his second and City's fourth and Andy Hinchcliffe completed the rout with a spectacular fifth goal for the home side. Chants of 'Fergie out' came from the terraces although it is believed that they came from City fans and not United supporters.

2006 A ROYAL ENGAGEMENT

Reading 1   Manchester United 1
United played Reading for the first time in a League football match when they visited the Madejski Stadium for a Premiership game. A goal from Cristiano Ronaldo was good enough to secure United a point against the Royals, who were managed by the former United hero, Steve Coppell.

2007 BLUES FEELING THE BLUES

Manchester United 2   Chelsea 0
The Premiership champions from the previous three seasons went head-to-head in this Premier League game at Old Trafford. The game came just three days after Jose Mourinho parted company with the Blues and United beat their London visitors 2–0 thanks to goals from Carlos Tevez, his first for United, and a penalty from Louis Saha. Former United target, Jon Obi Mikel, was sent off in the game, which was Avram Grant's first as manager of Chelsea.

24

1952 CHARITY IN SHORT SUPPLY AT OLD TRAFFORD

Manchester United 4   Newcastle United 2
The champions proved too strong for Cup-holders Newcastle in the Charity Shield. Goals from Jack Rowley (2), Roger Byrne and John Downie were enough to secure the victory.

1962

Michael Christopher Phelan (Defender 1989–94) was born in Nelson, Lancashire.

25

1911 HALSE HITS SIX

Manchester United 8   Swindon Town 4
In the 1911 FA Charity Shield Manchester United, the reigning First Division champions, annihilated Swindon Town 8–4 at Stamford Bridge. Harold Halse scored six goals for Manchester United in the game, a feat equalled by George Best in an FA Cup tie for the Reds against Northampton Town on 7 February 1970. The other scorers were Sandy Turnbull and George Wall.

1957 NO LUCK FOR THE IRISH

Shamrock Rovers 0   Manchester United 6
Manchester United recorded their best away win in Europe defeating the Irish champions Shamrock Rovers 6–0 in this first round, first leg European Cup tie played in Dublin. Tommy Taylor (2), Liam Whelan (2), Johnny Berry and David Pegg scored for the Reds.

1963 HERD'S MIXED FORTUNES

Willem II 1   Manchester United 1
This game was Manchester United's first ever game in the European Cup Winners' Cup. United drew 1–1 away to the Dutch side in the first round, first leg of the 1963–64 ECWC with David Herd scoring for United before later being sent off.

1968 DEFEAT IN THE FIRST LEG OF THE WORLD CLUB CHAMPIONSHIP

Estudiantes de la Plata 1   Manchester United 0
Manchester United lost the first leg of their World Club Championship clash 1–0 away to the South American champions Estudiantes de la Plata. The game was an ill-tempered affair with many bad tackles, mainly from the Argentinian side. Nobby Stiles was sent off 11 minutes from time after lashing out at an opposing player.

26

1956 UNITED'S RECORD SCORE

Manchester United 10   RSC Anderlecht 0

Manchester United played their first ever home European tie (played at Maine Road), defeating Anderlecht 10–0 in the second leg of their European Cup preliminary round encounter. The 10–0 scoreline still remains Manchester United's record win in all competitions. The scorers were Dennis Viollet (4), Tommy Taylor (3), Liam Whelan (2) and Johnny Berry. It was one of only two games since the Second World War where two United players scored a hat-trick in the same match (the other was when Dennis Viollet and Albert Quixall both scored three against Burnley in United's 6–0 win on 12 April 1961). Denis Law (v Waterford, 2 October 1968) and Ruud van Nistelrooy (v Sparta Prague, 3 November 2004) have since equalled Viollet's record of four goals in a European tie.

1990 WHEN GOLIATH BEAT DAVID

Halifax Town 1   Manchester United 3

Manchester United visited Halifax Town, bottom of the Fourth Division, for a second round, first leg League Cup tie. United came away with a 3–1 win (scorers: Clayton Blackmore, Brian McClair, Neil Webb) while The Shaymen's goal was incredibly their first of the 1990–91 season.

1995 SCHMEICHEL'S RESCUE ACT

Manchester United 2   Rotor Volgograd 2

A goal from Manchester United goalkeeper Peter Schmeichel in the very last minute of this second round, second leg UEFA Cup tie saved United's proud unbeaten home record in European competition. Paul Scholes scored United's first goal but, unfortunately, after drawing the first leg 0–0 in Russia, the Reds went out of the competition on the away goals rule.

2007 UNITED KIDS SENT TO COVENTRY

Manchester United 0   Coventry City 2

Coventry City from the Championship knocked an inexperienced Manchester United side out of the 2007–08 Carling Cup with a 2–0 win over the Premiership champions at Old Trafford. The attendance of 74,055 was a record for the competition outside of the final.

27

1983 AWAY DAY SPECIAL

Dukla Prague 2   Manchester United 2

Manchester United went into this European Cup Winners' Cup first round, second leg match having drawn the first leg 1–1 at Old Trafford (scorer: Ray Wilkins). Two goals from skipper Bryan Robson and Frank Stapleton gave United a 2–2 draw in the Czech capital and they progressed to the second round courtesy of the away goals rule. Remarkably, this is the only time in the club's history that Manchester United have won a European tie on the away goals rule.

2007 MARADONA HEAPS PRAISE ON TEVEZ

The legendary Argentinian striker Diego Maradona backed his fellow countryman Carlos Tevez to be a resounding success at Manchester United. 'He is a fantastic player. Very strong on the ball and amazing vision,' said the captain of Argentina's 1986 World Cup-winning team.

28

1895 LAST EVER MEETING

Crewe Alexandra 0   Newton Heath 2

This game marked the last occasion on which Newton Heath or Manchester United played Crewe Alexandra in a League game. Richard Smith scored both goals for the Heathens in the Second Division encounter. This gap remains a League record between two English League clubs.

1903 WEST RESIGNS

James West resigned from his position as secretary at Manchester United after three years with the club.

1968

Russell Peter Beardsmore (Midfielder 1988–91) was born in Wigan.

2004 ROONEY OFF TO A FLIER

Manchester United 6   Fenerbahce 2

Wayne Rooney's debut for United after his £20m-plus transfer from Everton could not have been more spectacular. The teenaged sensation had only just recovered from a broken metatarsal when he lined up for this Champions League Group fixture. His brilliant hat-trick immediately announced him as one of the great talents of the modern game, and he went on to become the PFA Young Player of the Year at the end of the season. The other scorers that night were David Bellion, Ryan Giggs and Ruud van Nistelrooy.

29

1957
Leslie Jesse 'Les' Sealey (Goalkeeper 1988–91, 1993–4) was born in Bethnal Green, London.

1992 SPARKY RECEIVES MARCHING ORDERS
Manchester United 0   Moscow Torpedo 0 (United lost 4–3 on penalties)
Mark Hughes was sent off in this goalless first round, second leg UEFA Cup encounter with Moscow Torpedo at Old Trafford. United went out of the competition, losing 4–3 in a penalty shoot-out as the first leg had also ended 0–0.

1993 NEW PLAQUE UNVEILED
Manchester United 2   Kispest Honved 1
Frank Taylor, the only surviving journalist from the 1958 Munich Air Disaster, unveiled a new Press Memorial plaque in the Press Lounge at Old Trafford prior to Manchester United's 2–1 win over Kispest Honved in the second leg of their first round European Cup tie. Steve Bruce scored both United goals to put them into the next round with an aggregate 5–3 victory.

2001 A GAME OF TWO HALVES
Tottenham Hotspur 3   Manchester United 5
When the half-time whistle blew at White Hart Lane in this Premier League game, United were 3–0 down. Sir Alex Ferguson could not wait to get the players into the dressing room for 'a quiet word'. Whatever Sir Alex said during the break should be sold as a motivational speech because United were a different side in every way in the second half, scoring five goals without reply (scorers: David Beckham, Laurent Blanc, Andy Cole, Ruud van Nistelrooy, Juan Sebastian Veron).

30

1903 MANGNALL ARRIVES

Two days after James West resigned as Secretary of Manchester United the club moved swiftly and secured the services of Ernest Mangnall, who had performed the same role at Burnley. Mangnall transformed United, guiding them to their first Division One Championship title in 1907–08, a feat he repeated in 1910–11, and their first FA Cup final win in 1909.

1967 BOBBY'S DAY

Manchester City 1   Manchester United 2

In what would prove to be one of the tightest title races in years, with the destination of the trophy uncertain till the last day, this early season encounter between the two Manchester sides, who would battle it out to the end, seemed a decisive pointer. Bobby Charlton scored both United goals in a 2–1 victory at Maine Road. Sadly, United were to lose the return fixture later in the season, and that proved to be the difference between the two teams with City clinching the title.

OCTOBER

1

1936 A GENTLE GIANT IS BORN

Duncan Edwards (Half-back 1952–8) was born in Dudley, Worcestershire.

1945 BUSBY'S REIGN BEGINS

On 1 October 1945, Matt Busby walked into Old Trafford and took charge of Manchester United for the first time, having accepted the post on 15 February 1945. Busby was unsure what the future held for him and his ex-army mate Jimmy Murphy, whom he made his assistant. Both men had recently been demobilised from the armed forces. Old Trafford was a mess, having been bombed during World War II, while Busby and Murphy were unsure what players they would have so soon after the war drew to a close. Added to this, the club was also in debt to the sum of £15,000. As a player, Busby represented two English clubs, joining Manchester City on 11 February 1928 and making his debut the following year against Middlesbrough. When he left City in March 1936 he signed for Liverpool for a fee of £8,000. Busby turned down the job of assistant manager at Liverpool to become United's boss and fill the post left vacant since the resignation of Scott Duncan in 1937, temporarily filled by club secretary Walter Crickmer. Together Busby and Murphy created United's first great post-war team, built around the defensive capabilities of Johnny Carey, John Aston and Allenby Chilton and the attacking skills of Charlie Mitten, Jack Rowley and Stan Pearson. United were FA Cup winners in 1948, defeating Blackpool 4–2. Then, after finishing runners-up four times in 1947–49 and 1951, Busby's men brought the title to Old Trafford in 1952.

Far from being blinded by their success, Busby and Murphy had the foresight to plan ahead and prepare for the day when their first great team would need replacing. The club's scouting system was expanded and reorganised and by the early 1950s the new youth policy was bearing its first fruit as Jeff Whitefoot, Jackie Blanchflower and Roger Byrne stepped up to the first team. By 1953 a new team was being blooded in the First Division as Bill Foulkes, Mark Jones, David Pegg, Liam Whelan, Eddie Colman and Duncan Edwards all broke through. League success soon followed as this new young side, soon christened the 'Busby

Babes', won the League title in both 1956 and 1957 and reached the FA Cup final in 1957. Busby was still looking to the future, trailblazing the way for English clubs by entering the European Cup in 1956–57 against the wishes of the Football League. United reached the semi-finals, losing to eventual winners Real Madrid. The following season, 1957–58, bristled with promise and United were still challenging in all three competitions by February when disaster struck. On 6 February 1958, the aeroplane bringing the team home from a European Cup match against Red Star Belgrade crashed after refuelling in Munich. Twenty-three people were killed, including eight of Busby's players. Busby almost lost his life as well; he was twice given the last rites while lying gravely ill in a German hospital. Fortunately, he survived and returned to Manchester 71 days after the crash. In the meantime, Jimmy Murphy, who missed the tragedy because of his commitments as manager of the Welsh national side, brilliantly guided a patched-up team to an emotionally charged FA Cup final. Bolton Wanderers beat United 2–0 at Wembley.

After taking up the managerial reigns again in August 1958, Busby began to add some big-money purchases to his homegrown talent. The likes of Albert Quixall, Noel Cantwell, Denis Law and Pat Crerand joined United in the late 1950s and early 1960s. This group of players reached the FA Cup final in 1963 and beat Leicester City 3–1 to claim the club's first trophy after Munich. League titles followed in 1965 and 1967, giving Busby the chance to try to conquer Europe in the following seasons. In 1965–66, United reached the European Cup semi-finals, just as they had done in 1956–57 and 1957–58. But in 1967–68 they went all the way to the final at Wembley where they faced Portuguese side Benfica. On another night of great emotion, United triumphed 4–1 after extra-time to win the European Cup for Busby. It was a fitting tribute to the players and staff killed and injured 10 years before and was Busby's crowning achievement as United manager. They looked like retaining the Cup in 1968–69, but eventually bowed out to AC Milan in the semi-final. Busby retired at the end of that season, but stayed on as general manager while Wilf McGuinness became the man in charge of the team on a day-to-day basis. The new arrangement lasted little more than a year and on 28 December 1970, Busby was invited by the directors to return to his old job and replace McGuinness until the end of the season.

A respected figure throughout his career, Busby was awarded the CBE in 1958 and made the 66th Freeman of Manchester in 1967. In 1968 he was named Manager of the Year and was knighted following United's European Cup triumph. In 1972 he was made a Knight Commander of St Gregory by the Pope. And in 1980 he became president of Manchester United and was elected vice-president of the Football League in 1982 before going on to become a life member. In 1993, Warwick Road North, the road that runs past the front of Old Trafford, was re-named Sir Matt Busby Way in honour of the man known as 'Mr Manchester United'. In addition to managing United, Busby also guided the British Olympic football team to a semi-final place in the 1948 Olympics and in 1958 was manager of Scotland, giving an 18-year-old by the name of Denis Law his first cap. Sir Matt Busby died on 20 January 1994 in Alexandra Hospital, Cheadle, after a short illness. For his funeral a week later thousands lined the streets of Manchester as his cortege drove from Chorlton to Old Trafford and finally to Manchester's Southern Cemetery. Five years after Sir Matt's death, the modern United side emulated his greatest feat by winning the European Cup. Poignantly, the date of that triumph, 26 May 1999, would have been Sir Matt's 90th birthday.

1960 STILES MAKES HIS UNITED DEBUT

Bolton Wanderers 1   Manchester United 1

Nobby Stiles, a Busby Babe and a product of United's successful 1950s youth team, made his debut in Manchester United's 1–1 First Division draw with Bolton Wanderers at Burnden Park (scorer: Johnny Giles). Stiles, infamous for his toothless smile, was an aggressive half-back for United and England. Nobby was born in Collyhurst, Manchester and as a young boy he stood on the Stretford End cheering on United, hoping one day he too would wear the famous red jersey of his beloved team. That dream came true shortly after he represented Manchester and Lancashire Schoolboys when he signed on as an amateur for Manchester United in September 1957.

From 1960–71 the hard, tough-tackling, expert man-marker (ask Eusebio) won two League Championship medals (1965, 1967) and a European Cup winner's medal (1968). And who can ever forget his victory jig holding aloft the Jules Rimet trophy at Wembley Stadium in 1966 after England beat West Germany 4–2 after extra-time to win the World Cup? However, he missed out on an FA Cup winners' medal in 1963, losing his place in the side to Paddy Crerand. Nobby may not have been big but when he took to the pitch he was a giant among men, a fearless competitor who never shirked a tackle while rallying his team-mates when required. In many ways he was Busby's general on the field, a quick-thinking player who could spot danger for his defence in an instant. Some commentators often described Nobby as a dirty player but in truth he played football without his glasses and therefore was prone to the odd mistimed tackle or two. In May 1971 he joined Middlesbrough for £20,000, spending two years with the Second Division outfit before joining up with Bobby Charlton at Preston North End, as a player-coach and later manager. In 1981 Stiles joined Vancouver Whitecaps and in 1984 he left Canada and returned to England to become manager of West Bromwich Albion. In 1989 Nobby returned to Old Trafford to take up the post of youth team coach and he worked with many of United's future stars including Ryan Giggs, David Beckham and Gary Neville. He left United for a second time in 1993 and in 2000 he received an OBE for playing his part in England's World Cup-winning team.

STILES, Norbert Peter 'Nobby' (Half-back 1960–71) – debut in the above game.
Appearances: FL: 311, goals 17   FAC: 38, goals 0   FLC: 7, goals 0   EUR: 36, goals 2
TOTAL: 395 apps, 19 goals.

1995 THE RETURN OF LE ROI

Manchester United 2   Liverpool 2

Eric Cantona made his long-awaited comeback for Manchester United after serving an eight-month ban for attacking a foul-mouthed Crystal Palace fan at Selhurst Park on 25 January 1995. The game could not have been bigger with United entertaining their bitter rivals Liverpool at Old Trafford in the Premier League. Two minutes into the game the enigmatic Cantona threaded a superb pass through to Nicky Butt whose low shot flew into the net past David James. However, Robbie Fowler looked certain to dampen Eric's return by firing the Merseysiders in front with goals in the 35th and 53rd minutes. But cometh the hour, cometh the man, and after Ryan Giggs was dragged down, up stepped Eric to take the resulting spot kick. Old Trafford held its breath as Eric, with his trademark upturned collar, carefully placed the ball on the spot. He took a few paces back and coolly caressed the ball into the net to earn United a 2–2 draw. Then Eric could not contain his emotions after his enforced sabbatical from the beautiful game, and he ran behind the net, grabbed hold of a metal pole and twirled in mid-air, screaming his delight at being back.

1997 JUVE BEATEN

Manchester United 3   Juventus 2

Manchester United exacted revenge for their UEFA Champions League defeat at the hands of the Italians in the previous season's competition by beating them at Old Trafford. Despite going a goal down in the opening seconds of the game, the Reds put on a powerful performance to win 3–2 (scorers: Teddy Sheringham, Paul Scholes, Ryan Giggs).

2

1944

William 'Willie' Morgan (Forward 1968–75) was born in Sauchie, near Alloa, Scotland.

1957 OLD TRAFFORD TASTES EUROPEAN FOOTBALL

Manchester United 3   Shamrock Rovers 2

Shamrock Rovers became United's first ever Old Trafford European opponents and victims, in a competitive tie, when the Reds beat the Irish champions 3–2 in the first round of the European Cup. Dennis Viollet (2) and David Pegg scored for the Reds.

1968 LAW SHATTERS WATERFORD

Manchester United 7   Waterford 1
Denis Law scored four times against the Irish champions Waterford in this European Cup first round, second leg tie at Old Trafford. Francis Burns, Bobby Charlton and Nobby Stiles also scored to give United an aggregate 10–2 victory. Law had bagged a hat-trick in the first leg.

1996 TEA ANYONE?

Manchester United officially opened their Red Café at Old Trafford.

2007 BLOODY RONNY

Manchester United 1   AS Roma 0
Cristiano Ronaldo was forced off in the final five minutes of United's 1–0 UEFA Champions League win (scorer: Wayne Rooney) over AS Roma and had four stitches to the head wound he suffered against the Italian Serie A leaders. The game was United's 182nd in the European Cup/Champions League, the most appearances in the competition by any English League club, while only Juventus (186), AC Milan (200), Bayern Munich (277) and Real Madrid (301) had played more (Liverpool with 143 games occupied 12th place in the Top 20).

3

1891 THE INAUGURAL MANCHESTER DERBY

Newton Heath 5   Ardwick 1
Newton Heath were drawn to play Ardwick in an FA Cup first qualifying round game and hammered their opponents 5–1 with goals from Alf Farman 2, Roger Doughty, John Sneddon and Alfred Edge. The game marked the first ever Manchester derby as the Heathens subsequently became Manchester United in 1902 while Ardwick became Manchester City in 1894.

1981 ATKINSON GETS HIS MAN, CAPTAIN MARVEL IS SIGNED

Manchester United 5   Wolverhampton Wanderers 0
Bryan Robson had made almost 200 League appearances for West Bromwich Albion, scoring 39 goals, when his old boss at the Baggies, now in charge of Manchester United, returned to The Hawthorns and paid a joint fee of around £2m to bring both Robbo and Remi Moses to Old Trafford. The transfer deal rated Robbo at a British record transfer fee of £1.5m. Many football pundits questioned Ron Atkinson splashing out a bank-breaking £1.5m on a player

labelled 'injury prone'. During his early days with Albion Robbo suffered three leg breaks inside a year, which threatened his future in the game, but with great determination – something United fans would later see from him in abundance – he somehow made a complete recovery. Or maybe it was the diet of raw eggs and Guinness the team at West Bromwich Albion gave the skinny Robbo to beef him up that did the trick. However, just before agreeing the deal for the 24-year-old midfield marauder, Atkinson telephoned the legendary Bill Shankly to seek his valued opinion. Shanks simply told Atkinson that if Robbo was the player Atkinson thought he was, then he should do all he could to secure his signature.

When Robbo arrived at Old Trafford the club broke with tradition and brought him out on to the pitch, where the official signing ceremony took place. United, minus Robbo, thrashed Wolverhampton Wanderers 5–0 in this First Division game with United's Irish international midfielder Sammy McIlroy, the player many thought Robbo was bought to replace, scoring a hat-trick. The other goals came from Garry Birtles and Frank Stapleton.

4

1958 LIGHTS GO OUT ON UNITED

Wolverhampton Wanderers 4   Manchester United 0
Manchester United were the visitors to Molineux for the first ever Saturday night English League game played under floodlights, and lost 4–0. On the same night, Wilf McGuinness won the first of his two England caps when they drew 3–3 in a British Home International Championship game with Northern Ireland in Belfast. Bobby Charlton scored two of England's goals.

1997 TEDDY TAKES ON THE PALACE

Manchester United 2   Crystal Palace 0
Teddy Sheringham scored his first home Premier League goal since signing for United from Spurs (the other goal was an own goal). Brought in as a replacement for Eric Cantona, he scored 14 goals in his first season, second only to Andy Cole. He would go on to score five more goals in the next four Premier League matches.

5

1934
Ronald Cope (Half-back 1956–61) was born in Crewe.

1940
John David Gaskell (Goalkeeper 1957–67) was born in Orrell, Lancashire.

1977 UNITED'S HOME PARK FROM HOME
Manchester United 2   AS Saint-Étienne 0
UEFA forced Manchester United to play this European Cup Winners' Cup first round, second leg tie at least 300 miles from Manchester after a number of United fans had thrown bread at the French supporters in the first leg on 14 September. There was a bread strike on in France at the time. So, Home Park, Plymouth was the chosen venue and United won 2–0 with goals from Steve Coppell and Stuart Pearson. United progressed to the next round on a 3–1 aggregate victory.

1985 UNITED FALL AT 11th HURDLE
Luton Town 1   Manchester United 1
Manchester United were in fabulous form at the start of the 1985–86 season with Ron Atkinson's men winning their opening 10 First Division games, 30 points from 30, 26 goals for and just 3 conceded. The search for the club's first Championship success in 19 years was being spoken of but in this 11th game the run came to an end with a 1–1 draw against Luton Town (scorer: Mark Hughes) at Kenilworth Road. If United had won they would have equalled the best ever start to a First Division campaign of 11 consecutive victories set by Tottenham Hotspur's Double-winning side of 1960–61.

1993
James Alan 'Jim' Holton (Half-back 1972–5) died in Baginton, near Coventry, aged 42.

6

1888 A VERY OLD PROGRAMME

Newton Heath 0   Canadian XI 2
Newton Heath played a Canadian XI at North Road in the club's first game against international opposition. A match programme was produced for the game and it is believed to be the oldest home programme in the club's history.

1948 HIGHBURY THRILLER

Arsenal 4   Manchester United 3
United lost out to Arsenal in a close-fought Charity Shield match at Highbury. It was United's first appearance in the Shield for 37 years, and goals from Ronnie Burke, Jack Rowley and an own goal were not enough to secure victory. United have met Arsenal more times in the Charity/Community Shield (6) than any other opponent.

1956 BOBBY CHARLTON MAKES HIS UNITED DEBUT

Manchester United 4   Charlton Athletic 2
Bobby Charlton made his Manchester United debut against his namesake, Charlton Athletic, and scored two goals in United's 4–2 victory (the other scorers were Johnny Berry and Liam Whelan). In the return game four months later he bagged a hat-trick! Bobby Charlton was a Busby Babe who survived the Munich Air Disaster and who 10 years later helped Matt Busby fulfil his dream of conquering Europe by scoring two of United's four goals in the 1968 European Cup final at Wembley Stadium. The young Charlton, a nephew of the famous Newcastle United forward Jackie Milburn, arrived at Old Trafford as an amateur in January 1953. In October 1954 he turned professional for the club and over the next three decades he became one of the greatest players in the club's history. Charlton won FA Youth Cup winners' medals in 1954, 1955 and 1956. Although he wore the No.9 shirt for United he was more at home in midfield where his surging runs were usually followed by a bullet-like shot into the back of the opponents' net. Bobby enjoyed unprecedented success for both club and country. With United he won three League Championship medals (1957, 1965, 1967), an FA Cup winners' medal in 1963 (as well as finalists' medals in 1957 and 1958) and a European Cup winners' medal in 1968. In 1966 Bobby helped England to World Cup glory and in the same year he was voted European Footballer of the Year. He won 106 caps for his country and holds the record for most England goals, at 49. Along with Best and Law, Charlton brought the glory years back to

Old Trafford during the swinging sixties. At the time of writing, his 757 appearances and 249 goals for the Reds are both club records, though Ryan Giggs is closing in on his appearance record.

CHARLTON, Robert 'Bobby' (Midfielder/Forward 1956–73) – debut in the above game. Appearances: FL: 604 (2), goals 199 FAC: 79, goals 19 FLC: 24, goals 7 EUR: 45, 22 goals TOTAL: 757 (2), 249 goals.

1982 PETER'S FIRST AND ONLY

Manchester United 2   AFC Bournemouth 0
Peter Beardsley made his Manchester United debut in this 2–0 League Cup second round, first leg tie at Old Trafford (scorers: Frank Stapleton, o.g.). Beardsley never played for United again but went on to have a successful career at Liverpool, Newcastle United and with England.

BEARDSLEY, Peter Andrew (Forward 1982–3) – debut in the above game. Appearances: FLC: 1, goals 0 TOTAL: 1 app, 0 goals.

2007 A BRICK WALL

Manchester United 4   Wigan Athletic 0
Two goals from Cristiano Ronaldo and one each from Wayne Rooney and Carlos Tevez gave United a 4–0 win over Wigan Athletic, a result which saw United go to the top of the Premiership table for the first time since they were crowned champions at the end of the 2006–07 season. Amazingly, it was only the second headed goal of Rooney's career while Wigan's blank sheet made it the first time in 26 years that United had prevented their opponents scoring for six consecutive games. Danny Simpson had an outstanding game in his Premier League debut for the Reds.

7

1920

John Frederick 'Jack' 'Gunner' Rowley (Forward 1935–55) was born in Wolverhampton.

1950 JONES MAKES HIS DEBUT

Manchester United 3   Sheffield Wednesday 1
Mark Jones made his debut for Manchester United, slotting in for Allenby Chilton, who was making his debut for England in a 4–1 win over Northern Ireland in Belfast. United won the game 3–1 (scorers: John Downie, Harry McShane, Jack Rowley). Sadly, Jones lost his life in the Munich Air Disaster.

7 OCTOBER

JONES, Mark (Defender 1950–58) – debut in the above game.
Appearances: FL: 103, goals 1 FAC: 7, goals 0 EUR: 10, goals 0 TOTAL: 121 apps, 1 goal.

1967 LAW BANNED

Manchester United 1   Arsenal 0
Denis Law received a six-week ban following his sending off for fighting with Ian Ure of Arsenal at Old Trafford in this First Division encounter. Ure, a former United team-mate of Law's, was also sent off in the Reds' 1–0 win (scorer: John Aston Jnr). Law and Ure were also team-mates in the Scotland national side.

1972 UNITED'S FIRST SUPER TED

West Bromwich Albion 2   Manchester United 2
In September 1972 Frank O'Farrell, the Manchester United manager, paid AFC Bournemouth £200,000 for the services of their prolific striker Ted MacDougall. The fee was a record transfer for a Third Division player at the time. He made his Manchester United debut in a 2–2 First Division draw against West Bromwich Albion at The Hawthorns (scorers: George Best, Ian Storey-Moore). However, he spent only five months at Old Trafford before being sold to West Ham United by the new United manager Tommy Docherty. MacDougall went on to have a successful career scoring 256 League goals, the first Scottish player to score more than 200 League goals since United's very own Denis Law. He was also capped seven times by Scotland.

MacDOUGALL, Edward John 'Ted' (Forward 1972–3) – debut in the above game.
Appearances: FL: 18, goals 5 TOTAL: 18 apps, 5 goals.

1981 ROBBO PULLS ON A UNITED SHIRT FOR FIRST TIME

Tottenham Hotspur 1   Manchester United 0
Bryan Robson made his debut for Manchester United in this 1–0 League Cup second round, first leg defeat away to Spurs. When Robbo arrived at United he quickly grew in stature, becoming club captain in place of Ray Wilkins, a player with whom he enjoyed such a fine understanding and one who helped develop Bryan's already mature reading of the game. Robbo motivated all those around him and possessed an insatiable desire to succeed harnessed to an aggressive style of play, a seemingly endless supply of stamina, superb creative passing skills in attack or defence, pace, and powerful shooting and heading ability. He could also score, notching up over a century of League goals in his career, many of them arising from his unerring ability to make late blind-side runs into the area. But above all else, he was an inspirational captain for both club and country, a natural born leader who led United to a hat-trick of FA Cup wins in 1983, 1985 and 1990. In the 1983 final against Brighton & Hove Albion he scored twice in the 4–0 replay victory. In 1991 he picked-up a League Cup runners-up medal

and captained the Reds to European Cup Winners' Cup success, becoming the first captain to hold aloft a European trophy since Bobby Charlton lifted high the European Cup in 1968. Robson won 90 caps for England, wearing the Three Lions in three World Cups. His 26 international goals included a hat-trick against Turkey in 1984, and a strike after just 27 seconds against France in the 1982 World Cup, which at the time was the second-fastest goal of the tournament's final stages. In his final two seasons at Old Trafford Robson started only 15 Premiership games but more often than not usually made a telling contribution when called upon. To the delight of everyone the loyal servant ended his illustrious career by helping United complete the coveted League and Cup Double for the first time in the club's history in 1994. He scored United's last FA Premier League goal of the 1992–93 season. Captain Marvel's place in the history books of Manchester United is assured.

ROBSON, Bryan (Midfielder 1981–94) – debut in the above game.
Appearances: FL/PL: 326 (19), goals 74 FAC: 33 (2), goals 10 FLC: 50 (1), goals 5
EUR: 26 (1), goals 8 TOTAL: 437 (24) apps, 99 goals.

8

1926 UNITED BOSS SUSPENDED FOR IRREGULARITIES

Manchester United's secretary-manager John Chapman was suspended by the Football League for alleged management irregularities at the club. United appointed Walter Crickmer as secretary while Clarence Hilditch was asked to take over as player-manager until a suitable replacement for Chapman could be found. Hilditch remains the only man in the club's history to be player-manager (in 1969 Wilf McGuinness played for United and managed them but not at the same time). On 13 April 1927 Hilditch handed over the manager's role to Herbert Bamlett, while he continued to play for United until he retired in 1932.

1927 PLAYING DIXIE

Everton 5   Manchester United 2
Dixie Dean, the legendary Everton centre-forward, single-handedly destroyed Manchester United in this First Division game at Goodison Park by scoring all of his side's goals in their 5–2 win over the Reds. Samuel Bennion and Joe Spence scored for United.

1955 WILF'S DAY

Manchester United 4   Wolverhampton Wanderers 2
Wilf McGuinness made his debut for Manchester United in a 4–2 home win over

Wolves (scorers: Tommy Taylor 2, John Doherty, David Pegg). Wilf was a Busby Babe and enjoyed success in United's youth team during the early 1950s, appearing in three FA Youth Cup-winning teams. He also captained the England Youth side. After making his first-team debut Wilf flittered in and out of the team as competition for the left-half position was intense. Wilf was at home recovering from a cartilage operation when the Munich Air Disaster ripped the heart out of Manchester United. In December 1959, during a Central League game versus Stoke City, he broke a leg and, sadly for all United fans, this proved to be the end of his playing career. He was only 22 years old. Wilf joined the United coaching staff where he contributed to the success of the team on the field during the magical 1960s. On 9 April 1969 Manchester United announced to the football world that Wilf had been appointed chief coach, a move made in expectation of Sir Matt's retirement at the end of the 1968–69 season. On 1 June 1969 Wilf became the tenth manager of Manchester United, but things did not quite work out for him and in December 1970 he was forced to step down. Wilf reverted to trainer-coach of United's reserve team.

McGUINNESS, Wilfred 'Wilf' (Half-back 1955–60) – debut in the above game.
Appearances: FL: 81, goals 2 FAC: 2, goals 0 EUR: 2, goals 0 TOTAL: 85 apps, 2 goals.

1997 MASTER FERGIE

Manchester University awarded Alex Ferguson an Honorary Master of Arts Degree.

9

1954 BIG TOMMY'S ON SONG

Manchester United 5   Cardiff City 2
Tommy Taylor scored four times for Manchester United in this 5–2 First Division victory over Cardiff City. Dennis Viollet also scored. The prolific Taylor also scored four other hat-tricks in his career.

1974 ARTHUR'S DAY

Manchester United 1   Manchester City 0
Arthur Albiston made his debut for Manchester United in this 1–0 (scorer: Gerry Daly) third round League Cup win over rivals Manchester City at Old Trafford.

ALBISTON, Arthur Richard (Full-back 1974–88) – debut in the above game.
Appearances: FL: 364 (15), goals 6 FAC: 36, goals 0 FLC: 38 (2), goals 1
EUR: 26 (1), goals 0 TOTAL: 467 (18) apps, 7 goals.

10

1891 FIRST DERBY MEETING IN LEAGUE

Newton Heath 3   Ardwick 1
The first League derby meeting between Manchester United and Manchester City (then Newton Heath and Ardwick respectively) ended in a 3–1 win for the Heathens (scorers: Alf Farman 2, Robert Donaldson). A crowd of 4,000 turned up at North Road to see the game.

1935

Albert Joseph Scanlon (Forward 1954–61) was born in Manchester. Scanlon was the nephew of Charlie Mitten who played for United from 1946–50.

1981 ROBBO'S LEAGUE BOW IN GOALLESS DERBY

Manchester City 0   Manchester United 0
Bryan Robson made his League debut for Manchester United in this First Division 0–0 derby game at Maine Road.

11

1937

Robert 'Bobby' Charlton (Forward 1956–73) was born in Ashington, Northumberland.

1958 UNITED'S GRANDSTAND GAME

Manchester United 1   Arsenal 1
The inaugural transmission of BBC TV's Saturday afternoon sports programme *Grandstand* reported on a 1–1 First Division draw at Old Trafford between Manchester United and Arsenal (scorer: Dennis Viollet).

1986 DAVENPORT TAKES OUT WEDNESDAY

Manchester United 3   Sheffield Wednesday 1
Peter Davenport scored two goals (Norman Whiteside scored the other) to help United to a comfortable home win. Having struggled in the previous campaign, in 1986–87 he was United's leading scorer, with 16, but the arrival of Brian McClair the following year meant he had few subsequent opportunities.

12

1895 HEATHENS TAUGHT A LESSON

Liverpool 7   Newton Heath 1

Newton Heath went down to an embarrassing 7–1 defeat to Liverpool in this Second Division game at Anfield. Joe Cassidy scored a consolation goal for the Heathens.

1957 RECORD CITY GROUND GATE

Nottingham Forest 1   Manchester United 2

United were the visitors to the City Ground, Nottingham, to commemorate the official opening of their East Stand at a cost of £40,000. The Busby Babes won the First Division encounter 2–1 thanks to goals from Dennis Viollet and Liam Whelan. All of the players signed the match ball, which can be seen on display today in Nottingham Forest's trophy room. The crowd of 47,408 was a club record home attendance at the time. It was beaten on 28 October 1967 when 49,946 turned up to watch United again.

1988 CHOCCY'S DELIGHT

Manchester United 5   Rotherham United 0

Brian McClair scored a hat-trick for Manchester United in this League Cup second round, second leg win over Rotherham United at Old Trafford. Steve Bruce and Bryan Robson also scored to give United a 6–0 aggregate win over the two legs (Peter Davenport had scored in the 1–0 away win).

1992 UNDER THE HAMMER

Bill Foulkes's collection of football memorabilia items raised £35,000 at auction in Christie's, Glasgow. Bill's 1968 European Cup medal was sold for £11,000 while his actual shirt from the 1968 final was sold for £1,800.

1996 BECKS TO THE RESCUE

Manchester United 1   Liverpool 0

David Beckham scored a thunderbolt for Manchester United in their 1–0 Premier League win over Liverpool at Old Trafford. Beckham's goal reduced Liverpool's lead at the top of the Premiership table to a single point.

2006 KEANO'S BOOTS

A pair of boots worn and autographed by United legend Roy Keane in the 1999–2000 Premier League season realised £1,550 at an auction held at Christie's in London. At the same auction, a pair of boots worn by Sir Stanley Matthews in 1951 attracted a mere £1,350.

13

1956 BEST UNDEFEATED RUN OF LEAGUE GAMES

Sunderland 1   Manchester United 3
Manchester United set their best run of League games without defeat when they beat Sunderland 3–1 (scorers: Liam Whelan, Dennis Viollet, o.g.) at Roker Park. It was the Reds' 26th consecutive League game without defeat, a run that began with a 2–0 home victory over Burnley on 4 February 1956.

1979

Wesley Michael 'Wes' Brown (Defender 1996–present) was born in Manchester.

1999 WHO ARE YOU?

Aston Villa 3   Manchester United 0
When Manchester United met Aston Villa in this third round League Cup tie at Villa Park, none of the 11 players who took to the pitch at the start of the game had played in the Reds' last game, the 5–0 thrashing they received from Chelsea in the Premiership at Stamford Bridge ten days earlier.

14

1972 SUPER TED HANDS BLUES THE BLUES

Manchester United 1   Birmingham City 0
Ted MacDougall's first goal of the 1972–73 season gave Manchester United a 1–0 home win over Birmingham City in the First Division.

1978

Aston Villa 2   Manchester United 2
Goals from Lou Macari and Sammy McIlroy gave Manchester United a share of the points at Villa Park.

1995 SCHOLESY'S DERBY JOY

Manchester United 1   Manchester City 0
A goal in the fourth minute from Paul Scholes gave Manchester United a 1–0 win in the Manchester derby at Old Trafford.

15

1892 HEATHENS SET NEW RECORD FOOTBALL LEAGUE WIN

Newton Heath 10   Wolverhampton Wanderers 1
Season 1892–93 brought with it League football for the first time in the 14-year history of the club, and in their seventh First Division game of the campaign the Heathens recorded their inaugural League victory. The team would have welcomed any score so long as it was more than the opposition's having failed to register a win in their opening six games, but everyone was surprised when the club that was to become Manchester United claimed their first League victory with a 10-goal hammering of Wolverhampton Wanderers (scorers: Robert Donaldson 3, William Stewart 3, Adam Carson, Alfred Farman, James Hendry, William Hood). The impressive 10–1 win remains to this day a club record score in the League, while at the time it was a new Football League record score. William Stewart was an all-round sportsman who played cricket during the summer for Forfar and Perthshire. It is also one of only six games in United's history where two players have scored a hat-trick.

1910 UNITED GO TOP

Manchester United 2   Newcastle United 0
Manchester United beat Newcastle United 2–0 (scorers: Harold Halse, Sandy Turnbull) to go to the top of the First Division. United went on to win the Championship at the end of the season, finishing one point clear of Sunderland.

1960 DUNNE IN

Burnley 5   Manchester United 3
Despite a hat-trick from Dennis Viollet, Manchester United lost this First Division game 5–3 to Burnley at Turf Moor. The game marked the debut of Tony Dunne for the Reds.

> DUNNE, *Anthony Peter 'Tony' (Full-back 1960–73) – debut in the above game.*
> *Appearances: FL: 414, goals 2 FAC: 54 (1), goals 0 FLC: 21, goals 0 EUR: 40, goals 0*
> *TOTAL: 534 (1) apps, 2 goals.*

1971

Andrew Alexander 'Andy' Cole (Forward 1995–2001) was born in Nottingham.

1974 ARTHUR THE SECOND

Manchester United 0   Portsmouth 0
Six days after making his Manchester United debut in their 1–0 League Cup third-round win over Manchester City at Old Trafford, Arthur Albiston made his League debut for the Reds at home to Portsmouth. The game ended goalless.

1993 DANNY TURNS BLUE

Danny Wallace left Old Trafford and joined Birmingham City. He had scored 11 goals in 71 appearances in four years at the club.

16

1893 HEATHENS ACCUSED OF DIRTY TRICKS

Two days after Newton Heath beat West Bromwich Albion 4–1 an article written by 'Observer' appeared in the *Birmingham Daily Gazette*, accusing some of the Newton Heath players of dirty play in the game. The article described the Heathens' play as 'rough, brutal and cowardly' and characterised by 'dirty tricks'. Newton Heath sued the newspaper for £200 libel damages and won their case at Manchester Assizes. Unfortunately for the Heathens, the jury decided that the damage sustained by the club should be compensated by the lowest value of coin of the realm, which amounted to a farthing. The judge ordered both parties to pay their own legal costs, in Newton Heath's case £145. The court's ruling put a severe financial strain on the club.

1954 11-GOAL THRILLER AT THE BRIDGE

Chelsea 5   Manchester United 6
Manchester United won this 11-goal First Division thriller against Chelsea at Stamford Bridge 6–5 (scorers: Dennis Viollet 3, Tommy Taylor 2, Jackie Blanchflower). It is the only time in United's history that this scoreline has been recorded.

1965 NO.10 YOUR TIME IS UP

Tottenham Hotspur 5   Manchester United 1
Denis Law scored for Manchester United in a 5–1 reversal against Tottenham Hotspur at White Hart Lane in this First Division match. However, Law was then

taken off by Matt Busby and replaced by John Fitzpatrick, who became United's first ever substitute to be used.

1968 UNITED LOSE WORLD CLUB CHAMPIONSHIP

Manchester United 1   Estudiantes De La Plata 1
Manchester United went into the game trailing 1–0 from the first leg and once again the Argentinian team looked more interested in kicking the United players than the ball. The first leg was a brutal affair with the Estudiantes players constantly kicking George Best and Bobby Charlton, while Denis Law came in for particularly relentless foul play. George Best could take no more and retaliated, resulting in both him and Medina being sent off. United drew 1–1 (scorer: Willie Morgan) before a packed house of 63,500 at Old Trafford but lost the tie 2–1 on aggregate.

17

1948

Francis Burns (Defender 1967–72) was born in Glenboig, Lanarkshire.

1997 THE KHAKI CUP FINAL

A 1915 FA Cup final programme from the game played at Old Trafford was sold at Christie's for £11,270. The match took place on 24 April, with Sheffield United defeating Chelsea 3–0, and was the last FA Cup final to be played before competitive football was suspended in Britain because of the First World War. Old Trafford was selected as the venue to avoid disruption in London. The 1915 FA Cup final is famously known as the 'Khaki Cup Final' as a huge number of uniformed soldiers attended the game.

2006 NO JOY FOR DANES

Manchester United 3   FC Copenhagen 0
This was United's first official fixture against the Danish club. The comfortable win in the UEFA Champions League, with goals from John O'Shea, Kieran Richardson and Paul Scholes, meant United needed only one point from the next three fixtures to qualify for the knockout stages. But they had to wait till the final game to secure it.

18

1930 WORST RUN OF DEFEATS

Manchester United 1   Arsenal 2

When Manchester United lost 2–1 to Arsenal (scorer: George McLachlan) at Old Trafford it was the club's sixth consecutive defeat at home, their 11th successive defeat in total, thereby creating the worst run of home defeats in the club's history. Even before the game was played many disgruntled United fans decided enough was enough and formed a Supporters' Action Group in an attempt to organise a boycott of the match. However, 23,406 fans, United's biggest home gate of the season, watched their team lose again. The Red Devils also lost their next League game, 4–1 away to Portsmouth (scorer: Jack Rowley).

1952 BEST OF SEASON

Preston North End 0   Manchester United 5

Manchester United completed the first of a League double over their Lancashire rivals Preston North End by beating them 5–0 (scorers: Stan Pearson 2, John Aston Snr 2, Jack Rowley) at Deepdale.

1997 PRIDE PARK RECOVERY

Derby County 2   Manchester United 2

Manchester United paid their first visit to Derby County's new Pride Park Stadium. After trailing 2–0 early in the game, the Reds bounced back to draw 2–2 with goals from Teddy Sheringham and Andy Cole.

19

1892 PLAYER DIES AFTER GAME

In a game between Newton Heath Reserves and Darwen Reserves, the Heathens' James Brown and Darwen's Joseph Apsden accidentally bumped into one another, Brown's knee catching his opponent in the stomach. Apsden had to leave the field and was treated before being sent home to nurse his sore stomach. However, later that night he died. Although Brown was subsequently called to give evidence before the Coroner's Court, no action was taken against him as the panel recorded the unfortunate incident as an accidental death.

1960 FIRST LEAGUE CUP STEPS

Exeter City 1   Manchester United 1

This 1–1 draw (scorer: Alex Dawson) away to Exeter City in the first round of the League Cup was Manchester United's first ever game in the competition. On the same night Bobby Charlton scored a hat-trick for England in their 9–0 mauling of Luxembourg in a World Cup qualifying game played in Luxembourg.

1994 A GLOBAL AUDIENCE

Manchester United 2   FC Barcelona 2

This UEFA Champions League game was beamed live to 107 countries with a global audience of 80 million tuning in to watch an exciting 2–2 draw. Mark Hughes and Lee Sharpe scored for the Reds while Fergie dropped skipper Steve Bruce for the visit of the Spanish giants.

20

1934 BAMFORD OFF TO MAGPIES FLYER

Newcastle United 0   Manchester United 1

Thomas Bamford got his Manchester United career off to a flying start, scoring on his debut for the club in this 1–0 win over Newcastle United at St James' Park in the Second Division.

> **BAMFORD, Thomas 'Tommy'** *(Forward 1934–8) – debut in the above game.*
> *Appearances: FL: 98, goals 53 FAC: 11, goals 4 TOTAL: 109 apps, 57 goals.*

1956 FIRST HOME DEFEAT IN 18 MONTHS

Manchester United 2   Everton 5

Manchester United lost their first game at Old Trafford in 18 months when Everton beat the Reds 5–2. The defeat brought an unbeaten run of 26 League games to a halt. Bobby Charlton and Liam Whelan scored for the Reds. It was Whelan's eighth goal in eight successive League games. Ironically, Everton had also been the last team to win at Old Trafford when they beat United 2–1 in March 1955.

1973 STEPNEY PENALTY GIVES UNITED VICTORY

Manchester United 1   Birmingham City 0

Manchester United's goalkeeper Alex Stepney scored the only goal of this First Division game at Old Trafford. When United were awarded a penalty, up went Stepney to take it and he scored from the spot. It was his second League goal of the season, having scored a penalty against Leicester City in a 2–1 home defeat on 12 September 1973. He would remain United's joint leading scorer until after Christmas.

1990 OLD TRAFFORD PUNCH-UP

Manchester United 0   Arsenal 1
This was an ill-tempered First Division affair between Manchester United and Arsenal, which turned nasty and resulted in 21 of the 22 players on the field fighting. Only Les Sealey in the Manchester United goal kept his calm and watched the punch-up erupt in front of him. Following an enquiry into the incident by the FA, United were deducted one League point for misconduct while Arsenal were slapped with a two-point deduction. Arsenal went on to be crowned champions at the end of the season, managed by former United player George Graham.

1993 UNITED FAIL TO WIN A HOME EUROPEAN CUP TIE FOR FIRST TIME

Manchester United 3   Galatasaray 3
Bryan Robson scored his last European goal for United in their 3–3 draw with Turkish side Galatasaray in a European Cup second round, first leg tie at Old Trafford. The other scorers were Eric Cantona and a Hakan own goal. Remarkably, it was the first time in United's history that they failed to win a European Cup game at Old Trafford.

1996 GEORDIE REVENGE FOR CHARITY SHIELD

Newcastle United 5   Manchester United 0
Kevin Keegan's side avenged their humiliating 4–0 FA Charity Shield defeat by Manchester United back in August by beating the Reds 5–0 in the Premier League at St James' Park.

2007 RONNY'S DOUBLE CENTURY

Aston Villa 1   Manchester United 4
Manchester United scored four goals for the second successive Premiership game when they beat Aston Villa 4–1 at Villa Park (scorers: Wayne Rooney 2, Rio Ferdinand, Ryan Giggs). The game marked Cristiano Ronaldo's 200th appearance for United.

21

1950 NAMING THE OPPOSITION

Manchester United 0   Portsmouth 0

This First Division 0–0 draw at Old Trafford was the first time Manchester United printed the name of the opposing team on the front cover of the official match programme, the *United Review*.

1967

Paul Emerson Carlyle Ince (Midfielder 1989–95) was born in Ilford.

1981

Nemanja Vidic (Defender 2006–present) was born in Uzice, Serbia.

1998 SLICED DANISH

Brondby 2   Manchester United 6

United registered a record-equalling six away goals in Europe when they easily defeated their Danish challengers in this Champions League Group game. Ryan Giggs (2), Andy Cole, Roy Keane, Ole Gunnar Solskjaer and Dwight Yorke all scored. Two weeks later, United put five past the Danes at Old Trafford.

22

1932 JOE'S LANDMARK 500th GAME

Manchester United 7   Millwall 1

The most remarkable thing about this 7–1 hammering of Millwall in Division Two was the fact that United's magical little winger Joe Spence was playing his 500th game for the Reds, the first player ever to achieve the landmark appearances figure for the club (Newton Heath or Manchester United). 'Give it to Joe', as he was affectionately nicknamed by the Old Trafford faithful, and as they chanted when they thought the game was lacking entertainment, scored in the game along with Thomas Reid (3), James Brown (2) and Stanley Gallimore. Joe ended his Old Trafford career the same season after 10 more appearances, scoring a total of 168 goals.

1937 GUNNER ARRIVES

Manchester United signed Jack 'Gunner' Rowley for £3,000 from Bourne-mouth & Boscombe Athletic.

1945 MATT BUSBY BEGINS WORK AT UNITED

After agreeing to become the new manager of Manchester United back in February 1945, Matt Busby settled into his first day in charge at Old Trafford.

1957 TAYLOR TAKES OUT VILLANS

Manchester United 4   Aston Villa 0
United retained the Charity Shield in this comfortable victory over the Villa side that had denied them the Double in the FA Cup final. Tommy Taylor became the last United player to score a hat-trick in this fixture, and Johnny Berry added the other goal.

1980 BIRTLES DEBUT

Stoke City 1   Manchester United 2
Garry Birtles made his debut for Manchester United in this 2–1 First Division away win over Stoke City. Joe Jordan and Lou Macari scored for United.

> **BIRTLES, Garry** *(Forward 1980–82) – debut in the above game.*
> *Appearances:* FL: *57 (1), goals 11* FAC: *4, goals 1* FLC: *2, goals 0*
> TOTAL: *63 (1) apps, 12 goals.*

2003 'BATTLE OF BRITAIN' CLASH

Rangers 0   Manchester United 1
Manchester United beat the Scottish champions Rangers 1–0, in this 'Battle of Britain' UEFA Champions League clash at Ibrox thanks to a rare goal from Phil Neville after just five minutes. 'It was a great game of football, the atmosphere was terrific, the pitch was great and Rangers gave it everything,' said a delighted Sir Alex Ferguson, a former Rangers player.

23

1937 GUNNER'S DEBUT

Manchester United 1   Sheffield Wednesday 0
Jack 'Gunner' Rowley made his Manchester United debut in this 1–0 Second Division win over Sheffield Wednesday at Old Trafford (scorer: Ronald Ferrier). Jack Rowley is one of the greatest ever strikers to pull on a Manchester United

shirt. In 1937–38, his first season at Old Trafford following his arrival from Bournemouth & Boscombe Athletic, the powerful and prolific Rowley helped United out of the Second Division as runners-up. When war broke out in 1939, Rowley joined the South Staffordshire Regiment and participated in the D-Day landings at Normandy on 6 June 1944. During the war Rowley guested for Wolverhampton Wanderers, Aldershot, Belfast Distillery, Folkestone, Shrewsbury Town and Tottenham Hotspur. Indeed, in one particular guest appearance for Wolves he scored eight goals. In 1948 he won an FA Cup winners' medal with the Reds (scoring twice in United's 4–2 win over Blackpool) and his goals helped fire them to the First Division Championship in 1951–52.

ROWLEY, *John Frederick 'Jack' (Forward 1935–55) – debut in the above game.*
Appearances: FL: 380, goals 182 FAC: 42, goals 26 TOTAL: 424 apps, 211 goals.

1971 BEST QUAD

Newcastle United 0 Manchester United 1
George Best scored in his fourth consecutive League game (his 11th League goal in 14 games) to give Manchester United a 1–0 win over Newcastle United at St James' Park.

2007 THE RED MARAUDERS

Dynamo Kiev 2 Manchester United 4
Wayne Rooney scored in his fourth consecutive game for Manchester United when he netted twice in their impressive 4–2 away win over Dynamo Kiev in their UEFA Champions League group game, with Rio Ferdinand and Cristiano Ronaldo also finding the Ukrainian net. It was United's third straight victory from their opening three group games.

24

1927 UNITED'S SAVIOUR DIES

John Henry Davies, widely regarded as the Saviour of Manchester United, and certainly a pivotal figure in the club's early history, died. When Newton Heath subsequently became Manchester United in April 1902, John H. Davies was elected as the club's first president and over the following 25 years he continued to back the club financially when times were tough. Along with Ernest Mangnall, who was appointed manager of United in 1903, Davies brought success to the club, winning the First Division Championship in 1908 and 1911 and the FA Cup in 1909. Davies also played a significant role in United moving to a new home in 1910, Old Trafford.

1956 YOUNG GASKELL REPAYS MATT'S FAITH

Manchester City 0   Manchester United 1

A unique Manchester derby took place during the 1956–57 season, the 1956 FA Charity Shield. United, the reigning League champions, faced City, the 1956 FA Cup winners, in the customary showpiece game. United as champions had the right to host the game (Wembley was not the venue until 1974) but since it was a midweek fixture it was played at Maine Road because Old Trafford did not have any floodlights at the time. United won the match 1–0 thanks to a goal 15 minutes from time by Dennis Viollet. Matt Busby rested his first-choice goal-keeper, Ray Wood, replacing him with the young and inexperienced David Gaskell who, aged 16 years 19 days, became United's youngest post-war player. However, Gaskell was a regular in the United youth team and had played in goal for them in May 1956 when they beat West Ham United 8–2 on aggregate over two legs to claim the club's fifth consecutive FA Youth Cup.

1964 LAW MURDERS VILLANS

Manchester United 7   Aston Villa 0

Denis Law hit four goals in United's 7–0 demolition of Aston Villa at Old Trafford in the First Division. David Herd (2) and John Connelly also scored for the Reds.

1985 WAZZA IS BORN

Wayne Rooney (Forward 2004–present) was born in Croxteth, Liverpool. Following Wayne's superb performances for England at the 2004 European Championship in Portugal, Manchester United signed the 18-year-old from his boyhood heroes Everton in August 2004. The £20m price tag (rising to a possible £30m) made him the world's most expensive teenager but did little to faze him. After recovering from a metatarsal injury, which he had picked up in Portugal, Wayne burst on to the Old Trafford stage on 28 September 2004 when he produced a stunning display to steer an unforgettable debut hat-trick past a shell-shocked Fenerbahce in the UEFA Champions League. It was a fairytale start to his Manchester United career and very much a sign of what was to follow. By the end of the 2004–05 Premiership campaign Wayne had amassed 17 goals in 43 appearances and was the Man of the Match in the 2005 FA Cup final, which the Reds lost to Arsenal on penalties. However, he was voted the 2004–05 PFA Young Player of the Year. In Rooney's second season at Old Trafford he again took huge strides, justifying his billing as one of the world's most exciting young talents. He netted the Reds' first goal of the season against Debreceni and ended the season with 19 goals in 48 matches. It was a contribution that saw him named both Sir Matt Busby Player of the Year by fans and PFA Young Player of the Year (again) by his fellow professionals. The young striker openly endeavours to better his goals tally each season, and in the 2006–07 Premiership campaign he achieved his aim with 23 goals as he shook off a difficult World Cup with England. A long goalscoring drought was emphatically ended with a stunning hat-trick at Bolton Wanderers as United regained their Premiership crown. However, the final word on Wayne must come from the man who signed him, Sir Alex Ferguson, who described him as 'the best young player I have seen in my time'.

2002 WAYNE TOPS BBC VOTE

Wayne Rooney (then at Everton) won the BBC Young Sports Personality of the Year Award. It was his 17th birthday the same day.

2004 BUFFET BATTLE

Manchester United 2   Arsenal 0
Arsenal arrived at Old Trafford looking for their 50th unbeaten game in the Premiership with many of their fans already sporting '50 NOT OUT' T-shirts in and around the stadium. However, United were in no mood to play second fiddle to the team with whom they had shared the last seven FA Premier League titles (five for United and two for Arsenal), and brought the high-flying Gunners crashing back down to earth with a 2–0 (scorers: Ruud van Nistelrooy, Wayne Rooney) win before a delighted home crowd. But it is what occurred after the match that will be remembered as much as United's scintillating performance. The media had a field day reporting that trouble between the two sides kicked off in the tunnel after the game. Food then started to be hurled out of the Arsenal dressing room with the United boss caught in the line of fire of flying slices of pizza, mixed sandwiches and even cartons of pea soup.

25

1930 UNITED SET RECORD FOR WORST START EVER

Portsmouth 4   Manchester United 1
Manchester United made the worst start to a First Division campaign by any club when they lost 4–1 at Portsmouth (scorer: Harry Rowley). It was their 12th successive defeat since the opening day of the season, a run during which they scored 14 goals and conceded 49. It would be November before United registered their first League points of the season. Added to two defeats in their last two home games of the previous season, it made it the worst losing sequence at home in the club's history at 14.

1932

Henry 'Harry' Gregg (Goalkeeper 1957–67) was born in Tobermore, near Magherafelt, Northern Ireland.

1937

Wilfred 'Wilf' McGuinness (Half-back 1955–60) was born in Manchester.

1997 COLE FIRES REDS TO VICTORY OVER TYKES

Manchester United 7   Barnsley 0
A hat-trick from Andy Cole, plus goals from Ryan Giggs (2), Paul Scholes and Karel Poborsky, gave United an emphatic 7–0 victory over Premiership newcomers Barnsley at Old Trafford.

26

1952

Arthur Graham (Forward 1983–5) was born in Castlemilk, Glasgow.

1960 UNITED'S LOWEST LEAGUE CUP CROWD AT OLD TRAFFORD

Manchester United 4   Exeter City 1
Manchester United's first home game in the League Cup ended in a 4–1 victory (scorers: Albert Quixall 2 pens, Johnny Giles, Mark Pearson) over Exeter City in a first round replay. The crowd of 15,662 is United's all-time record low in the competition for a home tie.

1961

John Sivebaek (Full-Back 1982–5) was born in Vejle, Denmark.

1986 DERBY TV STARS

Manchester City 1   Manchester United 1
The first Manchester derby game to be shown live on television coincided with the lowest post-war attendance for the fixture when 32,440 fans turned up at Maine Road for the game. Frank Stapleton scored for the Reds.

1996 UNITED FADE TO GREY

Southampton 6   Manchester United 3
Six days after conceding five goals away to Newcastle United, Southampton put

six past the Reds at The Dell. David Beckham, David May and Andy Cole scored for United against the Saints. To make matters worse for the Reds, Roy Keane was sent off. At half-time, the United players changed out of their grey kit into another away strip, claiming they could not pick out team-mates against the background of the crowd.

27

1964 UNITED'S FIRST INTER-CITIES FAIRS CUP VISITORS

Manchester United 6   Djurgardens IF 1
Djurgardens IF became the first team to visit Old Trafford for an Inter-Cities Fairs Cup tie. Manchester United had drawn the away leg 1–1 (scorer: David Herd) and sailed into the second round following this comprehensive 6–1 win (scorers: Denis Law 3, Bobby Charlton 2, George Best). The competition subsequently became known as the UEFA Cup. Bobby Charlton's first goal made him the first Manchester United player to score for the club in all three of Europe's major cup competitions: he scored his first European Cup goal in United's 2–2 home draw with Real Madrid on 25th April 1957 (played at Maine Road) and bagged his first European Cup Winners' Cup goal for the Reds in their 6–1 first round, second leg home win over Willem II on 15 October 1963.

1976 REDS' BEST EVER LEAGUE CUP WIN

Manchester United 7   Newcastle United 2
Having disposed of Newcastle United's neighbours, Sunderland, in the third round of the 1976–77 League Cup competition, the Reds powered past the Geordies in round 4. United's 7–2 victory (scorers: Gordon Hill 3, Jimmy Nicholl, Stewart Houston, Steve Coppell, Stuart Pearson) over Newcastle United is their best ever win in the competition.

1988 MAL'S ARRIVAL

Mal Donaghy, a Northern Ireland international, joined United from Luton Town.

1990 REDS' LATE COMEBACK IN DERBY CLASH

Manchester City 3   Manchester United 3
Manchester United drew 3–3 (scorers: Brian McClair 2, Mark Hughes) with neighbours Manchester City in a Barclay's League Division One game at Maine Road. United were trailing 3–1 with only 10 minutes of the game remaining.

2007 FIRST IN A CENTURY

Manchester United 4   Middlesbrough 1

Manchester United easily beat Middlesbrough 4–1 at Old Trafford to move to the top of the Premier League. The Reds took the lead in the third minute when Nani fired home a 30-yard thunderbolt before the visitors drew level. But it wasn't long before United slipped into top gear as Wayne Rooney added a second followed by two goals from Carlos Tevez. It was the first time in over 100 years that United scored four goals in successive games – Wigan Athletic (h) 4–0, Aston Villa (a) 4–1 and Dynamo Kiev (a) 4–2. In season 1907–08 the Reds beat Chelsea (a) 4–1, Nottingham Forest (h) 4–0, Newcastle United (a) 6–1 and Blackburn Rovers (a) 5–1 en route to winning the First Division Championship for the first time in the club's history.

28

1924

Edward W. Buckle (Forward 1946–50) was born in Southwark, London.

1992 VILLANS DUMP REDS OUT OF CUP

Aston Villa 1   Manchester United 0

Aston Villa put United out of the 1992–93 League Cup at Villa Park. It was the shape of things to come as the two clubs went head-to-head all season in the race for the inaugural Premier League.

2000 SUPER TED'S OLD HAT-TRICK

Manchester United 5   Southampton 0

Manchester United hammered the Saints 5–0 in this very one-sided Premiership encounter at Old Trafford. Teddy Sheringham scored three to make him at 34 years 6 months and 26 days the oldest player in the history of the club to score a hat-trick for United. Andy Cole scored the other two goals.

29

1970 FILLING SCHMEICHEL'S GLOVES

Edwin van der Sar (Goalkeeper 2005–present) was born in Voorhout, The Netherlands. He began his career with Ajax Amsterdam in 1990 and won UEFA

Cup (1992) and UEFA Champions League (1995) winners' medals with the Dutch club plus four League titles (1994, 1995, 1996, 1998), three domestic cups (1993, 1998, 1999), the European Super Cup (1995) and the World Club Championship (1995). His performacces for Ajax in season 1994–95 earned him Europe's Best Goalkeeper award. In 1999, after making 226 League appearances for Ajax and scoring one goal, he signed for Juventus in Serie A but stayed in Turin for only two seasons. In 2001 he made a £5m switch to Fulham where he stayed for four seasons (127 League appearances) helping the London outfit win the Intertoto Cup (2002) and retain their Premiership status before United came knocking at Craven Cottage in 2005 to lure him to Old Trafford. Edwin was signed by Manchester United for an undisclosed fee. In his first season with the club, Edwin started all but five of United's 56 games, keeping an impressive 24 clean sheets, including five on the spin from his debut. Van der Sar's solid presence, agility and reliability have been a major plus to United while his quick and inventive distribution aid the team's speedy attacking style. These qualities helped the Reds to their Carling Cup win in 2005–06, Premiership glory in 2006–07 and Community Shield success in 2007–08. His 12 clean sheets in the Premiership during the 2006–07 season included a late penalty save from Darius Vassell against Manchester City at Eastlands near the end of the campaign (United won 1–0), which was a defining moment, a veritable title-clinching stop. Edwin was voted into the 2007 Premiership Team of the Year.

2006 THE MILLENNIUM MAN

Middlesbrough 4   Manchester United 1
Cristiano Ronaldo scored Manchester United's 1,000th Premier League goal in a 4–1 away defeat to Middlesbrough.

30

1886 HEATHENS REFUSE TO PLAY

Fleetwood Rangers 2   Newton Heath 2
In season 1886–87 Newton Heath entered the FA Cup for the first time in the club's history and despite not losing a game they were put out of the competition in unusual circumstances. The Heathens were drawn away to Fleetwood Rangers in the first round and drew 2–2 (scorer: John Doughty 2). However, when the referee asked Newton Heath to play extra-time to decide who would progress to the next round the players refused and walked off the pitch, leaving the official with no other option but to award the tie to the home side. Fleetwood were drawn away to Partick Thistle in the second round and were thumped 7–1 (Scottish teams were allowed to enter the competition at the time).

1996 PROUD EUROPEAN HOME RECORD FALLS

Manchester United 0   Fenerbahce 1

Manchester United first entered European competition in 1956 and up until this game they had never been beaten at Old Trafford in a European game. Their proud record lasting 57 ties finally fell to the Turkish champions Fenerbahce in this 1996–97 UEFA Champions League group game. It was also the first time in 27 home European Cup matches that the Reds failed to find the back of the net.

31

1921 FROM MANAGER TO ASSISTANT

Manchester United were going nowhere fast in season 1920–21 and the board decided to 'ask' the manager John Robson to step down. Robson reluctantly agreed to vacate his managerial post and made way for the arrival of John Chapman as the new manager. When Chapman eventually took charge at Old Trafford Robson was appointed as his assistant.

1965

Denis Joseph Irwin (Full-back 1990–2002) was born in Cork, Ireland.

1988 PETER ON HIS WAY

Peter Davenport left Manchester United and signed for Middlesbrough.

1990 REDS DUMP REDS OUT OF CUP

Manchester United 3   Liverpool 1

On their way to the League Cup final in 1991, Manchester United disposed of Lancashire rivals Liverpool in the third round at Old Trafford. United won 3–1 (scorers: Steve Bruce pen, Mark Hughes, Lee Sharpe).

1994 INCEY THE FIRST

Paul Ince became the first Manchester United player to win the Premier League's Player of the Month Award, for October 1994.

NOVEMBER

1

1921 CHAPMAN TAKES THE HOT SEAT

John Chapman took up his position as manager of Manchester United after replacing John Robson in the Old Trafford hot seat. Robson was made his assistant while Chapman reverted to the dual role of secretary/manager last held by J. J. Bentley. Chapman had a disastrous start to his tenure in charge of the Reds and lost the services of the inspirational Billy Meredith, signed by ex-United manager Ernest Mangnall for Manchester City, despite the fact that he was 47 years old. It was perhaps no coincidence that United were relegated in their first season without him, winning only 8 of their 42 matches in season 1921–22. Chapman's United played in the Second Division for the next three seasons until, under the leadership of Frank Barson on the pitch, the team pulled together, resulting in promotion back to the First Division at the end of the 1924–25 season when Manchester United finished second to Leicester City, after losing only eight games. In season 1925–26 Chapman steered United to a respectable ninth place in the First Division but the board and the fans wanted more. A good FA Cup run in season 1925–26 put United on the brink of reaching the final only to lose 3–0 to Manchester City at Sheffield United's Bramall Lane ground in the semi-finals. However, the fortunes of the two Manchester sides underwent a role reversal as City lost the final and were relegated to the Second Division. Two months into the 1926–27 season the FA suspended manager John Chapman with immediate effect, the reasons for which never became public. Wing-half Clarence 'Lal' Hilditch took over as player-manager while the club looked for a permanent replacement, but Hilditch was reluctant to select himself as a starter and the team suffered.

1963 SPARKY ARRIVES

Leslie Mark Hughes (Forward 1980–86, 1988–95) was born in Wrexham. Mark Hughes's love affair with Manchester United began in March 1978 when, aged just 14, he signed on as a schoolboy at Old Trafford. However, it was United's youth team coach, Syd Owen, who recognised that his young Welsh dragon had the skills necessary to make it in senior football and how right he was. Sparky made a goalscoring debut against Oxford United in the fourth round of the League (Milk) Cup just 29 days after his 20th birthday. Six months later he won his first Welsh cap and celebrated his international debut with a goal against England. In 1985 he was named PFA Young Player of the Year and collected an FA Cup winners' medal after United's dramatic 10-man victory over Everton in the final at Wembley. However, in season 1985–86 Sparky had a fall-out with the club, and within a year he was off to Spain to join Terry Venables' new revolution at Barcelona. The young Welsh striker never really settled in Spain and Barca sent him out on loan to Bayern Munich during the 1987–88 season where he rediscovered his goalscoring touch.

In July 1988 Alex Ferguson managed to persuade Sparky to come home to Manchester. Fergie's £1.5m investment proved to be a masterstroke: Hughes was named PFA Player of the Year in his first season back and he helped United win the 1990 FA Cup final with two goals against Crystal Palace, forcing a replay that gave Fergie his first trophy. In 1991 he was once again named Player of the Year and experienced glorious retribution with a man-of-the-match display in the 2–1 European Cup Winners' Cup final win in Rotterdam over the club that rejected him, Barcelona, scoring both United goals (although Steve Bruce tried to claim the first!). Later that year he picked up a European Super Cup winners' medal when his striking partner, Brian McClair, scored the only goal of the game against the European Cup holders, Red Star Belgrade. More trophies followed; he won a League Cup winners' medal in 1992 (United's first ever League Cup win) and then in season 1992–93 Hughes and his new strike partner, Eric Cantona, fired the bulk of the goals that landed United their first Championship success in 26 long years. However, whereas the genius of Cantona attracted the headlines it was Hughes's 100th League goal for the Reds against Crystal Palace that helped clinch the inaugural FA Premier League Championship crown. Sir Alex once said: 'Hughes was the best big game player I have known,' and the Boss's prophetic statement was never better demonstrated than when Sparky scored an injury-time volley in the 1994 FA Cup semi-final against Oldham Athletic just as the Reds were staring defeat in the face. United beat Oldham in the replay and went on to hammer Chelsea 4–0 in the final with Hughes scoring the third goal to clinch the club's first ever Double.

In July 1995 Sparky signed for boyhood favourites Chelsea and he went on to collect a fourth FA Cup winners' medal and a second European Cup Winners' Cup medal with the Blues. After Chelsea he moved on to Southampton, Everton and later Blackburn, where he picked up the last gong of his playing career, another League Cup winners' medal. He finally hung up his playing boots at the age of 38. However, Sparky had his heart firmly set on testing himself as a manager, having launched his managerial career during his time at Southampton when he was appointed the part-time manager of the Welsh national team. Sparky masterminded a famous win for the Welsh over Italy and almost took

Wales to Euro 2004, before returning to Ewood Park to take up his current role as the full-time manager of Blackburn Rovers.

2

1888 UNITED MANAGER WINS LEAGUE AND CUP AS A PLAYER

Scott Duncan, manager of Manchester United from 1932–7, was born in Dumbarton, Scotland. Duncan began his playing career with his hometown club before joining Newcastle United in 1908 for a fee of £105. He played for the Geordies 81 times and won a First Division winners' medal with them in season 1908–09 and an FA Cup winners' medal in 1910. He also played for Glasgow Rangers. On 1 August 1932 he was appointed the new manager of Manchester United, taking over from Walter Crickmer. Prior to arriving at Old Trafford Duncan had been manager at Hamilton Academical and Cowdenbeath. He guided United to sixth place in Division Two in his first full season in charge (1932–33). However, the following season he almost took United into Division Three and only a 2–0 win away to Millwall in the final game of the season kept the Reds in Division Two – they finished 20th (22 teams) in the table. Then the following season things started to look up at United when he guided them to fifth place in Division Two. United finally came good under his leadership in season 1935–36 by winning the Second Division and returning to the top flight. However, the Reds went straight back down to Division Two at the end of the 1936–37 season after finishing in 21st place in the table. He left United in November 1937.

1895 PETERS SINKS POOL

Manchester United 5 Liverpool 2
James Peters scored a hat-trick for Newton Heath in their 5–2 win over Liverpool in the Second Division. John Clarkin and Richard Smith also scored for the Heathens but it was Liverpool who were smiling at the end of the season after winning the Championship, while Newton Heath could only manage a sixth-place finish.

1960 EMPTY SEATS

Bradford City 2 Manchester United 1
Bradford City beat Manchester United 2–1 (scorer: Dennis Viollet) in this League Cup second round tie at Valley Parade. The crowd of 4,670 represents United's lowest post-war attendance for a competitive fixture.

1974 PANCHO HAT-TRICK

Manchester United 4   Oxford United 0
Stuart Pearson scored a hat-trick for Manchester United in their 4–0 mauling of Oxford United at Old Trafford in the Second Division. The attacking performance was typical of United's play throughout the 1974–75 season as they made an immediate return to the top flight by winning the Second Division Championship. Lou Macari also scored in the game.

1977 A HELPING BOOT

Manchester United 5   FC Porto 2
Manchester United beat the Portuguese side FC Porto 5–2 at Old Trafford in this second round, second leg European Cup Winners' Cup tie. However, two goals from Steve Coppell, one from Jimmy Nicholl and two own goals from Porto defender Murca were not enough to see the Reds through to the third round, having lost the first leg 4–0 in Portugal.

3

1894 A PROLIFIC HEATHEN

Manchester City 2   Newton Heath 5
This game marked the first Manchester derby in the League. The Heathens had played Ardwick (renamed Manchester City) previously in the Football Alliance, FA Cup and Manchester Cup but this game played at Ardwick was a Second Division encounter. The Heathens won this historic game 5–2 thanks to four goals from striker Richard Smith and one from John Clarkin. It was the first time a player had scored four League goals for the club in a game, and the only time a United player has done it in the derby. Season 1894–95 was the first of Smith's two separate spells with Newton Heath (1894–8, 1899–1901) with five months at Bolton Wanderers (January–May 1899) sandwiched between. His first season with the Heathens was his most prolific – he scored 20 League and FA Cup goals, which meant the Heathens finished third in the Second Division and earned a Test Match play-off game with Stoke City, who had finished third from bottom of the First Division. The Heathens lost the game and remained in Division Two. In 1895–96 Smith missed just two games during the entire season, and one of them fell on his wedding day!

1962 THE IRRESISTIBLE LAWMAN

Ipswich Town 3   Manchester United 5
Denis Law scored four times for Manchester United in this 5–3 away win over

Ipswich Town at Portman Road in the First Division. David Herd also scored. Four days later Denis was on international duty for his beloved Scotland and bagged another four, this time against Norway.

1993 DEVILS VISIT HELL

Galatasaray 0   Manchester United 0
When Manchester United arrived at Istanbul Airport for their European Cup tie with Galatasaray, the Turkish fans gave them a hot welcome with some banners reading 'Welcome To Hell'. United drew 0–0 but were knocked out of the competition, having drawn the first leg 3–3 at Old Trafford. On a miserable night for the Reds, Eric Cantona was sent off after the final whistle had been blown and both he and Bryan Robson were attacked with batons by the Turkish police as they made their way down the tunnel to the relative safety of the dressing rooms.

2004 FOUR FOR RUUD

Manchester United 4   Sparta Prague 1
Ruud van Nistelrooy scored all four of United's goals in this 4–1 demolition of Sparta Prague in the UEFA Champions League at Old Trafford. His quad came in the 14th, 25th, 60th and 90th minutes. Amazingly, this was the third time a player had scored four goals on 3 November in just 14 fixtures played on this day.

4

1986 BIG RON'S SWAN SONG

Southampton 4   Manchester United 1
This League Cup third round replay defeat to Southampton at The Dell brought the curtain down on Ron Atkinson's time in charge of Manchester United. Peter Davenport scored the Reds' consolation goal.

2003 UNITED WIN 'BATTLE OF BRITAIN'

Manchester United 3   Rangers 0
Manchester United beat the Scottish champions Rangers 3–0 in this 'Battle of Britain' UEFA Champions League clash at Old Trafford to complete the double over the Scottish side. United's in-form Uruguayan striker Diego Forlan scored a spectacular goal in the fifth minute, followed by two goals from Ruud van Nistelrooy, one in each half (42nd and 59th mins). In the first leg of this tie Manchester United had beaten Rangers 1–0 at Ibrox on 22 October 2003.

5

1892 EIGHT-GOAL STALEMATE

Newton Heath 4   Blackburn Rovers 4
Newton Heath drew 4–4 with Blackburn Rovers in this First Division game played at the Heathen's North Road ground. Alf Farman scored twice for the Heathens with their other goals coming from Adam Carson and William Hood. The Heathens had a miserable 1892–93 season, finishing bottom of the First Division (16 teams) with just 18 points from their 30 League games. However, they managed to avoid the drop into the Second Division by winning their Test Match play-off encounter against Small Heath (renamed Birmingham FC in 1905 and Birmingham City in 1944).

1938 EX-SWAN BECOMES A DEVIL

Aston Villa 0   Manchester United 2
Jack Warner made his Manchester United debut in this 2–0 First Division win over Aston Villa at Villa Park (scorers: Jack Rowley, William Wrigglesworth). Manchester United had signed Warner from Swansea Town in June 1938 after the half-back scored a superb goal against the Red Devils.

> **WARNER, John 'Jack'** (Half-back 1938–50) – *debut in the above game.*
> *Appearances: FL: 102, goals 1 FAC: 13, goals 1 TOTAL: 115 apps, 2 goals.*

1997 COLE FOLLOWS IN THE KING'S FOOTSTEPS

Feyenoord 1   Manchester United 3
Andy Cole's hat-trick for United in this UEFA Champions League group win over Feyenoord was the first hat-trick scored by a United player in Europe since Denis Law walked off the Old Trafford pitch with the match ball after bagging four in their 7–1 win over Waterford on 2 October 1968.

6

1965 THE GLOVES ARE OFF

Manchester United 2   Blackburn Rovers 2
Bobby Charlton and Denis Law scored for Manchester United in this 2–2 First Division draw with Blackburn Rovers at Old Trafford. However, the game will be remembered more for the sending off of Harry Gregg, the United goalkeeper.

Gregg, a Northern Ireland international, became the first Manchester United goalkeeper to be sent off in a competitive fixture.

1971 BUSBY'S LAST BABE SHINES

Manchester City 3   Manchester United 3

Debuts don't come much more unnerving than the Manchester derby, but 17-year-old Sammy McIlroy, signed by Sir Matt Busby as a 14-year-old schoolboy on 1 August 1969, came through his baptism of fire with flying colours, scoring once and assisting twice at Maine Road to endear himself instantly to the United faithful. However, the Irish teenager's emphatic entrance to the first-team set-up didn't seal a regular starting berth, and McIlroy largely remained a substitute for the next year. Seriously injured in a car accident in January 1973, he fought his way back into the team against all odds the following season to earn himself a regular place in the starting line-up. That 1973–74 season ended with the gloom of relegation, but McIlroy was a permanent and crucial fixture in the side that secured an instant return to the top flight. His domestic importance was matched on the international scene, and he went on to win 88 caps for Northern Ireland. Sammy remained an integral part of the Reds side that went to Wembley three times in four years in the late 1970s. He tasted heartbreak in the 1976 and 1979 defeats to Southampton and Arsenal respectively, although he did score a fine equaliser in the '79 final only for Alan Sunderland to grab a dramatic late winner for the Gunners. Those disappointments sandwiched United's 2–1 win over Liverpool in 1977, the only major honour of Sammy's 11-year Old Trafford senior career. On 1 February 1982, Ron Atkinson sold McIlroy to Stoke City for £350,000. Three years later Sammy moved back to Manchester to join City on a free transfer before moving into management. Spells with Northwich Victoria, Ashton United and Macclesfield Town preceded the role of Northern Ireland boss, before Sammy took over at Stockport County. In 2005–06 he was appointed caretaker and then permanent manager at Nationwide Conference club Morecambe.

> **McILROY, Samuel Baxter 'Sammy'** *(Midfielder 1971–82) – debut in the above game.*
> *Appearances: FL: 320 (22), goals 57 FAC: 35 (3), goals 6 FLC: 25 (3), goals 6*
> *EUR: 10, goals 2 TOTAL: 391 (28) apps, 71 goals.*

1986 A DOUBLE SACKING

Manchester United terminated the contracts of manager Ron Atkinson and his assistant Mick Brown.

7

1978
Rio Gavin Ferdinand (Defender 2002–present) was born in Peckham, London.

1981 ROBBO OFF THE MARK
Sunderland 1   Manchester United 5
Bryan Robson scored his first goal for Manchester United in this 5–1 mauling of Sunderland at Roker Park in the First Division. Frank Stapleton (2), Garry Birtles and Kevin Moran also scored for the Reds, a result that sent them to the top of the League.

1986 FERGIE'S APPOINTMENT
Alex Ferguson was appointed the new manager of Manchester United following the sacking of Ron Atkinson the previous day. The new Reds boss enjoyed a playing career north of the border with Queen's Park, St Johnstone, Dunfermline Athletic, Rangers, Falkirk and Ayr United. After a brief spell as a publican, Fergie tried his hand at football management with his first appointment being manager of East Stirlingshire before moving on to St Mirren and then Aberdeen. During his time in charge of Aberdeen, Fergie broke the Glasgow dominance of Scottish football by Celtic and Rangers and brought unprecedented success to Pittodrie, winning three Scottish titles, four Scottish Cups, one League Cup and one European Cup-Winners' Cup. The Old Trafford directors pulled out all the stops to land Fergie as the new manager of Manchester United and have not looked back since.

1993 FIRST ON A SUNDAY
Manchester City 2   Manchester United 3
This Premier League derby game played at Maine Road was the first Manchester derby to be played on a Sunday. Manchester City took a 2–0 half-time lead but two goals in the second half from Eric Cantona and a late Roy Keane strike gave the Reds all three points and an 11-point lead at the summit of the Premiership for the defending champions.

8

1924 TOM JONES STARS FOR UNITED

Portsmouth 1   Manchester United 1

Tom Jones made his Manchester United debut in this 1–1 Second Division draw with Portsmouth at Fratton Park. Thomas Smith scored for the Reds. Amazingly, Smith was one of seven brothers, five of whom played League football and two of whom (Jack and Sep) were capped by England. Tom Jones went on to serve United for 13 seasons, making 200 appearances for the club but never scored.

> JONES, Thomas 'Tom' (Full-back 1924–37) – debut in the above game.
> Appearances: FL: 189, goals 0 FAC: 11, goals 0 TOTAL: 200 apps, 0 goals.

1930 FOXES OUTSMART REDS

Leicester City 5   Manchester United 4

Despite a hat-trick from Jimmy Bullock and another goal from George McLachlan, Manchester United still managed to lose this First Division game 5–4 to Leicester City at Filbert Street. During his career McLachlan played League football for English, Scottish and Welsh sides and when he retired from playing he managed Le Havre in France.

1986 BAD START TO FERGIE'S UNITED REIGN

Oxford United 2   Manchester United 0

Alex Ferguson lost his first game in charge of Manchester United, a 2–0 away defeat to Oxford United at the Manor Ground in the First Division. It was the only time United have ever lost to Oxford at this level.

2000 PRAWN SANDWICH BRIGADE

Manchester United 1   Dynamo Kiev 0

Following Manchester United's 1–0 win over Dynamo Kiev in the UEFA Champions League at Old Trafford (scorer: Teddy Sheringham), the United captain Roy Keane launched a blistering attack on some sections of the Old Trafford crowd. The talismanic Keano was responding to the reaction of some fans despite the fact that the result put the Reds into the second phase of the competition. In an interview with BBC Radio, Keane said: 'Away from home our fans are fantastic, I'd call them the hardcore fans. But at home they have a few drinks and probably the prawn sandwiches, and they don't realise what's going on out on the pitch. I don't think some of the people who come to Old Trafford can spell football, never mind understand it.' Keane's swipe at United's hospitality match attendees came one year after Sir Alex Ferguson himself pleaded with the Manchester United fans to improve the atmosphere at Old Trafford by making more noise.

9

1937 DUNCAN LEAVES

Manchester United announced that Scott Duncan had tendered his resignation as manager. He left the club to take over at Ipswich Town where he guided them to the Football League (Second Division). United won the Second Division Championship in 1935–36 under Duncan.

1963 LAW'S HAT-TRICK OF HAT-TRICKS

Manchester United 4   Tottenham Hotspur 1
Tottenham Hotspur were on the wrong end of a 4–1 drubbing in this First Division game played at Old Trafford. Denis Law was in majestic form for the Reds, scoring a hat-trick, his third of the 1963–64 season, while David Herd scored United's other goal. Law would go on to score a record seven hat-tricks that season.

1985 GOOD RUN COMES TO AN END

Sheffield Wednesday 1   Manchester United 0
At the start of the 1985–86 season Manchester United remained unbeaten in their opening 15 League games with 13 wins and 2 draws. However, in their sixteenth encounter of the campaign the Reds went down 1–0 to Sheffield Wednesday at Hillsborough.

2002 DERBY CURTAIN BROUGHT DOWN AT MAINE ROAD

Manchester City 3 · Manchester United 1
When the Red half of Manchester left the ground after the game, they had to endure taunts from the Blue half as the City fans celebrated a 3–1 victory over United in the last ever derby game between the two sides to be played at Maine Road. United's defending was sloppy and the only consolation came when Ole Gunnar Solskjaer scored. And to make matters worse for the United faithful, Peter Schmeichel was in goal for the Blues.

10

1976 CLARK'S MOMENT

Manchester United 3   Sunderland 3

Jonathan Clark made his Manchester United debut in this 3–3 First Division draw with Sunderland at Old Trafford (scorers: Brian Greenhoff, Gordon Hill, Stuart Pearson). Clark came on for Colin Waldron with 30 minutes of the game remaining but never played for United again. Despite his inexperience, Derby County paid £50,000 for his midfield services in September 1978.

1982 DEBUT OF THE BLACK PEARL

Bradford City 0   Manchester United 0

Paul McGrath made his debut for Manchester United in this goalless League Cup third round tie at Bradford City. Born in Ealing, London, to an Irish mother and a Nigerian father, Paul was given up for adoption when he was just four weeks old and he was brought up in several orphanages in Dublin before his mother later tracked him down. Paul was one of the greatest defenders of his time. He was a powerful, commanding centre-half who joined Manchester United from St Patrick's Athletic in 1982. To the Old Trafford fans he was known as 'The Black Pearl of Inchicore'. His greatest moment in a United shirt came in the 1985 FA Cup final, when after his defensive partner Kevin Moran had been sent off, he almost single-handedly kept Everton at bay for the 10-man Reds in the 1–0 win. However, when Alex Ferguson was appointed Manchester United manager in 1986 the new boss quickly stamped his authority on the club and what he perceived as a 'booze culture' among some of the players at the time. In August 1989 McGrath was sold to Aston Villa for £450,000, a sum deemed high at the time by the press for a player who had had serious knee injuries, requiring eight operations on his knees. Despite not being able to train fully because of his knee troubles McGrath flourished at Villa under his former Old Trafford boss, Big Ron Atkinson. Paul recovered his form and became a defensive bedrock of the Republic of Ireland's international success in both the 1990 and 1994 World Cups. He also became the Republic's first black captain. In season 1992–93 he helped Villa to runners-up spot in the inaugural Premier League season (won by United) and was voted the PFA Player of the Year the same season. He retired in 1998 after a brief spell at Sheffield United.

McGRATH, Paul (Defender 1982–8) – debut in the above game.
Appearances: FL: 159 (4), goals 12 FAC: 15 (3), goals 2 FLC: 13, goals 2 EUR: 4, goals 0
TOTAL: 192 (7) apps, 16 goals.

1994 UNITED GIVE CITY THE BLUES

Manchester United 5   Manchester City 0

Manchester United got revenge on their neighbours City for a 5–1 defeat at Maine Road in 1989 with this powerhouse display including a hat-trick from Andrei Kanchelskis. United's Russian winger became the first Manchester United player to score a hat-trick for the club in the Premier League. Eric Cantona and Mark Hughes also scored in the 5–0 derby victory. Andrei ended the 1994–95 season as the Reds' top scorer in the Premiership with 14 goals.

11

1911 A PALINDROMIC GAME

Manchester United 0   Preston North End 0

This 0–0 First Division draw with Preston North End is remarkable in that the game was played on a palindromic date i.e. the 11th day of the 11th month of the 11th year.

1964 UNITED RUN RIOT

Borussia Dortmund 1   Manchester United 6

Manchester United travelled to Germany to face Borussia Dortmund in the first leg of their second round Inter-Cities Fairs Cup tie. On the night, United played some of the best football they have ever played in Europe, sweeping aside the Germans 6–1 thanks to a Bobby Charlton hat-trick and goals from George Best, David Herd and Denis Law.

12

1881 DERBY RIVALRY BEGINS

West Gorton (St Marks) 0   Newton Heath 3

The first unofficial meeting between Manchester United (then Newton Heath) and Manchester City (then West Gorton, St Marks) took place on 12 November 1881 with the Heathens claiming a 3–0 away victory. The first Football League meeting between the clubs came during the 1894–95 season, Newton Heath beating Manchester City 5–2 at Hyde Road in Division Two. United's 2–1 defeat to City at Old Trafford on 10 February 2008 was the 150th Manchester derby meeting; United have won 60 and City 41, with 49 draws.

1955 SNAKE HIPS

Bolton Wanderers 3   Manchester United 1

Eddie Colman made his Manchester United debut in this 3–1 First Division loss to Bolton Wanderers at Burnden Park (scorer: Tommy Taylor). Eddie was born in Salford on 1 November 1936 and joined Manchester United's youth team when he left school in the summer of 1952. Eddie quickly established himself in the famous side at Old Trafford that won three FA Youth Cups from 1953–5, and proudly captained the team that beat West Bromwich Albion's youth team 7–1 in the 1955 final (he scored twice in a side that included those other famous Busby Babes, Bobby Charlton, Duncan Edwards and Mark Jones). He became a first-team regular during the 1955–56 season while his dazzling dribbling skills earned him the nickname of 'Snake Hips'. Over the next two-and-a-half years he made 107 first-team appearances, scoring two goals, the second of which was against Red Star Belgrade in the first leg of United's European Cup quarter-final against the Yugoslavian side on 14 January 1958. Aged just 21 years and 3 months, Eddie was the youngest person to die in the Munich Air Disaster. 'Eddie was a chirpy lad and a terrific player,' said Wilf McGuinness, who played alongside Eddie in the 1954 and 1955 FA Youth Cup finals. 'He pushed the ball – never kicked it – and he jinked past players. He was known for his swivel hips.'

COLMAN, Edward 'Eddie' (Half-back 1955–8) – debut in the above game.
Appearances: FL: 85, goals 1 FAC: 9, goals 0 EUR: 13, goals 1 TOTAL: 108 apps, 2 goals.

1990 FA HANDS OUT PENALTIES

Manchester United were hit with a £50,000 fine and deducted one League point by the FA following their part in the 21-man brawl during the First Division match against Arsenal at Old Trafford. The FA also handed the Gunners a £50,000 fine but deducted three points from their League tally.

13

1897 BOB'S FAREWELL

Newton Heath 0   Newcastle United 1

The legendary Robert Donaldson (147 appearances, 66 goals, 1892–7) made his last appearance for Newton Heath in this 1–0 defeat at home to Newcastle United in the Second Division.

1937 AN UNHAPPY REUNION

Chesterfield 1   Manchester United 7

In December 1936 Walter McMillen left Old Trafford and joined Chesterfield. On 13 November 1937 Manchester United played Chesterfield away in the Second Division and McMillen scored against his former employers. However, United replied with seven goals of their own, four of them from Tommy Bamford with Henry Baird, Billy Bryant and Thomas Manley also on target for the rampant Reds.

1968 THE LAWMAN AND THE KIDD

Manchester United 3   RSC Anderlecht 0

Denis Law scored twice for Manchester United against the Belgian champions, RSC Anderlecht, in the first leg of this second round European Cup tie played at Old Trafford. Brian Kidd also scored for United, his third and last European goal for the club. Law's goals, his 27th and 28th goals in Europe for United in just 33 European games, were also his last for the club.

14

1960

Remi Mark Moses (Midfielder 1981–8) was born in Miles Platting, Manchester.

1989 BUSBY'S FRIEND AND RIGHT-HAND MAN DIES

Jimmy Murphy, Matt Busby's assistant manager at Manchester United, died. During his playing career Murphy was a wing-half, who played for West Bromwich Albion (1928 to the outbreak of World War II in 1939), and a Welsh international. Murphy served in Italy, where he met Matt Busby, and when Busby was offered the vacant manager's job at Manchester United in 1945, Murphy became Busby's first 'signing'. The pair teamed up at Old Trafford as soon as they were demobbed from the army. During his first 10 years at Old Trafford, Murphy was employed as a coach before being given the title of assistant manager in 1955. Around the same time he was made the manager of Wales and as a result of his excellent work at United, particularly coaching the exciting Busby Babes of Charlton, Edwards, Whelan et al., he soon attracted the interests of foreign sides. However, Murphy rejected offers from Brazilian clubs and Juventus, prefering to work alongside Busby and continue nurturing the talent they had at United. Following the Munich Air Disaster on 6 February 1958, a flight Murphy missed as he was with Wales in Cardiff preparing for their game against Israel, he took temporary charge of United while Busby was recovering from his injuries, and steered them to the 1958 FA Cup final. In August 1958 Murphy stepped aside when Busby returned to resume control of United, only too glad to see his friend healthy once more. Murphy, an avid reader and a classical pianist, resigned as assistant manager in 1971 although he continued to scout for the club he had so loyally served for 26 years.

15

1895 THE GOLDEN OLDIE

Neil McBain (Half-back 1921–3) was born in Campbeltown, Argyllshire. McBain holds the unique distinction of being the oldest player in a Football League game: he was 51 years old when he played in goal for New Brighton Tower in a Third Division North match away to Hartlepools United. His football career spanned 32 years and two world wars.

1924 A HANSON DEBUT

Manchester United 2   Hull City 0
Jimmy Hanson made his debut in this Second Division win over Hull City at Old Trafford, celebrating with a goal. United's other goal in the game was scored by Francis McPherson. Interestingly, Hanson was brought to the attention of United by a reader of the *Manchester Football News* who wrote into the paper singing the praises of the 18-year-old Hanson, who was a striker for Bradford Parish Church in the Chester Amateur League. However, it was two years before United realised Hanson's talents and signed him from Manchester North End after the young striker had joined Stalybridge Celtic upon leaving Bradford Parish Church.

> HANSON, James 'Jimmy' (Forward 1924–30) – debut in the above game.
> Appearances: FL: 138, goals 47 FAC: 9, goals 5 TOTAL: 147 apps, 52 goals.

1987 BANANAS, COINS AND EGGS FOR THE GOALIE

Manchester United 1   Liverpool 1
Following this 1–1 First Division draw with Liverpool at Old Trafford (scorer: Norman Whiteside), Bruce Grobbelaar, the Liverpool goalkeeper, claimed that a number of fans in the Stretford End had hurled bananas, coins and eggs at him during the game. However, Manchester United escaped any punishment as the referee did not report any alleged incident to the FA.

16

1895 10 GOALS SHARED

Newton Heath 5   Lincoln City 5
Newton Heath drew 5–5 with Lincoln City in this Second Division encounter. The Heathens' goals were scored by John Clarkin (2), Joe Cassidy, Jimmy Collinson and James Peters.

1929 HIT FOR SEVEN

Sheffield Wednesday 7   Manchester United 2
Manchester United visited Hillsborough for this First Division game against Sheffield Wednesday and suffered a 7–2 hammering (scorers: John Ball, Jimmy Hanson).

1974

Paul Aaron Scholes (Midfielder 1994–present) was born in Salford.

17

1944 WAR COMMISSION'S COMPENSATION

Manchester United became the worst hit of all League clubs during the Second World War when on the night of 11 March 1941, during a raid on the nearby Trafford Park industrial estate, German bombs landed on Old Trafford and virtually destroyed the Main Stand, damaged part of the terracing and badly scorched the pitch. Makeshift offices were erected and Manchester United were faced with a major rebuilding task. They wrote to the War Commission seeking compensation and on 17 November 1944 the War Commission wrote to United informing them that they did not consider Old Trafford to be a 'total loss' and awarding the club the sum of £22,278 to clear the debris and rebuild the ground. The Manchester United directors had hoped for a much greater sum and had planned to make Old Trafford into a 120,000 capacity stadium, but the lack of sufficient funds meant that only the Main Stand was replaced.

1956 WHELAN BRACE

Manchester United 3   Leeds United 2
Manchester United beat Leeds United 3–2 in this First Division game at Old Trafford before a crowd of 51,131 (scorers: Liam Whelan 2, Bobby Charlton). Manchester United, the reigning League champions, went on to retain their title at the end of the season. Whelan would go on to be the leading scorer in the League that campaign, finishing with 26 goals.

1965 VICTORY BEHIND THE IRON CURTAIN

ASK Vorwaerts 0   Manchester United 2
Manchester United won 2–0 away to the East German side ASK Vorwaerts in this European Cup second round, first leg tie with goals from John Connelly and Denis Law.

1986

Luis Carlos Almeida da Cunha 'Nani' (Winger 2007–present) was born in Praia, Cape Verde, Africa.

18

1963 PETER SCHMEICHEL, GOALKEEPING LEGEND

Peter Boleslaw Schmeichel (Goalkeeper 1991–9) was born in Gladsaxe, Denmark. Without question Peter Schmeichel is the greatest goalkeeper ever to play for Manchester United. In his eight seasons at Old Trafford Schmeichel was a key player in Alex Ferguson's team that totally dominated English football during the 1990s. During his time with the Reds the glory years returned and Schmeichel won a host of honours including: five Premier League winners' medals (1992–93, 1993–94, 1995–96, 1996–97, 1998–99), three FA Cup winners' medals (1994, 1996, 1999) and a League Cup winners' medal (1992), and he famously captained United during their Treble-winning season in 1998–99. Schmeichel played his last game for the Reds in their UEFA Champions League final win over Bayern Munich. Individually, he also won the Best Goalkeeper in the World title twice and 87 caps for Denmark. A lot of United fans will not be too surprised to learn that during the early part of his career Schmeichel was a centre-forward with Danish side Hvidovre (1984–6). He scored six goals before realising his true potential lay in stopping the ball from going into the net. Schmeichel moved on to Brondby IF in 1987 where he was voted '1990 Danish Footballer of the Year' and on his international debut in 1987 he kept a clean sheet in a 5–0 win. In 1991 United moved quickly to sign Schmeichel for £500,000 after Newcastle United withdrew their initial offer to Brondby. As it turned out, and thankfully for all United fans, Schmeichel proved to be the transfer steal of the decade, although Eric Cantona's bargain price from

Leeds United runs it a close second. Schmeichel was simply awesome in a United shirt and made countless wonderful saves, perhaps none more important than his penalty save in the last minute of United's 1999 FA Cup semi-final replay against Arsenal. He was rock solid while his distribution of the ball led to many productive counter-attacks from the free-scoring Reds. One-on-one encounters usually resulted in Schmeichel saving the striker's shot or wrapping his body around the ball at the striker's feet. In 1992 he won the European Championship with Denmark. His name is firmly embedded in the United history books while his proudest moment for the Reds surely has to be that magical night in Barcelona when he lifted the European Cup with Alex Ferguson, the first United captain to lift European club football's most coveted prize in 31 years. In total he played 398 games for Manchester United and scored one goal (v Rotor Volgograd in the UEFA Cup in September 1995).

SCHMEICHEL, Peter Boleslaw *(Goalkeeper 1991–9)*
Appearances: FL/PL: 292, goals 0 FAC: 41, goals 0 FLC:17, goals 0 EUR:43, goals 1
TOTAL: 398 apps, 1 goal.

1995 LIGHTNING STRIKE AT OLD TRAFFORD
Manchester United 4   Southampton 1
Ryan Giggs gave Manchester United a lightning start to this Premier League game against Southampton at Old Trafford when he scored after just 15 seconds. It was, and remains, the fastest ever goal scored by a Manchester United player. Further goals from Andy Cole, Paul Scholes and a second from Giggsy sealed a comfortable 4–1 win. This was the first game of the 1995–96 season when away fans were permitted into Old Trafford as building work was ongoing.

19

1983 FRANKLY QUITE BRILLIANT
Manchester United 4   Watford 1
Watford visited Old Trafford for this First Division game against Manchester United and were sent packing on the back of a 4–1 hiding. United's Republic of Ireland international striker Frank Stapleton scored a hat-trick while skipper Bryan Robson also scored.

1991 SUPER CUP WINNERS
Manchester United 1   Red Star Belgrade 0
The European Super Cup was the brainchild of a Dutch reporter with *De Telegraaf* named Anton Witkamp. In 1972 he came up with the idea of pitting the

winner of the European Cup against the winner of the same year's European Cup-Winners' Cup, over two legs. Manchester United's first taste of the competition came in 1991 when, following the Reds' magnificent victory over FC Barcelona in the 1991 European Cup-Winners' Cup final, they faced the European champions Red Star Belgrade. However, as a result of Yugoslavia's unstable political climate at the time, UEFA decided that the 1991 Super Cup would be settled over one leg. A Brian McClair goal in the 67th minute of the game played at Old Trafford was enough to hand Manchester United a 1–0 win and give Alex Ferguson his third trophy.

1994 OOH LA LA

Crystal Palace 0   Manchester United 3
The highlight of this game was a superbly taken Eric Cantona half-volley goal, a typical piece of brilliance from the mercurial Frenchman. Denis Irwin and Andrei Kanchelskis also scored.

2005 KEANO QUITS UNITED

Roy Keane was still injured, having broken a metatarsal bone in his foot in United's Premiership match against Liverpool at Anfield on 18 September 2005, when the club announced that the Irishman's Old Trafford career was over and that Manchester United had reached agreement with Keane to end his contract immediately, enabling him to join Celtic. 'Whilst it is a sad day for me to leave such a great club and manager I believe the time has now come for me to move on,' said Keano. Sir Alex Ferguson labelled Keano the best he's ever worked with and described him as 'the best midfield player in the world of his generation' and 'one of the great figures in our club's illustrious history'.

20

1957 CZECH IT OUT

Manchester United 3   Dukla Prague 0
Goals from David Pegg, Tommy Taylor and Colin Webster gave Manchester United a 3–0 first leg home lead over the Czech side Dukla Prague in this European Cup first round tie.

1999 DARLINGTON REPLACE MANCHESTER UNITED

When Manchester United elected not to defend the FA Cup in season 1999–2000, opting instead to play in the inaugural FIFA Club World Championship in Brazil, it meant that a third round place had to be filled. Darlington, second round losers to Gillingham on 20 November 1999, were the 'Lucky Losers' and given a second bite at the cherry with a third round tie at Aston Villa. However, the Quakers lost 2–1 at Villa Park on 11 December 1999 to go out of the Cup for a second time in the space of 21 days. Former United player Dion Dublin scored one of Villa's goals. Villa made it all the way to the final, losing 1–0 to Chelsea.

2005 'DON'T DIE LIKE ME'

The *News of the World* published a photograph of George Best at the request of the Manchester United legend, showing him lying in his hospital bed, accompanied by what was reported to be his final message to his fans: 'don't die like me'.

21

1891 BIGGEST ALLIANCE VICTORY

Newton Heath 10   Lincoln City 1
Newton Heath recorded their biggest ever victory in the Football Alliance with this 10–1 annihilation of Lincoln City. Bob Donaldson scored a hat-trick with goals from Hood (2), William Stewart (2), Alf Farman, J. Sneddon and an own goal from Bates.

2006 TRIO TO BE IMMORTALISED

Celtic 1   Manchester United 0
Manchester United unveiled plans to recognise three of the club's greatest ever players: George Best, Denis Law and Sir Bobby Charlton. The trio are to be immortalised in a bronze statue, commissioned by the club from sculptor Philip Jackson, which will be located on Sir Matt Busby Way. On the same day, United lost their first-ever competitive match at Celtic Park to the Scottish champions Celtic, 1–0. The defeat meant United needed a result in their final group game to qualify for the knockout stages of the Champions League. United then beat SL Benfica 3–1 at Old Trafford to qualify for the knockout stages.

22

1902 THE SOLDIER'S DEBUT

Leicester Fosse 1   Manchester United 1
Lawrence 'Soldier' Smith made his debut for Manchester United in this 1–1

Second Division draw (scorer: Alex Downie) with Leicester Fosse (later renamed Leicester City). Smith, a soldier in the British Army before he joined United, was handed his debut because Daniel Hurst was injured, and another United debutant, Alex Downie, scored for the Reds. Both Downie and Smith had an eventful day as the train taking the United players from Manchester to Leicester was delayed due to a derailment at Nottingham and the United team had to change into their kits on board. The game kicked off late, there was no half-time interval and the match ended in semi-darkness.

SMITH, Lawrence 'Soldier' (Forward 1902–3) – debut in the above game.
  Appearances: FL: 8, goals 1 FAC: 2, goals 0 TOTAL: 10 apps, 1 goal.
DOWNIE, Alexander Leek Brown (Half-back 1902–10) – debut in the above game.
  Appearances: FL: 172, goals 12 FAC: 19, goals 2 TOTAL: 191 apps, 14 goals.

1997 GOALS GALORE

Wimbledon 2   Manchester United 5
This was United's biggest away win of the 1997–98 season and came in the middle of a golden spell for the club, as United scored 27 Premier League goals in just six games. On the day, goals came from David Beckham (2), Nicky Butt, Andy Cole and Paul Scholes.

23

1935 CANARIES NOT SINGING

Norwich City 2   Manchester United 5
A hat-trick from Jack Rowley and two goals from Thomas Manley gave Manchester United a deserved 5–2 win over Norwich City in this Second Division game played at Carrow Road. United were simply too hot to handle for most teams in the Second Division during the 1935–36 season as they romped their way to the title and promotion back into English football's top flight.

1946 UNITED TEAR TERRIERS APART

Manchester United 5   Huddersfield Town 2
Two goals each from Charlie Mitten and Johnny Morris and a fifth from Jack Rowley gave Manchester United a comfortable 5–2 win over Huddersfield Town in this First Division game played at United's rented home, Maine Road. United were in superb form throughout the 1946–47 season but missed out on winning the First Division Championship, finishing runners-up to Arsenal.

2002 BATTLE OF THE KNIGHTS

Manchester United 5   Newcastle United 3

This game marked the first time that two managers with knighthoods faced one another in a League game. However, it was Sir Alex Ferguson's Red Devils that claimed the spoils over Sir Bobby Robson's Newcastle United. Paul Scholes opened the scoring for the Reds in the 25th minute following some dazzling wing display by Ole Gunnar Solskjaer. Ruud van Nistelrooy scored a hat-trick, including his 50th goal for United, with Solskjaer also finding the gaping Newcastle net.

2004 SIR ALEX, THE MILLENNIUM MAN

Manchester United 2   Olympique Lyonnais 1

Sir Alex Ferguson celebrated his 1,000th game in charge of Manchester United when the Reds claimed win number 564 for the Boss after this 2–1 UEFA Champions League group victory over French champions Olympique Lyonnais at Old Trafford. Gary Neville and Ruud van Nistelrooy scored the goals to ensure a win for Sir Alex in this landmark game. 'All day I was a bit nervy but I kept saying to myself that it was the 999 before it that mattered. It was a fantastic night for me and I was very pleased with my players,' he said. In total, he had won 564 (56%), drawn 188 (19%) and lost 248 (25%) of his 1,000 games in charge of United. The 1,000 games included: League: 707, Charity Shield: 11, League Cup: 65, FA Cup: 78, European Cup/Champions League: 116, Cup-Winners' Cup: 13, UEFA Cup: 4, Super Cup: 2, World Club Championship: 3, Toyota Cup: 1.

Despite the success, including the Treble in 1999, Sir Alex got off to a bad start on the path to clocking up 1,000 games, losing his first one, 2–0 to Oxford United in the old First Division on 8 November 1986. Fergie joined an élite club as the only other men to have taken charge of an English club for 1,000 games or more at the time were Brian Clough, Graham Taylor, Joe Royle, Dario Gradi and Dave Bassett.

24

1951 BIRTH OF THE BUSBY BABES

Liverpool 0   Manchester United 0

A journalist for the *Manchester Evening News* wrote a brief report on Manchester United's 0–0 draw with Liverpool at Anfield in the First Division and within the body of his text he described the United team as Busby's Babes with Jackie Blanchflower and Roger Byrne, two products from United's blossoming youth team, making their senior debuts for United in the game.

BLANCHFLOWER, John 'Jackie' (Half-back 1951–8) – debut in the above game.
  Appearances: FL: 105, goals 26 FAC: 6, goals 1 EUR: 5, goals 0 TOTAL: 117 apps, 27 goals.
BYRNE, Roger (Full-back 1951–8) – debut in the above game.
  Appearances: FL: 245, goals 17 FAC: 18, goals 2 EUR: 14, goals 0
  TOTAL: 280 apps, 20 goals.

1984 TOO SPARKY

Sunderland 3 Manchester United 2

Manchester United's Mark Hughes and Sunderland's David Hodgson were both sent off for fighting in this First Division game at Roker Park. United lost 3–2 with Bryan Robson and Sparky scoring for the Reds.

25

1998 YORKE SETS UP CAMP

Barcelona 3 Manchester United 3

In a thrilling UEFA Champions League encounter United drew 3–3 with Barcelona in their magnificent Nou Camp Stadium. Dwight Yorke scored twice, with Andy Cole netting the other. It was the second time that season that the two European giants had drawn 3–3. United's next visit to the Nou Camp was even more memorable: the Champions League final at the end of the season.

2005 WHEN A DEVIL WENT TO HEAVEN

George Best died in the Cromwell Hospital, London following a titanic battle against liver disease. Treatment to the Manchester United legend had been stopped in the early hours of the morning and Bestie passed away at 1.05 p.m. from a lung infection and multiple organ failure. The Premier League announced that a minute's silence would be observed before all Premiership games played over the forthcoming weekend of his death. However, the traditional minute's silence was subsequently ignored at many grounds up and down England and replaced with a minute's applause in recognition of the Belfast Boy's contribution to the game he loved so much.

26

1960 UNITED'S FOOTBALLING CRICKETER

Cardiff City 2 Manchester United 0

Noel Cantwell made his Manchester United debut in this 2–0 First Division loss away to Cardiff City. When Cantwell arrived at Old Trafford he was a double international having played for Ireland at both cricket and football. United signed the Irish defender for £29,500 from West Ham United, a record transfer fee for a full-back at the time. In 1963 he captained Manchester United to FA Cup final glory, a 3–1 win over Leicester City at Wembley Stadium.

CANTWELL, *Noel Euchuria Cornelius (Full-back 1960–67) – debut in the above game. Appearances: FL: 123, goals 6 FAC: 14, goals 2 EUR: 7, goals 0 TOTAL: 146 apps, 8 goals.*

1966 A UNIQUE HAT-TRICK

Manchester United 5 Sunderland 0

David Herd scored four times and Denis Law also put his name on the score sheet for Manchester United in this 5–0 First Division win over Sunderland at Old Trafford. However, what was even more remarkable about Herd's feat in notching four goals in a First Division game was the fact that he did it against three different goalkeepers. His first goal was scored against Jim Montgomery who then left the field injured, his second was against George Herd, who also went off, and then he scored twice against the Rokerites' third goalkeeper in the game, Charlie Hurley.

27

1992 LE ROI TAKES UP HIS CROWN

Alex Ferguson made one of the most important signings in the history of Manchester United when he brought Eric Cantona to Old Trafford from Leeds United. The player described as '*l'enfant terrible*' of French football, despite title success with Marseille in 1991 and close on a half-century of caps for his country, had famously 'retired' from the game aged just 25 when a failed trial with Sheffield Wednesday alerted the attentions of Leeds United boss Howard Wilkinson, eager to bolster his side's title fortunes for the 1991–92 First Division run-in. Cantona helped the Yorkshire club pip United to claim the last ever 'old' First Division Championship. Astonishingly, given his success in Yorkshire and a Charity Shield hat-trick in Leeds' 4–3 win against Liverpool at Wembley in the 1992–93 curtain raiser, Alex Ferguson's enquiry as to whether the mercurial Frenchman might be for sale was met with a nod of approval from Elland Road. Ironically, Leeds had contacted Fergie to enquire if Denis Irwin was available. Within a matter of hours a £1.2m deal was agreed and Ooh Aah Cantona was on his way across the Pennines.

Over the following four-and-a-half seasons *Le Roi* would stamp his name indelibly on the club's history, his heart and soul seemingly in tandem with it. Reds everywhere will remember Eric for what he did on the field above all else, but who can forget the way he wore his No.7 shirt collar, stiffly upright as if it had been starched, that imperious look, theatrical swagger and poise, his prophetic pronouncements, his pure, well, *Frenchness*. Eric Cantona was born to play for Manchester United. At Old Trafford Eric admitted that he fell in love with football once more, and had found his spiritual home. The missing piece in the long-awaited Championship jigsaw, Cantona's 9 goals in 22 League games helped United end their 26-year Championship title drought and win the inaugural FA Premier League trophy in 1992–93. With his probing presence, United would fail to win the trophy just once in the following four campaigns. Cantona was leading scorer in two and second in the other two. However, it wasn't just his technical ability that fired the imagination, it was his talismanic qualities. He led by example, defiant, never giving in. It was a three-way relationship between player, team-mate and fans and in season 1993–94 United not only retained their Premiership title but beat Chelsea 4–0 in the FA Cup final at Wembley, Eric scoring two penalties, to secure the club's inaugural domestic Double.

When the FA threw the book at him with an eight-month ban in January 1995 following his infamous Kung-Fu spat with a foul-mouthed Crystal Palace fan at Selhurst Park, Cantona retained his dignity and did his 120 hours' community service with no complaints. United finished runners-up in both the Premiership and the FA Cup final minus Eric's presence for the last four months of the 1994–95 season. And of course, he scored on his return, against the old enemy Liverpool on 1 October 1995 in a 2–2 draw at Old Trafford, netting a penalty to salvage a point. With Cantona orchestrating the talents of a young David Beckham, Ryan Giggs, and Roy Keane in his pomp as midfield general, United proved irresistible in 1995–96. Cantona led the way with 19 goals in all competitions, one of four men to reach double figures. He scored in six consecutive Premiership games through March and April (four of them 1–0 victories) as United faced down the faltering challenge of Newcastle United to take the Premiership title, their third in four seasons. And it was Cantona again who fired through a crowd scene at Wembley when United saw off Liverpool in the FA Cup final to complete a second Double in three seasons. That season was the pinnacle of his time at Old Trafford. At the end of the 1996–97 season, he won his and the club's fourth Premiership crown, but with the disappointment of a European Cup semi-final exit proving a heavy cross to bear, he exited stage left. He made his final appearance in the last home game of the season against West Ham United at Old Trafford. Eric's days at United will never be forgotten, a United legend among legends.

28

1936 AN INAUSPICIOUS DEBUT

Leeds United 2   Manchester United 1
Tommy Breen made his debut in goal for United in this First Division 2–1 defeat by Leeds United (scorer: William Bryant). Less than one minute into the game at Elland Road the home side had scored and Breen's first touch of the ball came when he bent down to pick it out of his net.

> **BREEN, Thomas 'Tommy'** *(Goalkeeper 1936–9) – debut in the above game.*
> *Appearances: FL: 65, goals 0 FAC: 6, goals 0 TOTAL: 71 apps, 0 goals.*

1951 FERGIE LINK

Ian Richard Donald (Full-back 1972–3) was born in Aberdeen. Donald signed for United as an amateur in May 1968 and as a professional in July 1969 and served under four different managers at Old Trafford: Sir Matt Busby (twice), Wilf McGuinness, Frank O'Farrell and Tommy Docherty. Ian's father appointed a certain Alex Ferguson as the manager of Aberdeen in June 1978.

1990 GUNNERS DOWNED AT HOME

Arsenal 2   Manchester United 6
Manchester United beat Arsenal 6–2 at Highbury in this fourth round League Cup tie and went all the way to Wembley to win the trophy, defeating Brian Clough's Nottingham Forest in the final. Lee Sharpe scored a memorable hat-trick with Clayton Blackmore, Mark Hughes and Danny Wallace also scoring for the rampant Red Devils in the 6–2 victory.

29

1947 MORRIS GIVES BLUES THE BLUES

Chelsea 0   Manchester United 4
A hat-trick from Johnny Morris and a goal from Jack Rowley gave Manchester United a comfortable 4–0 victory over Chelsea in this First Division game played at Stamford Bridge.

1973

Ryan Joseph Giggs (Forward 1991–present) was born in Cardiff.

2006 CAPTAIN NEVILLES' FACE-OFF

Manchester United 3   Everton 0

Old Trafford welcomed the return of Phil Neville, now captain of Everton, to the ground he had graced for so long. With brother Gary captaining the Reds, it was the first time that two brothers had captained opposing sides in the top tier of English football. United's comfortable win, with goals from Cristiano Ronaldo, Patrice Evra and John O'Shea, was made all the more notable by the fact that it was the Frenchman's first Premier League goal for United, and his only one in his first 60 League appearances for the Reds.

30

1935 PREACHING THE UNITED GOSPEL

Manchester United 0   Doncaster Rovers 0

Herbert Whalley made his Manchester United debut in this Second Division goalless draw at Old Trafford. Although he never scored in the Football League for the Reds he did score in the Wartime League, most notably in a 3–1 win over Manchester City in May 1942, which gave United the Football League Northern Section (Second Championship). Bert Whalley was a Methodist lay preacher. When he was forced to retire through injury in 1947, Matt Busby gave him a place on his coaching staff where he helped nurture many young talents. Whalley took Jimmy Murphy's place on the ill-fated trip to Belgrade for a European Cup tie on 5 February 1958 and lost his life the next day in the Munich Air Disaster. Murphy was in Cardiff managing the Welsh national side in their game against Israel.

> **WHALLEY, Herbert 'Bert'** *(Half-back 1935–47) – debut in the above game.*
> *Appearances: FL: 32, goals 0 FAC: 6, goals 0 TOTAL: 38 apps, 0 goals.*

1999 UNITED CROWNED WORLD CLUB CHAMPIONS

Manchester United 1   Palmeiras 0

Manchester United became the first British club to be crowned World Club champions with a 1–0 win over the South American champions, Palmeiras of Brazil, in the Olympic Stadium, Tokyo. United's captain Roy Keane scored the all-important goal while Ryan Giggs won a brand new Toyota Celica car after being named Man of the Match. Ten minutes before the half-time interval Ryan Giggs went past the Palmeiras right-back and his superb high cross completely deceived keeper Marcos, whose error allowed Keano to side-foot the simplest of goals in at the far post.

DECEMBER

1

1935 STAN'S THE MAN

Stan Pearson, a 16-year-old Salford boy, was spotted playing for Adelphi Lads' Club by Manchester United's legendary scout Louis Rocca, who signed the young striker as an amateur for Manchester United on 1 December 1935. In May 1937 he turned professional and just six months later made the step up to first-team football. However, just as Pearson was establishing himself in the first team, his career was interrupted by the outbreak of the Second World War. During the six years that organised football (Football League) was suspended, Pearson served with the 2nd/4th Lancashires and also managed to make guest appearances for Newcastle United, Brighton & Hove Albion and Queens Park Rangers. At the end of the war Pearson resumed his Old Trafford career. Matt Busby, himself recently demobbed from the army and newly installed as manager, handed Pearson the inside-forward role in his new-look United, and Stan became one of the best of the day at a time when England had a wealth of talent to choose from. He was a key member of Busby's first great United team, which tasted success in the FA Cup in 1948 (Pearson scored a hat-trick in the semi-final against Derby County and one in the 4–2 final win over Blackpool), won the First Division League Championship in 1952 and was runner-up four times in 1947, 1948, 1949 and 1951. Ever reliable, Pearson missed only 13 first-team matches in seven seasons between 1946 and 1953, and proved the perfect foil for Jack Rowley. As well as his trademark consistency Pearson possessed a deadly and accurate shot. After losing his place to the young Jackie Blanchflower in the 1953–54 season, he moved to Bury in February 1954 for £4,500, after which he became player-manager at Chester where he continued to play until the age of 40. After hanging up his boots, Pearson became a sub-postmaster in Prestbury, Cheshire.

1965 HERD ON TARGET

Manchester United 3 ASK Vorwaerts 1
David Herd scored a European hat-trick for Manchester United in their second round, second leg 3–1 win over the East Berlin club ASK Vorwaerts at Old Trafford. The Reds progressed to the quarter-finals with a 5–1 aggregate victory.

2006 LARSSON SIGNS FOR UNITED

Manchester United announced the news all Red Devil fans had hoped to hear some six years earlier – the signing of Henrik Larsson. United confirmed that they had agreed a three-month loan deal for the former Celtic and Sweden striker, now with his hometown club Helsingborgs IF. The 35-year-old agreed to leave Helsingborg but would return to Sweden on 12 March when the Swedish football season commenced. United moved swiftly to capture Larsson following injuries to both Alan Smith and Ole Gunnar Solskjaer.

2

1907 UNITED PLAYERS PIONEER PFA

In 1898 a meeting was held in Liverpool and the Association Footballers' Union (AFU) was formed but dissolved within three years. On 2 December 1907, Manchester United's captain, Charlie Roberts, and the mercurial Billy Meredith held a meeting in the Imperial Hotel, Manchester, with a view to unionising footballers. The United pair were founder members of the AFU. And so the Association of Football Players' and Trainers' Union was established, which still exists today 100 years later as the Professional Footballers' Association. The principal reason why the union was successfully created was that the Football League had finally ratified the maximum wage in 1901 at £4 per week.

1964 GERMANS HIT FOR TEN

Manchester United 4   Borussia Dortmund 0
Manchester United beat the German side Borussia Dortmund 4–0 (scorers: Bobby Charlton 2, John Connelly, Denis Law) in their Inter-Cities Fairs Cup second round, second leg tie at Old Trafford. Having already won the away leg 6–1, the Reds comfortably progressed to the third round with a 10–1 aggregate victory.

3

1963 A SHORT EUROPEAN TRIP

Tottenham Hotspur 2   Manchester United 0
This game marked the first occasion on which Manchester United played a British team in one of the three major European competitions. This second round, first leg European Cup-Winners' Cup game was played at White Hart

Lane with United, the 1963 FA Cup winners, losing 2–0 to Spurs, the 1963 European Cup-Winners' Cup holders.

1969 LEAGUE CUP DERBY

Manchester City 2   Manchester United 1
Manchester City took the spoils in this first leg semi-final encounter of the 1969–70 competition. Bobby Charlton scored United's goal at Maine Road before a crowd of 55,799. It was the first time United had reached this stage of the tournament.

1994 FERGIE GOES SHOPPING

Alex Ferguson officially opened the new Manchester United Megastore situated behind the Stretford End at Old Trafford.

2007 RONALDO ON TARGET

Manchester United 2   Fulham 0
Cristiano Ronaldo was the star of the show with two goals, which took his season's total to 13. He could have had his first hat-trick for the Reds had strong claims for a penalty late on not been turned down. However, the return of Wayne Rooney, after an ankle injury that had kept him out of action for over three weeks, was a huge boost.

4

1920 ALL DOWNHILL FOR AVENUE

Manchester United 5   Bradford Park Avenue 1
Manchester United hammered Bradford Park Avenue 5–1 at Old Trafford in this First Division game (scorers: Thomas Miller 2, Joseph Myerscough 2, Edward Partridge).

1937 THE YOUNG GUNNER

Manchester United 5   Swansea Town 1
Manchester United's Jack Rowley scored four goals in this Second Division romp over Swansea Town at Old Trafford to become United's youngest ever hat-trick scorer aged 17 years and 58 days. William Bryant also scored for the Reds.

1959

Paul McGrath (Defender 1982–8) was born in Ealing, London.

5

1959 VIOLLET SHINES FOR REDS

Manchester United 3   Blackpool 1

Blackpool must have wished they had stayed at home at the seaside following this 3–1 beating by Manchester United at Old Trafford in the First Division (scorers: Dennis Viollet 2, Stan Pearson).

2001 LARRY WHITE'S STORY

Manchester United 3   Boavista 0

Manchester United ran out 3–0 winners over Portugal's Boavista in this UEFA Champions League group game played at Old Trafford. Ruud van Nistelrooy (2) and Laurent Blanc scored. Sir Alex Ferguson had unsuccessfully attempted to lure veteran French international defender Laurent Blanc to Old Trafford three times before finally landing his man at the fourth attempt. When Jaap Stam left Old Trafford in the summer of 2001 it left a huge void in the heart of the United defence and just five days before the Champions League transfer deadline Sir Alex persuaded Blanc to come to United. On 30 August 2001, the 35-year-old master defender and World Cup winner in 1998 signed a one-year contract for United, his ninth club, on a free transfer. At first the United faithful were sceptical of a player who lacked pace and was clearly in the twilight period of his career, but as the season progressed United shored up their defence and the fans quickly recognised that the cool-as-a-cucumber Blanc was indeed a class act. He was affectionately nicknamed 'Larry White' (the English translation of his name) and is famous for his pre-match ritual of kissing goalkeeper Fabian Barthez's head, both in international games for his country and in Champions League games for the Reds. In July 2002, after coaxing by Sir Alex, Laurent agreed to postpone his retirement and stay another season at Old Trafford. And what a season it proved to be as United 'got their trophy back' in winning the 2002–03 Premiership title. At the age of 37, Blanc finally retired, bringing to a close an illustrious career lasting two decades.

6

1975 18 IDENTICAL TEAMS

Middlesbrough 0   Manchester United 0
The Manchester United team that took to the pitch for this First Division goalless draw with Middlesbrough at Ayresome Park remained unchanged for the next 17 games (12 League, 5 FA Cup), ending with the 4–0 League home win over West Ham United on 28 February 1976 (scorers: Alex Forsyth, David McCreery, Lou Macari, Stuart Pearson).

1992 A DERBY FIT FOR LE ROI

Manchester United 2   Manchester City 1
This Manchester derby at Old Trafford was a landmark occasion for two reasons. It was the first ever meeting between the two bitter rivals in the Premier League, and United beat Manchester City 2–1 thanks to goals from Mark Hughes and Paul Ince. But of even greater significance was that it marked the League debut of *Le Roi*. When Eric Cantona trotted on to the pitch as a substitute for Ryan Giggs, United fans were witnessing the start of one of the most illustrious careers yet seen in the red shirt of United.

> *CANTONA, Eric (Forward 1992–7) – debut in the above game.*
> *Appearances: PL: 142 (1), goals 64 FAC: 17, goals 10 FLC: 6, goals 1 EUR: 16, goals 5*
> *TOTAL: 184 (1) apps, 82 goals.*

2003 FORLAN HERO

Manchester United 4   Aston Villa 0
Diego Forlan scored twice, as did Ruud van Nistelrooy, in this comfortable victory over Aston Villa. It was the first of eight successive wins in the Premiership and FA Cup.

7

1963 FOUR FOR LAW

Manchester United 5   Stoke City 2
Manchester United hammered Stoke City 5–2 in this First Division game played at Old Trafford. Denis Law scored four times, which, along with a goal from David Herd was enough to seal a comprehensive victory.

1974 MASS PITCH INVASION

Sheffield Wednesday 4   Manchester United 4

Following Manchester United's 4–4 draw (scorers: Lou Macari 2, Stewart Houston, Stuart Pearson) with Sheffield Wednesday in this Second Division game at Hillsborough, crowds invaded the pitch. More than 100 people were arrested and the FA took disciplinary action against both clubs. United's central defender Jim Holton broke his leg in the game and was replaced by Ron Davies. United went on to win the Second Division Championship at the end of the 1974–75 season while The Owls finished bottom of the table and were relegated to Division Three.

1993 NICELY ARRANGED

Manchester United 3   Sheffield United 0

When the Manchester United starting XI took to the Old Trafford pitch the fans witnessed something they had not seen since the introduction of Premier League squad numbers. The United side lined up numbers 1–11 while Roy Keane (No.16) came on as a substitute. The Red Devils won this Premiership encounter 3–0 with goals from Eric Cantona, Mark Hughes and Lee Sharpe.

2002 CHAMPS DETHRONED

Manchester United 2   Arsenal 0

Goals from Paul Scholes and Juan Sebastian Veron gave Manchester United all three Premiership points against Arsenal, the reigning Premier League champions. The two clubs were once again battling it out at the top of the table.

8

1894 ANONYMOUS HEATHEN

Newton Heath 5   Burton Swifts 1

Newton Heath hammered Burton Swifts 5–1 in this Second Division game (scorers: James Peters (2), Richard Smith (2), John Dow). When John Dow made his debut for the Heathens in March 1894 he did so under the pseudonym of M. J. Woods. This was common practice at the time and adopted to preserve the anonymity of trialists.

1963 CHOCCY'S BIRTH

Brian John McClair (Forward 1987–98) was born in Airdrie, Scotland. Brian McClair booked his place in the annals of Old Trafford history when he became the first player since George Best to score 20 League goals for the Reds. Numerous strikers had strived but failed to achieve the feat in the intervening 20 years, a plausible explanation, no doubt, for United's failure to win the title in that period. McClair might have scored 24 goals in his debut season but still the League was out of reach. For 1987–88 was also the season when a new-look Liverpool of Barnes, Beardsley and Aldridge went on the rampage, finishing nine points ahead of United and with a vastly superior goal difference. Like his 1970s and '80s predecessors, McClair had to settle for success in the cup competitions as the quest for the Holy Grail, the elusive League Championship, continued. As the spearhead in a thriving partnership with Mark Hughes, he more than played his part as the Reds won four trophies between 1990 and 1992. The honour of scoring the winning goal in the 1990 FA Cup final may have gone to the left-back Lee Martin but in the three previous rounds against Oldham Athletic (semi-final replay), Sheffield United and Newcastle United, McClair got his name on the score sheet. It was a similar story in the European Cup Winners' Cup the following season (1990–91) when McClair scored against every team that United faced until the final, when Hughes took over with his brilliant brace against FC Barcelona in Rotterdam. Cup final-winning goals would not elude McClair for long, however, as he was the only man on target when United won the European Super Cup against Red Star Belgrade in 1991 and the League Cup at Nottingham Forest's expense in 1992. These honours extended his already impressive CV because with his former club, Celtic, he had won the Scottish Cup in 1985 and the Championship in 1986.

Scotland's Player of the Year in 1987, he joined United for a fee of £850,000. The prolific striker, nicknamed 'Choccy', became a bustling midfield player following the arrival of Eric Cantona from Leeds United in November 1992. McClair achieved his League title ambition with United in 1993 and played his part in the club's first Double win in 1993–94 when, as a substitute, he scored the last goal in the 4–0 FA Cup final win over Chelsea at Wembley Stadium. Prior to leaving in 1998, McClair won a second Double in 1996 and another title in 1997, albeit with a decreasing number of appearances. After cutting his coaching teeth at Motherwell and then Blackburn Rovers, McClair returned to Old Trafford in 2001 for the start of a successful career on United's backroom staff.

2007 CENTURY FOR GIGGS

Manchester United 4   Derby County 1

Ryan Giggs scored his 100th League Goal for United with a tap-in late in the first half to set the Reds on their way to a comfortable 4–1 victory over bottom club Derby (scorers: Carlos Tevez 2, Cristiano Ronaldo). His first League goal was in May 1991, against Manchester City.

9

1950 BIRKETT SCORES

Huddersfield Town 2   Manchester United 3

Manchester United won this hard-fought First Division encounter away to Huddersfield Town 3–2 thanks to goals from John Aston Snr (2) and Clifford Birkett, the first of his United career.

2003 EUROPEAN JOY

Manchester United 2   VfB Stuttgart 0

Goals from Ryan Giggs and Ruud van Nistelrooy gave Manchester United a 2–0 win over the German side VfB Stuttgart in this UEFA Champions League group game played at Old Trafford. United were confirmed as group winners, conceding only two goals in six games.

2006 BLUES SENT PACKING

Manchester United 3   Manchester City 1

Manchester United extended their lead at the top of the Premiership table following this 3–1 win over Manchester City in the derby game played at Old Trafford. Wayne Rooney turned in Cristiano Ronaldo's cross after five minutes and Louis Saha made it 2–0 just before half-time after bundling home a cross from Gabriel Heinze. The Blues pulled a goal back in the 73rd minute before Ronaldo wrapped up all three points for the Reds with his second goal of the game six minutes from time. In the last minute City's Bernardo Corradi was sent off for diving.

10

1904 UNITED'S WINNING RUN

Manchester United 3   Gainsborough Trinity 1

Manchester United beat Gainsborough Trinity 3–1 in this Second Division game with goals from Thomas Arkesden (2) and John Allan. It was United's eighth consecutive League victory and the first goal they conceded in the eight games (scored 14). The Reds went on to win their next six League games, stretching the unbeaten run to 14 on their way to finishing third in the table at the end of the 1904–05 season.

1960 THRILLING DRAW

Fulham 4 Manchester United 4

Manchester United visited Craven Cottage for this First Division game against Fulham and despite finding the net four times (scorers: Albert Quixall 2, Bobby Charlton, Alex Dawson) they came away with just a point as the home side also rattled four past Harry Gregg in the United goal.

1963 SPURS SENT PACKING

Manchester United 4 Tottenham Hotspur 1

Exactly one week after Manchester United lost 2–0 to Tottenham Hotspur at White Hart Lane in their second round, first leg European Cup Winners' Cup game, the Reds beat Spurs 4–1 at Old Trafford in the second leg to proceed to the quarter-finals at the expense of the reigning European Cup Winners' Cup holders. Two goals each from Bobby Charlton and David Herd powered United to victory before an ecstatic 50,000 fans.

11

1954 BABE MAKES HIS DEBUT

Burnley 2 Manchester United 4

Geoffrey Bent, aged 22, made his Manchester United debut in this 4–2 First Division win against Burnley at Turf Moor. A hat-trick from Colin Webster and a goal from Dennis Viollet gave United both points. Bent was given his start in the side as a result of an injury sustained by the Manchester United and England captain Roger Byrne. Needless to say, as an understudy to Byrne, Bent's appearances were somewhat limited and he managed only 12 League appearances for the Reds before tragically losing his life in the Munich Air Disaster on 6 February 1958. Bent joined United from Salford Schoolboys as a trialist in August 1948 after captaining his schoolmates to glory in the 1947 England Schools Trophy final. He signed for the Reds as an amateur in May 1949 and as a professional in April 1951.

1974 CHANGE THE REF

Following Manchester United's 0–0 draw with Middlesbrough in the fifth round of the League Cup at Ayresome Park one week earlier, Boro's manager Jack Charlton lodged an official protest with the Football League against the match referee Peter Reeves, criticising his handling of the game. Big Jack, the older brother of the Manchester United legend Bobby Charlton, asked for another official to be appointed for the replay.

12

1896 THREE DOUBLES AMONG SEVEN STRIKES

Newton Heath 7   West Manchester 0

Newton Heath annihilated West Manchester 7–0 in this FA Cup third qualifying round tie with goals from Joe Cassidy (2), Matthew Gillespie (2), Charles Rothwell (2) and William Bryant. It was the only FA Cup match Rothwell played for the Heathens.

1959 FROM THE PITCH TO THE CHALKBOARD

Manchester United's Wilf McGuinness fractured a leg playing for the reserves against Stoke City at Old Trafford. The injury was so bad that it brought the half-back's playing career to an end, resulting in McGuinness taking-up a coaching position at Old Trafford. He began with the reserve and youth sides and eventually became manager of Manchester United in June 1969.

1970 SIR MATT BUSBY, THIS IS YOUR LIFE

Manchester United 1   Manchester City 4

Just before the kick-off to the first Manchester derby game of the season, Sir Matt Busby and the manager of Manchester City, Joe Mercer, received special awards in recognition of their services to their respective clubs. It was a day of mixed emotion for Sir Matt Busby, who used to play for City. Just as he was about to leave the pitch Eamonn Andrews came out of nowhere with his famous Big Red Book and, with a microphone in his hand, said, 'Sir Matt Busby. This is Your Life.' It was the second time the United manager had been invited to appear on the famous television show. United lost the game 4–1 (scorer: Brian Kidd, who would later play for City).

13

1952 UNITED'S COWBOY

Liverpool 1   Manchester United 2

Bill Foulkes (nicknamed 'Cowboy') made his Manchester United debut in this First Division 2–1 win over Liverpool at Anfield (scorers: John Aston Jnr, Stan Pearson). He played at right-back before moving to his favoured position of centre-half during his Old Trafford career. Foulkes was an old-fashioned stopper who loved the physical challenge of facing a bustling centre-forward. For 18 seasons he gave a granite-like solidity to the Reds' rearguard, so much so that during nearly two decades at Old Trafford it was rare for Matt Busby to omit him from his starting XI. Foulkes joined United as an amateur in March 1950 and turned professional in August 1951 after leaving his mining job at Lea Green Colliery, St Helens. The positional switch suited Foulkes, who preferred to keep things simple, passing to his more gifted team-mates at the first opportunity. It was an approach that served him well. A survivor of the Munich Air Crash, Foulkes captained a depleted United in the aftermath of the tragedy, leading the Reds to the 1958 FA Cup final. Defeat against Bolton Wanderers then was a bitter pill to swallow, but it was a rare one: in a distinguished career Foulkes won First Division Championship medals in 1956, 1957, 1965 and 1967 and was back at Wembley, this time a winner, in the FA Cup final of 1963. Add to that his part in the 1968 European Cup-winning team and it's somewhat surprising that he was capped only once by England, against Northern Ireland in October 1954. Although noted more for stopping than scoring goals, Foulkes is fondly recalled for his happy knack of getting critical strikes. One in particular stands out, his goal against Real Madrid at the Bernabeu in 1968, which helped put United into the European Cup final. He retired from playing in June 1970 but remained at Old Trafford as a coach, before moving on to coach and manage in other countries. Bill Foulkes trails only Sir Bobby Charlton and Ryan Giggs in United's all-time appearance list with a mammoth 688 appearances to his name and 9 goals.

> FOULKES, William Anthony 'Bill' (Defender 1952–70) – debut in the above game.
> Appearances: FL: 563 (3), goals 7 FAC: 61, goals 0 FLC: 3, goals 0 EUR: 52, goals 2
> TOTAL: 685 (3) apps, 9 goals.

2004 PAPA SPOILS THE DAY

Fulham 1   Manchester United 1
A spectacular long-range shot from Fulham's Papa Bouba Diop denied Manchester United all three points in this Premiership encounter at Craven Cottage. Alan Smith scored for the Reds.

14

1912 GEORDIE HAT-TRICK

Newcastle United 1   Manchester United 3
Enoch West scored a hat-trick for Manchester United in this 3–1 First Division win over Newcastle United at St James' Park. It was United's only hat-trick of the season and helped West on his way to 22 goals in the campaign.

1963 HERD HAT-TRICK

Manchester United 3   Sheffield Wednesday 1
David Herd scored a hat-trick for Manchester United in this 3–1 First Division win over Sheffield Wednesday at Old Trafford. He was on a run of scoring 12 goals in 12 games.

2002 ON THE MARCH TO TITLE GLORY

Manchester United 3   West Ham United 0
Manchester United hammered West Ham United 3–0 at Old Trafford in this Premiership game. Goals from Ole Gunnar Solskjaer, Juan Sebastian Veron and an own goal gave United all three points as they began a charge that would result in them winning back the Premiership crown at the end of the 2002–03 season.

2005 NEW BOYS WHIPPED

Manchester United 4   Wigan Athletic 0
Premiership new boys Wigan Athletic were on the receiving end of a 4–0 drubbing by Manchester United at Old Trafford. Wayne Rooney (2), Rio Ferdinand and Ruud van Nistelrooy all scored for the Reds.

15

1898

Joseph Waters 'Joe' Spence (Forward 1919–33) was born in Throckley, Northumberland.

1951 BABY SHARK BORN

Joseph Jordan (Forward 1977–81) was born in Carluke, Lanarkshire, Scotland. Jordan was already an established international striker for Scotland when he moved to Manchester United from Leeds United in January 1978 for £350,000. Big Joe was one of the most fearsome centre-forwards in the country while his famous gap-toothed grin and eye for goal (hence his nickname 'Jaws') made him a firm favourite with the United faithful. In total he scored 41 times in 126 games for the Reds before moving on to AC Milan and then Verona.

1962 LAW TAKES LAW INTO HIS OWN HANDS

West Bromwich Albion 3   Manchester United 0
Manchester United striker Denis Law complained to Matt Busby that the referee, Gilbert Pullin, was constantly abusive towards him throughout the game against

West Brom at The Hawthorns. Busby was furious and reported Pullin to the Football Association. At the subsequent hearing, and after hearing testimony from several other players who were involved in the game, the FA found in favour of the Lawman. Pullin was enraged. He refused to accept the decision that had gone against him and tendered his resignation as a Football League referee.

16

1972 O'FARRELL'S REIGN IS CLOSE TO AN END

Crystal Palace 5   Manchester United 0
Frank O' Farrell's last game in charge of Manchester United ended in defeat when the Reds were hammered 5–0 by Crystal Palace at Selhurst Park. The man who was about to succeed O'Farrell as manager, Tommy Docherty, was watching from the stands. After the game Sir Matt Busby approached Docherty to enquire whether or not he was interested in managing United. Docherty indicated that he had wanted the job for the last 25 years.

1983 HISTORIC LIVE GAME

Manchester United 4   Tottenham Hotspur 2
Manchester United's 4–2 win over Tottenham Hotspur in the First Division made football history when it was transmitted live by the BBC, the first League match to be beamed live into UK households. Manchester United were paid £50,000 by the Beeb. A crowd of just 33,616 attended the game, when United's average home attendance at the time was around 50,000. Arthur Graham and Kevin Moran both scored twice for the Reds.

2007 MERSEY JOY FOR TEVEZ

Liverpool 0   Manchester United 1
Carlos Tevez scored United's winner just before half-time in a fine, solid performance that prevented Liverpool from threatening Edwin van der Sar's goal too often. Later that day, Arsenal beat Chelsea 1–0 as all the 'Big Four' met each other.

17

1969 CITY DENY UNITED FINAL PLACE

Manchester United 2   Manchester City 2
A crowd of 63,418 poured into Old Trafford to see Manchester United draw 2–2 (scorers: Paul Edwards, Denis Law) with Manchester City in the second leg of their League Cup semi-final encounter. At the time, the gate was a

record attendance for a League Cup game. City had won the first leg 2–1 and so took the tie 4–3 on aggregate.

1987 BRUCEY SIGNS FOR UNITED

Manchester United signed defender Steve Bruce from Norwich City for £825,000. Pound for pound, the £825,000 Alex Ferguson paid the Canaries for their uncompromising centre-half two weeks short of his 27th birthday was one of the best deals Manchester United has ever done. Bruce's central defensive partnership with Gary Pallister – the pair were affectionately dubbed 'Dolly and Daisy' by Fergie – was the bedrock on which three Premier League-winning sides were built (1993, 1994, 1996) as well as successes in the European Cup-Winners' Cup (1991), FA Cup (1990, 1994, 1996) and the League Cup (1992). It was arguably Bruce's two critical late, late goals, a pair of towering headers against Sheffield Wednesday, that tipped the 1992–93 Premiership title race in United's favour and really got the ball rolling for United's dominance of the modern game. Bruce's was a steady climb to the football summit. A product of the famous Wallsend Boys Club that gave the game such talents as Alan Shearer, Peter Beardsley and more recently the United acquisition Michael Carrick, he represented Newcastle schoolboys, but was rejected at 16 by his boyhood idols, as well as Sunderland, Bolton Wanderers, Sheffield Wednesday and Southport, because he was perceived to be too small. He subsequently got a job at the Swan Hunter shipyard as a trainee plumber but a week before he was due to start he was offered an apprenticeship with Gillingham. After making his league debut for the Gills at the start of the 1979–80 season aged just 17, he went on to make more than 200 League appearances for the Kent club before Norwich paid £135,000 for his services in August 1984. At Carrow Road, Bruce won a League Cup winners' medal in 1985 and the Second Division Championship medal the following year. Remarkably, for all his subsequent honours at Old Trafford, Bruce was never selected for a full England cap, though he did lead his country at 'B' level. He finally left the Reds on a free transfer for Birmingham City in the 1996 close season after nine years, 414 appearances and a prolific 51 goals. Assisted by his accuracy from the penalty spot, he had finished as the club's joint top scorer in the League in 1990–91 with 13 goals. In 1998 he started out on the management trail with Sheffield United as player-manager, and has also been in charge at Huddersfield Town, Crystal Palace and Birmingham. He is currently the boss of Wigan Athletic, having previously managed them in a brief spell in 2001.

1994 UNITED'S DEFENCE FINALLY BREACHED

Manchester United 1   Nottingham Forest 2
Stan Collymore scored for Nottingham Forest in the 65th minute of his side's 2–1 FA Premier League win over Manchester United at Old Trafford. Amazingly,

it was the first goal conceded by United at Old Trafford in 1,135 minutes of competitive football. Eric Cantona scored for United.

18

1931 THE GIBSON GUARANTEE

Manchester United found themselves in such financial trouble in early December 1931 that the club did not even have enough money to pay for the players' annual Christmas dinner let alone their wages. But then along came a new saviour in the shape of local businessman James W. Gibson, who handed the club £30,000 in return for the chairman's position at United. The club gratefully accepted his kind gesture.

1974 LEAGUE CUP SUCCESS

Manchester United 3   Middlesbrough 0
After drawing 0–0 with Middlesbrough two weeks earlier in the fifth round of the League Cup, Manchester United progressed to the semi-finals of the competition for the third time in six years with this comfortable 3–0 win over Boro in the replay at Old Trafford (scorers: Sammy McIlroy, Lou Macari, Stuart Pearson). It meant that three Second Division teams (United, Aston Villa, Norwich City) and one Fourth Division team (Chester) were now in the semi-finals.

2004 A HANDFUL AGAINST THE PALACE

Manchester United 5   Crystal Palace 2
Manchester United beat Crystal Palace 5–2 at Old Trafford in this Premiership game, their highest scoring performance in the League that season. Goals from Paul Scholes (2), Alan Smith, John O'Shea and an own goal gave the Reds an easy win in the end.

19

1972 FRANK O'FARRELL IS SACKED AND GEORGE BEST RESIGNS

Manchester United's board of directors met at the offices of the chairman, Louis Edwards, and made their decision to sack the management team of Frank O'Farrell, Malcolm Musgrove and John Aston. They issued the following statement: 'In view of the poor position in the League, it was unanimously decided that Mr O'Farrell, Malcolm Musgrove and John Aston be relieved of their duties.' The statement also went on to say: 'Furthermore, George Best will remain on the transfer list and will not be selected again for Manchester United as it is felt it is in the best interest of the club and the player that he leaves Old Trafford.' A few hours later George Best handed in his letter of resignation. It was a sad end to a sad day in the history of Manchester United.

1972 TOMMY DOCHERTY TAKES CHARGE AT OLD TRAFFORD

A few hours after O'Farrell's sacking Tommy Docherty was unveiled as the new manager of Manchester United.

Docherty was viewed by many as the man to bring the glory years back to Old Trafford, having already proved his managerial ability at Chelsea, Aston Villa, Queens Park Rangers, Rotherham United and FC Porto of Portugal. Docherty was a breath of fresh air to the United faithful on the terraces and he did a remarkable job in steering the team away from the relegation zone. As it turned out, however, Docherty was only putting off the inevitable because the following season, 1973–74, United were relegated to Division Two. But the spell in the lower division enabled Docherty to blood many new young players and the team adopted a swashbuckling style that culminated in the 1974–75 Second Division Championship. United were back and the crowds poured into Old Trafford to watch one of the most exciting teams for many a season. In their first season back in the top flight United finished third in the League and lost the 1976 FA Cup final to Southampton. Under Docherty, United returned to Wembley the following year and this time they came away with the trophy after defeating Liverpool 2–1, thereby depriving the Merseysiders of the Double. The good days seemed to have returned. But then the news broke that Docherty was having an affair with the wife of the club's physio. United, with their strong Catholic traditions, felt compelled to ask Docherty to step down and so ended the reign of the man fondly remembered as 'The Doc'.

1987 FROM CANARY TO DEVIL

Manchester United 2   Portsmouth 1
Steve Bruce made his Manchester United debut following his £825,000 switch from Norwich City. United beat Portsmouth 2–1 (scorers: Brian McClair, Bryan Robson) at Fratton Park in the First Division. Brucey conceded a penalty and broke his nose in the game.

> BRUCE, Stephen Roger 'Steve' (Defender 1987–96) – debut in the above game.
> Appearances: FL/PL: 329, goals 36 FAC: 41, goals 3 FLC: 32 (2), goals 6
> EUR: 25 (1), goals 6 TOTAL: 411 (3) apps, 51 goals.

20

1947 ANDERSON DEBUT

Manchester United 2   Middlesbrough 1
John Anderson made his Manchester United debut in this 2–0 First Division home win (played at Maine Road) over Middlesbrough. Stan Pearson scored both United goals.

> ANDERSON, *John (Half-back 1946–9) – debut in the above game.*
>   *Appearances:* FL: *33, goals 1* FAC: *6, goals 1* TOTAL: *39 apps, 2 goals.*

1999 FA CUP WITHDRAWAL

Manchester United pulled out of the FA Cup after the FA put intense pressure on the Reds to take part in the inaugural Club World Championship, to be held in Brazil in January 2000, in the belief that it would help England's bid to host the 2006 World Cup. As soon as the decision to withdraw from the FA Cup was announced, United, the Cup holders, received a hammering in the press with many tabloids claiming they had 'damaged the history of the FA Cup.'

21

1907 FIRST RED TO EARN RED

Manchester United 3   Manchester City 1
Manchester United beat their neighbours Manchester City in this First Division derby with two goals from Sandy Turnbull and one from George Wall. However, the victory was spoilt when Turnbull was sent off in the game, earning the dubious distinction of becoming the first Manchester United player to be dismissed.

1957 BABES RAVAGE FOXES

Manchester United 4   Leicester City 0
The famous Busby Babes walloped Leicester City 4–0 in this First Division game played at Old Trafford. Dennis Viollet (2), Bobby Charlton and Albert Scanlon all scored for Manchester United.

1996 ERIC'S GLORY

Manchester United 5   Sunderland 0

Goals from Eric Cantona (2), Ole Gunnar Solskjaer (2) and Nicky Butt gave Manchester United a comprehensive 5–0 win over Sunderland in this Premier League game played at Old Trafford. Most United fans will remember Eric's audacious chipped goal over Lionel Perez (a former team-mate of Cantona's) resulting in Eric slowly turning with his arms half up in the air, milking the Old Trafford applause.

22

1956 FOGGED OFF

Manchester United were due to play West Bromwich Albion in the First Division at Old Trafford but the match had to be abandoned when The Baggies arrived at Old Trafford almost two hours late. The game was scheduled for a 2.15 p.m. kick-off but was delayed until 2.30 before finally being called off at 3.30. By the time the West Brom players and staff arrived at Old Trafford, 4.00 p.m., the crowd had gone home. The game was eventually played on 29 April 1957 and ended 1–1 (scorer: Alex Dawson). At the end of the latter game Manchester United paraded the First Division Championship trophy at Old Trafford for the second successive season.

1969

Mark Gordon Robins (Forward 1988–92) was born in Ashton-under-Lyne, Lancashire.

1979 JAWS MUNCHES FOREST

Manchester United 3   Nottingham Forest 0

Manchester United beat Nottingham Forest 3–0 in this First Division match at Old Trafford. The ex-Leeds United pair of Joe Jordan and Gordon McQueen scored for United with Big Joe grabbing two of the three.

2001 DEVILS MAUL SAINTS AT CHRISTMAS

Manchester United 6   Southampton 1

Manchester United hammered Southampton 6–1 in this Premiership encounter at Old Trafford. Ruud van Nistelrooy bagged a hat-trick while Roy Keane, Phil Neville and Ole Gunnar Solskjaer all scored against the Saints in a superb display of power and clinical finishing from the Reds.

23

1933 RELEGATION DRAW

Manchester United 1   Millwall 1

Manchester United drew 1–1 with Millwall in this Second Division game at Old Trafford (scorer: Neil Dewar). United endured an awful 1933–34 season and only a victory on the final day of the season away to Millwall prevented the Reds from dropping into the Third Division for the first time in their illustrious history. Millwall were relegated along with Lincoln City as United finished in a 'safe' 20th position from 22 teams.

1962

Terence Bradley 'Terry' Gibson (Forward 1986–7) was born in Walthamstow, London.

1970 KIDD WINS NOTHING

Aston Villa 2   Manchester United 1

Aston Villa dumped Manchester United out of the 1970–71 League Cup following this 2–1 semi-final, second leg win over the Reds (scorer: Brian Kidd). United had drawn the home leg 1–1 (scorer: Brian Kidd) but missed out on a place in the final after losing 3–2 on aggregate over the two legs.

24

1898 HEATHENS LACKING GOODWILL TO FELLOW MEN

Newton Heath 9   Darwen 0

Newton Heath hammered Darwen 9–0 in this Second Division game with William Bryant and Joe Cassidy both netting hat-tricks. The other Heathens goals came from Matthew Gillespie (2) and an own goal. This is one of only six games in the club's history where two players scored a hat-trick.

1904 REDS SPOIL REDS' CHRISTMAS

Manchester United 3   Liverpool 1

Manchester United beat Liverpool in this 1904 Christmas Eve Second Division game at Old Trafford. Thomas Arkesden, Charlie Roberts and Henry Williams all scored for United who ended the season third in Division Two while Liverpool were crowned champions.

25

1896 FIRST CHRISTMAS CLASH

Newton Heath 2   Manchester City 1
Newton Heath spoilt this Christmas Day for their local rivals Manchester City, winning their Division Two encounter 2–1 (scorers: Robert Donaldson, Richard Smith). It was the first time the club had played a fixture on Christmas Day.

1897 HEATHENS HEAP CHRISTMAS BLUES ON RIVALS

Manchester City 0   Newton Heath 1
Newton Heath beat their neighbours Manchester City for the second successive Christmas Day, only this time winning their Division Two encounter 1–0 away (scorer: Joe Cassidy).

1906 SCHOFIELD MAKES WAY FOR MEREDITH

Manchester United 0   Liverpool 0
On Christmas Day 1906, Manchester United drew 0–0 at home with Liverpool in the First Division. The game marked Alfred Schofield's 179th and last for United. Schofield had joined Newton Heath in August 1900 and was at the club when they changed their name to Manchester United in April 1902. In his 179 games for the club (157 League, 22 FA Cup) he scored 35 goals, 5 of them in the FA Cup. On New Year's Day 1907, the magician, Billy Meredith, made his Manchester United debut and even Schofield had to accept that his time was finally up and he decided to retire. The talented Schofield had played for Everton from August 1895 to August 1900 before becoming a Heathen.

1933 TWO TRANSFERS, A WEDDING AND A RESIGNATION

On Christmas Day Neil Dewar (Forward 1932–4) played his 36th and last game for Manchester United in their 3–1 home defeat by Grimsby Town (scorer: George Vose). Shortly after the game Dewar left United in an exchange deal with Sheffield Wednesday involving the return of John T. Ball to Old Trafford. However, Dewar had also eloped with the daughter of Councillor A. E. Thomson, a Manchester United director at the time. The couple were unaware of the residency requirement to qualify for a registry office wedding and such was the furore in the local press that Councillor Thomson tendered his resignation at Old Trafford.

26

1955 BOXING DAY KNOCKOUT

Manchester United 5   Charlton Athletic 1
Manchester United recorded their biggest League win of the season when Charlton Athletic were emphatically beaten 5–1 in the Boxing Day victory at Old Trafford in front of 44,611 fans. Dennis Viollet (2), Roger Byrne, Peter Doherty and Tommy Taylor all scored for United.

1977 TOFFEES FOR CHRISTMAS

Everton 2   Manchester United 6
Manchester United recorded a memorable Boxing Day victory over Everton at Goodison Park, beating The Toffees 6–2 in this First Division encounter. Lou Macari (2), Steve Coppell, Jimmy Greenhoff, Gordon Hill and Sammy McIlroy scored in the Goodison romp.

1986 SOLO TAKE AWAY

Liverpool 0   Manchester United 1
Amazingly, this 1–0 win over Anfield on Boxing Day was Manchester United's only success from 21 away games during the 1986–87 season. Norman Whiteside scored the all-important goal.

1992 BOXING HAT-TRICK

Sheffield Wednesday 3   Manchester United 3
When Manchester United drew 3–3 away to Sheffield Wednesday in the Premiership, Brian McClair scoring twice (Eric Cantona also scored), it meant that United's Scottish international striker had netted for the third consecutive year for the club on Boxing Day.

2006 SIR ALEX ACCEPTS HE WILL LOSE BET

Manchester United 3   Wigan Athletic 1
Cristiano Ronaldo came on as a half-time substitute with the score 0–0 in Manchester United's Premiership game against Wigan Athletic and immediately made an impact, scoring twice (47th and 51st minutes) to take his tally of League goals to 14. United won the game 3–1 with Ole Gunnar Solskjaer adding United's third in the 59th minute. After the game Sir Alex Ferguson accepted that he would lose his wager with his young Portuguese international winger – he had bet Ronaldo £300 that he would not score 15 times in the Premiership.

27

1902 THREE GOALKEEPERS FOR CHRISTMAS

Manchester United beat Barnsley 2–1 at United's Clayton ground with goals from Hubert Lappin and John Peddie. Remarkably, their goalkeeper in the game, James Saunders, was the third one used in as many games, played over three consecutive days, all at home. On Christmas Day Herbert Birchenough stood between the posts for the 1–1 draw with Manchester City (scorer: Ernest 'Dick' Pegg) while on Boxing Day it was James Whitehouse's turn in goal for the 2–2 draw with Blackpool (scorers: Alexander Downie, Thomas Morrison).

1955 DOUBLE WHAMMY

Charlton Athletic 3   Manchester United 0
Having recorded their biggest League win of the season the previous day against Charlton Athletic (5–1), Manchester United were on the receiving end of their heaviest League defeat of the season when they lost 3–0 away – to Charlton Athletic! However, United lost only one more League game of the 1955–56 campaign and won the First Division Championship.

1997 KAREL ON HIS WAY OUT

Manchester United agreed to sell their Czech international winger Karel Poborsky to the Portuguese side SL Benfica. Poborsky had spent an unsuccessful 18 months at Old Trafford.

28

1914 UNITED'S FIRST EVER MANAGER

John Robson succeeded Ernest Mangnall to become the new manager of Manchester United. In May 1899 Robson was appointed the secretary-manager of Middlesbrough but in May 1905 he took charge at Crystal Palace where he spent two seasons and then assumed control at Brighton & Hove Albion. In season 1909–10 Robson guided Brighton to the Southern League Championship. On 28 December 1914 he was appointed manager of Manchester United, the first man ever to hold the position of manager at the club as all the previous incumbents had the title of secretary-manager. Robson stayed at Old Trafford for seven years although for four of these during World War I the club played only Regional League football. In the two seasons (1919–20 and 1920–21) when proper League football resumed following the end of the Great War, United finished in 12th and 13th place respectively. In October 1921 Robson retired on the grounds of ill-health and on 11 January 1922 he died of pneumonia following a heavy cold.

1963 SKINNY KID SCORES

Manchester United 5   Burnley 1

Manchester United beat Burnley 5–1 at Old Trafford in the First Division thanks to goals from David Herd (2), Graham Moore (2) and a 17-year-old skinny kid named George Best. It was Bestie's first goal for United but the first of many as he went on to become a Manchester United legend scoring 179 times in 470 appearances for the club he loved. William John Anderson made his Manchester United debut in the game.

> *ANDERSON, William John 'Willie' (Forward 1963–7) – debut in the above game.*
> *Appearances: FL: 7 (2), goals 0 FAC: 2, goals 0 EUR: 1, goals 0*
> *TOTAL: 10 (2) apps, 0 goals.*

1999 FAREWELL TO THE 20th CENTURY

Sunderland 2   Manchester United 2

Manchester United's last game of the 20th century was in the FA Premier League at Sunderland. The match ended 2–2 (scorers: Nicky Butt, Roy Keane) at the Stadium of Light.

2005 SCHOLESY SEEING DOUBLE

Birmingham City 2   Manchester United 2

Paul Scholes sustained a blow to the head in this 2–2 Premier League draw (scorers: Ruud van Nistelrooy, Wayne Rooney) with Birmingham City at St Andrews and was taken off suffering from double vision in his right eye.

2006 RONALDO BEATS MOURINHO TO AWARD

Manchester United's sensational 21-year-old Portuguese winger Cristiano Ronaldo was named Portugal's Sportsman of the Year ahead of Benfica's Nuno Gomes and Chelsea boss Jose Mourinho, who finished third. The prestigious award, presented annually by the Portuguese newspaper *A Bola*, recognised the United player's 'contribution to the expansion of Portuguese football across the world'. The young star replied: 'I'm very happy with what I've achieved and want to continue at this level in 2007.'

29

1956 POMPEY NO PROBLEM FOR BABES

Portsmouth 1   Manchester United 3
Matt Busby's famous Busby Babes visited Fratton Park to take on Portsmouth in a First Division game. Manchester United, the reigning First Division champions, played some beautiful football to win the game 3–1 thanks to goals from Duncan Edwards, David Pegg and Dennis Viollet. United went on to retain their title at the end of the 1956–57 season.

1970 SIR MATT COMES OUT OF RETIREMENT

After just six months in the job, Wilf McGuinness was asked to step down as manager of Manchester United and revert to a coaching position at Old Trafford. The board lured Sir Matt Busby out of retirement to take charge of his beloved Manchester United for a second time until a suitable manager could be found to take over from the Great Man.

1993 PREMIER TON

Oldham Athletic 2   Manchester United 5
Goals from Ryan Giggs (2), Steve Bruce, Eric Cantona and Andrei Kanchelskis gave Manchester United a 5–2 Premiership victory over Oldham Athletic at Boundary Park. It was United's last game of 1993. They had begun it with a 4–1 win over Tottenham Hotspur in the Premiership on 9 January (scorers: Eric Cantona, Denis Irwin, Brian McClair, Paul Parker) and the three points against Oldham Athletic gave them a total of 100 Premier League points for the calendar year.

30

2001 GIGGS BRACE

Fulham 2   Manchester United 3
Ryan Giggs scored twice in this close-fought victory, with Ruud van Nistelrooy scoring the other goal. United were in the middle of a run of eight successive Premier League victories, but ended the season in third place, their worst Premier League finish to that point.

2006 FIRST ROYAL VISIT

Manchester United 3   Reading 2

Reading, managed by Steve Coppell, visited Old Trafford for the first time in a League game and went home pointless thanks to two goals from Cristiano Ronaldo and one from Ole Gunnar Solskjaer.

31

1941 SIR ALEX IS BORN

Alexander Chapman Ferguson was born in Govan, Glasgow. After a successful period as manager of Aberdeen, where he broke the dominance of the big Glasgow clubs, Ferguson joined United in November 1986. At first, trophies were hard to come by, but once he won the FA Cup in 1990, beating Crystal Palace 1–0 in the final replay, thanks to a Lee Martin goal, the honours kept on coming. By the end of the 2006–07 season, Sir Alex Ferguson had won nine Premier League titles (1993, 1994, 1996, 1997, 1999, 2000, 2001, 2003, 2007), five FA Cups (1990, 1994, 1996, 1999, 2004), two League Cups (1992, 2006), the Champions League (1999) and the European Cup-Winners' Cup (1991). In that time, he won three domestic Doubles (1994, 1996 and 1999) and a unique Treble of Premier League, Cup and Champions League in 1999. His collection of 18 major honours makes him the most successful manager in the history of English football, ahead of Bob Paisley, who won 13 with Liverpool. The first leg of the Champions League quarter-final in 2008 was his 1,200th match in charge of the club, beating the 1,141 matches in charge by Sir Matt Busby. The defeat to Portsmouth in the FA Cup on 8 March 2008 was his 101st FA Cup tie, over-hauling Sir Matt's record of 100 ties. However, Sir Alex will have to wait until the end of November 2011 before he will match Sir Matt's total of 972 League games as boss.

1955 OLD TRAFFORD PACKED

Manchester United 2   Manchester City 1

A post-war record crowd of 60,956 turned up to Old Trafford to see the Reds achieve a 2–1 victory over their neighbours. United's goals were scored by Tommy Taylor and Dennis Viollet. The record was broken later in the season when 62,277 saw United beat Blackpool 2–1 on 7 April.

1960

Stephen Roger Bruce (Defender 1987–96) was born in Corbridge, near Hexham, Northumberland.

1966

Joseph Waters 'Joe' Spence (Forward 1919–33) died.

1999 OVER THE CLIFF

The Manchester United first team had their last training session at The Cliff training ground before moving to their new state-of-the-art complex at Carrington.

2006 BACK-TO-BACK AWARDS FOR RONNIE

Cristiano Ronaldo was named the Barclays Player of the Month for the second successive month, becoming only the third player in the Premiership to claim back-to-back awards after Arsenal's Dennis Bergkamp in 1997 and Liverpool's Robbie Fowler in 1996.

BIBLIOGRAPHY

Websites

http://www.manutd.com/
http://www.stretfordend.co.uk
http://www.manutd.zone.com/
http://www.sportinglife.com/football/news
http://www.mirror.co.uk/news
http://www.npg.org.uk/live/prelcent.asp
http://archive.theboltonnews.co.uk/1996/12/4/839488.html
http://www.sportinglife.com/football/news
http://freespace.virgin.net/heroes.villains1/68/3.htm
http://www.manureds.co.uk/managers.html
http://www.redcafe.net/
http://www.unitedonline.co.uk/
http://www.englandfootballonline.com/
http://www.englandfc.com/
http://www.redissue.co.uk/footydb/loadotd.asp
http://www.carryduffmusc.com/
http://www.prideofmanchester.com

Essential reading

Bogota Bandit by Richard Adamson, Mainstream Sport, 2005

The Official Manchester United Miscellany by John White, Carlton Books Limited, 2005

Manchester United, Player by Player by Ivan Ponting, Hamlyn Publishing, 1998

The United Miscellany by John White, Carlton Books Limited, 2007

The England Football Miscellany by John White, Carlton Books Limited, 2007

England – The Football Facts by Nick Gibbs, Facer Publishing Limited, 1988

A Football Compendium: An Expert Guide to the Books, Films & Music of Association Football; Second Edition compiled by Peter J. Seddon, Redwood Books, 1999

Record Collector: Rare Record Price Guide 2002 by Sean O'Mahony, Parker Mead Ltd, 2002

BIBLIOGRAPHY

British Hit Singles & Albums (Edition 17) by David Roberts, Guinness World Records Ltd, 2004

The Daily Telegraph Football Chronicle compiled by Norman Barrett, SevenOaks, 2004

The Official Illustrated History of Manchester United by Alex Murphy, Orion Publishing Group Limited, 2006

Manchester United Almanac by Dean Hayes, Yore Publications, 1997

The United Alphabet by Garth Dykes, Polar Publishing (UK) Limited, 1994

Manchester United A Complete Record by Ian Morrison and Alan Shury, Breedon Books Publishing Company Limited, 1992

The Champions' Story, The Players' Own Account of their Premiership winning triumph in 2006-2007, Orion Publishing Group Limited, 2007

The Definitive Newton Heath FC by Alan Shury and Brian Landamore, Tony Brown Publishing, 2002

The Complete Manchester United Trivia Fact Book by Michael Crick, Penguin Publishing, 1996

European Glory 1968-1999: United's European Triumphs by Barney Chilton, Juma Publishing, 1999

Irish Reds by Iain McCartney, Britespot Publishing, 2002

Tartan Reds by Iain McCartney, Britespot Publishing, 2002

Man United – The Red Army – Five Decades of Player Profiles by Ivan Ponting, Hamlyn Publishing, 2000

Back Page United – Over 100 Years of Newspaper Coverage by Stephen F. Kelly, Virgin Publishing, 1998

Great Derby Matches – Man Utd v Man City – Complete History by Michael Heatley and Ian Welch, Dial House Publishing, 1996

United – The Story Of Manchester United in the FA Cup by Steve Cawley, Champion Publishing, 1994

The Gibson Guarantee – The Savings of Man United 1931-1951 by Peter Harrington, Imago Publishing, 1994

Manchester United – The Official History 1878-1992 by Tom Tyrrell and David Meek, Hamlyn Publishing, 1992

The Pride of Manchester – History of Manchester Derby Matches by Steve Cawley and Gary James, ACL & Polar Publishing, 1992

A-Z of Manchester Football – 100 Years of Rivalry 1878-1978 by Derek Brandon, Boondoggie Publishing, 1978

There's Only One United – The Official Centenary History of Manchester United by Geoffrey Green, Hodder & Stoughton Publishing, 1978

Manchester United – Pictorial History and Club Record by Charles Zahra, Joseph Muscat, Iain McCartney and Keith Mellor, Temple Nostalgia Publishing, 1986

Manchester United, The Complete Record, First Edition by Andrew Endlar, Orion Publishing Group Limited, 2007

INDEX OF NAMES

Albinson, George 15
Albiston, Arthur 151, 154, 155, 159, 188, 191, 203, 270, 275
Aldridge, John 323
Allan, John 4, 324
Allardyce, Sam 127
Allen, Reg 101, 167, 218
Anderson (Anderson Luis de Abreu Oliveira) 105, 163, 168, 170, 180, 186
Anderson, George 92, 121
Anderson, John 118, 119, 333
Anderson, Trevor 171, 237
Anderson, Viv 12, 149, 214
Anderson, Willie 339
Andrews, Eamonn 137, 326
Apsden, Joseph 277
Arkesden, Thomas 8, 14, 324, 335–6
Asquith, Beaumont 231
Aston Jnr, John 66, 80, 102–3, 108, 161, 179, 268, 326
Aston Snr, John 76, 102, 119, 126, 232, 247, 259, 277, 324, 331
Atkinson, Ron 12, 34, 79, 87, 112, 134, 154, 169–70, 183, 192, 203, 224, 227, 263–4, 265, 294, 297, 300

Babbel, Markus 172
Bailey, Gary 64, 148, 151, 155, 159, 208
Bailey, Trevor 31
Bainbridge, William 11
Baird, Henry 24, 303
Ball, John 66, 76, 305
Bamford, Thomas 133, 240, 241, 278, 303
Bamlett, Herbert 31, 69, 104, 133, 165, 269
Banks, Gordon 157
Bannister, Jimmy 1, 2, 149, 230
Barnes, John 323
Barnes, Peter 170, 228

Barrera, Marco Antonio 177
Barson, Frank 40, 99, 237–8, 290
Barthez, Fabien 30, 111, 171, 172, 194, 320
Basler, Mario 159
Bassett, Dave 311
Batson, Brendon 169
Battistuta, Gabriel 78
Beale, Robert 230–1
Beale, Walter 231
Beardsley, Peter 20, 268, 323, 330
Beardsmore, Russell 2, 181, 256
Beckenbauer, Franz 155
Beckham, David
    birth 133
    career record 185
    signs as trainee 188
    signs apprenticeship forms 185
    in youth team 137, 185, 220, 261
    signs professional terms 25
    awards and honours 106, 173, 179, 185
    injured by boot kicked by Ferguson 47
    transfers to Real Madrid 176, 185
    matches:
        in 1994 250–1
        in 1995 92, 185, 220
        in 1996 58, 90, 144, 185, 211, 216, 272, 286
        in 1997 6, 15, 205, 310
        in 1998 5, 185
        in 1999 66, 106, 150, 156, 159, 203
        in 2000 7, 31, 91, 115
        in 2001 61, 158, 257
        in 2003 117, 135, 145
        in 2004 171
        in 2006 178
        in 2007 174–5
    brief mention 105

INDEX

Beckham, Victoria 185
Behan, Billy 66
Bell, Alexander 1, 89, 118
Bell, Colin 124
Bellion, David 257
Benitez, Rafael 195
Bennett, Steve 214–15
Bennion, Ray 133
Bennion, Samuel 269
Bent, Geoff 39, 47, 50, 325
Bentley, J.J. 290
Berbatov, Dimitar 116
Bergkamp, Dennis 106, 342
Berry, Johnny 18, 38, 39, 40, 47, 64, 83, 97,
   164, 233, 254, 255, 266, 281
Best, George
  birth 156
  career record 243–5
  signs as amateur 233
  turns professional 243
  matches:
    in 1963 243–4, 339
    in 1964 20, 286, 301
    in 1965 12, 122, 126, 213
    in 1966 74, 221, 244, 247
    in 1967 139
    in 1968 21, 35, 86, 108, 143, 161, 217,
     244, 276
    in 1969 150, 195
    in 1970 41, 98, 110, 207, 244
    in 1971 137, 200, 244, 248, 282
    in 1972 62, 129, 268
    in 1974 2
  superstar status 75
  awards 244
  misses training 4
  misses match 10
  refuses to play in Charlton's
    testimonial 248
  resigns 331
  in hospital 309
  death 312
  movie about 132–3
  band plays tribute to 72–3
  shirt sold at auction 242
  statue commissioned 309
  brief mentions 43, 47, 56, 205, 254
Bielby, Paul 77
Birchenough, Herbert 338

Birkett, Clifford 324
Birtles, Garry 17, 149, 192, 198, 249, 264,
   281, 297
Bishop, Bob 243
Bishop, Ian 253
Black, William 39
Blackmore, Clayton 10, 94, 146, 149, 158,
   219, 252, 255, 315
Blanc, Laurent 257, 320
Blanchflower, Danny 232
Blanchflower, Jackie 11, 39, 40, 70, 136,
   232, 259, 275, 311–12, 317
Blomqvist, Jesper 159
Bosnich, Mark 16, 181
Boyd, Henry 233, 239–40
Bradley, Warren 31, 120, 130, 238
Brazil, Alan 173
Breen, Tommy 24, 315
Brennan, Shay 51 74, 85, 139, 161, 196,
   205
Brightwell, David 44
Brightwell, Ian 44
Bronckhorst, Giovanni van 210
Brook (1944 team) 107
Brown, James (1892 Newton Heath
   team) 238, 277
Brown, James (1932 Manchester United
   team) 280
Brown, Lawrie 154
Brown, Mary 154, 186
Brown, Mick 296
Brown, Wes 18, 60, 85, 156, 177, 273
Browne, Michael 3
Bruce, Steve 5, 38, 52, 58, 100, 103, 135,
   139, 146, 147, 149, 151, 165, 219, 235,
   257, 272, 278, 289, 291, 330, 332, 340,
   341
Bryant, Billy (player in 1934–9) 107, 228,
   241, 303, 315, 319
Bryant, William (player in 1896–1900) 86,
   229, 233, 326, 335
Buchan, George 133, 216
Buchan, Martin 62, 67, 69, 77, 103, 133,
   154, 215–16
Buckle, Edward 37, 135, 287
Bullock, Jimmy 298
Burgess, Herbert 1, 2, 149
Burke, Ronald 10, 44, 266
Burns, Francis 263, 276

INDEX

Busby, Sir Matt
  birth 158
  career and achievements 46–7, 259–61
  takes on job as manager 46, 259, 281,
    317
  building of teams 46–7, 64, 259–60
  offers job of assistant manager to Jimmy
    Murphy 303
  players signed by 23, 33, 34, 56, 64, 70,
    93, 182, 196, 216, 228, 229, 296
  gives Herbert Whalley a job on coaching
    staff 316
  wins first trophy success as manager 118
  rests players between games 114
  appearances on *This Is Your Life* 6, 326
  injured in Munich Air Disaster 39, 51,
    260
  pays tribute to Duncan Edwards 54
  returns home after hospital treatment in
    Munich 110
  unveils Munich memorial plaque 57
  reports referee to FA 328
  receives telegram about George Best 243
  European Cup Final win 160–1, 260,
    266
  visits Denis Law in hospital, with
    trophy 162
  announces retirement 17
  last European game as manager 148
  final game as manager 150
  Wilf McGuinness takes over from 164,
    260
  returns for a short time as manager 260,
    340
  final game after second spell as
    manager 137
  Frank O'Farrell takes over from 187
  approaches Tommy Docherty about job
    as manager 329
  made a Knight Commander of St
    Gregory 82, 260
  elected as president of Manchester
    United 65
  death 22, 24, 261
  statue unveiled 125
  brief mentions 20, 27, 48, 49, 55, 68, 99,
    107, 122, 124, 133, 153, 157, 162, 197,
    217, 233, 236, 247, 276, 283, 304, 315,
    341

Busst, David 65
Butt, Nicky 10, 16, 23, 25, 58, 62, 137, 144,
  156, 159, 185, 188, 199, 211, 220, 235,
  251, 262, 310, 334, 339
Byrne, Roger 31, 34, 37, 39, 41, 47, 50, 122,
  152, 195, 253, 259, 311, 312, 325, 337

Canio, Paolo di 30
Cantona, Eric
  birth 157
  signed by Alex Ferguson 313
  career record 313–14
  matches:
    in 1992 321, 337
    in 1993 81, 135, 246, 279, 294, 297,
      322, 340
    in 1994 5, 53, 78, 80, 82, 147, 206,
      214, 301, 308, 331
    in 1995 12, 25, 28, 262
    in 1996 68, 137, 144, 211, 216, 220,
      235, 334
    in 1997 69, 104, 145
  alleged involvement in punch up 191
  attack on Crystal Palace fan 28
  suspension 28, 52, 57, 153, 200, 219,
    250, 314
  charged with assault, 55
  sentenced, 83
  press conference following appeal 89
  begins community service 110
  awards 90, 179
  announces retirement 145, 146, 209
  depicted in painting 3
  predicts success for Manchester
    United 29
  brief mentions 63, 105, 264, 291, 323
Cantwell, Noel 26, 61, 158, 190, 196, 260,
  312–13
Cape, John 137
Carey, Johnny 24, 25, 46, 49, 71, 77, 101,
  118, 119, 232, 259
Carlos, Roberto 223
Carrick, Michael 90, 101, 174, 199, 200,
  206, 215, 223–4, 330
Carroll, Roy 156
Carson, Adam 238, 274, 295
Carvalho, Ricardo 186
Case, Johnny 154
Casper, Chris 15, 25

Cassidy, Joe 63–4, 79, 123, 233, 239, 272, 305, 326, 335, 336
Castillo, Jose Luis 177
Cavanagh, Tommy 77–8
Cech, Petr 152
Chapman, John 31, 138, 165, 269, 289, 290
Chapman, Lee 59
Charles, Prince 195
Charlton, Sir Bobby
  birth 271
  career record 266–7
  signs as amateur 2
  injured in Munich Air Disaster 39
  misses European Cup matches 141, 147
  pays tribute to Duncan Edwards 54
  matches:
    in 1956 266, 278, 306
    in 1957 49, 83, 120, 333
    in 1958 27, 33, 34, 37, 85, 264
    in 1959 81, 94, 238
    in 1960 31, 88, 243, 278, 325
    in 1961 225
    in 1962 49
    in 1963 158, 167, 325
    in 1964 20, 79, 286, 301, 318
    in 1965 93, 122, 248, 295
    in 1966 74, 198, 247
    in 1967 80, 139, 190, 211, 258
    in 1968 21, 35, 108, 161, 263, 266, 276
    in 1969 148, 195, 319
    in 1970 98, 172
    in 1971 137, 221, 248
    in 1972 62, 129, 248
    in 1973 16, 21, 89, 116, 127, 133
  announces retirement 116
  awards 162, 266
  receives knighthood 171
  unveils memorial in Munich 252
  statue commissioned 309
  pays tribute to Ryan Giggs 173
  brief mentions 47, 56, 133, 156, 164, 217, 218, 244, 250, 251, 261, 268, 302, 303, 327
Charlton, Jack 156, 325
Chilton, Allenby 30, 119, 231, 246, 247, 259
Chisnall, Phil 73, 195, 232
Clarke, Alf 39
Clarkin, John 292, 293, 305

Clegg, Michael 186, 187
Clegg, Stephen 198
Clemence, Ray 206
Clough, Brian 103, 169, 209, 311, 315
Cochran, C.B. 192
Cochrane, Jimmy 151
Cockburn, Henry 119, 128
Cohen, George 190
Cole, Andy
  birth 275
  transfer from Newcastle United 13
  matches:
    in 1995 25, 36, 44, 67, 80, 108, 143, 220, 307
    in 1996 58, 90, 138, 144, 286
    in 1997 30, 52, 69, 104, 111, 166, 277, 285, 295, 310
    in 1998 5, 280, 312
    in 1999 18, 40, 113, 150, 156, 159
    in 2000 78, 91, 100, 287
    in 2001 62, 107, 257
    in 2003 111
  brief mentions 153, 251, 264
Collina, Pierluigi 159
Collinson, Jimmy 239, 305
Collymore, Stan 330
Colman, Eddie 34, 37, 39, 47, 50, 259, 302
Connelly, John 74, 93, 99, 173, 190, 283, 306, 318
Connor, Edward 24
Cooke, Stacey 235
Cooke, Terry 184
Cooper, Davy 83
Cope, Ronald 51, 265
Coppell, Steve 17, 72, 145, 146, 154, 173, 189, 226, 242, 253, 265, 286, 293, 337, 341
Corradi, Bernardo 324
Coton, Tony 21
Coupar, James 63, 116, 123, 232, 238
Cowan, Sam 238
Cracked Flag (band) 72–3
Craven, Charlie 225–6
Crerand, Paddy 50, 56, 74, 111, 139, 148, 158, 161, 167–8, 183, 260, 261
Crickmer, Walter 39, 133, 259, 269, 292
Crompton, Jack 66, 101, 119, 192
Crooks, Garth 74
Cross, Graham 80

INDEX

Crowther, Stan 51
Cruyff, Jordi 42, 144, 224
Cudicini, Fabio 148, 189
Culkin, Nick 222
Cunningham, Laurie 72, 169, 192
Curry, Tom 39

Dale, Joe 186
Dalglish, Kenny 13, 194, 217, 219
Daltrey, Roger 133
Daly, Gerry 8, 94, 104, 130
Davenport, Peter 84, 94, 103, 271, 272, 289, 294
Davies, Alan 36, 155, 159
Davies, Don 39
Davies, John Henry 60–1, 121, 125, 282
Davies, Ron Tudor 55, 322
Davis, Rhain 204
Dawson, Alex 4, 34, 51, 54, 55, 85, 114, 128, 130, 226, 325, 334
Dean, Dixie 269
Delaney, Jimmy 13, 33, 69, 97, 119, 132, 228, 236
Desailly, Marcel 172
Dewar, Neil 335, 336
Dida 119
Diop, Papa Bouba 327
Docherty, Michael 136
Docherty, Tommy 2, 56, 72, 77, 104, 118, 149, 154, 169, 183, 186, 192, 203, 217, 241, 268, 315, 329, 332
Doherty, John 269
Doherty, Ken 144
Doherty, Peter 337
Donaghy, Mal 242, 286
Donald, Ian 315
Donaldson, Robert 98, 99, 232, 238, 271, 274, 302, 309, 336
Dong Fangzhou 28
Doughty, Jack 9, 97, 288
Doughty, Roger 9, 97, 263
Dow, John 322
Downie, Alex 309, 310, 338
Downie, John 68, 71, 114, 126, 253, 267
Doyle, Mike 77
Drogba, Didier 115, 116, 152
Duberry, Michael 212
Dublin, Dion 95, 115, 231, 252, 309
Duncan, Scott 259, 292, 299

Dunn, David 111
Dunne, Tony 122, 158, 161, 196–7, 203, 274
Duxbury, Mike 94, 151, 155, 159, 181, 229

Eagles, Chris 127, 196
Edge, Alfred 263
Edmonds, Hugh 230
Edwards, Duncan 33, 34, 39, 40, 47, 50–1, 54, 93–4, 111, 114, 128, 152, 259, 302, 303, 340
Edwards, Louis 59, 82, 186, 197, 331
Edwards, Martin 36, 59, 82, 132, 172, 197, 215, 218
Edwards, Paul 329
Erentz, Fred 9, 96, 238
Erentz, Harry 9, 96
Eriksson, Sven Goran 62, 220
Eusebio 73–4, 161, 247
Evans, Jonny 223
Evra, Patrice 13–14, 60, 101, 115, 149, 316

Farman, Alf 63, 113, 123, 230, 232, 263, 271, 274, 295, 309
Ferdinand, Les 150
Ferdinand, Rio Gavin 3, 7, 60, 115, 125, 177, 178, 196, 206, 279, 282, 297, 328
Ferguson, Sir Alex
  birth 341
  career before joining Manchester United 297
  as Aberdeen manager 149, 224, 297, 315
  appointed as manager of Manchester United 297
  career as manager 341
  loses first game 298
  players signed by 12, 23, 117, 125, 147, 165, 170, 171, 183, 194, 200–1, 224, 291, 313, 320, 330
  awards and honours 62, 83, 90, 115, 163, 270
  sells Paul McGrath 300
  media anticipates sacking, 8
  first trophy success 150–1
  becomes first manager to win European Cup-Winners' Cup with two different British sides 149
  opens Manchester United Megastore 319

Ferguson, Sir Alex—*contd*
publishes book 197–8
loses star players and forms successful
team with youthful players 219–20
causes injury to Beckham 47
Queiroz appointed assistant manager
to 184
visits Munich for unveiling of
memorial 252
celebrates 1,000th game as manager 311
bets with Ronaldo 187, 337–8
18th major trophy win 139
objects to Heinze's transfer to
Liverpool 195
assaulted 239
100th FA Cup tie as manager, 48
comments on players 115, 174, 284, 308
brief mentions 21, 38, 59, 68, 76, 84, 92,
94, 100, 117–8, 142, 145, 159, 169,
176, 179, 206, 209, 223, 251, 253, 257,
278, 281, 299, 306, 307, 308
Ferguson, Darren 17, 42, 65, 183
Ferguson, John 231
Ferrier, Ronald 281
Fevre, David 170
Fitzpatrick, John, 98, 116, 276
Fitzsimmons, Thomas 98
Fletcher, Darren 34, 45, 48, 76, 156, 193,
223
Fletcher, Peter 133
Flynn, Jerome 133
Follows, George 39
Forlan, Diego 294, 321
Forsyth, Alex 26, 31–2, 321
Fortune, Quinton 10, 52, 100
Foster, Ben 93, 223
Foulkes, Bill 5, 11, 29l 34, 39, 47, 51, 54,
73, 122, 139, 148, 158, 161, 259, 272,
326–7
Fowler, Robbie 158, 262, 342

Gallimore, Stanley 66, 133, 280
Gaskell,John David 158, 265, 283
George VI, King 119
Gerrard, Steven 116
Gibson, Colin 42, 84, 94, 96, 167
Gibson, Darron 223
Gibson, James W. 5, 21, 331
Gibson, Terry 26, 335

Gidman, John 13, 151
Giggs, Ryan
birth 315
matches:
in 1991 65
in 1992 10, 103, 137, 321
in 1993 135, 340
in 1994 5, 24, 78, 95, 147, 152, 200
in 1995 25, 29, 152, 262, 307
in 1996 105, 138, 144, 152
in 1997 30, 69, 262, 285
in 1998 280
in 1999 106–7, 152, 156, 159, 316
in 2000 100
in 2001 107, 340
in 2003 28, 58, 96, 104, 109, 324
in 2004 152, 156, 257
in 2005 45, 59, 152
in 2006 60
in 2007 53, 67, 71, 139, 152, 196, 206,
279, 323
in 2008 53, 97
awards and honours 106, 115, 162, 163,
173
sponsorship deal 196
opens new training complex 198
retires from international football 162
marriage 235
brief mentions 169, 174, 215, 220, 248,
250–1, 261, 267, 314, 327
Giles, Johnny 3, 49, 153, 158, 261, 285
Gill, Anthony 25
Gill, David 194
Gillespie, Keith 6, 13, 49, 137
Gillespie, Matthew 326, 335
Glazer, Malcolm 48, 157, 177
Godsmark, Gilbert 1, 45–6
Gomes, Nuno 339
Gonzalez, Albert 190
Goodwin, Freddie 51
Gouw, Raimond, van der 179, 184
Gowling, Alan 10, 52, 78, 98, 221
Graca, Jaime 161
Gradi, Dario 311
Graham, Arthur 221, 285, 329
Graham, Deiniol 25
Graham, George 6–7, 83, 279
Grant, Avram 253
Grassam, William 14

Gray, Andy 115
Greaves, Jimmy 182
Greenhoff, Brian 20, 97, 126, 154, 237, 300
Greenhoff, Jimmy 17, 94, 97, 123, 154, 175, 237, 337
Gregg, Harry 34, 39, 51, 285, 295–6, 324
Griffiths, William 54, 233
Grimes, Ashley 17, 204, 242
Grobbelaar, Bruce 304
Grundy, John 125

Haaland, Alf-Inge 209
Hadfield, Emma 174
Halse, Harold 1, 18, 69, 84, 113, 118, 119, 127, 240, 248, 254, 274
Hamill, Michael 42–3, 77, 127–8
Hanlon, John 28, 55
Hanot, Gabriel 241
Hansen, Alan 139, 144, 220
Hanson, Jimmy (James) 42, 304, 305
Hardman, Harold 112, 248–9
Hargreaves, Owen 22, 155, 163, 170, 181, 184, 210, 220, 225
Hart, Ian 133
Hatton, Ricky 177
Hayes, James 89, 118
Healey, William 11
Heinze, Gabriel 171, 187, 191, 195, 210, 222–3, 324
Henderson, William 249
Hendry, James 274
Henry, Thierry 210
Herd, David
  birth 107
  career record 182
  joins Manchester United 182
  matches:
    in 1958 33
    in 1961 225
    in 1962 216, 294
    in 1963 153, 157–8, 254, 299, 321, 325, 328, 339
    in 1964 27, 73, 252, 283, 286, 301
    in 1965 93, 102, 162, 213, 317
    in 1966 73, 221, 245, 313
    in 1967 80
  brief mentions 114, 244
Higson, James 64

Hilditch, Clarence 'Lal' 31, 104, 165, 202, 227, 228, 269, 290
Hill, Alexander 26, 43, 72, 78, 91, 136, 149, 154, 160, 221
Hill, Gordon 286, 300, 337
Hinchcliffe, Andy 253
Hine, Ernest 240
Hoddle, Glenn 147, 166
Hodge, James 187
Hodgson, David 312
Hogg, Graeme 8, 174
Holden, Dick 171
Holt, Edward 125
Holton, Jim 21, 29, 89, 101, 183, 265, 322
Homer Thomas 8, 50
Hood, William 99, 238, 274, 295, 309
Hooper, Arthur 24
Houghton, Eric 51
Houston, Stewart 2, 83, 203, 286, 322
Howard, Tim 60, 156, 172, 210
Howcroft, Jack 237
Hughes, Mark
  birth 290
  career record 23, 290–2
  signs as apprentice 23, 161
  signs professional forms 164
  rejoins Manchester United after a period at Barcelona 23, 177, 291
  matches:
    in 1983 23
    in 1984 23, 312
    in 1985 74, 83, 109, 151, 228, 265
    in 1989 2, 219, 246, 253
    in 1990 146, 151, 286, 289, 291, 315
    in 1991 23, 28, 148–9, 291
    in 1992 103, 231, 257, 321
    in 1993 113, 207, 322
    in 1994 23, 59, 76, 78, 87, 100, 106–7, 147, 278, 291, 301
    in 1995 12, 52, 67, 83
    in 1997 205
  medals and awards 23, 162, 163, 173, 291
  leaves Manchester United to join Chelsea 23, 163, 177, 219, 291
  brief mentions 144, 169, 250, 323
Hughes, Richard 215
Hurst, Daniel 234, 235, 242, 310
Hurst, Geoff 200

Iddon, Richard 177
Ince, Paul 16, 44, 53, 55–6, 59, 67, 78, 80,
  95, 103, 108, 113, 135, 142, 144, 146,
  147, 149, 151, 153, 170, 176, 214, 219,
  250, 280, 289, 321
Irwin, Denis 5, 29, 53, 59, 65, 91, 103, 105,
  144, 147, 149, 159, 169, 180, 216, 219,
  289, 308, 313, 340

Jackson, Philip 309
Jackson, Tom 39
Jackson, Tommy 171
James, David 111, 262
Jansen, Wim 9
Jeffers, Francis 210
Jennings, Pat 145, 211
Johnsen, Ronny 15, 156, 159, 170, 204
Johnston, William 36, 42, 231
Johnstone, Paul 73
Jones, Mark 34, 39, 47, 50, 173, 259, 267–8,
  302
Jones, Tom 298
Joorabchian, Kia 188
Jordan, Joe 32, 41–2, 58, 91, 120, 192, 281,
  328, 334
Jovanovic, Nikola 35, 242
Juninho 172

Kainer, Karl 37
Kaka 119
Kanchelskis, Andrei, 10, 25, 38, 44, 55, 76,
  83, 87, 103, 105, 132, 144, 147, 185,
  195, 206, 219, 235, 250, 301, 308,
  340
Keane, Roy
  career record 209–10
  joins Manchester United 194, 209
  meets the Pope 180
  matches:
    in 1993 207, 246, 297, 322
    in 1994 80, 147, 175
    in 1995 67, 103
    in 1996 115, 144, 211, 286
    in 1997 138
    in 1998 280
    in 1999 106, 113, 156, 222, 316, 339
    in 2000 78
    in 2001 57, 334
    in 2002 21
  in 2004 156
  in 2005 34, 38, 155, 209
  in 2006 142–3
  attacks behaviour of crowd 298–9
  leaves Manchester United to join
    Celtic 210, 308
  boots sold at auction 273
  brief mentions 13, 59, 152, 172, 176,
    201, 223, 314
Keegan, Kevin 137, 154, 166, 279
Kennedy, Fred 40
Kennedy, William 93
Keyworth, Ken 157
Kidd, Brian 6, 21, 41, 61, 100, 116, 128,
  160, 161, 179, 219, 221, 247, 303, 326,
  335
Kinnaird, Lord 155
Kinsey, Albert 12
Knighton, Michael 218, 252
Knox, Archie 179
Kopel, Frank 87
Kuszczak, Tomasz 81, 186, 210

Langford, Leonard 161
Lappin, Hubert 338
Larsson, Henrik 9, 71, 318
Law, Denis
  birth, 57
  career record 56, 216–18
  given his first cap 261
  joins Manchester United 190, 216
  matches:
    in 1960 226
    in 1962 293–4, 328–9
    in 1963 124, 157, 158, 232, 299, 321
    in 1964 20, 27, 73, 79, 120, 283, 286,
      301, 318
    in 1965 122, 126, 162, 248, 275–6,
      295, 306
    in 1966 73, 221, 223, 246, 313
    in 1967 80, 139, 179, 211, 268
    in 1968 21, 248, 263, 276, 303
    in 1969 150, 329
    in 1970 205
    in 1971 137
    in 1974 124, 129, 217
  visited in hospital by team with
    trophy 162, 217
  signs for Manchester City 184, 217

Law, Denis—*contd*
  awards and honours 162, 186
  statue 56, 217–18, 309
  brief mentions 7, 47, 102, 133, 180, 182,
    212, 244, 255, 260
Lawton, Norbert 84
Ledbrooke, Archie 39
Lee, Francis 124
Leighton, Jim 98, 146, 147, 150,
  197
Leitch, Archibald 50
Lenglen, Suzanne 192
Lewis, Edward 31, 37, 49
Ljungberg, Freddie 34
Lofthouse, Nat 134
Lowrie, Thomas 97
Lydon, George 178
Lynam, Des 220
Lynch, John 132

Macari, Lou 5, 17, 20, 21, 32, 77, 96, 123,
  154, 166, 183, 221, 227, 242, 273, 281,
  293, 321, 322, 331, 337
McBain, Neil 304
McCalliog, Jim 14
McClair, Brian
  birth 322
  career record 322–3
  joins Manchester United 183, 323
  matches:
    in 1987 214, 332
    in 1988 103, 142, 272
    in 1989 2, 25, 219
    in 1990 102, 146, 151, 255, 286
    in 1991 43, 149, 291, 308
    in 1992 38, 103, 337
    in 1993 252, 340
    in 1994 100, 147
    in 1995 29, 52, 143, 148
  1997 testimonial match 108
  leaves Manchester United 184
  brief mentions 12, 60, 177, 271
McClaren, Steve 179
McCreery, David 154, 171, 246, 321
MacDougall, Ted 9, 268, 273
McGarvey, Scott 115
McGrath, Paul 139, 142, 151, 300, 319
McGregor, Jim 170
McGuinness, Wilf 2, 54, 99, 150, 164, 217,
  246, 260, 264, 269–70, 285, 302, 315,
  326, 340
McIlroy, Sammy 8, 23, 26, 32, 34, 35, 43,
  58, 136, 145, 154, 171, 203, 264, 273,
  296, 331, 337
McKay, William 140
McLachlan, George 277, 298
McLenahan, Hugh 36
McMahon, Steve 95
McManaman, Steve 46
McMillen, Walter 303
McNaught, James 93, 168
McParland, Peter 70, 136
McPherson, Francis 40, 304
McQueen, Gordon 58, 145, 155, 159, 178,
  192, 213, 334
McShane, Harry 126, 267
McShane, Paul 210
Malouda, Florent 206
Mangnall, Ernest 127–8, 258, 282, 290,
  338
Manley, Thomas 128, 137, 236, 240, 241,
  303
Maradona, Diego 82, 256
Marsden, Dan 57
Martin, Lee Andrew 20, 37, 146, 150, 151,
  323, 341
Mather, Dave 73
Mathieson, William 238
Matthews, Stanley 76, 118, 273
Maxwell, Robert 36, 218
May, David 28, 69, 138, 141, 144, 156, 178,
  184, 220, 286
Meek, David 2–3, 68
Mercer, Joe 326
Meredith, Billy 1, 24, 109, 110, 118, 123,
  127–8, 130, 140, 149, 199–200, 229,
  230, 290, 318, 336
Mikel, Jon Obi 253
Milburn, Jackie 2, 266
Miller, Thomas 15, 319
Milne, Ralphn 146, 181
Mitchell, Andrew 238
Mitten, Charlie 10, 19, 26, 44, 69, 71, 119,
  128, 140, 224, 228, 236, 240, 259, 310
Moger, Henry 118, 230
Moir, Ian 180, 232
Molby, Jan 213
Moncur, John 80

Moore, Charlie 166, 202
Moore, Graham 120, 339
Moran, Kevin 17, 128, 130–31, 151, 155, 159, 226, 297, 300, 329
Morgan, Willie 10, 52, 62, 133, 150, 241, 262, 276
Morgans, Ken 39
Morley, Trevor 253
Morris, Johnny 13, 26, 64, 158, 236, 310, 315
Morrison, Thomas 338
Mortensen, Stan 118
Moses, Remi, 40, 169, 263, 303
Mourinho, Jose 253, 339
Muhren, Arnold 155, 159, 165, 232
Muntari, Sulley 214–15
Murphy, Jimmy 46, 51, 54, 55, 70, 259, 260, 303–4, 316
Musgrove, Malcolm 331
Mutch, George 128, 236, 250
Myerscough, Joseph 319

Nakamura, Shunsuke 242
Nani (Luis Carlos Almeida da Cunha) 48, 163, 168, 170, 186, 196, 210, 225, 249, 287, 306
Neal, Phil 139
Needham, David 8
Neville, Gary 14, 16, 25, 34, 46, 49, 59, 60, 62, 76, 101, 115, 137, 138, 141, 142–3, 144, 156, 159, 166, 169, 174, 179, 185, 188, 220, 251, 261, 311, 315
Neville, Phil 16, 23, 28, 44, 62, 106, 127, 141, 144, 156, 165, 185, 187, 220, 281, 316, 334
Nicholl, Jimmy 61, 154, 171, 286, 293
Nistelrooy, Ruud van
  birth 182
  career record 211–12
  signs with Manchester United 117, 212
  matches:
    in 2001 211, 257, 320, 334, 340
    in 2002 15, 21, 56, 125, 311
    in 2003 28, 58, 96, 104, 109, 111, 117, 135, 145, 294, 321, 324
    in 2004 32, 41, 46, 156, 257, 284, 294, 311
    in 2005 59, 209, 328, 339
  signs with Real Madrid 199, 212

second place in European Golden Boot Award 175
brief mentions 70, 215, 223, 234, 255

O'Farrell, Frank 62, 187, 216, 217, 268, 315, 329, 331, 332
O'Kane, John 25
Oldfield, David 253
Olive, Les 101, 123
Olsen, Jesper 81, 94, 151, 213
O'Reilly, Gary 145–6
O'Shea, John 60, 67, 127, 130, 156, 177, 196, 316, 331
Owen, Syd 290

Paisley, Bob 139, 341
Pallister, Gary 103, 111, 135, 144, 146, 147, 149, 151, 170, 181, 184, 330
Palmer, Roger 98
Pape, Albert 40, 114, 172
Park, Ji-Sung 58, 60, 90, 101, 193, 209
Parker, Paul 76, 94, 103, 147, 340
Partridge, Edward 15, 319
Patterson, Darren 103
Paul VI, Pope 82
Pearce, Ian 221
Pearson, Mark 34, 78, 285
Pearson, Mike 17
Pearson, Stan 10, 13, 22, 31, 33, 37, 76, 106, 119, 122, 132, 135, 158, 218, 236, 259, 277, 317, 320, 326, 333
Pearson, Stuart 20, 72, 123, 149, 154, 240, 265, 286, 293, 300, 321, 322, 331
Peddie, John 4, 88, 126, 234, 235, 338
Pegg, David 39, 47, 49, 50, 70, 152, 250, 254, 259, 262, 269, 308, 340
Pegg, Dick 170, 338
Pelé, 102, 244
Perez, Lionel 334
Perrins, George 238
Peters, James 35, 292, 305, 322
Phelan, Mike 6, 103, 146, 149, 151, 176, 181, 183, 253
Picken, John 8, 88, 89, 126
Pires, Robert 210
Poborsky, Karel 65, 88, 235, 285, 338
Podolski, Lukas 188
Pointon, Neil 100
Poll, Graham 34

Preston, Stephen 116
Pullin, Gilbert 328–9
Queiroz, Carlos 179, 184
Quigley, Eddie 64
Quinn, Jack 193
Quixall, Albert 4, 51, 130, 158, 208, 225, 243, 255, 260, 285, 325

Ramsden, Charlie 65
Ramsey, Sir Alf 172, 190, 200
Rattin, Antonio 190
Rawlings, Bill 42, 97
Rayment, Captain Kenneth 38, 39, 40
Ramsden, Charlie 65
Redwood, Hubert 10
Reeves, Peter 325
Regis, Cyrille 169
Reid, Andy 223
Reid, Peter 151
Reid, Thomas 19, 31, 133, 280
Rennox, Clatworthy 25
Revie, Don 122
Reyes, Jose Antonio 155
Ricardo, Felipe 111
Richards, Chas 234, 235
Richardson, Kieran 60, 107, 276
Richardson, Lancelot 55
Rideout, Paul 153
Rimmer, Jimmy 43, 108
Ritchie, Andy 84, 130
Rivaldo 185
Roberts, Charlie 24, 91, 96, 118, 318, 335–6
Robins, Mark Gordon 8, 84, 102, 146, 334
Robinson, Paul 172, 225
Robinson, Pete 73
Robson, Sir Bobby 311
Robson, Bryan
  birth 14
  joins Manchester United 263–4
  career record 268–9
  matches:
    in 1981 268, 271, 297
    in 1982 148, 166
    in 1983 155, 158, 159, 221, 256, 307
    in 1984 82, 312
    in 1985 109, 151
    in 1986 27, 68
    in 1987 332

  in 1988 94, 103, 272
  in 1989 25, 246
  in 1990 98, 146, 151
  in 1991 149
  in 1993 135, 142, 197, 279, 294
  in 1994 105, 142
  awarded OBE 173
  leaves Manchester United and joins
    Middlesbrough 163, 181
  signs Gary Pallister for
    Middlesbrough 184
  brief mentions 17, 169, 220, 251, 252
Robson, John 14, 71, 138, 202, 289, 290, 338–9
Rocca, Louis 36, 60, 104, 126, 317
Roche, Paddy 4, 148
Romario 10
Ronaldo, Cristiano
  birth 37
  matches:
    in 2003 117
    in 2004 46, 156
    in 2005 10, 20, 52, 81, 209
    in 2006 60, 186, 221, 222, 253, 288, 315, 324, 337, 341
    in 2007 101, 107, 119, 138, 193, 196, 215, 249, 263, 267, 279, 282, 319
    in 2008 88, 92, 97
  raises funds for tsunami victims 12
  opens own fashion store 43
  awards 115, 116, 121, 125, 146–7, 151, 162, 188, 191, 339, 342
  bets with Sir Alex Ferguson 187, 337–8
  statement issued about future of 191
  meets up with Rooney again 201
  signs new contract 105
  brief mention 220
Rooney, Wayne
  birth 283
  career record 283–4
  signs for Manchester United 171, 283
  matches:
    in 2004 171, 256–7, 283, 284
    in 2005 18, 20, 38, 45, 59, 209, 328, 339
    in 2006 60, 129, 178, 186, 221, 222, 324
    in 2007 95, 101, 107, 119, 127, 196, 206, 212, 249, 263, 267, 279, 282,

Rooney, Wayne—*contd*
  287, 319
  in 2008 88, 92, 97
  injuries 129, 168, 212
  awards 162, 191, 283, 284
  depicted in painting 3
  signs publishing deal 74
  attends boxing match 177
  sent off at World Cup Quarter-final
    186
  meets up with Ronaldo again 201
  allocated No. 10 shirt 180, 210
  brief mentions 174, 220, 230
Rose, Henry 39
Rothwell, Charles 326
Roughhead, Lisa 174
Roughton, William George 168
Rous, Sir Stanley 214
Rowley, Jack
  birth 267
  career record 236, 281–2
  matches:
    in 1935 310
    in 1937 281, 319
    in 1938 295
    in 1941 71, 106, 228
    in 1944 107
    in 1946 11, 228, 240, 310
    in 1947 55, 158, 315
    in 1948 13, 19, 26, 69, 79, 118, 119,
      266
    in 1949 10, 44, 140, 224
    in 1950 71, 128
    in 1951 22, 126, 236
    in 1952 122, 253, 277
    in 1953 31, 37, 70
    in 1955 15
  brief mentions 259, 317
Royle, Joe 311
Rush, Ian 7, 217
Ryan, Jimmy 222

Sadler, David 36, 80, 161, 232, 243
Sagar, Charles 88, 89, 126, 230
Saha, Louis 32, 60, 101, 207, 212, 221, 223,
  242, 253, 324
Sapsford, George 140
Sar, Edwin van der 60, 115, 138, 186,
  194–5, 206, 214, 287–8, 329

Saunders, Dean 87
Saunders, James 338
Scanlon, Albert Joseph 34, 39, 94, 130, 238,
  243, 246, 271, 333
Schmeichel, Caspar 220
Schmeichel, Peter 52, 75–6, 87, 103, 106,
  143, 144, 147, 150, 156, 159, 172, 179,
  207, 255, 299, 306–7
Schofield, Alf (Alfred) John 45, 89, 229,
  336
Scholes, Paul
  birth 305
  career record 250–1
  signs as trainee 188
  signs professional terms 25
  matches:
    in 1994 250
    in 1995 220, 255, 274, 307
    in 1996 58, 144
    in 1997 6, 104, 157, 166, 251, 262,
      285, 310
    in 1998 251
    in 1999 156, 167, 251
    in 2000 91, 100
    in 2001 62, 152, 158
    in 2002 15, 251, 311, 322
    in 2003 111
    in 2004 32, 46, 156, 331
    in 2005 10, 155, 339
    in 2007 3, 67, 90, 214, 215
    in 2008 129–30
  medals and awards 115, 250, 251
  eye problems 27
  brief mentions 101, 169, 174, 185, 223
Sealey, Les 76, 87, 149, 151, 181, 257, 279
Seaman, David 106, 207
Setters, Maurice 158, 225, 232
Sexton, Dave 58, 96, 120, 131, 169, 183,
  192, 213, 237, 243
Shankly, Bill 183, 217, 264
Sharpe, Lee 43, 57, 80, 82, 83, 103, 108,
  147, 149, 160, 162, 165, 170, 246, 252,
  278, 289, 315, 322
Shearer, Alan 67, 106, 330
Sheringham, Teddy 5, 26, 30, 57, 92, 150,
  156, 158, 159, 173, 251, 262, 264, 277,
  287, 298
Sidebottom, Arnold 116–17
Silcock, Jack 202, 227, 228

INDEX

Silvestre, Mikael 34, 60, 156, 171, 208, 210
Simeone, Diego 66
Simpson, Danny 4, 267
Sivebaek, John 285
Smith, Alan 10, 49, 81, 101, 139, 204, 208, 276, 318, 327, 331
Smith, David 124
Smith, Gordon 155
Smith, John 71, 106, 107, 140, 225, 228
Smith, Lawrence 309–10
Smith, Richard 35, 256, 292, 293, 322, 336
Smith, Thomas 112, 298
Sneddon, John 263, 309
Solskjaer, Ole Gunnar
  birth 59
  joins Manchester United 199
  career record 226
  matches:
    in 1996 224–5, 334
    in 1997 15, 52, 138, 144
    in 1998 280
    in 1999 13, 26, 40, 156, 159
    in 2000 91, 115
    in 2001 57, 334
    in 2002 15, 299, 311, 328
    in 2003 28, 96, 104
    in 2004 156
    in 2006 223, 242, 276, 337, 341
    in 2007 9, 90
  retirement 226
  brief mention 318
Smith, Lawrence 309–10
  joins Manchester United 199
  career record 226
  matches:
    in 1996 224, 334
    in 1997 15, 52, 138, 144
    in 1998 280
    in 1999 13, 26, 40, 156, 159
    in 2000 92, 115
    in 2001 57, 334
    in 2002 15, 299, 311, 328
    in 2003 28, 96, 104
    in 2004 156
    in 2006 223, 242, 276, 337, 341
    in 2007 9, 90
  retirement 226
  brief mention 318
Southall, Neville 151

Spence, Joe 42, 54, 140, 227, 228, 239, 269, 280, 328, 342
Spink, Nigel 108
Stafford, Harry 11, 60–1, 93, 121, 125
Stam, Jaap 18, 125, 156, 159, 208, 320
Stapleton, Frank 17, 68, 82, 142, 145, 151, 155, 159, 189, 226, 228, 256, 264, 267, 285, 297, 307
Steele, Luke 210
Stefano, Alfredo Di 70
Stepney, Alex 74, 108, 124, 154, 161, 164, 211, 229, 241, 246–7, 278–9
Stevens, Gary 155
Steele, Luke 210
Stiles, Nobby 17, 133, 161, 190, 200, 221, 254, 261, 263
Stokes, Bobby 132
Storey-Moore, Ian 32, 129, 268
Strachan, Gordon 26, 42, 83, 94, 151, 208, 224
Sunderland, Alan 145, 296
Sutcliffe, John 233–4
Swift, Frank 39
Sylva, Tony 53

Talbot, Brian 145
Taylor, Christopher 112
Taylor, Ernie 51, 122, 129
Taylor, Frank 39, 257
Taylor, Gordon 215
Taylor, Graham 311
Taylor, Pete 185
Taylor, Tommy 11, 30, 33, 34, 38, 39, 49, 50, 64, 70–1, 97, 101–2, 111, 114, 120, 128, 130, 136, 152, 234, 241, 254, 255, 269, 270, 275, 281, 302, 308, 337, 341
Tevez, Carlos 37, 53, 88, 92, 170, 188, 194, 204, 210, 214, 225, 249, 253, 256, 267, 287, 329
Thain, Captain James 38, 39
Thomas, Danny 87
Thomas, Harry 112
Thomas, Mickey 15, 35, 82, 84, 167, 187, 188
Thompson, Eric 39
Thomson, A.E. 21, 336
Thomson, Arthur 54
Thornley, Ben 25, 59, 112, 137
Tilden, Bill 192

Tognini, Guido 191
Totti, Francesco 175
Turnbull, Jimmy 69, 118, 240
Turnbull, Sandy 1, 2, 18, 50, 63, 92, 118,
    134, 149, 227, 235, 248, 254, 274,
    333

Ure, Ian 268

Van: for names beginning with Van *see*
    under final part of surname
Vassell, Darius 138, 288
Venables, Terry 166, 291
Venison, Barry 27
Vennegoor of Hesselink, Jan 242
Veron, Juan Sebastian 190, 251, 257, 322,
    328
Vidic, Nemanja 6, 60, 90, 101, 115, 125,
    193, 280
Vieira, Patrick 34, 106
Viollet, Dennis
  birth 250
  career record 101–2
  matches:
    in 1954 11, 275, 325
    in 1955 15, 337, 341
    in 1956 112, 227, 241, 251, 255, 273,
      283, 340
    in 1957 38, 233, 262, 272, 333
    in 1958 33, 34, 37, 122, 271
    in 1959 81, 94, 238, 320
    in 1960 88, 226, 243, 274, 292
  injured in Munich Air Disaster 39
  sold to Stoke City 2
Vose, George 176, 336

Waldron, Colin 177, 300
Walker, Dennis 153
Walker, Ian 150
Vose, George 176, 336

Wall, George 8, 50, 126, 227, 230, 235, 240,
    254, 333
Wallace, Danny 22, 98, 146, 151, 275, 315
Walsh, Gary 82, 143
Walton, Joseph 167
Warburton, Arthur 19
Warner, Jack 108, 114, 168, 295
Warner, Jimmy 7–8, 238
Webb, Neil 98, 146, 151, 183, 195, 219, 255
Webster, Colin 15, 51, 68, 114, 246, 308,
    325
West, Enoch 92, 127–8
West, James 119, 125, 256, 258
Whalley, Arthur 92
Whalley, Herbert 39, 160, 316
Whelen, Liam 22, 39, 47, 50, 91, 110, 111,
    114, 128, 233, 234, 251, 254, 255, 259,
    266, 272, 273, 278, 303, 306
Whelan, Ronnie 86
Whitefoot, Jeffrey 107, 114, 259
Whitehouse, James 338
Whiteside, Norman 13, 74, 83, 85–6, 94–5,
    139, 140, 148, 151, 155, 158–9, 178,
    Whelan, Ronnie 86
Wilkins, Ray 155, 159, 160, 169, 192, 213,
    224, 243, 256, 268
Wilkinson, Howard 166, 235, 313
Williams, David 97
Williams, Henry 4, 335–6
Willis, Peter 151
Wise, Dennis 156
Witkamp, Anton 307–8
Wood, Ray 39, 49, 70, 101, 136, 283
Woodcock, Wilfred 202, 227
Worrall, Harold 160
Wrigglesworth, William 11, 295
Wright, Ian 52, 146

Yorke, Dwight 7, 13, 18, 26, 40, 57, 66, 78,
    107, 113, 156, 159, 280, 312